The Human Use of Human Resources

McGraw-Hill Series in Management

Keith Davis and Fred Luthans,
Consulting Editors

Allen: Management and Organization
Allen: The Management Profession
Argyris: Management and Organizational Development: The Path from XA to YB
Beckett: Management Dynamics: The New Synthesis
Benton: Supervision and Management
Brown: Judgment in Administration
Buchele: The Management of Business and Public Organizations
Campbell, Dunnette, Lawler, and Weick: Managerial Behavior, Performance, and Effectiveness
Cleland and King: Management: A Systems Approach
Cleland and King: Systems Analysis and Project Management
Cleland and King: Systems, Organizations, Analysis, Management: A Book of Readings
Dale: Management: Theory and Practice
Dale: Readings in Management: Landmarks and New Frontiers
Davis: Human Behavior at Work: Organizational Behavior
Davis and Newstrom: Organizational Behavior: Readings and Exercises
Davis, Frederick, and Blomstrom: Business and Society: Concepts and Policy Issues
DeGreene: Systems Psychology
Dunn and Rachel: Wage and Salary Administration: Total Compensation Systems
Edmunds and Letey: Environmental Administration
Fiedler: A Theory of Leadership Effectiveness
Finch, Jones, and Litterer: Managing for Organizational Effectiveness: An Experiential Approach
Flippo: Personnel Management
Glueck: Business Policy and Strategic Management
Glueck: Readings in Business Policy from *Business Week*
Glueck: Strategic Management and Business Policy
Hampton: Contemporary Management
Hicks and Gullett: Management
Hicks and Gullett: Modern Business Management: A Systems and Environmental Approach
Hicks and Gullett: Organizations: Theory and Behavior

Prasow and Peters: Arbitration and Collective Bargaining: Conflict Resolution in Labor Relations

Reddin: Managerial Effectiveness

Sartain and Baker: The Supervisor and the Job

Sayles: Leadership: What Effective Managers Really Do . . . and How They Do It

Schroeder: Operations Management: Decision Making in the Operations Function

Shore: Operations Management

Shull, Delbecq, and Cummings: Organizational Decision Making

Steers and Porter: Motivation and Work Behavior

Sutermeister: People and Productivity

Tannenbaum, Weschler, and Massarik: Leadership and Organization

Walker: Human Resource Planning

Werther and Davis: Personnel Management and Human Resources

Wofford, Gerloff, and Cummins: Organizational Communications: The Keystone to Managerial Effectiveness

The Human Use of Human Resources

Marvin Karlins
Professor of Management
University of South Florida

McGraw-Hill Book Company

New York St. Louis San Francisco Auckland Bogotá Hamburg
Johannesburg London Madrid Mexico Montreal New Delhi Panama
Paris São Paulo Singapore Sydney Tokyo Toronto

This book was set in Optima by Black Dot, Inc. (ECU).
The editors were Kathi A. Benson and Peggy Rehberger;
the production supervisor was Leroy A. Young.
The cover was designed by Charles A. Carson.
R. R. Donnelley & Sons Company was printer and binder.

THE HUMAN USE OF HUMAN RESOURCES

Copyright © 1981 by McGraw-Hill, Inc. All rights reserved. Printed in the
United States of America. No part of this publication may be reproduced,
stored in a retrieval system, or transmitted, in any form or by any means,
electronic, mechanical, photocopying, recording, or otherwise, without the
prior written permission of the publisher.

1 2 3 4 5 6 7 8 9 0 D O D O 8 9 8 7 6 5 4 3 2 1

Library of Congress Cataloging in Publication Data

Karlins, Marvin.
      The human use of human resources.

      Bibliography: p.
      Includes index.
      1.   Personnel management.   I.   Title.
HF5549.K268   658.3   80-25582
ISBN 0-07-033298-3
ISBN 0-07-033297-5 (pbk.)

About the Author

MARVIN KARLINS, Professor of Management at the University of South Florida, received his Ph.D. from Princeton University. He is a prolific writer, having authored, coauthored, or edited fourteen books, including *Psychology and Society*, *The Other Way to Better College Grades*, and *Biofeedback*, and contributed numerous articles on the subjects of psychology and business to various professional journals. He has also been a consultant to a wide variety of businesses and governmental agencies, including the Peace Corps, the U.S. Air Force, State Farm Insurance, and Graham-Jones. He has served on the faculties of the University of Pittsburgh, City College of the City University of New York, and Southern Illinois University. In 1980 Professor Karlins was voted the outstanding teacher of the year in the School of Business at the University of South Florida.

In loving memory of Sheldon Weinberg,
a man who always practiced what this book preaches.

Contents

Preface

This book is about management and how *you* can become a better manager. It is also a book about psychology and how you can use it to accomplish both management *and* labor objectives on the job. And, finally, it is a book about the human use of human resources: an opportunity to transform the workplace into a *worth* place, a place where personal and economic growth can coexist.

A manager's job isn't easy. If 20 years as a consultant, psychologist, and professor of business has taught me anything, it is a profound sense of respect for the men and women who choose management as a career. Theirs is often a thankless job requiring unwavering dedication and boundless energy to deal with seemingly endless problems and crises. Yet, it is also an occupation of crucial importance, where a person *can* make a difference in the world. Management, in short, is "where the action is" . . . and that's where you probably want to be.

Although a manager's job is difficult, it can be mastered, and mastered well. The purpose of this book is to make you a better manager by showing you how to use human resources both effectively *and* humanely.

The first section of the text, "A Theoretical Orientation," will provide you with the philosophical and conceptual basis for human resource management. How to actually manage those resources effectively will be discussed in Section Two, "How to Be an Effective Human Resource Manager in the Real World." It is here that I will be teaching you the skills necessary to function successfully in the workplace—skills that can be learned, and have been, by thousands of individuals just like yourself. Finally, Section Three will be devoted to making *you* happier and more satisfied as a manager and is entitled, pointedly, "How to Succeed in Business without Really Dying."

There are today a growing number of individuals and corporations dedicated to making the job environment a better place to work. I salute their efforts. Yet, there is still a long way to go in the struggle for the human use of human resources. Being a manager in our changing world is a challenging mixture of opportunity and responsibility. I hope the information in this book will help make work more rewarding to both you and those you manage, and hasten the day when all labor and management can work together in a productive and personally satisfying manner.

Marvin Karlins

Acknowledgments

First and foremost, I recognize with gratitude the contributions of my students and colleagues to this effort. I would like to single out Dr. Keith Davis for his support and valuable contributions to the manuscript. Then, too, there is Dr. Harold Schroder, my doctoral adviser at Princeton University and associate at the University of South Florida School of Business. I acknowledge my continuing intellectual debt to him. Thanks are also due those authors whose published research reports I utilize throughout the text. Finally, I would like to express my appreciation to two fine editors at McGraw-Hill, John F. Carleo and Kathi A. Benson. Without their enthusiasm and insights this project would still be on the drawing board.

Marvin Karlins

"The No. 1 survival skill for today's business manager is the human relations skill—the ability to understand human behavior and to deal with it intelligently."

Karl Albrecht

The Human Use of Human Resources

Section One

A Theoretical Orientation

Chapter 1

A Story with a Moral

I will pay more for the ability to deal with people than any other ability under the sun.

John D. Rockefeller

A patient is dying. For 13 years the vital signs have deteriorated—a profile of life ebbing inexorably toward oblivion. Everyone familiar with the case is frustrated; intensive examinations and treatments have done little to alleviate the condition. With time running out, a specialist is called in to save the patient where others have failed. He is advised that the patient is in need of major surgery "to remove the malfunctioning organs and replace them with new ones."

The specialist doesn't agree. He believes that the organs can function effectively without surgery if properly treated. He's right. Three years later the patient's vital signs have clearly improved, and the patient is growing at a healthy, robust rate.

3

Would it surprise you to find out the patient was a *corporation* and the specialist a *manager?* You most likely know the patient: Avis Rent-A-Car. And the specialist? None other than Robert Townsend, the peppery chief executive who engineered Avis's recovery and wrote about it in his irreverant best-seller *Up the Organization.*[1]

When Townsend took command of Avis in 1962 the floundering company hadn't turned a profit in 13 years of life. The rest is corporate history. In 3 years Avis had more than doubled its sales (from $30 million to $75 million) and amassed earnings in excess of $9 million.

How did Townsend do it? With some unorthodox philosophy, hard work, and a deep, abiding faith in his employees. Claims Townsend:

> When I became head of Avis, I was assured that no one at headquarters was any good, and that my first job was to start recruiting a whole new team. Three years later, Hal Geneen, the President of ITT (which had just acquired Avis), after meeting everybody and listening to them in action for a day, said, "I've never seen such depth of management; why, I've already spotted three chief executive officers!" You guessed it. Same people. I'd brought in only two new people, a lawyer and an accountant.[2]

There was nothing wrong with the "internal organs" of Avis's corporate body—and Townsend knew it. Rather than "cutting out" the people he had, he worked with them, provided them with a corporate environment that satisfied their needs, and encouraged them to be productive. And he succeeded.

There is a profound lesson to be learned from the story of Robert Townsend. It is this: Success or failure in the business world often turns on a manager's ability to utilize human resources effectively (see Box 1-1). Townsend had that ability, and he used it to turn Avis around. When it came to human resource management, Townsend tried harder. He fully understood the need for motivating workers and made the effort to fire them up at work rather than fire them out of work. (Not a bad strategy when you consider that an attempt to dismiss a single federal employee can tie up half of a manager's workday for 18 months at a cost of $100,000 to the taxpayer.[3])

[1] Robert Townsend, *Up the Organization,* Fawcett-Crest, New York, 1970.
[2] Ibid., p. 123.
[3] *Forbes,* July 24, 1978, p. 22 (quoting *Time*).

BOX 1-1

THEY HAD THEIR PIE—AND ATE IT, TOO

History books are bulging with examples of businesses—large and small—which faltered or failed because of poor human resource management. One of the most spectacular examples is also one of the most recent: the bankruptcy of the giant W. T. Grant Company. The executives of this company didn't have a monopoly on poor human resource practices; but if the following quote from *The Wall Street Journal* is true, they went a long way toward establishing a base line against which management incompetence can be measured. Let us hope that their idea of management incentives will be a kind of "custard's last stand."

Managers for W. T. Grant Co. stores were hit in the face with custard pies or suffered other indignities if they didn't meet their credit quotas.

The hazing procedure was discussed by John E. Sundman, former senior vice president and treasurer of Grant, in his deposition discussing the problems besetting the chain before it went bankrupt.

It was called a Steak and Beans program and had "negative incentives," which consisted of, besides the pie-in-the-face, store managers having their ties cut in half, being forced to run around their stores backward, pushing peanuts with their noses, and not being promoted to larger stores, he said.

Asked if it also had come to his attention that a losing district manager was required to walk around a hotel lobby dressed in nothing but a diaper, Mr. Sundman answered that he had never heard of that one.*

Contrast the human resource practices at the bankrupt Grant's with those of a highly successful company, McDonald's. In another *Wall Street Journal* article, reporter James Hyatt discusses the human use of human resources beneath the "golden arches."

Individuals deserve a break at McDonald's, the fast-food chain declares.

To preserve the human touch, the corporation creates a "vice president of individuality." The new official, James S. Kuhn,

*The Wall Street Journal, Feb. 4, 1977, p. 6.

formerly a personnel officer, says the idea is to "maintain the growth and identity" of the individuals responsible for the company's success. He listens to employee complaints and offers advice. And he tries to consider an employee's personality, as well as abilities, in career planning.

One innovation: an annual "Store Day" when top management from the chairman on down works in restaurants cooking hamburgers and cleaning up, to "keep in touch" with workers. Mr. Kuhn also is studying impact of corporate life on employee families. "We're writing to spouses and some of the older kids for any suggestions," he says.†

†*The Wall Street Journal*, February 1, 1977, p. 1.

JUST HOW IMPORTANT ARE HUMAN RESOURCES IN THE CONTEMPORARY ECONOMY?

Vitally important. Just *how* vital we are only now beginning to appreciate. Unfortunately, early American managers tended to focus most of their energy and attention on developing the production side of management, ignoring or downplaying the human dimension in the workplace. This bias was understandable considering the temper and knowledge of the times. In the first place, "people resources" were plentiful and easily exploitable (rights of labor were yet to be realized). The early managers tended to treat workers much as the early pioneers tended to treat the natural resources on the frontier: as unlimited, cheap, and always replaceable. Conservation of resources just didn't seem relevant in an environment where supply overwhelmed demand and management power over the labor force was so absolute. Secondly, there was the problem of *recognizing* the value of human resources. There was no reason for a manager to grasp the dollar-and-cent value of human resources because profit and loss statements didn't include "people costs" in the balance sheets.[4]

[4]We are just now realizing the significance of this oversight. Recently, for example, twelve executives of a "big board" company tried to assess how much its people really cost. Considering recruiting, hiring and training costs, the amount equaled 75 percent of the corporate net profit before taxes a year earlier. The "people costs" had been hidden because there was no calculation for turnover in the company's financial statements. For an excellent discussion of the financial value of human resources, see J. Rosnow, "Solving the Human Equation in the Productivity Puzzle," *Management Review*, August 1977, pp. 40–43.

In effect, then, the true value of human resources lay hidden—lost in an era of cheap, easily exploitable labor and bookkeeping systems that ignored the impact of human resources in "bottom-line" profit and loss considerations.

How times have changed! Today the effective utilization of human resources is being touted as a major development in maintaining the health of the American economy—a point of view I heartily endorse. Just as our nation has come to understand that the pioneer view of natural resources is no longer viable—that we must now develop a new respect and working plan for our physical environment—so, too, has management come to realize that the early attitudes toward human resources are obsolete and that a new "ecology" of people as a precious commodity must be instituted.

Think of human resource development as a whole new frontier. Unlike production factors, which have been widely explored and developed, human resource development is still largely unexplored and represents a fertile new area for discoveries and progress.

It is imperative that you—a future manager—make the effort necessary to familiarize yourself with this new frontier, so that you may discover how to get the most out of your human resources—how to encourage sustained high levels of productivity at work. This is particularly true today because American business faces foreign challenges unknown in earlier times. If we are to meet successfully the market thrust of other industrialized nations, we must maintain a productive stance at home that will keep us competitive abroad.

Keep in mind the words of management expert Robert Lazer: "If, in fact, the goals of an organization are maintenance and growth, then the productive use of human resources becomes imperative. It is probably in the area of human resource utilization that the greatest short-term improvement in organizational productivity can be obtained."[5]

GETTING THE MOST OUT OF YOUR HUMAN RESOURCES

Once we recognize the importance of human resources for succeeding in the contemporary business world, the next logical question is, "As a manager, how can I get the most out of the human resources

[5]Robert Lazer, "Behavior Modification as a Managerial Technique," *Conference Board Record*, January 1975, p. 22.

under my direction?" Or, simply, "How can I get the most productivity out of my workers?"

The answer to this question will occupy us for the rest of this book. We will be learning to use the motivational techniques developed by behavioral scientists to keep workers productive *and* satisfied. We will also be exploring some new ways of conceptualizing labor-management relations. Before we do this, however, it will be instructive to observe the average working environment, for it is from the contemporary workplace that our strategy of effective human resource management will evolve.

Chapter 2

Work Is a Four-Letter Word

Am I worried about going to hell? Why should I be, I already work there five days a week.

Heavy-equipment operator

Victor Ruiz is a musician residing in Tampa, Florida. He is also a polished amateur golfer with a low handicap and a high degree of dedication to the game. How high? Well, consider one of his rounds as detailed in *Sports Illustrated:*

> Ruiz was going quite well after a few holes at the Rocky Point course. Suddenly pain gripped his chest and he doubled over. His partners suggested that he go back to the clubhouse.
>
> "I was playing too good to quit," says Ruiz, "so I hit myself in the gut and the pain went away. I kept on."

9

The pain came back, but between pars Ruiz slapped at himself some more. He shot 37 on the first nine and was not about to quit. A friend gave him a Coke and some Rolaids.

"I began to feel better," Ruiz recalls, "but soon the pain returned again. This time it was in my arm."

He putted for birdies on the last three holes, making one on the 18th green for 74. Then he all but fell down in a faint. He was rushed home and from there to a hospital, where he was given emergency treatment for the heart attack that had been striking him. He was hospitalized for almost three weeks and is now convalescing.

The incident taught him a lesson, Ruiz says.

"That pain in my arm," he explains, "was one reason I was hitting my long irons so straight. It made me shorten my swing."[1]

Picot Floyd also lives in Tampa, Florida, where he works as a county commissioner. Unfortunately, some of the county employees weren't quite as devoted to their work as Mr. Ruiz was to his golf. Recently, Mr. Floyd attempted to stir his workers from their lethargy with a little "wake-up reminder" called the "Employee Death Tag." The yellow tag suggested:

> Because of the close resemblance between death and the normal working attitude in some departments, all supervisors should extend a paycheck as the final test to determine if a worker is really deceased or just snoozing. If the employee does not reach for the paycheck, it reasonably may be assumed that death has occurred.[2]

Things aren't always as they appear, however, and Mr. Floyd cautioned the supervisors: "In some cases, the paycheck-reaching instinct is so strongly developed in the worker that a spasmodic clutching reflex may occur. Don't let this fool you."

Talk about differences in behavior! Mr. Ruiz was highly motivated to pursue his golf game; he played willingly with zest. Contrast this kind of dedication and that of Mr. Floyd's Death Tag recipients, who approached work with all the enthusiasm of bears in hibernation.

Now I am not suggesting that Mr. Floyd's employees throw themselves into their work with reckless abandon—nor, for that

---

[1]Martin Kane, "The Game's the Thing," *Sports Illustrated,* July 24, 1972, pp. 6–7.
[2]Picot Floyd, personal communication, 1978.

matter, do I think Mr. Ruiz should play the links in the midst of a coronary. It would be nice, however, if Commissioner Floyd's yellow-tagged employees could somehow display a bit of Mr. Ruiz's enthusiasm in their work, be a more productive human resource on the job.

Actually, the contrasting behaviors of Mr. Ruiz and the Death Tag employees of Mr. Floyd disturbs those of us involved in the business community. With increasing frequency we observe individuals displaying lackluster performance on the job. What makes matters worse is that many of these listless employees are active, alert, and performing to the best of their ability *outside* the workplace. It is almost as if these individuals possess two personalities: one for weekends and evenings, the other for working hours. Why should this be? Are avocational pursuits inherently more interesting and motivating than work? Is the workplace devoid of challenge and stimulation?

The sad truth is that for an increasing segment of employees work is becoming a four-letter word (see Box 2-1). More and more, labor is seen as an activity to be endured, not enjoyed—an unpleasant necessity of life to be done as quickly as possible and forgotten equally as quickly. Consider, for example, these dismal statistics:

- One poll reports that five out of six workers claim their jobs put them under tension.[3]
- Another survey indicates that about 75 percent of the people who consult psychiatrists are suffering from problems that can be traced to a lack of job satisfaction or an inability to relax.[4]
- Business consultant Ronald Barnes claims that "about half of all working people are unhappy with their careers, and as many as 90 percent may be spending much of their time and energy at jobs that do not help them get any closer to their 'goals in life.'"[5]

A COST WE CAN'T AFFORD

What is the cost of such attitudes and feelings about work? Tremendous, for *both* the nation's economy and its employees. For the individual worker it means the squandering of one-third of a lifetime in

[3]Ronald Kotulak, "Stress: A Small Reward of the Good Life," *Miami Herald,* June 1, 1976, sec. F.
[4]"Cracking Under Stress," *U.S. News & World Report,* May 10, 1976, p. 59.
[5]Ibid.

BOX 2-1

THANK GOD IT'S FRIDAY

Work might be as American as apple pie, but judging from some current employee attitudes, it certainly isn't as enjoyable.

Humorous cartoons are popular vehicles for portraying the very *un*funny condition of contemporary work. For example, judging from the *Frank and Ernest* cartoon included below, do you think the cartoon character will be very enthusiastic about *any* new job?

Consider also the facing "Work Week" sketch. If a picture is worth ten thousand words, this cartoon should tell you a lot about current worker attitudes toward their jobs. In this comic view of labor, the weekend is seen as an oasis, a refuge, a "safe place" where the employee can escape from the miseries of the workplace and store up enough energy to face Blue Monday. Wednesday becomes "hump" day—the day an employee must "get over" to be more than halfway through the workweek. And Friday? It becomes the vestibule to salvation—or as a movie title has suggested: *Thank God It's Friday*.

If you wish to become an *effective* manager, you must learn how to enhance worker satisfaction *and* productivity on the job. This is what skilled human resource management is all about.

FRANK AND ERNEST

Reprinted by permission. © 1978 NEA, Inc.

THE WORK WEEK

SUNDAY

MONDAY

TUESDAY

WEDNESDAY

THURSDAY

FRIDAY

SATURDAY

13

activity which is distasteful and limiting to personal growth. For American business it means all the evils associated with job dissatis-faction: low morale, absenteeism, reduced productivity, and, in extreme cases, sabotage.

It is a well-established fact that unhappy workers (those whose needs are not being met) are less productive workers; they reduce the ability of American business to survive and prosper in the increasingly competitive world marketplace. In 1972, then Undersecretary of the Treasury Charles E. Walker put it bluntly: "If we don't get increased productivity in this country, we might as well put up a sign saying 'going out of business.' Our economic survival is at stake."[6]

Are things hopeless?

Certainly not! I am firmly convinced that it is possible to create a work environment that will stimulate employees to perform to the best of their ability, to their fullest work potential. And I believe that it is the job and responsibility of management to take the steps necessary to create such a work environment. I call such a workplace a *worthplace,* and it is in this worthplace that we will have the best chance to develop workers who want to work.

[6]Elaine Scott, "Motivation, Productivity and the American Worker," unpublished manuscript, 1978.

Making the Workplace a Worthplace: The Role of Behavioral Science and the Plus-Plus Relationship

As the next generation of managers it will be your responsibility to create the worthplaces where your employees can reach their full potential as workers and as human beings. To fashion such an environment you must become a *human resource director*, a person who can encourage optimal job performance in your subordinates through *effective leadership* (gaining the respect and cooperation of those you direct) and *motivational practices* (practices that encourage employee productivity and satisfy employee needs).

THE IMPORTANCE OF BEHAVIORAL SCIENCE FOR MAKING THE WORKPLACE A WORTHPLACE

Behavioral science research findings reveal how you can most effectively lead and motivate your employees—how, in short, you can be a successful manager. Combined with on-the-job experience, these findings can help you optimize your human resource skills, assuming, of course, you are willing to use them in the first place (see Box 3-1).

Becoming an effective human resource director is no small accomplishment! As management consultant Karl Albrecht emphasizes: "The #1 survival skill for today's business manager is the human relations skill—the ability to understand human behavior and to deal with it intelligently."[1]

That's *your* survival Albrecht is talking about. And he's right: A

[1]Karl Albrecht, personal communication.

BOX 3-1

SCIENCE FRICTION

Longstanding prejudices and superstitions die hard—like the belief that behavioral science has nothing to contribute to management effectiveness. Some managers really believe this. You can show them actual cases of scientific insights enhancing managerial performance, and they'll nod and smile; then they go right on managing "by the seat of their pants." It's downright maddening. It reminds me of people who would rather wade through a puddle than walk under a ladder and risk "bad luck." You can tell them the ladder idea is superstition, and they'll nod and smile; then, the minute you leave, they'll detour around the ladder as if they hadn't heard a word you said.

A person can afford to walk around ladders, but a manager cannot afford to ignore the scientific insights that lead to superior on-the-job performance. Management theorists Harold Koontz, Cyril O'Donnell, and Heinz Weihrich grasped the importance of behavioral science for effective management in this powerful statement:

Physicians without a knowledge of science become witch doctors; with science, they may be artful surgeons. Executives who attempt to manage without theory, and without knowledge structured by it, must trust to luck, intuition, or what they did in the past; with organized knowledge, they have a far better opportunity to design a workable and sound solution to a managerial problem.*

*Harold Koontz, Cyril O'Donnell, and Heinz Weihrich, *Management*, Seventh Edition, McGraw-Hill, New York, 1980, p. 9.

For contemporary managers, scientific advances have come none too soon! At the same time workers have gained the power to eliminate some of the older, ethically questionable management practices for controlling job performance, behavioral science has provided new techniques for encouraging high levels of productivity in the workplace.

Gone are the days when managers could simply "pink-slip" unsatisfactory employees, confident that fresh supplies of labor waited to do their bidding. Today's workers are more educated, both in skills and knowledge of their rights. They demand more from their labor than simply a salary, and they know how to get it. They realize that their legal rights make it extremely difficult for management to carry out threats of punishment or dismissal—and that in many cases mediocre work can be sufficient to keep a job. In dealing with these new workers, with their new expectations and powers, behavioral science has given the contemporary manager new ways to stimulate employee productivity and satisfy employee needs on the job.

1979 study by Henchey & Company revealed that 76 percent of the executives in its "outplacement" program lost their jobs because of "difficulties in interpersonal relationships." Only 14 percent of the terminations were attributed to failures in job performance.[2]

PLAYING THE ROLE OF PSYCHOLOGIST

It is recognized in Hollywood that the great movie stars are proficient at playing many different kinds of roles. The same can be said for skilled managers. Throughout your career you will be called upon to play different roles, to wear "different hats" in performing your duties. One of those roles is *psychologist*. As Dr. Harry Levinson has so astutely observed: "We're going to have to go a lot deeper into what makes people tick. Managers will have to know and understand as much about the psychology of motivation as they know about marketing, EDP, and other increasingly functional areas."[3]

[2]Personal communication, 1980.

[3]John Roach, "Managing Psychological Man," *Management Review,* June 1977, p. 27.

Now I am *not* suggesting that to be an effective manager you must be trained as a psychologist to direct the activities of others. Nor, for that matter, am I recommending that you have to be a professional accountant to work with a budget or a trained economist to make company forecasts. What I *am* suggesting is that you gain a basic familiarity with some of the concepts of psychology, accounting, economics, and so forth—so that when the need arises on the job, you will have the information necessary to effectively manage the situation.

Harold Leavitt, managerial psychologist, has argued:

> Some kind of psychological theory is just as necessary for the manager dealing with human problems as is electrical and mechanical theory for the engineer dealing with machine problems. Without theory the engineer has no way of diagnosing what might be wrong when the engine stops, no way of preestimating the effects of a proposed change in design. Without some kind of psychological theory, the manager cannot attach meaning to the red flags of human disturbance; nor can he predict the likely effects of changes in organization or personnel policy.[4]

In Section 2 of this book I will be giving you some of the psychological and behavioral science findings Dr. Leavitt believes you will need to deal most effectively with the human problems you are bound to encounter. We will be focusing on those findings that can be *readily applied* on the job to help you manage your human resources with the highest proficiency—in the words of management pioneer Mary Parker Follett, "get things done through other people." For now it is sufficient for you to recognize the importance of behavioral science findings in helping you develop into a humane and effective manager.

THE SPECTER OF BEHAVIOR CONTROL

A major goal of contemporary psychology is the *control of human behavior*. And, yes, one of *your* major goals as a manager who studies psychological theories and techniques will be to learn how to control

---

[4]Harold Leavitt, *Managerial Psychology*, rev. ed., University of Chicago Press, Chicago, 1964, p. 7.

more effectively the behavior of your subordinates—to get them to do what you want them to do.

Does this sound sinister? Machiavellian? To many of you it might smack of "1984ism" and be repugnant. Yet let me point out that each of you *already* tries to control the behavior of others. The woman who tries to persuade a friend to carry out some task or the man who spanks his child are practicing rudimentary forms of behavior control— rudimentary in comparison with the more sophisticated, effective behavior control techniques used by individuals trained in psychology or in the use of psychologically based behavioral science techniques. You will be learning in this book how to regulate human behavior in a more systematic, scientific, powerful manner—in short, how to control your human resources more effectively.

There is nothing wrong with attempting to control the behavior of others *as long as it is done in a responsible manner.* I do ask you, however, always to remember the following:

I will be giving you information that will make you a more powerful behavior controller (more proficient in your ability to regulate the actions of your employees). With this increased proficiency comes an increasing obligation to use your behavior-changing power in an ethical, humane way—in a manner which will benefit both the behavior controller *and* the controllee. That is what I mean when I speak of the human use (should I say *humane* use?) of human resources.

Sometimes we become so accustomed to our behavior-changing power as to forget we possess it and use it in a careless or callous fashion. This is an unforgiveable error. One can never afford to be casual with behavior-changing power.

Remember that to possess behavior-changing power is both a privilege and a burden. Don't use it unless you are willing to do so in a responsible and ethical way that will benefit your employees as well as you.

ESTABLISHING THE PLUS-PLUS RELATIONSHIP

In the spirit of what I have just said, we come to a major concept in the effective *and* ethical use of behavior control on the job: the creation of the ++ *(plus-plus)* relationship. The ++ (also called *win-win*)

Condition	Management	Labor	Result
"plus-plus" High job productivity High need satisfaction	+	+	"win-win"
"plus-minus" High job productivity Low need satisfaction	+	−	"win-lose"
"minus-plus" Low job productivity High need satisfaction	−	+	"lose-win"
"minus-minus" Low job productivity Low need satisfaction	−	−	"lose-lose"

Figure 3-1 The four possible types of relationships that can occur in the workplace. Management should strive to create the ++ (win-win) relationship, as it leads to the greatest worker productivity and satisfaction. The +− (win-lose) and −+ (lose-win) relationships can occur for short periods of time, but they create imbalances between the needs of management and labor, usually resulting in the development of a −− condition. This lose-lose relationship occurs, sadly, all too often in the present-day workplace. It should be eliminated if business is to survive.

relationship refers to the establishment of a work environment whereby the needs of management and labor are both fulfilled: specifically, an environment where productivity (management goal) and satisfaction of personal needs (employee goals) coexist (see Figure 3-1).

Why worry about satisfying employee needs anyway? One reason for this emphasis is my belief in human dignity: the assumption that management has a moral obligation to treat people as individuals, not objects. But for those who would label me a "bleeding heart" and rail at the "wastefulness" of this approach, let me emphatically say that such a practice is eminently pragmatic (economically sound).

Study after study, from automobile assembly lines to major department stores, reveals that managers who know how to satisfy workers—how to fulfill their needs—are those who get superior performance from their employees. And no wonder! It has long been known and accepted that to sell your product you must satisfy your customers' needs. Is it so surprising, then, that to sell production to your workers you must satisfy their needs?

The bottom line is clear: humanism and productivity are not incompatible. We can no longer afford to squander our human resources. We must learn to improve the morale and productivity of the workers so that we can effectively compete from a position of strength in the new world economy. Highly respected business expert John Gardner warns that ". . . we must discover how to design organizations and technological systems in such a way that individual talents are used to the maximum, and human satisfaction and dignity are preserved. We must learn to make technology serve man not only in the end product, but in the doing."[5]

Although my appeal for establishing ++ relationships may sound revolutionary, it isn't. As a matter of fact, the ++ concept has been around for quite a while, although judging from current management practices, it seems to have been largely ignored or forgotten. Frederick Taylor, the father of scientific management, had a basic appreciation of the ++ relationship when he spoke of his "mental revolution," in which labor and management would work harmoniously to maximize profits rather than argue about how they should be divided.

The problem is, of course, how you as a manager can go about creating a ++ work environment. It requires a lot of effort, application of the behavioral science principles presented in Section 2, and a belief that work can be something more than a four-letter word. It also involves developing a different conception of the *power relationships* between management and labor, a topic we will turn to in the next chapter. In the meantime you might want to read and ponder the passage in Box 3-2. It seems that young Tom Sawyer had a keen understanding of (and appreciation for) the ++ relationship, which he set out to use in creating a win-win situation on the job.

[5]William Dowling, "At General Motors: System 4 Builds Performance and Profits," *Organizational Dynamics,* Winter 1975, p. 37.

BOX 3-2

BRUSHING UP ON THE PLUS-PLUS RELATIONSHIP

Sometimes a job that seems devoid of any satisfaction can, with skillful management, be made to appear in a different light. Case in point: Tom Sawyer and his famous fence-painting encounter. How he got out of doing the job (which he didn't want in the first place) and, most important, got someone else interested in doing it makes interesting reading in the context of the ++ relationship.

We pick up the story where Ben, Tom's friend, spots him whitewashing the fence.

"Hello, old chap, you got to work, hey?" Tom wheeled suddenly and said:

"Why, it's you, Ben! I warn't noticing."

"Say—I'm going in a-swimming, I am. Don't you wish you could? But of course you'd druther *work*—wouldn't you? Course you would!"

Tom contemplated the boy a bit, and said: "What do you call work?"

"Why, ain't *that* work?"

Tom resumed his whitewashing, and answered carelessly:

"Well, maybe it is, and maybe it ain't. All I know is, it suits Tom Sawyer."

"Oh, come, now, you don't mean to let on that you *like* it?"

The brush continued to move.

"Like it? Well, I don't see why I oughtn't to like it. Does a boy get a chance to whitewash a fence every day?"

That put the thing in a new light. Ben stopped nibbling his apple. Tom swept his brush daintily back and forth—stepped back to note the effect—added a touch here and there—criticized the effect again—Ben watching every move and getting more and more interested, more and more absorbed. Presently he said:

"Say, Tom, let *me* whitewash a little."

Tom considered, was about to consent; but he altered his mind:

"No—no—I reckon it wouldn't hardly do, Ben. You see, Aunt Polly's awful particular about this fence—right here on the street, you know—but if it was the back fence I wouldn't mind and *she* wouldn't. Yes, she's awful particular about this fence; it's got to be done very careful; I reckon there ain't one boy in a thousand, maybe two thousand, that can do it the way it's got to be done."

"No—is that so? Oh come, now—lemme just try. Only just a little—I'd let *you*, if you was me, Tom."

"Ben, I'd like to, honest injun; but Aunt Polly. . . . If you was to tackle this fence and anything was to happen to it—"

"Oh, shucks, I'll be just as careful. Now lemme try. Say—I'll give you the core of my apple."

"Well, here—No, Ben, now don't. I'm afeard—"

"I'll give you *all* of it!"

Tom gave up the brush with reluctance in his face, but alacrity in his heart. And while . . . Ben . . . worked and sweated in the sun, the retired artist sat on a barrel in the shade close by, dangled his legs, and munched his apple . . .*

*From Mark Twain, *The Adventures of Tom Sawyer,* The Heritage Press, New York, 1936, pp. 26–28.

Chapter 4

A New Conception of Managerial Power and Labor-Management Relations

I believe in power; but I believe that responsibility should go with power.

Theodore Roosevelt

In this chapter I want to talk with you about the power—the ultimate power—to influence human behavior. This brings to mind a demonstration popular in college classrooms. At the beginning of class the professor introduces a Dr. Hans Schmidt to the students, informing them that the guest is a "research chemist of international renown currently employed by the United States government to study the properties of gas diffusion." Dr. Schmidt, clad in a full-length white lab coat and sporting a well-tended goatee, then steps forward and, in a heavy German accent, tells the class he wishes to test the properties of a new chemical vapor he has developed. "Specifically," he says, "I wish to determine how quickly the vapor diffuses throughout the room and how readily people can detect it."

Pointing to a small glass beaker the doctor continues:

Therefore I would ask your cooperation in a little experiment. I am going to pull this stopper and release the vapor. It is completely harmless but purposely treated to smell like gas—the kind you smell around a stove when the burner doesn't ignite. This particular sample is highly odorous so no one should have any trouble detecting its presence. What I want you to do is raise your hand as soon as you smell the vapor. Are there any questions?

At this point the chemist pulls the stopper and releases the vapor. Very soon, and in a very orderly manner, hands begin going up—first in the front rows and then on back—like a wave rolling through the lecture hall.

Obviously satisfied, the visiting scientist replaces the stopper, thanks the class for its cooperation, and leaves the room. Later on the professor informs his class that the "chemist" was in reality a faculty member from the German Department and the "vapor" nothing more than odorless distilled water.

Why, then, did nearly everyone smell gas? Power of suggestion, you might answer. Certainly the power of suggestion had something to do with it—but that wasn't the only or most important factor at work. Do you think, for example, that a student getting up before the class and making the same appeal could have received the same response as Dr. Schmidt? I've tried it: the answer is no. The power of suggestion worked so well because it was backed up by the *authority* of the person making the suggestion. After all, didn't a famous chemist say the gas would be odorous and readily detected? A *German* chemist at that (we all know how good German scientists are), wearing a white lab coat and referred to by the title of *Dr.* Schmidt.

THE AUTHORITY FIGURE AS A POWER SOURCE

Yes, Dr. Schmidt had all the trappings we associate with an *authority figure*—and a person perceived as an authority can be very persuasive indeed. As a matter of fact, authority figures have tremendous power in our society: they can mold opinions, command obedience, regulate the behavior of others. The most telling and awesome demonstration of this fact was provided by a social psychologist in a series of celebrated experiments at Yale University.

In the early 1960s Dr. Stanley Milgram had been wondering about the role of obedience in man's inhumanity to man, particularly the kinds of inhuman atrocities committed by the Nazis who were "acting under orders." Could the same obedience that made a child dutifully obey his parents and respond in socially acceptable fashion be turned around to make a person commit antisocial acts at the prodding of another authority figure? Dr. Milgram went into his laboratory to find out.

The Milgram experiment was a masterpiece of simplicity and deception. Two subjects were ushered into the laboratory to participate in a "learning experiment, ostensibly designed to study the effect of punishment on memory." One subject was to be the "teacher," the other the "learner." The subjects drew lots to determine their roles, but unbeknown to one of them, the drawing was rigged. One participant, the naive subject, was always given the role of the teacher; the other subject, a confederate of the experimenter, was given the role of the learner.

Once the drawing was completed, the learner was strapped into an "electric chair" and outfitted with electrodes capable of delivering powerful electric shocks to his body. The teacher, after observing this macabre scene, was ushered into an adjacent room containing an intercom and an imposing "shock generator." The generator, an impressive array of dials and switches, was outfitted with a control panel that gave the voltage readings for thirty separate levers (voltage levels went up in 15-volt steps, from 15 to 450 volts). Subjective descriptions of shock intensity were also included on the panel, ranging from Slight Shock at the lower intensities to Danger: Severe Shock at the 400-volt level. To convince the teacher of the authenticity of the shock generator and also to let him experience the painful properties of shock, he was administered a 45-volt stimulation.

The teacher's instructions were quite simple. He was told to teach the learner a list of word pairs over the intercom and punish him with an electric shock whenever he made a mistake, increasing the shock intensity one level (15 volts) for each new mistake. As the experiment progressed, the learner purposely made errors so that the teacher would have to shock him with increasingly severe shocks. As the shock level went up, the learner often made "increasingly insistent demands that the experiment be stopped because of the growing discomfort to him."

Although the teacher didn't realize it, *the learner never received any shocks.* Nor were his pleas real; they were in actuality a tape recording preprogrammed to deliver specific inputs when certain shock levels were reached. "They started with a grunt at 75 volts, proceeded through a 'Hey, that really hurts,' at 125 volts, got desperate with 'I can't stand the pain don't do that' at 180 volts, reached complaints of heart trouble at 195 (the learner had informed the teacher and the experimenter that he had heart trouble before the experiment began), an agonized scream at 285, a refusal to answer at 315, and only heartrending, ominous silence after that."[1]

If the teacher became concerned with the learner's agony, the experimenter ordered him to continue and to disregard the learner's protests. If the teacher balked and tried to quit, the experimenter commanded, "You have no choice, you must go on!" It should be emphasized that the teacher was free to quit the experiment and leave whenever he wanted to; the only way the experimenter could try and keep him at the task was by verbal commands that he must go on.[2]

The teacher's performance score was the highest level of shock intensity he was willing to administer to the learner. Thus his score could range from 0 (unwilling to administer any shock) to 450 (for a subject who gave the highest voltage on the shock generator).

When Dr. Milgram began his experiment, using townspeople from New Haven, Connecticut, he didn't expect many of the teachers to administer very high shocks to the learners. "I'll tell you quite frankly, before I began this experiment, before any shock generator was built, I thought that most people would break off at 'Strong Shock' (135–180 volts) or 'Very Strong Shock' (195–240 volts). You would get only a very, very small proportion of people going out to the end of the shock generator (450 volts), and they would constitute a pathological fringe."[3]

---

[1] P. Meyer, "If Hitler Asked You to Electrocute a Stranger, Would You? Probably," *Esquire*, February 1970, p. 130.

[2] If the teacher expressed concern that he might be held liable for anything that happened to the learner, the experimenter could also attempt to keep him in the study by saying he (the experimenter) would take responsibility for anything that happened.

[3] P. Meyer, op. cit., p. 128

Dr. Milgram's colleagues and his students agreed with his assessment. In fact, when he asked a class of Yale University psychology students to estimate how many of a hypothetical group of a hundred subjects would give the most intense (450-volt) shock, the average answer was 1.2 percent. In other words, the Yale students felt that less than two subjects in a hundred would remain in the experiment to the end.

If only Dr. Milgram and his students had been correct! Unfortunately, their optimistic faith in human nature would find no support in the obedience study. Of the first forty subjects tested not *one* quit the experiment prior to administering 300 volts (at which point the learner is kicking the wall in agony); and twenty-six of the forty teachers (over 60 percent of the subjects tested) obeyed the experimenter to the end, punishing the hapless learner with the full 450 volts.

Many of these teachers displayed extreme tension and misgivings about their behavior, but when prodded on by the stern voice of the experimenter/authority over the intercom, they went on shocking the hell out of the protesting learner.

How much power do authority figures wield in this society? Listen to Dr. Milgram's summary of what he observed in his laboratory: "With numbing regularity, good people were seen to knuckle under to the demands of authority and perform actions that were callous and severe. . . . A substantial proportion of people do what they are told to do, irrespective of the content of the act and without limitations of conscience, so long as they perceive that the command comes from a legitimate authority."[4]

MANAGERIAL AUTHORITY AND POWER

There is no doubt that many people who hold positions of respect and authority can and *do* exert powerful control over the behavior of their fellow citizens. This brings us to the topic of managerial authority and power.

Managers, by the very nature of their position in society, have a degree of authority which gives them power in dealing with their subordinates. There are two reasons for this.

[4]Stanley Milgram, "Some Conditions of Obedience and Disobedience to Authority," *Human Relations,* vol. 18, 1965, pp. 74–75.

1 The title "manager" carries with it a built-in recognition of legitimate authority, particularly for those working within the business hierarchy.

2 Managers have a degree of "fate control" over their subordinates (for instance, hiring, firing, promotion, discipline) which lends credence to their position as authority figures.

As a manager you, like Dr. Schmidt and Dr. Milgram, will have the authority to control the behavior of your subordinates to a certain degree, depending in part on how effectively you utilize your power in the work environment.

But, is a manager's power absolute? That is, can managers control workers' behavior at will—totally, without challenge?

The answer is no. As a manager you are not the only power factor in a worker's life. There are other persons and institutions that the worker also respects, and those other sources of authority and power can also influence the worker's behavior (see Figure 4-1).

At various times any or all of these other power sources can influence your employees' behavior; but, for all practical purposes, the only power sources that need concern us here are those of the

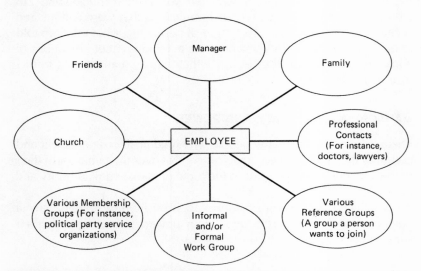

Figure 4-1 Some examples of power sources that can influence a worker's behavior.

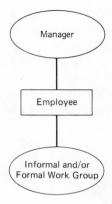

Figure 4-2 The major power focus in the workplace.

manager and the work group (see Figure 4-2). It is between manager and work group that the potential for power conflict and cohesion are greatest; we will therefore examine this most critical relationship in greatest detail.

THE WORK GROUP AS A POWER SOURCE

How many of you have taken a new job and experienced the tug-of-war feeling that occurs when your boss wants you to behave one way and your new coworkers want you to behave another? You're caught right in the middle—a very unpleasant and unfortunately not very uncommon experience.

I vividly remember just such an experience, even though it happened to me long ago. Having taken a summer job on a loading dock, I reported to work the first day and was assigned to load 50-pound sacks of grass seed into a large van. I took to the task with the enthusiasm of a new employee wanting to prove himself to management. Only 2 hours into the workday a fellow employee approached me and suggested that I might be working a bit too fast. This message was delivered in a very effective manner: the 6-foot 6-inch, 250-pound old-timer hoisted all 165 pounds of me into the air and shook me like a rag doll while communicating his recommendation for a work slowdown. Needless to say, I complied with his wishes, and, after checking my body for wear and tear, I returned to the sack loading at a significantly reduced pace. Chalk one up for the work group as a power source!

As a manager you must remember that all groups—including work groups—attempt to regulate members' behavior by the application of rewards and punishments. That is, the individual group member is rewarded for conforming to the standards of the group and punished for deviating from them. Sometimes the rewards and punishments are highly structured, formal, and clearly understood, as in the military. Other times they are more flexible, informal, and open to interpretation, as in the academic profession.

Work groups in industrial plants are notorious for their application of rewards and punishments to keep members in line. These sanctions are so powerful they often take precedence over the reward and punishment system imposed by management in the same plant.

Consider, for example, a classic series of studies at the Hawthorne Division of Western Electric Company in about 1930. One such investigation focused on a bank wiring room, where a group of fourteen workers (nine wiremen, three solderers, and two inspectors) assembled terminal banks for use in telephone exchanges. These workers were paid on the incentive system—the more they produced, the more they were paid.

The assumption behind the wage system was simple enough: every employee would work harder to amass a higher wage. The system failed. Why? Because the informal social organization of the workers in the bank wiring room had established a more powerful set of rewards and punishments (than money) to keep output at a fixed level and successfully challenge the power of management.

In discussing the Western Electric investigations, George C. Homans gives an excellent description of how work-group sanctions operate to control the behavior of individual laborers:

> The working group had also developed methods of enforcing respect for its attitudes. The experts who devised the wage incentive scheme assumed that the group would bring pressure to bear upon the slower workers to make them work faster and so increase the earnings of the group. In point of fact, something like the opposite occurred. The employees brought pressure to bear not upon the slower workers but upon the faster ones, the very ones who contributed most of the earnings of the group. The pressure was brought to bear in various ways. One of them was "binging." If one of the employees did something which was not considered quite proper, one of his fellow workers had the right to

"bing" him. Binging consisted of hitting him a stiff blow on the upper arm. The person who was struck usually took the blow without protest and did not strike back. Obviously the virtue of binging as punishment did not lie in the physical hurt given to the worker but in the mental hurt that came from knowing that the group disapproved of what he had done. Other practices which naturally served the same end were sarcasm and the use of invectives. If a person turned out too much work, he was called names, such as "Speed King" or "The Slave."[5]

WHEN POWERS COLLIDE

On the one hand, you as a manager possess power to influence the actions of your subordinates. On the other hand, work groups also have power which can be brought to bear on employee behavior. You can be sure that at certain times (often many times) during your career, the interests of the work group (or individual workers) and your interests as manager will be "out of sync," in opposition, in conflict. When this happens, we have a situation in which *powers collide*. Such power conflicts will truly test your mettle as a human resource director, for, in the final analysis, skillful handling of your power and the power of your subordinates is what effective managerial leadership is all about. How should you deal with such power problems? What are your options? You have several.

1 You Can Give in to the Opposing Power

What this means, basically, is that you acquiesce to the demands of the work group.[6] At times this is not a bad strategy. Capitulation to work-group power, if done appropriately, can make a manager look flexible, compassionate, and understanding of employees' needs. Also, in the long run of business operations, managers can afford to lose a few skirmishes with employees as long as they win the major battles. I know managers who purposely lose certain labor-management struggles so that they will be in a better position to gain their employees' allegiance on major issues.

[5]G. Homans, "The Western Electric Researches," in Hoslett (ed.), *Human Factors in Management,* Harper, New York, 1951.

[6]In this section I speak of power conflicts between you as manager and the work group; however, these options also hold true in a power conflict between you and an individual worker.

The problem, however, with yielding to work-group demands *too* often is an undermining of managerial power. Managers who consistently adopt the "give in" strategy in labor-management power conflicts are seen as weak and ineffectual, and eventually lose any semblance of authority on the job.

2 You Can Fight Power with Power

Here, the managers' strength is pitted against that of the work group and, as in a tug of war, the strongest power source pulls the opposing force "screaming and dragging their feet" across the finish line. Again, as in the case of the yielding strategy, fighting power with power is a workable policy *at times.* Used properly (and not too often) it can lead to increased worker respect for a manager and also compliance with specified orders.

Now for the difficulties. The problems with pitting power against power are potentially even more lethal than those encountered with the compliance approach. First of all, it can be a tremendous drain of energy for both labor and management, leaving little strength for job-relevant productivity. Secondly, the manager may lose the power struggle, and at that point the manager's authority will be seriously (if not irreparably) damaged. Finally, the manager may win the power battle and still lose the productivity war. Workers who are "beaten" into compliance often exhibit signs of bitterness and hostility long after the power struggle has ostensibly ended. This can lead to all kinds of critical management headaches—including loss of employee morale, reduced productivity, higher absenteeism and job turnover, and in extreme cases even physical confrontations with the manager or sabotage in the workplace.

3 You Can Reach a Compromise with the Opposing Power

Compromise means that nobody is a total winner, but, then, nobody is a total loser either. As a strategy for dealing with power confrontations, compromise can be effective in getting things accomplished and maintaining the peace, particularly if other power alternatives have been attempted and found unsuccessful.

Yet there is a major difficulty with the compromise approach: used too frequently, it often leads to a feeling on the part of management and labor alike that their needs are not being met. One business manager put it this way: "Compromise is a lot like having Chinese food—you eat it, but ten minutes later you feel hungry again."

4 You Can Harness the Opposing Power

When you harness the opposing power, you are basically using it to accomplish your own goals. This is not easily achieved, but if it can be done, it is the *best* way to deal consistently with conflicts of power.

In a business context the best method of harnessing the opposing power is to convince workers or work groups that it is in their best interest to carry out the actions that you, the manager, wish them to perform. Tom Sawyer did this with a flourish in the example presented in Box 3-2 (see pp. 21–23). You will be able to do it, too, once you put into practice the behavioral science techniques you will be learning in Section 2.

Harnessing employee power for your own ends might seem strange and new in business, but there is, in fact, nothing unusual or novel in this approach. There are many physical and human examples of this process—for instance, in the harnessing (with dams) of water power for electricity or the use of solar energy to heat homes and offices. Practitioners of the martial arts have long recognized that you can turn another person's power to your service. Thus, an individual skilled in the art of self-defense will readily utilize the attacking thrust of an adversary's arm to help throw the opponent off balance or to the ground.

HARNESSING POWER AND THE PLUS-PLUS RELATIONSHIP

In Chapter 3 I spoke of the need to establish a ++ relationship in the workplace—a condition whereby the needs of management and labor are both fulfilled; specifically, a condition in which productivity (management goal) and need satisfaction (employee goal) coexist. I suggested that until the ++ goal was met, relations between labor and management would be strained and work would continue to be viewed as a four-letter word.

In the present discussion, you can now see how important establishment of the ++ relationship becomes. Without the development of this win-win environment, suspicion and hostility between employee and employer will persist. As a matter of fact, the idea of harnessing worker power seems so farfetched in the business world exactly because of the antagonistic historical relationship that has evolved between manager and subordinate—making the idea of mutual cooperation seem unworkable, even unthinkable.

As long as this "adversarial" posture endures, the chance of harnessing worker power will remain remote. There will be too much distrust, too much hostility, too much of a win-lose attitude. It is only through the creation of the ++ relationship that the old conceptions will give way to a more cooperative labor-management relationship, paving the way for you as future managers to harness worker power in the service of higher productivity.

A NEW MODEL FOR LABOR-MANAGEMENT RELATIONS

Steps must be taken, and taken now, to find the formula for establishing the ++ relationship, for reducing conflict between labor and management—a productivity-draining interaction we can no longer afford in the light of current economic realities. One person who has taken such a step—and it is a giant one—is Muzafer Sherif, who, like Stanley Milgram, is a social psychologist. In the 1950s, Dr. Sherif conducted an innovative experiment with groups that, in my opinion, represents the most important psychological contribution ever made to the understanding of how to reduce hostility between labor and management and establish a healthy ++ business environment. First let me present the experiment, and then I'll discuss its importance for contemporary management-labor relations.

The Sherif Experiment

Every year hundreds of thousands of city kids make their annual migration to that treasured American institution, the summer camp. There they swim, fish, shoot, canoe, learn arts and crafts, and go on overnights. At a camp in Oklahoma they unknowingly became experimental subjects in Dr. Sherif's study of intergroup relations.

A psychology experiment in a summer camp? It sounds strange. Yet, in actuality, Dr. Sherif chose this particular "laboratory" for sound scientific reasons: isolated from the outside world, the summer campsite provided a place where scientific control could be more readily achieved, a place where Sherif and his staff could manipulate the environment and observe the campers in a naturalistic setting, without fear that disturbances from the outside world would confound their results.

The campers that Sherif chose for his experiment were a counselor's dream: twenty-two healthy, well-adjusted 11-year-old boys, all from stable, middle-class families and in the upper half of their classes in scholastic standing. None of the boys had been problem children at home, in the neighborhood, or in school. They were basically peaceful preteenagers. Yet in a matter of weeks, they would be aggressively embroiled in a full-scale camp war under the watchful eye of the camp staff.

The camp war did not occur accidentally. It was an outgrowth of carefully planned experimental manipulations designed to help Dr. Sherif answer two basic questions: (1) How does intergroup conflict arise? (2) How can such conflict be reduced? In answering these inquiries, Dr. Sherif divided his camp study into three basic parts.

1 Stage of Group Formation Before you can study intergroup relations, you have to have groups. In the group-formation stage, two independent cohesive groups were created. This involved, first, an attempt by Dr. Sherif and his staff to divide the twenty-two campers into two equal units, making sure that the physical skills and sizes of the campers were roughly equivalent in each unit. Once this was done, the boys were transported, in separate buses, to opposite ends of the campsite and billeted in separate cabins. Then, for about a week the boys in each cabin participated in activities designed to foster the growth of well-developed groups. These activities included canoe trips over rough terrain and cookout overnights, the kinds of highly appealing tasks that require concerted, cooperative effort to carry out and build esprit de corps among the participants. Once each cabin unit had developed into a well-defined group, both groups were brought together for the first time, and the second stage of the experiment commenced.

2 Stage of Intergroup Conflict Just as you cannot study intergroup relations without groups, neither can you study the reduction of intergroup conflict without first producing that conflict. The question is, "How do you go about producing conflict between two groups of campers who are basically well-behaved and peaceful?" Dr. Sherif gives us an important hint with the following hypothesis:

> When members of two groups come into contact with one another in a series of activities that embody goals which each urgently desires, but which can be attained by one group only at the expense of the other, competitive activity toward the goal changes, over time, into hostility between the groups and their members.[7]

Now what "series of activities" can be conducted at a summer camp that "embody goals which each [group] urgently desires, but which can be attained by one group only at the expense of the other"? For those of you who have been to camp, one answer probably comes to mind immediately: a color war. For those unfamiliar with this term, a color war is a kind of junior Olympics, a time when the camp is divided into teams (each team designated by a color) that compete in a series of athletic events lasting from a day to a week or more. When all the events are completed, the team with the highest total score wins the color war. As any camper or counselor who has gone through such an experience will attest, a color war creates a fierce sense of competition and team pride that permeates the whole camp while the contest is in progress.

Making use of the color war potential for creating intergroup hostility, Dr. Sherif and the camp staff arranged for the boys of the two cabins to oppose each other in a tournament that included baseball, football, tent pitching, and tug-of-war contests. Observes Dr. Sherif:

> The tournament started with a great deal of zest and in the spirit of good sportsmanship to which these American boys had already been thoroughly indoctrinated. . . . As the tournament progressed from event to event, the good sportsmanship and good feeling began to evaporate. The sportsman-like cheer for the other group, customarily given after a game, "2-4-6-8, who do we appreciate," turned to a derisive chant: "2-4-6-8, who do we appreci*hate*."[8]

[7]M. Sherif and C. Sherif, *Social Psychology,* Harper & Row, New York, 1969, p. 239.

[8]Ibid., p. 240.

In a very short time, what had begun as friendly relations between two groups of peaceful boys deteriorated into an intercabin donnybrook, replete with name-calling, fisticuffs, cabin raids, and property destruction. Dr. Sherif notes: "If an outside observer had entered the situation after the conflict began . . . he could only have concluded on the basis of their behavior that these boys (who were the 'cream of the crop' in their communities) were either disturbed, vicious, or wicked youngsters."[9] That's how bad things got.

There was no question about it: Intergroup conflict had been solidly achieved at Dr. Sherif's summer camp. The problem now was to end it. The whole purpose of the experiment was to find a way of reducing intergroup conflict; and judging from the behavior of Dr. Sherif's campers, there would never be a better time to find the solution.

3 Reduction of Intergroup Conflict Through experimental manipulation, Dr. Sherif had first created conditions conducive to the formation of groups and then to the onset of hostilities between them. Now, in the final stage of the experiment, Dr. Sherif set out to answer this question: "How can two groups in conflict, each with hostile attitudes and negative images of the other and each desiring to keep the members of the detested outgroup at a safe distance, be brought into cooperative interaction and friendly intercourse?"

Several approaches were tried. One approach was an *appeal to the moral values* shared by members of both groups. This appeal was contained in sermons given by the camp minister at religious services. In these sermons, he talked of brotherly love, the value of cooperation, and the need for forgiving one's enemies. "The boys arranged the services and were enthusiastic about the sermons," Dr. Sherif writes. Nevertheless, "upon solemnly departing from the ceremony, they returned within minutes to their concerns to defeat, avoid, or retaliate against the detested outgroup."[10]

A second approach involved *bringing the groups together at events that were very enjoyable.* Thus, the groups were brought

[9] Ibid., p. 254.
[10] Ibid., p. 254.

together to eat, see movies, shoot off fireworks on the Fourth of July, and so forth. Unfortunately, this approach also failed. "Far from reducing conflict, these situations served as occasions for the rival groups to berate and attack each other. . . . The mealtime encounters were dubbed 'garbage wars' by the participants,"[11] who used their food for ammunition rather than nourishment.

The one approach that Dr. Sherif believed would work—*and did*—involved the use of *superordinate goals* in the reduction of intergroup conflict. "Superordinate goals are those goals that have a compelling appeal for members of each group, but that neither group can achieve without participation of the other."[12]

To demonstrate that accomplishing superordinate goals leads to reduced intergroup hostility, Dr. Sherif and his staff rigged the camp program so that highly desirable activities and outcomes could be realized only through the joint cooperation of the two groups. For example, one day on an outing, the two groups of boys were faced with a terrible problem: Hot, tired, and hungry, they reached their campsite only to discover that the truck which was to go for food and water was stalled and needed to be pulled onto the road. One group of campers got a rope, tied it around the truck's fender, and began to tug. The vehicle didn't move, and it became obvious that one group working alone couldn't accomplish the task. When both groups pulled on the rope together, however, they were able to get the truck started and on its way.

Joint efforts in situations such as the stalled truck episode did not immediately dispel hostility between the two groups. "But gradually," Dr. Sherif notes, "the series of activities requiring interdependent action reduced conflict and hostility between the groups. . . . In the end, the groups were actively seeking opportunities to intermingle, to entertain and 'treat' each other."[13]

All's well that ends well. On the last day of the camp session, the boys were given the choice of returning home together on one bus or on two separate buses, one for each group. They voted to return together.

[11]Ibid., p. 256.
[12]Ibid.
[13]Ibid.

SUPERORDINATE GOALS AND
LABOR-MANAGEMENT RELATIONS

From peace to war and back to peace again. At least in his summer camp, Dr. Sherif seemed to create conflict or cooperation at his bidding. Now nobody is suggesting that what Dr. Sherif did with a group of boys in Oklahoma he could do as easily with labor and management. But what Dr. Sherif learned about the induction and reduction of intergroup hostility might very well be applicable to improving labor-management relations.

In contemporary business, we are confronting productivity problems that can be solved only through the *cooperation* of labor and management. Just as Dr. Sherif's campers could not move the truck without intergroup cooperation, neither can we move the economy forward without the cooperation of employer and employee working together.

This currently leaves us in an extremely ironical state of affairs. Labor and management are, in fact, partners in progress—they are irrevocably yoked together in a common effort to survive and prosper. One can not succeed without the other. Yet, through the years these two groups have behaved as if they were natural foes, enemies to be defeated.

Please don't get me wrong. I am not saying that it is unhealthy or unnatural to allow an "adversarial" position between labor and management (the Western nations have squabbles even though they are allies). Disagreements and differences of opinion can be healthy to all parties, if carried out in the proper spirit and context. What I am saying is that as future managers your perception of labor-management relations (one you should attempt to transmit to labor and one which labor should embrace as well) should be more in keeping with the true reality of the situation. Labor and management are like Siamese twins, joined together in a struggle for survival. You can't cut off one half and expect the other half to survive and prosper.

Management and labor should think in terms of cooperation rather than conflict, harmony rather than tension. Business presents employer and employee with a "natural" superordinate goal. It would be a shame if labor and management didn't grasp at the opportunity to cooperate in the achievement of that goal.

Remember the all-important Sherif hypothesis:

When members of two groups come into contact with one another in a series of activities that embody goals which each urgently desires, but which can be attained by one group only at the expense of the other, competitive activity toward the goal changes, over time, into hostility between the groups and their members.[14]

It would be the height of unnecessary tragedy if labor and management waste their energy fighting each other on the mistaken assumption that only one group can win at the expense of the other, when in fact the only way either group can win is through the mutual cooperation of both.

As long as management and labor insist on viewing their interaction in terms of a win-lose situation, only a lose-lose result can occur, particularly in today's world, where business faces harsher international competition than ever before. When, on the other hand, both groups come to see their roles as cooperative, interdependent, and win-win in nature, then the potential for a productive ++ relationship will be enhanced, along with the opportunity for management to effectively harness worker power in the service of higher productivity (see Box 4-1).

[14]Ibid., p. 239.

BOX 4-1

**AN EXAMPLE OF COOPERATION
IN LABOR-MANAGEMENT RELATIONS**

Sometimes it takes a crisis to move labor and management from an "adversarial" position to one of cooperation. As discussed in the following excerpt from an article in *Time* magazine, just such a crisis occurred at the General Motors Corporation's factory in Tarrytown, New York, and just such a cooperative effort was undertaken. The results of the effort speak well for a superordinate approach to labor-management relations.

STUNNING TURNAROUND AT TARRYTOWN*

American-made automobiles last week were again selling like Edsels. Mid-April car sales by General Motors, Ford and Chrysler dropped 32% from the same period a year earlier. Detroit continues to struggle with the dark reputation that it turns out cars inferior to those made by Japanese or West German manufacturers and that American workers are not sufficiently productive. But one Big Three plant belies such notoriety. The General Motors factory in Tarrytown, N.Y., one of the plants where the company assembles its hot-selling front-wheel-drive Chevrolet Citations, has earned the reputation of being perhaps the giant automaker's most efficient assembly facility. Tarrytown's current renown is more surprising because in the early 1970s the 55-year-old plant was infamous for having one of the worst labor-relations and poorest quality records at GM.

The turnaround at Tarrytown grew out of the realization by local management and union representatives that inefficiencies and industrial strife threatened the plant's continued operation. Automakers sometimes use forced plant closings caused by sluggish auto sales to unload a lemon facility. Ford, for example, decided two weeks ago to shut the gates of its huge Mahwah, N.J., plant largely because it had a poor quality record. After Tarrytown lost a truck production facility in 1971, bosses and workers became fearful for their jobs and got together to find better ways to build cars. At first hesitantly but later with enthusiasm, they embarked on an unusual joint experiment to improve work and to tap shop-floor expertise for running the factory.

The setting for the initiative could hardly have been more dismal. Some 7% of the plant's workers were regularly failing to appear for work, and the number of outstanding employee grievances against management totaled 2,000. The result of the confrontation and conflict was sloppy work, rapidly rising dealer complaints, and an unprecedented number of disciplinary and dismissal notices. "Workers and bosses were constantly at each other's throats," recalls Gus Beirne, then general superintendent

*From "Stunning Turnaround at Tarrytown" *Time,* May 5, 1980, p. 87. Reprinted by permission from TIME, The Weekly Newsmagazine; Copyright Time Inc. 1980.

of the plant. Agrees Larry Sheridan, the former United Auto Workers shop chairman at Tarrytown: "It sure as hell was a battleground."

The first significant payoff from the new mood at the plant came at model changeover time in 1972 and then again the following year. GM management showed workers the proposed changes in the assembly line and invited their comments. Says Beirne: "A lot of good ideas came forward, and we were shown a lot of problems we didn't realize existed. Things we had missed were picked up, and we had time to implement them before the start of the new models."

The cost savings produced by simply sharing information with the shop floor encouraged Tarrytown's executives to move further. In 1972, the plant's supervisors began holding regular meetings with workers on company time to discuss worker complaints and ideas for boosting efficiency. In order to turn the gripe sessions into something more substantive, both sides agreed to bring in an outside consultant to organize worker-participation projects. They chose Sydney Rubinstein, 52, a former blue-collar tool-and-die worker and white-collar engineer, who had become an expert on worker innovation and productivity.

Rubinstein's first breakthrough came in a trial project with Tarrytown's 30 windshield installers. Half of the workers had been disciplined during the previous six months for poor work. During discussions it was revealed that each worker selected a different point around the windshield to begin applying the sealant. One worker explained that he started at the spot where the radio antenna wires emerged from the windshield because "you get a little extra adhesive, a puddle, and that stops leaks." That little trick was new to the other workers, the foreman and the plant engineers. The method was immediately adopted and resulted in a rapid reduction in the number of dealers' complaints. Later, the plant's body-shop workers held informal discussions on welding problems. Within a few months, the percentage of bad welds dropped from 35% to 1.5%. When the small voluntary program of worker participation was expanded to the plant's 3,800 employees, 95% of them took part. The plan eventually cost GM $1.5 million.

As a result of these projects, workers say, they now readily inform supervisors that they would rather discuss problems than knock heads. "The evolution that has taken place is terrific," says Ray Calore, president of the local U.A.W. "There are no longer any hidden-ball tricks. If management has a problem, we sit and discuss it." The U.A.W. insists that job-participation programs like those at Tarrytown are neither a panacea to end all labor disputes nor just a management tool to boost output. But giving workers a greater voice in their job can improve productivity by bringing about declines in grievances, absenteeism and waste.

The benefits of the new attitudes are clear. Since 1976, the Tarrytown plant has turned out high-quality products. There are now only about 30 outstanding worker grievances, while absenteeism has fallen by two-thirds, to 2.5%. Disciplinary orders, firings, worker turnover and breakage all show significant declines. The clear lesson from Tarrytown is that both management and workers can cooperate to their mutual advantage to boost job satisfaction and increase productivity. Says Dartmouth Business Administration Professor Robert H. Guest: "Tarrytown represents in microcosm the beginnings of what may become commonplace in the future—a new collaborative approach on the part of management, unions and workers to improve the quality of life at work in its broadest sense."

GETTING THINGS STARTED

The road leading to harmonious, productive relations between labor and management will be long and, at times, treacherous. In a sense, I envision each of you as an "Ambassador of Goodwill," sent out on a mission to reduce the distrust and hostility built up between labor and management in the past. Being apprised of the necessity for creating a ++ relationship in the workplace is the first step in your journey. The second step involves acceptance of the superordinate approach to business success. The third step involves the application of behavioral science findings to enhance worker productivity and satisfy worker needs. Learning how to take that third step will occupy our attention as we turn now from theory to practice: the actual things you can do to be a more effective manager on the job.

Section Two

How to Be an Effective Human Resource Manager in the Real World

Chapter 5

The Need to Know

The need to know is your employee's need.

First-line supervisor

Having just finished the theoretical section of this book, you now have a philosophical and conceptual basis for effective human resource management. But, I hear you asking, how can I apply that theory in practice and make myself a more effective manager on the job? In other words, how do I translate theoretical ideas into action programs in the workplace?

The answer is, by utilizing behavioral science techniques to satisfy worker needs and enhance worker output. I will be discussing these techniques in the next few chapters, showing you how to use them to harness worker power and create the ++ relationship so vital to making the workplace a productive worthplace. First, however, you must know the following.

49

HOW TO UNDERSTAND AND IDENTIFY
INDIVIDUAL WORKER NEEDS

Before you can satisfy worker needs, you must know what they are. If you think you already do, then spend a moment to take the test in Box 5-1.

BOX 5-1

TEST DIRECTIONS

Below, you will find a list of 10 things people want from their work. Your task is to rank the items in order from 1 (most important) to 10 (least important) on the basis of how you think the average worker (*not* manager) would rate the items. In other words, try to predict how a worker would respond to the 10 items on the basis of their job-related needs.

Here are the 10 items. Remember, 1 is most important, 10 is least important.

YOUR ESTIMATE OF WORKER'S RANKING	WHAT PEOPLE WANT FROM THEIR WORK
_____	Full appreciation of work done
_____	Feeling of being in on things
_____	Sympathetic help on personal problems
_____	Job security
_____	Good wages
_____	Interesting work
_____	Promotion and growth in the organization
_____	Personal loyalty to employees
_____	Good working conditions
_____	Tactful disciplining

Once you have finished taking the test (and not before!) I think you'll find it instructive to look at two other sets of responses shown here: one from an actual group of employees, the other from a group of supervisors. Put your own estimates in the blanks provided and then make a few comparisons.

The employee rankings represent the actual expression of what a group of workers felt were important wants to be satisfied on the job. How did you do in comparison with their rankings? Did you

What people want from their work	Employee ranking	Supervisor ranking	Your ranking
Full appreciation of work done	1	8	_____
Feeling of being in on things	2	10	_____
Sympathetic help on personal problems	3	9	_____
Job security	4	2	_____
Good wages	5	1	_____
Interesting work	6	5	_____
Promotion and growth in the organization	7	3	_____
Personal loyalty to employees	8	6	_____
Good working conditions	9	4	_____
Tactful disciplining	10	7	_____

accurately assess what they wanted most from their work? If you didn't, don't feel bad—you weren't alone. When you glance at the supervisors' ranking it's obvious that they, too, were way off when it came to guessing what workers want most on the job.

Commenting on these data, Professor Kenneth Kovach notes:

> The ranking of items is not necessarily the important thing to observe, since conditions have changed since . . . the survey was taken. The significant point is the wide variance between what workers consider to be important in their jobs and what their supervisors think workers believe to be important. Research indicates that a wide gap still exists between what workers want from their jobs and what management thinks they want.[1]

Unfortunately, it has been this management misreading of worker needs that has led to so many problems in labor-management relations now and in the past.

As I indicated earlier, to increase worker productivity you must satisfy worker needs, and to satisfy worker needs you must know what

[1]Kenneth Kovach, "Improving Employee Motivation in Today's Business Environment," *MSU Business Topics*, Autumn 1976, p. 7.

they are. Different workers have different needs at different times. If you can ascertain each employee's needs with accuracy, you'll be in a better position to satisfy the employee and encourage higher productivity on the job.

Assessing the needs of individual workers is not as difficult as it sounds. In the first place, many workers have the same needs. Then, there aren't that many different needs to worry about. Moreover, by conscientiously observing your employees you can usually ascertain their needs. Finally, behavioral scientists have provided us with some good "models" of human needs, models that will help you understand and assess workers' needs more accurately. Here I would like to present one such model: the so-called need hierarchy of Abraham Maslow.[2] Although the model is a gross oversimplification of complex human behavior and doesn't hold true for every employee you'll confront, it still provides us with some useful guidelines for identifying worker needs and understanding how they operate.

THE MASLOW MODEL OF HUMAN NEEDS

Think for a moment: If I were to ask you to explain your behavior—to tell me why you pursued a certain goal or acted in a certain way—how would you answer? Abraham Maslow spent a career considering this kind of question, and here is how he would reply:

1 People have needs and they will act in ways to satisfy their needs. As long as our needs remain unfulfilled they act as *motivators,* stimulating us to behave in ways that will lead to the satisfaction of those needs. Once a need is satisfied, however, it no longer motivates a person and other unfulfilled needs take its place.

2 Some needs are more pressing (more important) than others. For instance, the need to breathe is more crucial than the need to gain public recognition for a job well done.

3 The basic, most survival-relevant needs must first be satisfied before other, more psychologically oriented needs become motivators of behavior. In other words, a person will seek to satisfy the rumblings of an empty stomach before turning to the challenges of an inquisitive mind.

[2]Abraham Maslow, *Motivation and Personality,* Harper, New York, 1954.

It was Maslow's realization that human needs vary in importance and behavioral priorities which led him to postulate his "need hierarchy" concept (see Figure 5-1).

It will help you understand the need hierarchy if you view it as a kind of stepladder people climb on their way to total fulfillment as human beings.

The first rung on the ladder represents the *physiological needs.* These are very urgent needs that must be satisfied before any higher-rung needs can come into play. There are very few physiological needs, but they must be satisfied if the individual is to survive. Examples of these needs are air, water, food, and—in certain climates—clothing and shelter. In contemporary North America most people have been successful in satisfying their survival needs; but for the millions of people throughout the world who haven't, life is little more than a grim day-by-day struggle for survival.

The second rung on the ladder represents the *safety needs.* Once

Figure 5-1   Maslow's hierarchy of human needs.

people have won the day-to-day struggle to stay alive, they start looking for longer-term solutions to the survival problem. People with safety needs are motivated to seek *security:* to protect themselves against misfortune and put distance between themselves and the daily scramble for survival.

The third rung on the ladder represents the *social needs.* Here the individual is concerned with *affiliation:* being around other people and being accepted by them. People with social needs want to belong—they desire social relationships and the chance to interact with others.

The fourth rung on the ladder represents *esteem needs.* People with esteem needs seek external validation of their worth; that is, they want others to recognize their competence and accomplishments. Individuals with these "ego" needs are concerned with prestige, status, and a sense of self-respect that comes with recognized achievement.

The fifth rung on the ladder is *self-actualization* and represents, according to Maslow, the highest level of human development. People with self-actualization needs are motivated to seek internal validation of their worth; that is, their values are defined in terms of personal beliefs and philosophies. People who attempt to self-actualize are striving to become all they are capable of becoming—in short, to reach their full potential as human beings. It is in this stage that individuals grapple with the age-old questions: Who am I? Where am I? Where am I going? Self-actualization is the pursuit of self-fulfillment, the quest for personal growth and the development of the total self.

From what I have just said, it becomes evident that a person's position on the Maslow hierarchy will determine, in large part, what that person wants out of life in general and from the workplace in particular (see Figure 5-2). Consider, for example, a person on the "first rung" of the Maslow hierarchy. Certainly this individual will be more satisfied receiving a living wage than recognition as "employee of the month." And, as we know, a satisfied employee is a more productive employee.

It is important to note that movement up the Maslow hierarchy of needs is progressive; that is, "lower" needs must first be satisfied before "higher" needs make themselves felt. Further, if people operating at a higher need level are suddenly confronted by conditions which push them back to a lower level, then those lower needs will

What a Person Wants out of Life	Maslow's Hierarchy of Needs	What a Person Wants out of a Job
Freedom Personal growth (self-development) Achieve full human potential	Self-actualization needs	Creative and challenging work Responsibility for decision making Flexibility and freedom
Status Prestige Recognition for achievement	Esteem needs	Promotion Praise (recognition) by supervisor Merit pay increase
Social relationships Acceptance by others Affiliation	Social needs	Compatible work group Social activities at work Friendship at work
Security Safety "Nest egg"	Safety needs	Safe and healthy working conditions Job security Reasonable wages and fringe benefits
Food Water Clothing and shelter	Physiological needs	Meals Shelter from the elements Subsistence wages

Figure 5-2 What people want out of life and work at various levels of Maslow's need hierarchy.

once again predominate. An example: Suppose you're a wealthy businessperson who functions at the esteem level of human needs. One afternoon your pleasure boat is blown out to sea and suddenly you're forced to fight for survival on a day-to-day basis. Under such conditions you would revert to functioning at the level of physiological needs until the crisis was resolved.[3]

Some Limitations of the Maslow Model

As I pointed out earlier, Maslow's need hierarchy isn't a precise scientific instrument for predicting human behavior; rather, it is a descriptive model that gives us general guidelines for classifying and understanding human needs.

When considering Maslow, you should be aware that not all people behave according to his model. For instance, some people are motivated by more than one need at a time—like the person who strives for social relationships (social need) and prestige (esteem need) at the same time. There are also people who don't fit into the five-step progression of needs in the need hierarchy. Some people skip over certain need levels entirely (as when a person moves from safety

[3]For a good example of what happens when people are suddenly thrust into a survival situation read Paul Piers, *Alive*, Lippincott, Philadelphia, 1974.

needs directly to esteem needs); others voluntarily move *down* the need hierarchy (for instance, well-paid executives who quit their jobs in favor of subsistence farming on an agricultural commune). Finally, there is the factor of *rising expectations*.

> As people partially satisfy each need, they tend to require more of it for full satisfaction. This . . . phenomenon of rising expectations . . . partially explains why workers today are unhappy with their earnings even though earnings have never been higher. A starving factory worker of the 1800s was overjoyed to earn enough to buy an extra potato. A factory worker today becomes angry if he cannot afford steak.[4]

So much for the limitations of the Maslow model. Even with such shortcomings, it can still be an extremely valuable ally in your efforts to manage more effectively. Do, however, keep those limitations in mind.

Using Maslow to Manage

A basic premise of this book can be expressed in the statement: *if you want worker productivity you must satisfy worker needs.* I began this chapter by suggesting that many contemporary managers can't satisfy worker needs because they don't know what they are. I then presented the Maslow model to help you understand the types of human needs and how they function, an understanding that should put you in a better position to identify your workers' needs more accurately. Let me explain why this is so.

Based on what Maslow has said, you now know the types of needs workers have and the corresponding factors that can be used to satisfy those needs on the job (Figure 5-2). Further, you realize that once a need is satisfied it ceases to motivate a person and other needs "take over." Finally, you are now aware that a person normally satisfies needs step by step, starting with the basic physiological (survival) needs and moving up to the psychological needs of esteem and self-actualization.

Given this information, plus your knowledge of current economic conditions, you might well decide that most contemporary American workers will be motivated by higher (as opposed to lower) level needs. And you would be right (see Box 5-2). Of course, this wasn't always

---

[4]Michael Mescon and David Rachman, *Business Today,* Random House, New York, 1976, p. 159.

BOX 5-2

HOW BOSSES GET PEOPLE TO WORK HARDER*

Despite inflation's bite, most workers put job satisfaction ahead of a raise, says a noted industrial psychologist, Arthur Witkin. He asserts that recognition by the boss, the opportunity to participate in management decisions and a feeling that one's work is useful are more important in motivating employees than is salary or job security. Management often doesn't get its money's worth from fringe benefits, he adds, and promotions aren't always welcomed.

The following is an excerpt, reprinted from *U.S. News and World Report,* from an interview with Witkin, who is chief psychologist for the Personnel Sciences Center in New York City and an associate professor at Queens College.

Q: Professor Witkin, how do people's attitudes toward their jobs differ from attitudes in the past?

A: Workers today are far more interested in personal satisfaction, in "doing their own thing." They put less stress on cash pay and on long-term job security. They are motivated by far more complex things than was true of jobholders a generation or so ago.

The greatest mistake management can make is to fail to understand this complexity of motivation. Often an employer will say: "Workers want money. We'll pay them more, and that will do the trick." Of course, that doesn't do the trick. It's the sort of thing that might work with Pavlov's dogs—where you have a simple stimulus-response relationship—but it won't work with humans.

Q: What accounts for the marked change in work attitudes recently?

A: A whole series of factors have come into play: Our country has a higher level of education than ever before, and a higher standard of living. Youngsters are more sophisticated; they want to throw off parental shackles and get away from school discipline. And, of course, none of today's young people has had any contact with an economic setback as severe as the Depression of the 1930s.

*Excerpt from an interview with Arthur Witkin, "How Bosses Get People to Work Harder," *U.S. News & World Report,* Jan. 29, 1979, pp. 63–64. Copyright 1979 U.S. News & World Report, Inc.

The result of all this is that younger workers feel they can pretty much call their own tune on a job; if they don't like what they see, they'll pick up their marbles and walk away. They figure they can always find something else, or maybe collect unemployment insurance.

Q: Has the rise of two-income families spurred the idea of worker independence?

A: I'm sure it has. If one partner wants to change jobs, it's not the traumatic situation that it would be if there were only a single breadwinner.

It's no longer as hard to survive in this country as it was years ago. Workers once were so preoccupied with making enough money to provide food and to keep a roof over their heads that they never had time to contemplate whether there was anything beyond that— something more to the job than just earning a living. Today's affluence has made all the difference. And, of course, the job-satisfaction idea cuts two ways: A working wife wants to be happy at work just as does her husband.

Q: How can management deal with this?

A: Perhaps the single most important thing is to be aware of a worker's need for self-esteem. Everyone needs to feel good about himself; if he doesn't, he'll not only turn in a poor job performance, he'll keep others from doing their best.

One way to deal with this involves worker participation in decisions that concern them. Some matters, for instance, must be solely a management prerogative, such as where a new plant should be located; but there are many other decisions in which workers can be given a say.

the case. In earlier times, when labor rights were nonexistent and wages desperately low, workers could not have cared less about prestige or the opportunity for self-esteem—their concern was survival and security, pure and simple.[5] With the rise of labor unions and

---

[5]For a depiction of workers struggling to stay alive in early industrial America read Upton Sinclair's novel *The Jungle.*

social legislation, however, plus four decades of unprecedented prosperity, working conditions changed. Labor won better wages and job security. Many workers found their physiological and safety needs were satisfied—*and a satisfied need ceases to motivate an individual.* These workers began looking to different kinds of satisfactions, satisfactions connected with needs higher on the Maslow hierarchy— the needs for social interaction, esteem, and self-fulfillment. This quest continues into the 1980s. Of course, should economic conditions take a dramatic downturn to a point where survival or job security once again becomes a meaningful concern, then (as Maslow predicted) we can expect many workers to again be motivated by physiological and safety needs.

HOW CAN I IDENTIFY MY OWN WORKERS' NEEDS?

In general, when it comes to today's workers you can be fairly certain (all things being equal) that most of your full-time employees will be striving to fulfill higher-level needs on the Maslow hierarchy.

Of course, there will always be exceptions to any general rule; and for that reason your ability to assess accurately any *specific* worker's needs will be improved if you get to know your employees individually and any personal circumstances that might affect their needs (see Chapter 6, pp. 72–73). For example, those who might normally be concerned with self-esteem will focus instead on security needs if they suddenly finds their financial nest egg destroyed by an unexpected (and costly) medical problem.

Sometimes the only way to be sure about the particular needs of individual workers is to offer them several different on-the-job *rewards,* each designed to satisfy a different need on the Maslow hierarchy, and then watch to see which is the most effective. To do this successfully you'll want to learn more about which rewards go with which needs and how you can administer those rewards effectively in the workplace. This involves the use of behavior modification—a technique you can learn to use once you read Chapters 6, 7, and 8.

Chapter 6

Give the Nod to Behavior Mod

Behavior modification isn't magic, but it sure works like it on the job.

Manager of a fast-food restaurant

You can't satisfy worker needs if you don't know what they are. In Chapter 5 we found out what they are, and now we're ready to satisfy those needs through the use of *behavior modification,* a powerful and exciting behavioral science technique that can be used to fulfill worker needs and enhance worker productivity at the same time.

WHAT IS BEHAVIOR MODIFICATION?

Behavior modification is a *scientific* procedure for systematically changing behavior through the use of rewards or punishments or both. Defined in such a manner, free of academic jargon, the method

61

seems, to some people, to offer nothing new. In one sense, those people are correct: The man who purchases flowers for his wife or spanks his child is practicing a rudimentary form of behavior modification (rudimentary in comparison with the more sophisticated, systematic, and effective behavior modification used by scientists). Nevertheless, these people are incorrect in assuming that behavior modification is "old hat." What makes the approach novel (and effective) is the use of psychological learning principles in the reinforcement of behavior.

Although the major thrust of behavior modification only began in the 1960s, the impetus for the movement came from investigations in the earlier decades of this century. One classic and influential study was performed in 1920 by John Watson, father of psychological behaviorism and advocate of human behavior control. Watson was convinced that such control was feasible and, not one to hide his convictions, once boasted:

> Give me a dozen healthy infants, well formed, and my own specified world to bring them up in and I'll guarantee to take any one at random and train him to become any type of specialist I might select—doctor, lawyer, artist, merchant-chief, and, yes, even beggar-man and thief, regardless of his talents, penchants, tendencies, abilities, vocations, and race of his ancestors.[1]

Unlike many of his contemporaries who speculated on such matters but went no further, Watson set out to substantiate his claims in the laboratory. His proof was gathered at the expense of Albert, a normal, healthy infant. Albert was basically stolid and unemotional. He cried infrequently, didn't scare easily, and, except when confronted with loud sounds, showed no signs of fear. At 9 months of age, he was suddenly presented with objects he had never seen before, including a white rat, a rabbit, a dog, a monkey, cotton, and wool; and he approached these objects without apprehension.

At this juncture, Watson set out to prove his point: that he could control Albert's behavior at will and, specifically, make him afraid of the white rat he now approached fearlessly. The animal was admitted into Albert's playroom, as it had been before, but now each time the

---

[1]John Watson, *Behaviorism,* People's Institute, New York, 1924, p. 82.

child reached for the animal, a loud gong was struck nearby. After a very few of these encounters, Albert began to cry and scurry away whenever he saw the rat, even when the gong did *not* sound. Furthermore, the child showed fear of other objects that looked like a rat, for example, the white rabbit he had earlier approached without fear. By a few pairings of a negative reinforcer (loud sound) with an initially attractive plaything, Watson was effectively able to condition little Albert's behavior and make him afraid of a whole class of objects similar to and including a white rat.[2]

My First Experience with Behavior Modification

I've always had an "I'm from Missouri . . . show me" attitude about things, so when I first heard about behavior modification as an undergraduate, my first reaction was skepticism. My second reaction was to test it and see what would happen. I was a psychology major and I remember thinking: If this really works, it should work for me. I checked with some of my classmates. They felt the same way. So, in the true spirit of science, we set out to see whether we could control human actions using behavior modification. Our little experiment was conducted on a particularly unpopular teacher, a chap we dubbed Mr. Monotone.

Mr. Monotone was the kind of instructor whose lectures should have been recorded and sold to hardcore insomniacs. I am sure the cure rate would have been astounding. Three times a week, an hour a day, he gave his dreadful little lectures, delivered in a dronelike monotone from a mouth that hardly seemed to move. To make matters worse, Mr. Monotone stood rigidly behind the podium and stared straight ahead when he spoke. In fact, the only real evidence that he was alive (besides the steady stream of words tumbling colorlessly from his lips) was his tendency to scratch his head with his left hand. This little gesture occurred five or six times an hour, usually at 8- to 10-minute intervals.

We decided to see if we could increase the frequency of Mr. Monotone's head-scratching gesture through behavior modification. First we enlisted the aid of a few students in his class (in addition to ourselves) to participate in the "investigation." Once everyone knew

[2]John Watson and R. Rayner, "Conditioned Emotional Reactions," *Journal of Experimental Psychology*, vol. 3, 1920, pp. 1–14.

what to do, we situated ourselves in a row near the front of the class, and here's what we did: Every time Mr. Monotone lectured in his normal, motionless manner we showed no real interest in the lecture. But whenever he made his head-scratching gesture we immediately went into action, nodding our heads in approval, smiling, furiously scribbling notes—everything we could to reward Mr. Monotone with something we figured he needed: social approval.

Sure enough, in a matter of hours, Mr. Monotone was scratching his head like a dog with fleas. Not only did he scratch more frequently, but his hand stayed in his hair longer each time he did.

The results of our little study spoke well for the power of behavior modification to control certain kinds of behavior. It took only a few lectures before Mr. Monotone had increased his head scratching in response to our reward of social approval. Furthermore, when we ended the experiment (stopped giving approval for the head-scratching behavior), it gradually returned to its normal prereinforcement levels.

Little Albert and Mr. Monotone Compared

John Watson's experiment with little Albert and our investigation with Mr. Monotone share one important characteristic: the use of *reinforcement* to change behavior. Behavior modification works by increasing or decreasing the likelihood of a specified behavioral response through systematic reward and punishment. Little Albert received negative reinforcement (loud sound), and it is assumed that such punishment will eventually lead to cessation of the negatively reinforced behavior. In the case of Mr. Monotone, the reinforcement was positive (social approval), and it is expected that rewarded behavior will be maintained (and often increase in frequency). The process by which reinforcement becomes associated with certain behaviors is called *conditioning*. The psychologist uses his knowledge of conditioning principles to make his efforts more effective.

One can get a feeling for the power of conditioning procedures, for how such methods can systematically change a wide variety of human actions, by reading B. F. Skinner's novel *Walden Two*. Although it is labeled a work of fiction, it is grounded in scientific facts, using the established learning principles underlying behavior modification to regulate human behavior and create a utopian community. In reality, the book is a reflection of Skinner's scientific thinking from start to finish, an application of his operant conditioning methods to the design of a society created and governed by psychologists.

In *Walden Two,* everyone is well-behaved, happy, and productive. Citizens are controlled, but they are not aware of being controlled. Control is achieved by procedures similar to those employed by Watson with little Albert and the undergraduates with Mr. Monotone. Explains the novel's psychologist-hero: "When he behaves as we want him to behave, we simply create a situation he likes, or remove one he doesn't like. As a result, the probability that he will behave that way again goes up, which is what we want. Technically it's called 'positive reinforcement.' "[3] *Walden Two* is deeply grounded in the principles of behavior modification.

In the years since the early work of Watson and Skinner, scientists have made behavior modification a far more powerful system for controlling behavior. At the same time, they have used it to change increasingly complex and diverse types of human activity. Some behavior modification takes place in clinical settings, where it is used to eliminate or modify dysfunctional personal behavior. The ability of behavior modification to change entrenched, highly resistant forms of human activity reminds us of its potency as a behavior control device.

USING BEHAVIOR MODIFICATION IN THE WORKPLACE

It was only a matter of time before the behavior-changing power of behavior modification attracted the attention of the business community. Would the technique be effective in the workplace? Ask Emery Air Freight Corporation. In the early 1970s the company embarked on a pioneering behavior modification program which saved it over $2 million in 3 years.[4]

Part of the program centered on the customer service department, where employees were charged with the responsibility of answering all customer inquiries within a 90-minute time frame. (If you had a question about shipping rates, the goal of the customer service

[3]B. Skinner, *Walden Two,* Macmillan, New York, 1948.
[4]Herbert Huebner and Alton Johnson, "Behavior Modification: An Aid in Solving Personnel Problems," *The Personnel Administrator,* October 1974, p. 34.

representative was to get back to you with an answer within 90 minutes.) When customer service representatives were asked how often they met the 90-minute goal, their response was optimistic: 90 percent of the time. Research, however, revealed that the goal was being achieved only 30 percent of the time.

To try and improve employee performance, each customer service representative was asked to record the actual time it took to answer each incoming inquiry on a log sheet. The log sheets were then checked daily by management, and feedback was given to employees concerning how well they were doing. Anytime an employee showed improved performance (more calls answered within the 90-minute limit) they were *rewarded* with praise from their supervisor. Even those who didn't improve their performance received a reward of sorts: they were praised for their honesty and accuracy in filling out their log sheets and were then reminded of the 90-minute goal.

The results of the behavior modification program were dramatic. After a few days of feedback and praise, customer service representatives were meeting the 90-minute time limit 90 percent of the time—and some employees were even setting higher goals for themselves.

The same basic behavior modification design was utilized by Emery Air Freight Corporation in its shipping department. Using the log-sheet approach, shipping department employees monitored their performance and received feedback and praise from their supervisors. The result? Container-packing efficiency jumped from 45 percent to 90 percent, saving the company over half a million dollars per year in shipping costs.[5]

How has the business community reacted to Emery Air Freight's pioneering experience with behavior modification? Being basically conservative, business leaders haven't suddenly embraced the technique as the ultimate cure-all. Yet the developments of the past decade make one thing clear: behavior modification will become an increasingly important management tool for shaping profits and worker satisfaction in the coming years (see Box 6-1). This should come as no

---

[5]Ibid. See also: "New Tool: Reinforcement for Good Work," *Psychology Today,* April 1972, pp. 67–69 (digested from article in *Business Week,* Dec. 18, 1971).

BOX 6-1

PRODUCTIVITY GAINS FROM A PAT ON THE BACK*

When Edward J. Feeney pioneered the systematic use of "positive reinforcement" to cut costs by $2 million . . . at Emery Air Freight Corporation a decade ago, few in the mainstream of management innovation paid much attention. They concentrated instead on other newly evolving techniques, such as job enrichment and management by objectives which seemed easier to implement and freer of dark psychological overtones. Now, though still in an evolutionary stage in business, the Feeney techniques—commonly called "behavior modification" and identified with Harvard psychologist B. F. Skinner—are increasingly being recognized as a valuable tool with which managers can combat slumping productivity growth rates, reduce absenteeism and turnover, and, in most cases, provide increased job satisfaction for employees.

Skinner's theories, which hold that all behavior can be affected by positive rewards such as praise or recognition, may seem too obvious to be called a management technique. Indeed, Skinnerians contend, successful managers have always been using behavioral principles, but only now are they attempting to systematize the approach. And many are reporting dramatic results.

"A conservative estimate of our cost savings in 1977 alone is $3.5 million, and that is not including employee morale, which is difficult to quantify," says Jay L. Beecroft, who runs a program using Skinner principles at 3M Co. Other major companies adopting such programs, which experts estimate at more than 100, include Frito-Lay, Addressograph-Multigraph, B. F. Goodrich, Weyerhaeuser, and Warner-Lambert. Many are in trial stages, however, or in selected divisions. At 3M, for instance, one program was applied to the specific task of unloading trailers, while at A-M it is being used largely with office workers. Still other companies, such as Ford, American Telephone & Telegraph, and General Electric, are using a modified form of Skinner concepts, incorporating them with other management techniques.

SETTING STANDARDS

Like 3M, most companies using behavior modification have recorded sizable cost savings, along with huge gains in worker productivity. And nearly all have achieved at least a 200% return on investment. In fact, one California firm, Carl Pitts Associates, of Del Mar, guarantees in writing to save companies twice the firm's $15,000 fee in one year.

To structure the approach, successful programs typically begin with a series of meetings in which managers and employees discuss mutual needs and problems and propose solutions. These diagnostic sessions are considered critical because it is in them that managers set standards for job performance and determine how they will be met. At the same time, employees identify their needs and provide their managers with a list of reinforcers that should "modify" the employees' behavior. A-M, for example, holds a three-day session. What workers, such as clerk typists, want most is a sense of belonging, a sense of accomplishment, and a sense of teamwork, says program director C. Eugene Dickerson. In return, managers ask for quicker filing of reports with fewer errors.

The second step is to arrange for worker performance to be observed with a reliable follow-up; the third is to give feedback often, immediately letting employees know how their current level of performance compares with the level desired. At Western Air Lines Inc., for instance, five telephone reservation offices, employing about 1,800 people, keep track of the percentage of calls in which callers make flight reservations. Then they feed back the results daily to each employee. At the same time, supervisors are instructed to praise employees for asking callers for their reservations. Since the program started, the ratio of sales to calls has soared from one in four to one in two.

BONING UP

Contributing to the technique's appeal are a growing number of consultants specializing in the field. Many have jumped into the arena behind Feeney, who set up shop in Ridgefield, Connecticut, in 1974 after his successes at Emery. Behavioral Systems Inc., however, began operating in 1971, and now claims to be the largest in the field, with $2 million a year in business. It employs 35 consultants and is being bankrolled by Minnesota Viking quarterback Fran Tarkenton. Interest has also spread to business schools. At the University of Michigan, for example, reinforcement seminars are constantly overbooked, a turnaround from a couple of years ago. Many companies, such as B. F. Goodrich, are sending managers to class to bone up on the subject. "The organization of the future is learning that productivity can be improved by managing the most important resource, and that is the human resource," says Roger Howe, director of personnel and organizational development at Goodrich, which started using behavior techniques three years ago to reduce scrap costs, among other things.

SUCCESSFUL USERS

Another company that has chalked up good results is Los Angeles–based Collins Foods International Inc., which started a program in 1974 for 70 clerical employees in its accounting staff. After determining the staff's actual performance in such areas as billing error rates, supervisors and employees got together to discuss and set goals for improvement. Employees were praised for reports containing fewer errors than the norm, and results were charted on a regular basis. According to Gerald R. Wahlin, controller, improvements have been dramatic. For instance, the error rate in the accounts payable department fell from more than 8% to less than 0.2%.

Malcolm Warren is another successful user of the technique. He ran behavior modification programs at Questor Corp. and Dayton Hudson Corp. before forming his own company, Performance Technologies Inc., a few months ago, with Saks & Co. among his new clients. While at Dayton Hudson, however, he set up a program to increase sales in the men's department of one of the company's stores. The average sale was $19. Warren established a standard of $25. Employees were taught how to make extra sales and were congratulated by supervisors each time a sale went above $19. Within two months, department sales averaged $23.

With success, quite naturally, comes expansion. At Dallas-based Frito-Lay Inc., a division of PepsiCo. Inc., behavior modification programs are now in place at 23 of 37 plants and soon will be under way at the remainder. Techniques are used only in manufacturing operations, such as the packaging machine assembly line, but the company is looking at applications elsewhere, including sales and distribution. Dr. David A. Lyman, associate manager of management development, stresses that programs must be used carefully, recognizing all the subtle conditions that must accompany them to make them work properly. "Our experience is that we can't go into a plant without some other things occurring first," cautions Lyman. "For instance, in a union plant you have to have an element of trust and cooperation between the personnel manager and union leaders." Another consideration, he says, is the personality of managers. "If you have a bunch of Attila the Huns running the plant, they're more likely to use the system as a club."

GAINING ACCEPTANCE

Lyman also points out that in Frito-Lay plants using behavior modification procedures, the average time required for a first-line supervisor to earn a promotion to a shift manager is 14 to 20 months. And one supervisor, he says, made the jump in nine months. This compares with an average of 24 to 30 months' promotion time in the company's other plants.

This move toward motivating employees to greater productivity is a move in the right direction, but it will be a slow and perhaps painful process for some, warns Kenneth L. Sperling, director of organization and career development at Warner-Lambert Co. The company has been successfully experimenting with Skinnerian principles in packaging operations at plants in Puerto Rico and Mexico, and will be introducing programs at other plants this year. In five or ten years, Sperling says, Skinner principles will be a much more accepted way of doing business. Managers will soon realize that an employee's involvement in determining his own best output level should provide the highest return to the bottom line. "There is a general feeling among managers that Skinner's concepts are undermining what they perceive to be their right to manage," Sperling observes. "But what managers must realize is that managing is not a right, it's a responsibility."

surprise, particularly when you consider the increasing number of psychologists and psychologically trained managers entering the business world. They're familiar with the power of behavior modification, and they'll be in a position to use it on the job. No doubt they will, and I hope you do, too.

INSTITUTIONAL VERSUS PERSONAL BEHAVIOR MODIFICATION PROGRAMS

In reality, there are two kinds of behavior modification programs that can be used in the workplace. One kind I call the *institutional* behavior modification program; it is amply described in Box 6-1. Normally, such a program is a highly formalized, large-scale affair, requiring coordinating and directing skills that come from years of specialized education and training. If as a manager you should be asked to participate in such a program, feel free to do so. But I don't recommend that you *start* one. The responsibility for creating and directing institutional behavior modification programs is best left to professional consultants or in-house organizational development (OD) directors. They have the proper training for the job, you don't.

Do not despair, however. There is still the second kind of program, called the *personal* behavior modification program, that you *can* start; in fact, it is labeled personal because you can use it with your employees even if no other manager in the entire organization follows suit. And, best of all, you don't need the specialized skills of the trained psychologist or professional consultant to make a personal behavior modification program function effectively in the workplace.[6] What you do need is a willingness to commit some time and effort to the undertaking, a caring attitude toward your employees, an unwavering commitment to use behavior modification in an ethical manner and a set of guidelines for applying personal behavior modification on the job. Let us turn to those guidelines now.

HOW YOU CAN UTILIZE BEHAVIOR MODIFICATION WITH YOUR EMPLOYEES

From our discussion of Maslow's need hierarchy and the experiments in behavior modification, you now possess two vital pieces of information:

1 Individual workers have individual needs, and they will behave in ways that lead to the satisfaction of those needs.

2 Behavior that is rewarded will be maintained or will even increase in frequency.

---

[6]This is primarily because personal behavior modification programs (unlike institutional programs) do not present the complex design and coordination problems that require the attention of more highly trained personnel. Let's face it, there are many people who can serve up an excellent feast for ten to twenty guests at home, but that doesn't qualify them to walk into the local restaurant and prepare a banquet for six hundred.

Putting this information together, your goal as a manager is to reinforce appropriate work behavior with rewards that satisfy the particular needs of individual employees. This should enhance worker productivity and satisfy worker needs, thus establishing the ++ relationship essential to making the workplace a worthplace.

To accomplish this goal will require you to successfully complete a three-step process:

Step 1   You will have to identify the specific needs of your individual workers.

Step 2   You will have to satisfy each worker's specific need(s) with the appropriate reward(s).

Step 3   You will have to administer worker rewards effectively.

Step 1, which has already been discussed in Chapter 5, will be examined again in the next few pages.

Step 2 will be discussed in Chapter 7, where you will find the various reinforcements you can use in motivating your workers. You can use any or all of these rewards, depending on your circumstances and the particular needs of your various employees.

Step 3 will be discussed in Chapter 8, where you will learn the basic rules for administering rewards in a manner that maximizes worker productivity and satisfaction.

A FINAL NOTE ON IDENTIFYING WORKER NEEDS

In Chapter 5 I gave you Maslow's behavioral science model to help you understand and identify your workers' needs more accurately. I also pointed out that many workers have the same needs, which tend to cluster on the higher rungs of the Maslow hierarchy. Thus, if you simply assume that *all* your employees have social, esteem and self-actualization needs, you'll probably be right in most instances.

If, however, you want to obtain greater accuracy in identifying your individual workers' needs, then it will be necessary to conscientiously observe them on the job. It doesn't take long to determine a worker's needs once you watch that person in action—in fact, once you have a little observational experience under your belt, you'll be amazed at just how quickly and accurately you can "read" an individual's needs.

Do you want to obtain the *greatest* accuracy in identifying your workers' needs? If so, observe your employees as you give them various rewards. That way you can pinpoint the reinforcements that work best for each employee. Such information is particularly valuable because, in most instances, you'll have to pick from a number of different rewards to use at any given need level of the Maslow hierarchy.

Finally, continue to observe your subordinates even *after* you have ascertained their needs and the rewards they value most. This is crucial, because workers' needs can change over time and so can their attitudes toward particular rewards. For example, some workers get bored with certain rewards if they're used too often, causing them to lose their effectiveness. If you continue to observe your subordinates, you will be alerted to these changes and be able to take corrective action. Otherwise you might miss such changes entirely and wonder why you ended up with a disgruntled, unproductive employee.

It is interesting to note that identifying worker needs with accuracy and practicing effective behavior modification both require the manager to *pay attention to the worker:* to observe, to be aware, to *see* (not look through) the people whom they supervise. I am not exaggerating when I say that paying attention to your employees is a basic prerequisite to becoming an effective human resource manager. Not only does it help you understand your workers, but it motivates them as well—as you shall soon see.

Chapter 7

Fourteen Rewards You Can Use in the Workplace

I feel more like working now that my manager seems to recognize my existence.

Shoe store salesperson

I'd like you to play scientist for a moment and consider what you'd do in the following circumstances.

Here is the situation. A major corporation has called you in to determine if variations in working conditions can influence employee productivity on the job. To find out, you begin by studying illumination in the workplace. Your hypothesis is simple enough: an increase in illumination will lead to an increase in productivity. Your experiment is simple, too. You designate one set of employees the test group and subject it to deliberate changes in illumination while it works; a second set of workers, called the control group, works under the original lighting throughout the experiment. The only problem is that the results are anything but simple; in fact, they are downright perplexing. Here is what you find:

1 Test group productivity rises when illumination is improved (increased)—as predicted by your hypothesis.
2 Test group productivity also rises when illumination is worsened (decreased). (No hypothesis ever predicted that!)
3 Output also increases in the control group—even though illumination remains constant. (Something definitely strange is going on here.)

All right, what do you do? If you answer, "Drop the experiment," you will be doing exactly what *was* done back in 1927 when a group of scientists from the Massachusetts Institute of Technology puzzled over the same results and finally abandoned the project. If, on the other hand, your curiosity is aroused and you decide to investigate further, then you will be doing exactly what was done between 1927 and 1932 by a new team of investigators headed by Elton Mayo, Fritz Roethlisberger, and William Dickson.[1]

Let us assume that you, like the Mayo team, choose to investigate further. You set up a new experiment, this time with a group of employees who assemble telephone relays. You are still concerned with how variations in the working conditions can influence employee productivity on the job. So now you vary several factors and observe what happens. Here is what you discover:

1 You institute rest periods of various durations. Result: Productivity goes up.
2 You provide soup and a sandwich on the job. Result: Productivity goes up.
3 You shorten the workday by an hour. Result: Productivity goes up.

How do you explain your findings? You might reasonably surmise that rest periods, refreshments, and a shorter workday are highly conducive to productivity. If you do, in fact, subscribe to such an

[1]E. Mayo, F. Roethlisberger, and W. Dickson, *Management and the Worker,* Harvard University Press, Cambridge, Mass., 1939.

explanation, then you might be a bit hard-pressed to account for this additional experimental finding:

4 For three months all rest periods, refreshments and shortened working days are eliminated, and the employees return to the work schedule they followed before the experiment began. Result: Productivity reaches a new high—and stays there during the entire 12 weeks.

What *is* going on here? And if that's not enough to raise havoc with your scientific theories, consider the final investigative result:

5 Rest periods and refreshments are reintroduced. Result: Output climbs higher still.

O.K., scientist—what's the verdict? It seems that no matter what changes you introduce, worker output increases. Why? Elton Mayo and his associates were faced with the same question over a half century ago when they actually conducted the study with the employees who assembled telephone relays in the Hawthorne Division of the Western Electric Company. They came up with the findings I just described.

How did the Mayo team explain the results? First, they realized that something more than changed working conditions was influencing worker productivity on the job. Then they identified what that "something more" was: the *human dimension*—the social and psychological condition of the employees in the workplace. The results of the Hawthorne studies seemed to indicate that the employees ·were more satisfied and worked harder because Mayo and his associates were *paying attention to them,* making them feel more worthwhile and important on the job. By creating changes in the workplace, the Mayo team was altering the *physical* environment; but more important as far as productivity was concerned, it was also transforming the *psychological* environment by fulfilling the social and personal needs of the workers.

Now, did you guess that it was the human element producing all those strange results at the Hawthorne plant of Western Electric? If you didn't, don't feel bad—neither did Mayo and his colleagues when they first puzzled over their unexpected experimental results. In fact, it took 5 years of experimentation with over 20,000 employee-subjects before they were reasonably sure of what exactly *was* accounting for the increases in productivity.

We all owe a debt of sorts to Mayo and his associates. Even though their work has received some critical brickbats among the bouquets, they were responsible for focusing managerial attention on the human dimension in the workplace. They were also among the first behavioral scientists to recognize that workers can be motivated by social and psychological (as well as economic) needs.

USING REWARDS TO PAY ATTENTION TO THE WORKER

The Mayo team discovered the importance of paying attention to the worker, how it could increase employee output and satisfaction at the same time. Their discovery remains relevant today. In fact, as I pointed out in the previous chapter, paying attention to the worker is basic to determining worker needs and practicing effective behavior modification.

On the following pages I will be discussing fourteen different rewards you can use in satisfying your employees' needs and encouraging their productivity. These rewards are:

1 Praise
   a Job-relevant
   b Non-job-relevant
2 Public recognition
3 Job security
4 Money
5 Fringe benefits
6 Employee development programs
   a Job enrichment
   b Personality (and leadership) development
   c Mental and physical health
7 Employee involvement in decision making
8 Leisure time
9 Feedback
10 Social participation
11 Company spirit (pride)
12 Opportunity to achieve and advance in the organization
13 Degrees of freedom at work
14 Pleasant forms of moderate distraction

Every time you administer a reward you are, in effect, paying attention to the worker; your goal will be to give your subordinates those rewards that best satisfy their particular needs. In other words, you want to achieve a match between workers' needs and the rewards they receive on the job.

Before I turn to a discussion of the various rewards, I will list some points that should help you choose and administer your rewards more effectively. A more complete discussion of these points will be found in Chapter 8.

1   Most of the fourteen rewards are geared to satisfying social, esteem, or self-fulfillment needs. This reflects our thinking that most contemporary workers have needs that fall in the upper ranges of the Maslow hierarchy.

2   The reward that works best is the reward that satisfies a worker's need(s) most successfully.

3   Many workers have several different needs at once, allowing you to use several different kinds of rewards in such circumstances.

4   Certain rewards can satisfy more than one human need. That is, some rewards overlap need levels in the Maslow hierarchy (for instance, money can satisfy physiological, safety, and esteem needs).

5   Certain needs can be satisfied by more than one reward. Choose the reward that works best for the individual worker in question.

6   Be on the lookout for boredom effects if you use the same reward frequently for a particular employee.

7   Don't be afraid to experiment with using the various rewards. The more rewards you can utilize effectively, the better manager you'll be.

REWARD 1: PRAISE

There are two kinds of praise you can use to satisfy worker needs: *job-relevant* praise and *non-job-relevant* praise. Let me discuss each in turn.

Job-Relevant Praise

Complimenting a worker for a job well done is probably the simplest and most basic reward you can administer—and it is also one of the most effective. Remember the survey in Chapter 5? Number 1 on the workers' "want parade" was full appreciation of work done. Praising an employee for superior job performance can show that appreciation, and unlike some rewards, such as money, it doesn't cost you anything.

Nationally recognized management consultant Dr. John F. Mee had this to say when asked if praise pays with today's employees: "Recognition for a job well-done reinforces an individual's self-image and self-satisfaction. . . . Praise increases an individual's pride and . . . hopes of making a contribution. Praise and recognition for a job well-done make for better employees."[2]

With all the benefits accruing from the use of praise, you'd think that contemporary managers would use it frequently. Right?

Wrong! Very few managers use praise or use it often enough; in fact, some are stingier with compliments than Scrooge was with money. Managers who have this attitude toward praise can usually be classified into one of two types. If you've ever had a job, you'll probably think I knew some of the managers you worked for.

Type 1: The Negativistic Manager   This is the type of person who seems to have mastered the now-you-see-him, now-you-don't routine. You see him when things go wrong, and you don't when things go right. Here's how one employee described the behavior of her negativistic manager:

> I work in sales at a large department store, and my manager has plenty of opportunity to observe my performance. On Monday I came to work and had a very good morning. My manager said nothing. Monday afternoon I sold about normal, and still my manager said nothing. On Tuesday I had an exceptional day: I sold way over average. My manager said nothing. On Wednesday I had an average sales morning and a good afternoon. My manager said nothing. Thursday I got to work a bit early for the storewide sale and put in a busy, high-sales day. My manager said nothing. Friday started O.K., I sold about normal. My manager said nothing. Then at 2:15 Friday afternoon I made a mistake that lost us a sale. Bam! The ceiling fell in. From out of nowhere the manager came racing up and began hounding me about losing the sale. *All I'd like to know is where the hell was she all week long when I was doing great?*

[2]J. Mee (interview), "Understanding the Attitudes of Today's Employees," *Nation's Business,* August 1976, p. 24.

The negativistic manager is the person responsible for the often-heard worker lament: The only time my manager talks with me about my work is when I do something wrong. Is it any wonder the worker gripes? The negativistic manager is a real motivation-destroyer. Nobody likes to feel that good work is ignored while any mistake receives maximum management attention. As one worker so aptly told her manager: "At least if you're going to criticize my mistakes, give equal time to my successes."

Type 2: The Perfectionistic Manager This type of person isn't unwilling to praise a worker for a job well done *as long as the job is done perfectly.* The problem is, the perfectionistic manager's standards are so high that hardly anybody reaches the competence level required to trigger a kind word.

I have had many perfectionistic managers approach me and ask, "Why should I praise workers if they don't measure up to my standard of excellence? Didn't you say that praise should be given only when you think a person honestly deserves it?"

My answers to such inquiries are always the same. Yes, you should only praise a worker when you can do so honestly, but there are ways you can honestly praise a person for work not yet up to your standards while, at the same time, encouraging that person to reach those high standards in the future. Here is what you do. Note the employee's work performance over a period of time. You will see that it varies; that is, sometimes it is better than other times. Now it might be true that even when the worker is performing best, the work might not measure up to your standards; but that shouldn't stop you from congratulating the worker for a better work performance.

There is a difference between saying, "Hey, Ms. Jones, I want to congratulate you on doing better" and "Hey, Ms. Jones, you're doing great work." Possibly, by rewarding a worker for an improvement in work performance you'll encourage that worker to keep improving until reaching, someday, a level a competence that justifies compliments without qualifications. (By the way, rewarding a worker for performance that approaches an ideal standard is called reinforcement by "successive approximations" and is an effective way to increase worker performance and satisfaction on the job.)

Make sure you don't get trapped in the pitfalls of either negativistic or perfectionistic managing when it's your turn to step into a supervisory role. Be prepared to use praise as an effective reward for deserving employees, particularly when those employees have either social or esteem needs, or both.

There are many ways to give praise on the job (see, for example, Box 7-1), but it should always be (1) honest (the employee should deserve the praise), (2) fair (everyone should have an equal chance of getting praise for similar performance), and (3) not so frequent that it loses its effectiveness. When an employee's performance is so great that you feel too much praise might become a problem, then alternate praise with another of the fourteen rewards. That should help reduce the danger of any one reward losing its potency through overuse.

BOX 7-1

THE COMPLIMENTARY INTERVIEW

When most employees think about interviews, they conjure up images of tough-minded corporate recruiters grilling nervous job applicants about their credentials; or else they think about performance appraisals where tough-nosed managers interrogate them about every facet of their job performance. The thought of going through such interviews is not very appealing to most workers; in fact, some find them downright unnerving.

Imagine, then, the pleasant surprise in store for employees who report for interviews with their managers and find out the purpose of the interview is to praise them for their performance on the job. Talk about the intertwining of relief and reward! What these workers have just experienced is the *complimentary interview,* a technique highly recommended by management experts Joseph Cangemi and Jeffrey Claypool.

The complimentary interview is an excellent way to provide deserving workers with praise reward. As the authors observe:

> The complimentary interview program allows management to share respect, praise, concern, trust and appreciation with employees in a formal way. There is evidence that this sort of management/employee communication tends to produce a strong, committed and efficient work force. This approach does not require direct financial investment on the part of the company—only time. On the contrary, even the smallest de-

crease in waste, cost or absenteeism, or an increase in safety, production, quality, is a good return on the investment of complimentary interviews.*

*Joseph Cangemi and Jeffrey Claypool, "Complimentary Interviews: A System for Rewarding Outstanding Employees," *Personnel Journal,* February 1978, p. 90.

Non-Job-Relevant Praise

Praise, to be effective, doesn't have to be limited to job performance. People like to be complimented on a whole range of behaviors, and that is where non-job-relevant praise comes in.

Let us presume that you're a manager, and one day you spot a subordinate walking into the office wearing a new outfit. If you honestly think the clothes are attractive, why not compliment the employee for having good taste? Such praise accomplishes two things:

It clearly demonstrates to your employees that you are aware of them (many workers complain that their supervisors don't even know who they are).

1 It satisfies the workers' need for social approval or external validation of their personal worth or for both.

There are many instances in which you as a manager will have the opportunity to practice non-job-relevant praise. For example:

1 Changes in a worker's personal appearance you find suitable for praise

2 Acquisitions by a worker (for instance, a new car, house, briefcase, or watch) you find suitable for praise

3 Significant occasions in a worker's life (for example, birthdays, weddings, graduations)

4 Significant off-the-job achievements in a worker's life (for instance, civic awards, election to office in a social or fraternal organization, religious activities, outstanding performance in sports)

Normally, workers are proud of their non-job-relevant activities, and they will be pleased that you chose to share their pride; however, let me make a few cautionary recommendations:

1 Some workers feel strongly about keeping their work life and personal life separate. Thus, they may feel offended by a manager who invades the privacy of their off-the-job world. This is a relatively rare problem, but one you should keep in mind when giving out non-job-relevant praise.

2 If you are going to congratulate one worker on a special occasion (birthday, graduation, marriage, or other occasion), then you should acknowledge every other worker when similar events occur. The only way you can do this is to gather information from the same source(s) and to be sure to do so regularly.

3 Most workers are pleased to be remembered for positive, happy occasions but might be miffed if a manager was to bring up a negative, I'd-like-to-forget-the-whole-thing event. For example, it would be the height of bad taste for you as a manager to send your employee a note congratulating him for beating a drunken driving rap.

This brings us to a sensitive issue. What should a manager do about an employee's personal tragedy, for instance, a death in the immediate family? There is no general rule I can give you to cover that kind of situation, except possibly to warn you to handle each incident with great tact and care. Under normal circumstances I see no reason why a condolence card cannot be sent, or possibly flowers or a contribution according to the wishes set forth in the obituary. I also feel it is within the bounds of good taste to express your sympathy upon the employee's return to work and your willingness to be of help should any help be desired. An employee will normally appreciate such a considerate gesture and show appreciation in on-the-job performance.

REWARD 2: PUBLIC RECOGNITION

One of my friends is an engineer with an interesting story to tell. It seems that a few years back he was working at a large company that combined public recognition with employee parking in a unique fashion. Here is what happened.

At that particular company parking was a problem, with employee lots strung out a good distance from the main plant. In fact, some of the outlying parking spaces were a 20-minute walk away, which meant that closer-in parking was coveted by all the workers. Then there were the six assigned parking places as close-in as one could get, three on either side of the main plant door, where all employees entered the building. Five of the six slots were reserved for company officers, and each bore the name of the particular executive painted on a large wooden sign. And the sixth space?

It was reserved for the "employee of the month," complete with name painted in bold letters on the parking sign nearby. The benefits of such an honor were clear to the winners: (1) they saved up to 40 minutes a day walking to and from their cars; (2) they got the opportunity to "rub shoulders" with top company officials every day; and (3) all employees walking into the plant saw the name of the employee of the month.

Now that's public recognition! Of course, such recognition doesn't have to be so elaborate to be effective—for instance, simply praising a person in front of others is a form of public recognition that can be very successful. What makes public recognition effective is sharing the news of a worker's meritorious service with others. Individuals with social and esteem needs want the approval of their supervisors and their peers; they want the external validation of their worth that leads to a sense of self-respect and personal pride. And they get it through public recognition.

There are many ways you can give public recognition on the job, some of which you may already be familiar with.

1 Employee of the month. This is one of the most common forms of public recognition and can be utilized for any number of reasons (for example, highest sales, best suggestion, least absenteeism, highest output, least errors).

2 Secretary for a day. This is normally a promotion sponsored by radio stations. The winner is publicly recognized over the air and often gets a packet of treats (such as dinner and gift certificates) as well. Normally, managers nominate their own secretaries for the contest.

3 Million-dollar round table or similar types of "clubs." Hence, people are publicly recognized for achieving significant sales in a calendar year. Often insurance companies will publish pictures of their million-dollar round-table representatives in a periodical like *Time*. Not only does this reward the employee, it also affords the opportunity to cut the picture out and have it framed for the office, where customers will be duly impressed.

4 Write-ups in the company periodical or the local newspaper.

5 Public praise.

6 Various performance charts or posters showing how an employee is doing on the job. (Sometimes performance charts or posters are used to show sales or other work indices as part of company contests.)

7 Administering honors or awards. Some companies have annual banquets where top employees receive special gifts or praise for superior performances (see Box 8-1).

8 Change in job title.

9 Publicly announced merit raises or bonuses.

10 Bestowing status symbols when appropriate.

The topic of status deserves special mention. There is a whole range of items that can be given to employees for superior performance, some of which are recognized by those employees and their coworkers as *status symbols*. What is recognized as a status symbol can vary from company to company and person to person; yet, some items seem to be almost universally recognized as status-relevant. Normally, we say something is a status symbol when (1) people want it, (2) not everyone can have it, and (3) possession of it gives the owner a degree of prestige.

In the business world there are many generally recognized status symbols, ranging all the way from the old favorite, the executive washroom key, to the ever popular company car, bigger desk, and larger office.[3] Remember almost anything can become a status symbol if it is recognized in those terms by the workers in the company.[4]

[3]Speaking of nicer offices, I had an interesting experience with this type of status symbol at the university. The building where I worked had two kinds of offices: windowed outer offices and windowless inner offices. One of my students pointed out that he thought the more desirable windowed offices were status symbols given out to professors of the highest rank. I checked out the hypothesis, and sure enough, almost every windowed office was occupied by a full professor, whereas the inner offices were assigned to faculty of lower ranks (associate and assistant professors).

[4]Whenever you give a worker some special privilege or equipment be aware that other workers might perceive this as a status symbol—even if you don't intend it that way. A few years ago a telephone company installer was replacing phones in the secretarial pool. The order called for several dozen black phones, one per desk—all in plain view of every other desk in the room. Unfortunately, the installer ended up one black phone short. "No problem," he muttered. He took a yellow phone from the truck and put it on the last desk. By noontime the next day there was almost a general strike by the secretaries who were enraged that one of their colleagues had gotten a yellow phone—a status symbol she didn't "deserve."

Using public recognition as a reward can be very effective in motivating workers and satisfying their needs, particularly if those needs are in the social and esteem range of the Maslow hierarchy. But certain precautions must be taken lest such rewards lead to serious difficulties.

1 When giving public recognition, do it fairly across the board; in other words, don't play favorites. Every employee should have an equal chance to gain public recognition for work performed.

2 Be wary of possible conflict between workers over public recognition. Particularly in small businesses you must be sure that public recognition doesn't stir up jealousies or destructive competitive rivalries between employees.

3 Be concerned if one employee gets a disproportionate share of public recognition. Not only can this lead to distress, frustration, and even "giving up" in other workers; it can also cause public recognition to lose its effectiveness for the recipient when it is overused or, worse, when the recipient shuns it to avoid rejection by the "overlooked" coworkers.

4 Most employees welcome public recognition, but some are shy about being placed in the limelight. If you have a subordinate who feels uncomfortable in the glare of public attention, use other rewards to motivate him.

REWARD 3: JOB SECURITY

As somebody who has battled for academic tenure, the issue of job security is dear to my heart. It's dear to the hearts of labor union representatives, too, and they have repeatedly struggled to gain contractual recognition of job security for workers.

From our earlier discussion it is evident that job security is not the motivator it once was. This is partially due to the fact that many contemporary workers already *have* that security. Then, too, until recently jobs were relatively abundant, and people could find employment if they were willing to look for it. Finally, with the advent of social legislation (for instance, unemployment compensation and welfare) people realized that being out of a job didn't mean being out of a meal. How vital is job security when the unemployed can depend on governmental programs to satisfy their basic needs? (This is particularly true for low-income workers, who can sometimes make more on welfare than on a job.)

Of course, should the economic picture turn bleak (high unemployment, tight money, and so forth), then the reward value of job security will increase once again. Thus your decision to use job security as a reinforcement will hinge, in part, on your reading of current economic conditions. Here are some other factors you'll want to consider when contemplating the use of job security:

1 The reward of job security is most appreciated by individuals who are lower on the Maslow hierarchy, particularly those with *safety* needs.

2 Job security as a reward will be most effective in industries hit hardest by unemployment and economic turmoil (for instance, at the beginning of the 1980s job security became a big issue to workers in the automobile industry).

3 Job security works least effectively for workers who are highly competent or have marketable skills, as they know they will have an easier time finding another job should the need arise.

4 In some companies, job security is already guaranteed in the employment contract, at which point it ceases to be an effective reward.

5 If you satisfy a worker's safety need by giving job security, recognize that new needs will predominate and change your rewards accordingly.

6 The need for job security tends to be highest when people get older (it's not as easy to find another job at an advanced age) and when they experience an upsurge in financial obligations (such as young children and unexpected bills).

REWARD 4: MONEY

With all this talk about workers' "higher needs" and the importance of psychological rewards, some of you might think I'm down on good old-fashioned money as an effective reinforcement. Nothing could be further from the truth. Money is still a very basic consideration in any jobholder's mind, and at least one management authority believes: "Money may not be the only people motivator, but many realists believe it's still the strongest one around. Apart from the material things, money buys education and opportunity, peace of mind, dignity, and more. In large measure, if you know what to do with it, money buys happiness."[5]

The same author recognizes, however, that money is not "the *only* motivator—people respond as well to interesting and meaningful work, humane treatment, or a feeling of importance and belonging."[6] In other words, there's more to life than cash.

When is it best to use money as a motivator on the job? When your employees require it to satisfy either physiological or safety needs or both. In general, workers who have financial hardships (because of unexpected costs, additional expenses, downturns in the economy, or low wages) find money more rewarding than employees who are more financially secure. There is, however, an exception to this rule. Some people equate money with self-worth and attempt to accumulate as much as they can to satisfy their esteem needs. For them, money is always a valuable reward, no matter how much they get.

Money can also be an effective motivator when it is given in a way that satisfies more than one need at a time. For example, a merit raise, publicly announced, can satisfy lower- *and* higher-level needs simultaneously (see Box 7-2).

[5]R. Dreyfack, "Dismal Disincentives," *Management Review,* December 1976, p. 51.
[6]Ibid., p. 49.

BOX 7-2

MONEY FOR MERIT

Many managers believe that money rewards can only be used to satisfy lower-level needs in the Maslow hierarchy. Not so. Money can also satisfy higher-level needs, and sometimes two or more needs at one time. It all depends on how the money is utilized with employees. At Xerox Corporation two cash merit award programs mix money with a dash of public recognition and a sprinkling of personal achievement. The result: a winning recipe for employee satisfaction and productivity.

The first type of merit award, called the Special Merit Program, is given to about 1 percent of the employees for significant contributions to the company. The amount? A lump sum of cash not less than 5 percent or more than 10 percent of the employee's annual salary.

The second type of award, called the President's Award, recognizes only the most outstanding contributions to Xerox. Very few of these awards are given, but for those employees who do receive them, the cash rewards are substantial: from 10 percent to 50 percent of annual base salary. In addition, award recipients are honored in an annual awards ceremony held at corporate headquarters, just the thing to satisfy even the most discriminating esteem need!

This information was reported in *Management Review*, June 1978, p. 44.

Finally, money rewards are often effective with part-time employees, particularly those who don't see their part-time job leading to full-time employment. Part-time employees often take work *specifically* to make money and, lacking any long-term commitment to the job, are not as excited by rewards that appeal to the career needs of full-time employees. It's like the difference one sees between a house renter and a house buyer. The person who buys a house sees it as a long-term investment and takes pride in that investment. A renter, on the other hand, has no such long-term commitment to the house and often treats it differently for that reason.

What are the problems with using money as a reward? There are two basic difficulties:

1 In most cases, if you use it too often or give out too much, it tends to lose some of its reinforcing effectiveness (even a starving person can get too much to eat).

2 Many times your financial resources will be limited, and you won't have funds available to use as rewards. In these circumstances it is imperative that you have other rewards ready for use with your employees.

In summary, money can be an effective reward, but it's not the *only* effective reward, and it shouldn't be used exclusively to increase worker productivity and satisfaction on the job. Remember, man does not live by bread alone.

REWARD 5: FRINGE BENEFITS

There are numerous kinds of fringe benefits employees can receive on the job—and, like money, how they are presented will determine what needs they can fulfill. In general, fringe benefits help satisfy safety (security) needs; but when they are tangible objects like company cars, then they can act as status symbols or a form of public recognition which can lead to satisfaction of esteem needs.

When asked if fringe benefits play a role in motivating workers, management adviser Arthur Witkin had this to say:

> Some recent studies show that fringes, when absent, can serve to demotivate, but when they're present, they aren't a positive motivating force. . . . Many psychologists, including myself, have accepted the fact that there are so-called hygienic factors involved in job satisfaction. If those factors aren't there, the company's in trouble because workers will feel their absence. But to pile on more of them has no noticeable effect in making workers more satisfied or more productive.[7]

This is an interesting point of view and seems to suggest that a certain number of fringe benefits are necessary because employees expect them, but that beyond that number they don't have much motivational impact. The vital question becomes: How *many* fringe benefits does the employee expect? There is no easy answer to this inquiry, as different workers in different industries have different needs and expectations.

In today's business world, most workers have come to expect fringe benefits like vacations, sick leave, and good group health insurance; beyond that, however, you will have to test and see whether additional benefits are worth the cost in terms of increased satisfaction and productivity in your employees.

REWARD 6: EMPLOYEE DEVELOPMENT PROGRAMS

There are three kinds of employee development programs you can use to satisfy worker needs: (1) job enrichment, (2) personality (and

[7]A. Witkin (interview), "How Bosses Get People to Work Harder," *U.S. News & World Report,* Jan. 29, 1979, p. 64.

leadership) development, and (3) mental and physical health. Let me discuss each in turn.

Job Enrichment

Let me introduce this topic with a personal story. A few years ago I was on a promotional tour, appearing on various radio and television programs to discuss a book I had written. Most of these programs were talk shows, involving 10 to 15 minutes of discussion between the host and myself. It was a comfortable, easygoing format. There was one exception, however: somehow I had been scheduled to discuss my book on a morning rock show—the kind with a disc jockey who plays "Top Ten" music to legions of rock fans listening frenetically by their radios. The idea of discussing my book between hit records, weather reports, and local ad spots—all at the hyperspeed preferred by disc jockeys—was a trifle disconcerting, but I knew it would be worth it. You see, most of my youth was spent dreaming about becoming a disc jockey, and now, at last, I was going to meet one face to face.

And I wasn't disappointed—at least, not at first. In fact, I was so fascinated with the disc jockey and his control room antics that I hardly remember the actual program. Afterward he invited me to lunch in the station's cafeteria. I gladly accepted. We ate at a small table by ourselves, and I waited patiently until he was finished before I asked him *the* question.

"Tell me," I asked, "How does it feel?"

He looked at me blankly. "What do you mean?"

"How does it *really* feel to be a disc jockey?"

His expression didn't change.

I decided to elaborate. "I mean, how does it feel to be right in the center of things—with rock stars on the one side, and the fans on the other . . . and you right in the middle of the action?"

The disc jockey—my hero—stared straight ahead with tired eyes and shattered my little illusion with one verbal shot. "It feels boring," he said flatly, "all I want to do is go home and go sailing." And with that he nodded goodbye and walked out of the cafeteria.

I sat stunned for several minutes before I got up and headed for the exit. On my way out I passed an observation window where I could see the afternoon disc jockey spinning records and talking into his microphone. I stopped to watch his frantic activity and then it hit me: Yes, it would be great to be a disc jockey for a while—a year, maybe two—but then how interesting would it be to sit in a little cubicle and tout the local pizza palace while spinning little discs on a turntable and making the weather sound as exciting as the play by play of the superbowl? Not very exciting at all, I decided, and I began to understand what my host had meant about boredom a few minutes before.

You know, boredom is a very important factor in the human condition. It can motivate us to expand our horizons as we seek new kinds of stimulation; yet, it can also be the "rust of human emotion," leading to dissatisfaction with people, jobs, and activities as we become used to them.

Let us consider boredom and its relationship to work. Any job, no matter what kind it is, has the potential to become boring to the jobholder if the job remains basically the same over a long period of time. This is because, as we learn a job, the skills that were once a challenge become automatic, and the things that were novel and exciting when we started work become mundane and predictable after being repeated day after day.

How *fast* a job becomes boring will vary, depending in part on the complexity of the job, how much the job changes over time, the personality of the employee, and the skills of the manager in keeping the employee satisfied and productive. (I have often heard a worker comment: "I'd quit this boring job if it wasn't for my manager.")

Only recently have behavioral scientists begun to recognize the significance of boredom in affecting worker satisfaction and productivity. To combat this motivation crippler they have come up with an antidote: *job enrichment*. They have studied the effectiveness of this antidote in the workplace, usually on the assembly line type of job, where the repetitive, relatively simple kinds of tasks invite boredom (see Box 7-3).

Do not think, however, that the assembly line is the only place where boredom can strike with devastating results. Remember *any* job can bet boring if a person stays on it long enough and the job doesn't change. And that goes for blue-collar work, white-collar work, unskilled labor, professional work, and—yes—managerial work, too.

BOX 7-3

JOB ENRICHMENT—"AUTO"MATICALLY

When it comes to job enrichment, the automotive industry takes a back seat to no one! Big name automakers like General Motors, Ford Motor Company, and Volvo have already implemented job enrichment programs on their assembly lines as a way to combat boredom and increase worker satisfaction and productivity. For example, at Volvo's new automobile assembly plant workers can listen to popular music, choose to work in teams, and even read a book or go for coffee while waiting for additional work. At some General Motors plants employee opinions are actively solicited by management. Workers are asked how they would go about solving various defect problems that arise during car assembly. Says John Mollica, assistant director for labor relations, "We try for an interchange of ideas and principles— something more than a boss-employee relationship—in order to involve the worker."

The job enrichment experiences of the major automakers has encouraged other industry groups to get involved in the approach—an approach you might find profitable to use in your workplace. For more information on job enrichment and how it is used, see the references listed below.

- "Big Firms Start to Talk Job Enrichment," *Industry Week,* July 9, 1973, pp. 42–46.
- B. Northrup, "Working Happier: More Swedish Firms Attempt to 'Enrich' Production-Line Jobs," *The Wall Street Journal,* Friday, Oct. 25, 1974.
- R. Schrank, "How to Relieve Worker Boredom," *Psychology Today,* July 1978, pp. 79–80.
- J. Robins, "Firms Try Newer Way to Slash Absenteeism as Carrot and Stick Fail. More Try 'Job Enrichment,' Seeking to Raise Morale; A Box Plant Gets Results. All 'Cures' Seem Temporary," *The Wall Street Journal,* March 14, 1979, p. 1ff.

As a manager what can you do about boredom? How can you combat this potentially destructive factor and keep worker satisfaction and productivity high? By utilizing job enrichment when possible— that is, when your efforts are allowed by upper management and existing contractual obligations.[8] Here are two objectives you'll want to accomplish in overcoming boredom.

Objective 1: Identify Bored Workers   Not all workers are bored with their jobs. You'll have to determine which ones are bored before you can take corrective action. (Trying to modify the work conditions of a person who is *not* bored on the job can create a terrible hassle.) If a worker has been assigned a specific job for a long time, and if that job is relatively easy for that particular worker to master, then the possibility of boredom increases. Watch for telltale signs, such as listlessness and lack of interest at work, increasing complaints and absenteeism, and loss of morale and productivity. Of course, these signs can also be indications of problems other than boredom—and if they remain after Objective 2 is attempted, then you'll want to look for other causes of the worker's dissatisfaction.

Objective 2: Help Workers Overcome Their Boredom through Job Enrichment   There are several ways you as a manager can help workers enrich their work world. The best way is to expand job responsibilities at a rate which keeps the employee challenged but not overwhelmed. Thus, as a person masters job skills, additional or different ones are assigned. Sometimes this means expanding a specific job to include new responsibilities and skills; other times it means promoting an employee to a new job "up the line." In either case, the emphasis is on giving the employee job enrichment to maintain interest and fend off boredom in the workplace.

"But," some of you may be asking, "what if an employee doesn't want new responsibilities? What if that person is happy the way things are?"

These are reasonable questions and deserve careful answers. Let me deal with the second question first: If the worker *is* happy the way things are, then my recommendation is to "let sleeping dogs lie"— don't tamper with an employee's job if he likes it the way it is. Normally, happy workers are *not* bored workers; they are usually

---

[8]Sometimes upper management or the employee contract (or both) very specifically limits the degree to which a job can be expanded. Be sure you know how much you can change a person's job before you start a job enrichment program with your employees.

interested, satisfied, and productive in the workplace—which means that you, the manager, will have reason to be happy, too.

Now, for the first question, there will probably be some workers who are bored and do not want new or additional responsibilities. You will have to use your best judgment as to whether forcing changes on these workers will later be met with a "Thank you, I wish you had done that earlier" or with even greater dissatisfaction on the job. Fortunately, you won't have to make this judgment very often, because in most cases bored workers welcome a chance to get out of their rut into work that is more challenging and stimulating.

Boredom is not an enjoyable human condition—people normally strive to avoid or eliminate it. If you can help them in their quest, all the better for you and for the worker. Just make sure that the workers don't feel you're ripping them off in the process. A worker who can readily take on new job challenges as a means of overcoming boredom may pass up the chance completely if that worker senses the manager is merely trying to get more work without paying for it. The best way to approach the idea of job enrichment, then, is in a voluntary context—giving the worker the option to accept or reject the job opportunities. That way, the employee will see the offer in the positive way it was intended, rather than as simply another attempt to get more work at no extra pay.

There are numerous job enrichment programs you can utilize with your employees (see, for example, the ones discussed in Box 7-3). Some require additional education or training programs, which in themselves help combat boredom.[9] Here are some job enrichment approaches you can use to help combat boredom on the job. Whichever ones you choose should be adapted to your particular work circumstances for maximum effectiveness.

1   On some jobs (for instance, on assembly lines) it is possible to rotate workers through several types of jobs, thus relieving the boredom of doing the same task time after time.

2   You can continually expand a person's job to encompass new skills and responsibilities.

3   You can promote an individual to a new job that may be more demanding.

[9]See, for example, J. Velghe and G. Cockrell, "What Makes Johnny Mop," *Personnel Journal*, June 1975, pp. 324ff.

4 You can change a person's working environment, to keep it novel and stimulating (see Reward 14).

5 You can let the worker get involved in team production efforts (see Reward 10).

6 You can give the worker more "degrees of freedom" in controlling the job (see Reward 13).

7 You can let the worker participate in the managerial decision-making process (see Reward 7).

Before moving on to the other forms of employee development programs, let me make one final point about job enrichment.

It is sometimes tempting to look at certain kinds of jobs—particularly repetitive ones like those on assembly lines—and automatically label them boring. This is a bad mistake you shouldn't make. A job that seems boring to one person might be perfectly satisfying and even highly challenging to someone else; it will depend to a great degree on the ability of the person to perform the task in question. There are always some individuals who enjoy doing the very jobs that others would find boring the minute they walk in the door.

As a manager, you should be striving for successful job-worker matches—in other words, jobs that fit the needs of the individual workers performing them. In doing this, don't ask yourself, "Would I find this job boring?"; ask yourself, rather, "Would my employee find this job boring?" After all, it's the worker who is going to have to do the work.

Personality (and Leadership) Development

Almost all major corporations and many smaller businesses offer their employees the opportunity to attend various seminars and workshops designed to improve job performance through the development of personal strengths (for example, creativity development, and assertiveness training). These programs can run from a few hours to a full week of intensive "marathon" sessions, and they are normally conducted by in-house specialists (usually the organizational development staff) or outside consultants hired for training purposes.

Because personality and leadership development programs normally require the direction of specialists, you probably won't be called upon to conduct any workshops unless you've had specialized training to do so. Therefore, I simply call these programs to your attention as another approach to improving worker satisfaction and productivity on the job. If your particular company doesn't have such programs, you might want to recommend their implementation—if you think they would be of value in your particular work environment.

Mental and Physical Health Programs

American business is waking to the profound personal and financial waste that occurs when a valued employee is mentally or physically incapacitated at the height of a productive career. In many cases, such mental or physical breakdowns could have been prevented had the proper preventative steps been taken. Major American corporations are now committed to developing programs to help safeguard the health and mental well-being of their employees. For example, corporations like Exxon, Mobil Oil, and General Motors are beginning to implement "executive fitness" programs in an attempt to lessen dramatically the risk of premature death among their executives. The investment of time and money is well spent. As William DeCarlo, manager of recreation services for Xerox Corporation, observes: "The death of a top executive means loss of what is stored in his mind. If we can prevent one fatal heart attack, we will have paid for our physical fitness program for several years."[10]

Good mental and physical fitness is vital to employee satisfaction and productivity on the job. And this applies to *all* employees—managers as well as their subordinates. A full discussion of this topic will be found in Section 3: *"How to succeed in business without really dying."*

All three employee development programs share a common characteristic—they are rewarding because they make workers' feel better about themselves. This "feeling better" can take many forms. Sometimes a worker feels more enthusiastic and less bored with life (job enrichment), other times more self-confident (personality development) or robust and alert (physical health). Whatever form it takes, however, can be rewarding to the individual, and for that reason employee development programs provide an effective method for increasing worker satisfaction and productivity on the job.

[10]W. DeCarlo, personal communication, 1977.

REWARD 7: EMPLOYEE INVOLVEMENT IN DECISION MAKING

The following incident took place many years ago in a company that manufactured wooden toys. One part of the process consisted of spraying paint on partially assembled toys, and then hanging them on an overhead belt of continuously moving hooks which carried the toys into a drying oven. The eight employees who did the painting sat in a line in front of the hooks. The plant engineers had calculated the speed of the belt so that a trained employee would be able to hang a freshly painted toy on each hook before it passed out of reach. The employees were paid on a piece rate basis, determined by their performance as a group. New employees were put on a learning bonus, which decreased every month. At the end of 6 months, the learning bonus was cut off and the employees were on their own.

The painting operation was a management headache. High turnover, low morale, and frequent absenteeism were the symptoms. The employees complained that the hooks were moving too fast and that the time study engineers had set the piece rates wrong. Many of the hooks were moving into the oven without toys on them.

A consultant was hired by the plant management to study the situation. After preliminary investigation, the consultant tried several times to persuade the supervisor to call a meeting of the toy painters to discuss working conditions with them. The reluctant supervisor finally agreed, and the first of several meetings was held right after the end of a shift. At the meeting a spokesperson for the employees elaborated on their complaints about the speed of the hooks. She explained that they could keep up with the moving hooks for short periods of time but purposely held back for fear that they would be expected to maintain the pace all day long. What they wanted was to "adjust the speed of the belt faster or slower, depending on how we feel." The supervisor agreed to pass this request along to the engineers and superintendent.

As might be expected, the engineers reacted unfavorably to the proposal, and only after much persuasion did they agree to try out the idea. The supervisor had a graduated control dial with points marked low, medium, and fast installed at the booth of one of the employees. The speed of the belt could now be adjusted within these limits.

What happened? The toy painters were delighted with this arrangement and spent much of their free time during the first few days deciding how the speed of the belt should be varied from time to time during the day. Within a week the pattern had been established. The productivity of the group as well as their morale went up considerably. The quality of their work was as satisfactory as it had been previously. And it is interesting to note that the average speed at which the toy painters were running the belt was *higher* than the constant speed they had been complaining about to the supervisor.[11]

For our purposes, the true story of the toy painters illustrates an extremely important principle for effective managing. If you want to increase worker satisfaction and productivity on the job, then involve your employees in the managerial decision-making process (see Box 7-4).

[11]Reported in W. Whyte, *Money and Motivation,* Harper, New York, 1955.

BOX 7-4

GUESS WHO'S COMING TO DINNER

It's not your ordinary business lunch. Joe and Mary from purchasing are there. So are Diane, Sue, and Steve from the accounting department. Cynthia is there too, along with two other secretaries from the central office. Not an executive in the bunch, clerical workers all. Why, then, are they eating with the president of the corporation?

Because the president wants to talk with them about the company. He wants to listen to their gripes and note their suggestions. He wants to examine their feelings about company issues and give them a chance to ask questions about company actions that affect them. In short, he wants to get rank and file involvement in decision making; he wants to encourage employees to add their voice to company policy.

This face-to-face approach by upper management to discover what is on the minds of the rank and file is called *deep sensing* and has two potential benefits:

1 *It can increase worker satisfaction and productivity.* Many executives who have utilized deep sensing report an across-the-board boost in employee morale. Workers feel that someone "up there" cares about them and is giving them a chance to participate in the creation of the policies that will affect their lives. One clerical worker put it this way: "I feel I'm heard now, that I'm not just a number."

2 *It can bring to upper management's attention useful employee ideas that might otherwise go unnoticed.* For instance, ". . . Shell Canada . . . has been holding meetings to 'sense' employee feelings on specific issues such as career planning and cost reduction. Marjorie Blackhurst, employee communications manager, says that the 600 employees involved in the sessions turned up ideas that yielded the company more than $1 million in savings."*

Deep sensing is one way managers involve their employees in the decision-making process. There are other ways as well, and skillful managers will want to use the approach that works best with their particular employees.

Here are some other articles on employee involvement in decision making that you might find interesting:

• "Participative Management, Bonuses Boost Productivity for Michigan Firm," *Commerce Today,* Nov. 11, 1974, pp. 12–13.

• D. Curley, "Employee Sounding Boards: Answering the Participative Need," *The Personnel Administrator,* May 1978, pp. 69ff.

• J. Donnelly, "Participative Management at Work," *Harvard Business Review,* January-February 1977, pp. 117–127.

• E. Lawler, "Workers Can Set Their Own Wages Responsibly," *Psychology Today,* February 1977, pp. 109–112.

• M. Ways, "The American Kind of Worker Participation," *Fortune,* October 1976, pp. 168ff.

*From "Deep Sensing: A Pipeline to Employee Morale," *Business Week,* Jan. 29, 1979, p. 126.

In the toy factory, the employees were given the opportunity to become involved in the decision-making process. They made recommendations about how the conveyor belt should move, and those recommendations were followed. What happened? Worker satisfaction and productivity increased.

The toy factory results are not unique. In fact, the value of employee involvement in decision making (also referred to as "participative management" in some circles) is one of the most documented and replicated findings in all behavioral science.

By involving your employees in the decision-making process, three benefits can result:

1 Workers who play an active role in the decision-making process will be more likely to go along with whatever decision is reached.

2 Workers who play an active role in the decision-making process will carry out those decisions in a more enthusiastic, motivated manner.

3 By involving your workers in the decision-making process you increase your chances of finding the best possible solution to any given problem. (This is because an employee may come up with a solution which is better than any you were able to devise.)

Many contemporary managers balk at the suggestion that they involve their workers in the decision-making process. They usually base their opposition on arguments that fall apart when held up to close scrutiny. Let me present these arguments and reveal why you as a manager don't have to worry about them if you decide to use employee involvement in decision making as a reward in the workplace.

Argument 1   I can't let my employees share in decision making because they might come up with a recommendation I can't live with.

My Response   Involving employees in the decision-making process doesn't mean that you have to accept every recommendation they make. There are times when your employees will come up with the same recommendation you favor or with a suggestion that you think is better than your own. In such cases you can use their inputs. Other times they won't have any ideas on the problem or their suggestions will be unacceptable (or inferior to your own). In those cases, thank your subordinates for their assistance and go with your own best suggestion.

Argument 2   I can't let my employees share in decision making because if I reject their recommendations they'll become frustrated and demotivated on the job.

My Response   Not necessarily so. If you consistently ask employees for their suggestions and never use any of them, or if you accept employee suggestions on minor issues and ignore them on every major problem that comes along, then you might have a problem with employee morale. On the other hand, no employees expect a manager to accept every suggestion they make; in fact, they might question your managerial competence if you did. As long as your subordinates feel you are asking for their help in good faith—accepting suggestions which are appropriate and rejecting those which are not—you'll be in good shape.

Argument 3 I don't want to involve my employees in decision making, because then I'll have to check with them every time a problem comes up.

My Response This isn't true. You can involve your employees in decision making as often or as little as you want. There will be some times and problems where soliciting employee inputs will be irrelevant or inappropriate. Also, situations will arise where there is not time to consult with subordinates or where subordinates have no desire to be involved in the decision-making process. Don't let such instances hassle you. Involve your employees when you think it will increase their satisfaction and productivity on the job.

Argument 4 I don't want to involve my employees in decision making because they aren't capable of making decisions.

My Response Often employees are more capable of assisting in decision making than managers realize. This is not because they are brighter than managers, but, rather, because they can bring different perspectives to bear on the problem in question. Let me give you an example. During World War II, an Allied airbase in the Pacific was having supply problems. One item in short supply was protective glass encasements for the landing lights. The ranking officer on the base was at a loss to solve the problem, so he decided to solicit recommendations from base personnel. Within a few hours the problem was solved. A cook in the mess hall, hearing of the problem, quickly realized that empty peanut butter jars would fit perfectly over the landing lights. Not only did the jars fit as well as the original encasements, but they were also stronger and withstood more pounding before breaking. Who would have figured a cook could solve a problem a base commander couldn't crack? The reason he could was that he brought a different perspective to the problem. He worked with peanut butter jars every day, the commanding officer did not. Remember, don't sell your employees short when it comes to giving aid in problem solving. More and more companies are realizing that when it comes to solving work problems, who should know better than the people who do the work (see Boxes 7-3 and 7-4).

Argument 5 I can't let my employees share in decision making because decision making is my job as a manager.

My Response It is your job to make decisions, but that doesn't mean you can't have help. Remember, by involving your employees in the decision-making process you gain additional input for solving the problem. You also create more motivated, satisfied, and productive workers—and that's your job as a manager, too.

Argument 6 I can't let my employees share in decision making because they'll think I'm incompetent and can't solve problems on my own.

My Response If you sat quietly by and let your employees solve every problem that came along, maybe this would be a possibility. If, however, you get actively involved in the decision-making process, sharing your ideas with your employees and vice versa, then you will not be seen as incompetent but, rather, a concerned manager who values what your employees have to say.

Argument 7 I can't let my employees share in decision making because if I accept their recommendation and it turns out badly, I'll be held responsible for it.

My Response It is true that you will be held responsible for any bad decision made, whether it be your own or that of your subordinates. But why should this cause any special difficulties? You simply don't accept poor decisions, whether they be yours or your subordinates.

When you add up all the arguments and counter-arguments, one simple conclusion stands clear: Managers have much more to gain than lose by involving their subordinates in the decision-making process. Workers like to feel they have a say in their destiny, that they are "in on things" and can claim some ownership of the policies that affect their lives. That's the way employees are, and refusing to accept them as they are isn't going to change them—it will simply frustrate and demotivate them. When it comes to giving out rewards in the workplace, don't forget the value of involving your employees in the decision-making process.

REWARD 8: LEISURE TIME

Item A worker in Wisconsin decides to share his job with another employee. His pay is cut in half, but he explains, "I want more time to fool around with my tenor sax."[12]

---

[12]Quoted in K. Sawyer, "Work Habits in U.S. Changing," *St. Petersburg Times,* Jan. 1, 1978, p. 1-A.

Item A certified public accountant limits her practice so that she has time to write the great American novel.

Item A husband and wife both cut their working hours so that they can spend more time at home with their family.

Item A successful salesman takes a whopping cut in commissions so that he can have ample opportunity to fish and hunt.

The salesman, the husband and wife, the accountant, the Wisconsin employee—all have one thing in common: they want to cut their working hours so that they'll have more time to do other things. And they're willing to take a corresponding cut in pay to get their wish. "People say time is money; well, I say less money is more time," is the way one worker explained it.

Such attitudes should come as no surprise. As I indicated earlier, as workers have found their basic needs satisfied, they have developed other, higher level needs—and the need for *leisure time* is one such need.

There are several ways that you as a manager can take advantage of this need for leisure time and use it to create greater worker satisfaction and productivity on the job. It involves using leisure time as a reward. Let me give you two examples of how this can be done.

Tactic 1: Leisure Time Tied to Production Rate With this tactic, employees are free to leave the workplace once they have produced a specified number of products or completed a defined amount of work. As an example, let's assume you manage a group of employees who produce wickets for the international market. Let us assume further that ten wickets is the daily acceptable production output per worker. Using the leisure-time-tied-to-production-rate tactic, you allow employees to leave the workplace once they have produced their ten wickets. Thus an employee who has worked diligently can leave early and gain more leisure time. Of course, the quality of wicket production has to remain satisfactory—and to make sure it does, you will probably want to institute a quality control check to maintain standards.

Tactic 2: Redistribution of Working Hours This tactic allows you to give workers more leisure time by rearranging work hours rather than reducing time.[13] You determine an acceptable number of hours per week a worker should be on the job; then you let the individual employees determine when each will put in those hours. Of course, this tactic can only be utilized in situations where hours can be shifted without a deleterious effect on the business.

Here is an example of how Tactic 2 might be utilized in the workplace. Let us assume you are a manager in a company where the following conditions exist: (1) your subordinates currently work a 40-hour week: 8 hours a day, 5 days a week; (2) their work is the kind that can be conducted in a 4-day workweek without any loss in profits; and (3) it is also the kind of work that can be done, without additional personal risk or loss in quality, for 10 hours a day. If these three conditions exist, you meet with your subordinates and give them the choice of working four 10-hour days or five 8-hour days per week. If your workers favor the 4-day week and the accompanying 3-day weekend, then you have just established a $++$ relationship. Your employees get a redistribution of working hours they find more to their liking (employee goal); and you still get 40 hours of work from your subordinates (management goal). Everybody wins, nobody loses. And that's what good management is all about.

This redistribution-of-time tactic can also be used to set starting and stopping hours for daily work. For instance, some employees might hate coming to work at 8 A.M. but would be very glad to stay at work until 7 P.M. Why not let them come in at 10 A.M. and work until 7 P.M. Again, assuming their work won't be affected by the different hours, this might be a viable way to satisfy a worker's special time needs and still get the required number of work hours.

In today's energy-conscious world, the redistribution of time is becoming increasingly popular. Already the rigid, fixed-hour work-week is giving way to more flexible time spans based on individual company and employee requirements. This new development is called "flextime" in the literature, and don't be surprised if you see a lot more of it in the years to come. This is as it should be. As one politician wisely observed: "The standard 40-hour workweek has been a sacred cow since the depression. Well, we have different

---

[13]Technically, you are not really giving workers more leisure time by rearranging work hours, but *psychologically* it seems that way to the worker, and that's what counts.

problems now."[14] One of those problems is the present-day worker who has a need for more leisure time. When you use time as a reward, you'll be able to satisfy that need and get more productive employees in the bargain.

REWARD 9: FEEDBACK

I'd like you to stop for a moment, close your eyes, and try to re-create in your memory several recent cartoons you have seen that deal with business people. Try to re-create as much of each cartoon as you can remember. Now—did you notice any similarities among the cartoons? Any common elements? Let me suggest one: the business chart. In almost every business cartoon I've seen, particularly those featuring a business manager, there is a performance chart in the scene. It may be on the back wall of the office, on a desk, or maybe on an easel or blackboard—but somewhere there is a business performance chart, jagged lines and all.

It's no accident that the business manager and the business chart have been linked in the cartoonist's art and the public's eye. To business managers, *knowledge of how they are doing* is very important—and the business chart is one way that knowledge is recorded and displayed.

This brings us to the topic of *feedback*. Feedback is knowledge of results—information that lets us know how well we're doing at a specific task. Here's an example. Imagine you are visiting your first English pub and your host challenges you to a game of darts. Never having played, you graciously decline and then—in the finest American spirit—run out, buy a set, and begin practicing in your hotel. After the first hundred tosses you begin getting a feel for the game; by the next day, you're ready to go out and challenge the Queen's finest.

You have learned your dart game well. But let us pretend you were forced to practice your throws blindfolded and with plugs in your ears. Could you ever perfect your toss under these conditions? No. Improvement would be impossible because you lacked the vital component of learning: feedback concerning your performance.

[14]Quoted in Sawyer, op. cit., p. 12-A.

Deprived of visual feedback—unable to gain knowledge of the results of your dart throwing—your plight would be hopeless.

We use feedback so regularly in our everyday life that we seldom realize how pervasive and important it is. Yet as one eminent scholar has pointed out: "Every animal is a self-regulating system owing its existence, its stability and most of its behavior to feedback controls."[15] It is only when we are suddenly deprived of our normal opportunity to receive feedback—for instance, in the case of sudden blindness—that we come to understand its momentous value for our very survival.

Because feedback is essential for improving performance, one would think it would be used extensively in the business world. Sadly, most managers don't even come close to providing their employees with adequate knowledge of results to maximize effective performance. And what makes this doubly tragic is that feedback, for many employees, is more than simply a way to improve performance, it is also a *reward* that can satisfy personal needs and lead to greater satisfaction and productivity in the workplace. In other words, workers need feedback to improve their performance, and they want feedback to know how they're doing. The need to know is deeply ingrained in the human character, and particularly in the character of the business manager. Managers have their business performance charts on the wall—why shouldn't subordinates have feedback, too?

In a very informative article, Professor Robert Kreitner identifies three different kinds of feedback you can give your employees to help bolster their satisfaction and productivity in the workplace.

Types of Feedback

1 Informational Feedback This type of feedback helps employees find out how well they are performing on the job. For example, a professor might be handed her course evaluation results or a telephone solicitor could be given information on how many of his contacts actually purchased a particular product. Such knowledge of results should help the professor and solicitor improve job performance in the future. Informational feedback is *non*evaluative—in other words, it should be transmitted to the employee without judgments as to how good or bad the performance was.

[15]O. Mayr, "The Origins of Feedback Control," *Scientific American,* 1970, no. 223, p. 111.

2 Corrective Feedback A manager can be evaluative (judgmental) in providing an employee with knowledge of results. The purpose of corrective feedback, however, is not to criticize and punish but, rather, to inform and correct. The famous basketball coach John Wooden, of the University of California, Los Angeles, was a master at using corrective feedback effectively:

> Observation of Wooden's behavior in practice sessions showed that while 50% of his contacts with his players amounted to straightforward instructions, no less than 75% of his contacts were instructive in nature. He used instructions to simultaneously point out a mistake and indicate the correct way of performing. Wooden's corrective feedback centered around the task at hand, not around the personality of the player. . . . An effective manager, like an effective coach, must not only point out mistakes but also get the individual headed in the right direction with appropriate instructions.[16]

3 Reinforcing Feedback When an employee is successful (productive) in the workplace, reinforcing feedback is used to reward the job performance. The praise given to employees at Emery Air Freight Corporation (see p. 66) is an example of reinforcing feedback (simply telling them how they did would be an example of informational feedback). Which kind of reinforcing feedback you give your workers will depend on their particular needs. As Kreitner correctly observes:

> Managers can . . . diagnose the specific reinforcing consequences to which subordinates currently respond. Careful observation of job performance soon reveals whether or not an individual responds to praise, money, additional responsibility, job rotation, status symbols, formal recognition, peer approval, or any other of the many consequences of job behavior. In a manner of speaking, managers must "fine-tune" reinforcing feedback to suit the individual. No quick and easy panaceas exist in this area.[17]

Providing Feedback

There are many opportunities for you to provide employees with feedback on the job. It can be done during formalized time periods set

[16]R. Kreitner, "People Are Systems, Too: Filling the Feedback Vacuum," *Business Horizons*, November 1977, pp. 56–57.
[17]Ibid., p. 57.

aside for it (for instance, during performance appraisals) or spontaneously during the workday in response to particular employee behavior. To be most effective, feedback should be *specific* and *clearly understandable* to the worker. Feedback won't help if your employees can't identify it with the behavior you're talking about; likewise, telling subordinates how they have performed in statistical terms won't make a difference if they don't understand statistics in the first place.

Don't forget that feedback is essential to learning—and it can be rewarding, too. When you manage, why not make it a part of your worthplace; if you do, you'll increase the chances that your business charts will be looking up.

REWARD 10: SOCIAL PARTICIPATION

Do you recall Mr. Monotone, the professor who liked to scratch his head? We got him to increase his little habit by giving him social approval—a reward that satisfied his social needs.

Many workers—managers as well as their subordinates—respond with greater productivity and satisfaction when their social needs are fulfilled in the workplace. This is because many of us are concerned with *affiliation:* being around other people and being accepted by them. People with social needs want to "belong"; they desire social relationships and the chance to interact with others—desires that can be satisfied in the worthplace if a manager provides the proper environment for social participation to take place.

Basically, there are two types of social participation that can be rewarding for a worker on the job: interaction with peers and interaction with the manager.

Types of Social Participation

1 Interaction with Peers We have already seen (in our discussion of job enrichment) how autonomous work teams are created to help fend off boredom and make the working experience more rewarding. In your own managerial situation there will normally be ample opportunity to encourage the development of compatible work groups as a means of satisfying social needs through social participation. One way to do this is participative management (see Reward 7), having subordinates meet as a group with the supervisor to discuss various issues that affect them. Another way is the development of "company spirit" (see Reward 11), encouraging social participation through various social events and team-building efforts. For an example of how one company has encouraged social participation with gratifying results, see Box 7-5.

2   Interaction with the Manager   This is an area many supervisors overlook, sometimes with serious consequences. It is important to realize that in many cases the social relationships you establish with your subordinates can have a definite impact on their productivity level and job satisfaction. Managers who are also *leaders* develop effective interpersonal relationships with employees—they are able to

---

BOX 7-5

IF THE SHOE FITS, WEAR IT*

The R. G. Barry Corporation manufactures footwear out of Columbus, Ohio. In 1969 the company decided to use social participation (in the form of "teamwork") as a way to increase worker productivity and satisfaction on the job. This required conversion of an individual, every-worker-for-himself incentive system to a team process. Three hundred production workers were organized into teams ranging from eight to twelve employees. Each team was then responsible for product manufacture from cut stock to finished product. Teams were also allowed to participate in the company's decision-making activities (see Reward 7), an opportunity that was well received by the workers.

After a rocky start, the team approach took hold. The results? "Absenteeism and personnel turnover declined by 50 percent; products sent back for reworking have been cut by two-thirds; downtime diminished significantly; training costs are down 50 percent; and total output is up 35 percent. Wages also increased 35 percent from 1969 to 1973."

One machine operator summed up employee feelings toward the new social participation in these words: "Before, everyone was on his own and no one cared about helping their fellow employee. Now everyone is dependent upon everybody else. I know in my case I think twice before taking a day off because I know if I do it will affect my team."

*The material in Box 7-5 was based on the following article: B. Shelton, " 'Team Spirit' Results in Higher Productivity, Job Satisfaction," *Commerce Today,* Sept. 30, 1974, pp. 5–6.

transmit a sense of caring and interpersonal enthusiasm which workers appreciate (see pp. 132–135).

Of course, there are times when interpersonal interaction won't be a vital factor in the workplace. First of all, not all workers have social needs, and if they don't, then the reward value of social participation will be diminished. Secondly, not all jobs allow for social participation. How, for example, can a manager who oversees a group of salespeople working separate territories encourage social participation on the job? Finally, on some jobs the employees might prefer to work alone or, when placed together, become too competitive or hostile with each other.

As with all the rewards in this chapter, you as manager will have to test social participation to see if it's effective in your particular work environment. Does social participation make your subordinates more productive and satisfied? If it does, then fine—it can be used with good results. If it doesn't, well—there are thirteen other rewards waiting to be used. Chances are excellent that some of them will help you get the results you're looking for.

REWARD 11: COMPANY SPIRIT

In central Florida there is a company that makes small aircraft, the kind that hold four to six passengers. It is not a large-scale operation—but it is a spirited one. Each time a plane rolls off the assembly line, the employees are given time off to gather around the finished aircraft and have a celebration (sometimes a picnic), a kind of "product send-off party" when the new owner comes to take delivery of his plane.

Across the country, California-based Kaiser Aluminum & Chemical Corporation gives its employees "inspirational" gifts—everything from frisbees to T-shirts—in an attempt to "motivate the work force" and "make people aware that their small unit is part of a large company."[18]

What do the aircraft company and Kaiser Aluminum have in common? Both organizations are directly fostering esprit de corps among company employees—attempting to increase worker production and satisfaction through the development of company spirit.

[18]Kaiser's efforts are described in D. Clutterbuck's article "Motivation Programme Is a Give-Away," *International Management,* August 1977, pp. 40–41.

BOX 7-6

COMPANY SPIRIT—IBM STYLE*

What image comes to mind when you hear the initials IBM? A huge computer? A massive building housing thousands of employees? Most people think of IBM as a big, impersonal corporation relentlessly spreading technology around the globe. These individuals would no doubt be surprised to learn that International Business Machines Corporation is called "Mother IBM" by many of those who work for it—recognition of the fact that IBM very actively and successfully develops company spirit among its employees.

In a *Newsweek* article, Allan Mayer and Michael Ruby describe some of the ways IBM establishes *esprit de corps* among its employees:

> More than any other major corporation in America, IBM smothers its employees with a dazzling array of womb-to-tomb benefits, ingenious motivational perks and sophisticated self-improvement programs. Not only does IBM pay its 300,000 employees generous salaries and cover their medical bills, it also counsels, trains and entertains them, supports their favorite charities and helps with their children's education. And uniquely among American corporations, it virtually guarantees its workers lifetime job security.

What is the result of all this "mothering"? A great many loyal, productive and satisfied employees. And some happy spouses, too. The wife of one IBM employee expressed her feelings this way: "IBM embodies all the values we hold sacred—worth of the individual, pursuit of excellence, brotherhood, the work ethic. . . . And over the years, the children absorb this. I do feel that the company takes a personal interest in me and my children, that it provides us with security and cares about us."

Want a good example of company spirit? Read the wife's comments again, and you'll reach the bottom line.

*The material in Box 7-6 is based on A. Mayer and M. Ruby, "One Firm's Family," *Newsweek,* Nov. 21, 1977, p. 82ff.

Exactly what is company spirit? Company spirit is a sense of pride, dedication, and loyalty to the organization one works for. It's kind of like patriotism, but in this case employees feel a sense of commitment to their employer. When workers feel this way about the company they work for—when they have company spirit—chances are they will be highly productive and satisfied on the job (see Box 7-6).

By now you are probably asking "How can I, as a manager, create a sense of esprit de corps among my employees?" You might want to try one or more of the suggestions below. Each has been used successfully in the business community. Whether any or all of these approaches work for you will depend, to a great degree, on the size of your work force, the needs of your particular employees, your budget, and the willingness of your organization to actively support "company spirit" programs in the workplace.

1 Develop work teams throughout the company or among the employees you supervise (see Reward 10 and Box 7-5).

2 Involve employees in the decision-making activities of the company (see Reward 7).

3 Sponsor various social functions for company employees (for example, picnics and outings).

4 Sponsor company sports teams.

5 Undertake activities that will make your employees proud to be associated with the company. For example, some businesses sponsor little league teams or civic activities; others conduct advertising campaigns that emphasize the "good deeds" they are doing in the community.

6 Conduct friendly competitions between various work teams in the company (for example, give an award to the team with highest output or best safety record). Be careful, however, to make sure the competition doesn't get out of hand.

7 Help your employees identify with the products they produce. Some businesses, like the aircraft company in the earlier example, do this by inviting all employees to see the product once it's completed. Other organizations encourage employee identification by having them sign the product they produce or in a like manner have them take personal responsibility for what they have created.

In many ways, a caring organization—one that practices the human use of human resources—will almost automatically increase its chances of developing company spirit. A caring company is like a caring manager—it brings out the best in workers, including higher productivity and job satisfaction.

REWARD 12: THE OPPORTUNITY TO ACHIEVE AND ADVANCE IN THE ORGANIZATION

When employees reach the upper rungs of the Maslow hierarchy, they become responsive to rewards that satisfy their esteem and self-actualization needs. The opportunity to achieve is important to these individuals; so is the opportunity to advance—to be promoted, to rise in the organization.

Time and time again I have watched businesses lose their most capable employees because they failed to provide them with jobs where accomplishment and advancement were possible. Don't make such a mistake. Keep apprised of your employees' progress and check with them frequently to see how they feel about their development within the company.

Do your best to see that all employees have job assignments where achievement and advancement are possible. Many times this will require changing your workers' assignments and responsibilities to keep pace with their growth and development in the workplace (see the discussion of job enrichment under Reward 6). This will require some effort, but it will be effort well invested—particularly when you consider that the people who want to achieve and advance in the organization are normally the most motivated and capable employees you'll be supervising. You don't want to lose them, and making it possible for them to achieve and advance in the organization is one good way to keep them productive, satisfied—and around.

REWARD 13: DEGREES OF FREEDOM AT WORK

I recently spoke with a department store buyer who was angry because she might have to punch in and out of work on a time clock. "I didn't have to do that under the old manager," she argued.

"What about the other people in your office," I inquired, "don't they have to punch in and out?"

"They're hourly workers," the buyer scoffed, "I'm a professional, I don't work by the clock."

Although this particular employee sounds a bit egotistical and spoiled, her concern does reflect a problem common to many workers as they climb the organizational ladder and the Maslow hierarchy: the need for more degrees of freedom on the job.

When I speak of degrees of freedom in work, I am referring to the level of personal autonomy and responsibility a person has on the job. Employees with high degrees of freedom in the workplace are pretty much their own boss when it comes to organizing their work and making decisions. Employees with low degrees of freedom have very little say in what they do or how they do it—they are, as some managers are fond of saying, "closely watched."

Now it is true that some types of jobs require closer supervision than others. It is also true that certain workers prefer to be closely supervised and shun the opportunity for more personal autonomy in the workplace. In these cases, giving workers degrees of freedom can cause difficulties. But what about those jobs that *can* be effectively performed by employees working under their own "recognizance"? And what about those workers who covet more degrees of freedom in the workplace? In these circumstances managers would be well-advised to loosen the reins of control and let employees have more say in the conduct of their work.

To determine what level of freedom you should give your workers, ask (and answer) these two questions:

1 Are my employees doing the kind of work that requires constant managerial supervision, or can I step back and let them have more control over their job activities?

2 Do my employees want more degrees of freedom on the job?

As far as the second question is concerned, you won't go very far afield if you follow this guideline. Generally, employees with higher level needs will be most rewarded by greater degrees of freedom on the job. If you turn back to Figure 5-2 you will note three things self-actualizing people want out of a job: (1) creative and challenging work; (2) responsibility for decision making; and (3) flexibility and freedom. These three wants can be satisfied by giving your employees greater degrees of freedom in the workplace. And if they're capable workers, giving them greater freedom will make your job easier in the bargain!

REWARD 14: PLEASANT FORMS OF MODERATE DISTRACTION

In 1965 a team of behavioral scientists conducted an interesting study with some Yale University undergraduates. One group of students read a series of four persuasive messages in a room well stocked with soft drinks and peanuts. The students were encouraged to sample the refreshments as they read—which they all did. A second group of students was presented with the same four messages to read, but in a room where no refreshments were available. Both groups of students were asked, before and after reading the four messages, certain key questions, which enabled the investigators to assess their degree of opinion change (if any) in response to the persuasive appeals. In other words, the scientists were able to ascertain if any of the students had been swayed by the four persuasive appeals.

What were the results of the study? The students who ate while they read were more persuaded by each of the four messages than were those students who read the same messages without food.[19]

On the basis of this study and several others,[20] behavioral scientists now believe that, in general, *persuasive appeals become more powerful when presented in conjunction with moderately distracting stimuli (for example, food) which positively reward the individual.*

How can this information be of use to you as a manager on the job? It suggests that if you want to be more persuasive with your employees (have them do what you want them to do), it might help if you utilize some pleasant forms of moderate distraction while making your requests. Even more important, pleasant forms of moderate distraction can increase worker satisfaction, not only because they are rewards in themselves, but also because they act as a boredom reducer in the workplace (see *Job Enrichment* under Reward 6).

There are several kinds of pleasant distraction you can use in the workplace (such as music and workspace alterations), but the most practical, versatile, and effective one for our purposes is . . . *food.*

[19]I. Janis, D. Kaye, and P. Kirschner, "Facilitating Effects of 'Eating-While-Reading' on Responsiveness to Persuasive Communications," *Journal of Personality and Social Psychology,* vol. 1, 1965, pp. 181–186.

[20]See M. Karlins and H. Abelson, *Persuasion: How Opinions and Attitudes Are Changed,* Springer, New York, 1970.

BOX 7-7

SOME FOOD FOR THOUGHT

For many years Fran Tarkenton was a superstar in the National Football League. As a quarterback for the Minnesota Vikings, he led his team all the way to the Superbowl on several occasions. Many people wonder how he did it. Some say it was his scrambling ability under pressure. Others speak of his pinpoint passing. Would you believe me if I told you it was because he used pleasant forms of moderate distraction? Probably not. But all-star, veteran quarterback Fran Tarkenton was known to give out candy to his teammates after they made a good play.* Now there's a man who understands the relationship between productivity and satisfaction on the job!

*Reported in L. Moore's article, "Motivation through Positive Reinforcement," *Supervisory Management,* October 1976, p. 8.

Salespeople have long recognized and utilized the power of food. The selling power of the client lunch is widely accepted in business circles. When it comes time to sign the contract—to close the deal—it is often accomplished over dessert. "A well-fed customer is a purchasing customer," as one salesperson expressed it.

Does this mean you'll have to take your subordinates to dinner every time you want to use pleasant forms of moderate distraction? Definitely not. The bent-elbow-and-heaping-forkful approach might be suitable for special occasions, but it is certainly inappropriate as an everyday kind of reward at work. It is appropriate, however, to serve coffee and doughnuts at staff meetings—particularly if the meetings are early in the morning. Even if you have to pay for these "goodies" out of pocket, I think you will find the benefits far outweigh the costs. It is amazing how a few doughnuts and cups of coffee can perk people up and put them in a cooperative, productive frame of mind. I know managers who also have coffee and small bowls of snacks in their offices, to offer to subordinates when they come in to discuss items of business. According to the managers, this helps open channels of communication and creates good feelings.

Like all the rewards we have discussed in this chapter, pleasant forms of moderate distraction will work better in some job settings than others. How effective will the reward be with your employees? The best way to find out is give pleasant distractions a try in your workplace.

Some Recommendations

1 Use Moderate, Not Intense, Distractions If a distraction is too strong, it can cause a decrease (rather than an increase) in productivity. For example, some companies pipe music over their intercoms. If this music is too distracting, employees end up concentrating on the tunes rather than on their work.

2 Use Pleasant, Not Unpleasant, Distractions Research studies clearly show that unpleasant distractions (even moderate forms of unpleasant distractions) reduce worker satisfaction and productivity—exactly the opposite of what you want. In this context, be sure you *know* what your individual employees consider pleasant or unpleasant distractions. For example, some employees might find hard rock music a pleasant form of moderate distraction, while others might consider it an unpleasant form of intense distraction. Play it safe: observe your workers' reactions to the distractions you use. That way you'll know what they think about them.

WORK AS ITS OWN REWARD

In this chapter I have described fourteen rewards you can use to make your employees more productive and satisfied in the workplace.

"But," you ask, "what if my employees are already satisfied with their work?" In that case, count yourself among the fortunate. As management expert Lewis Moore indicates: "The more rewarding the work is perceived to be by the worker, the less the need for supervision—except to specify results wanted."[21]

Unfortunately, not that many workers are naturally turned on by their jobs, and "in order to get the same level of motivation from employees who perceive less reward in their work, the difference in reinforcement must come from management. . . ."[22]

[21]L. Moore, "Motivation through Positive Reinforcement," *Supervisory Management,* October 1976, p. 9.
[22]Ibid.

This is where you come in. If your workers are not already satisfied with their jobs, you can help them by utilizing the fourteen rewards to create an environment that fulfills their needs and turns the workplace into a worthplace. In other words, your goal is to use rewards to create a worthplace more satisfying and meaningful to each individual employee.

Work does not have to be a four-letter word. Through such techniques as job enrichment, social participation, and employee involvement in decision making, you can encourage employees to get "into" what they are doing—help build a job to a point where it will become intrinsically interesting and motivationally self-sustaining.

Of course, you won't always be successful in getting an employee to the point where work becomes its own reward; but even then you can use rewards like praise, public recognition, and leisure time to make the job more palatable. Either way, you accomplish your ultimate goal: making the workplace a worthplace, where employees can satisfy their needs and be more productive at the same time.

Chapter 8

How to Administer Workplace Rewards Most Effectively

Knowing the rewards you can use on the job is important, but you must also learn the rules for using those rewards most effectively.

Aerospace industry manager

Before I present the rules for administering workplace rewards most effectively, let me briefly restate the major points discussed earlier.

A BRIEF REVIEW

From our discussion of behavior modification and Maslow's need hierarchy you now know that (1) individual workers have individual needs and will behave in ways that lead to the satisfaction of those needs and that (2) behavior which is rewarded will be maintained or even increase in frequency. Putting this information together, your goal as a manager is to reinforce appropriate work behavior with rewards that satisfy the particular needs of individual employees. This should enhance worker productivity and satisfy worker needs, thus establishing the ++ relationship essential to making the workplace a worthplace.

Accomplishing this goal will require you to complete successfully a three-step process:

Step 1   You will have to identify the specific needs of your individual workers.

Step 2   You will have to satisfy each worker's specific need(s) with the appropriate reward(s).

Step 3   You will have to administer worker rewards effectively.

Step 1 is discussed in Chapter 5 and at the end of Chapter 6. Step 2 is discussed in Chapter 7, where you will find the fourteen rewards you can use in motivating your workers. Step 3 is discussed below. Here you will find the basic guidelines for administering rewards in a manner that maximizes worker productivity and satisfaction on the job.

SOME MAJOR GUIDELINES FOR ADMINISTERING REWARDS EFFECTIVELY

Guideline 1   Know what kind of performance you want from your employees and let them know what your expectations are.

To administer rewards effectively, both you and your employees should have a common understanding of what is considered effective behavior (good output) on the job. This means you should first determine in your own mind the kinds of employee action that will lead to good job performance, and then you should explain to your subordinates what steps they can take to achieve that good performance and receive rewards.

If you don't take the time to tell your employees what your performance goals are and how they can be reached, then your subordinates will have to find out for themselves, usually through trial-and-error behavior on the job—and that is a tremendous waste of time, effort, and productivity. It doesn't do much for creating job satisfaction either.

Here are three questions I'd like you to ask yourself as a manager:

1 Have I determined what constitutes good performance in the workplace?

2 Have I communicated to my employees (a) my definition and standard of good performance; (b) the kinds of job behavior they should undertake to achieve good job performance; and (c) what they must do to receive the various rewards?

3 Do I have a method of accurately and fairly assessing the level of worker performance on the job?

If you can answer yes to all three questions, then you're in good shape as far as Guideline 1 is concerned.

Guideline 2 Give your subordinates those rewards that best satisfy their particular needs.

Put another way, the reward that works best is the reward that satisfies a worker's need(s) most successfully (see Box 8-1). Your goal should be the achievement of a match between workers' needs and the rewards they receive on the job. To do this effectively, you should know about the kinds of needs employees have and the rewards associated with them (see Chapters 5–7).

BOX 8-1

THE SOLID PINK CADILLAC

Mary Kay Ash retired as training director for World Gift, a decorative accessories company, in 1963. Not satisfied with the "life of leisure," she decided to start her own company, which in 14 years has turned into a $50 million cosmetics business.

How did she do it? One way was by giving her employees rewards that best satisfied their particular needs. For the women who sold her beauty products, such rewards ran the gambit from pocket calculators to pink cadillacs.

> Recognizing that many women "haven't had a round of applause since they graduated from school," Ms. Ash made sure there were plenty of plaudits for her personnel. "On Awards Night," she explains, "we get 8,000 people, all of whom come to Dallas at their own expense. Thousands of prizes are awarded, ranging from the keys to a Cadillac to diamond bumblebee pins. We crown the queens of sales and recruitment and present them with prizes and flowers and scepters, accompanied by standing ovations and musical fanfares."*
>
> Mary Kay Ash understood her employees' needs and the kinds of rewards that would satisfy those needs. And that's good business—from everyone's point of view.
>
> *Quote taken from an interview with Mary Kay Ash, "Flying High on an Idea," *Nation's Business*, August 1978, pp. 41ff.

Some managers try to guess what needs their workers have and what rewards they'd like to receive. As we saw on page 51, this can lead to some very inaccurate estimates. If you want to obtain greatest accuracy in identifying which rewards work best with which employees, observe your subordinates as you give them reinforcement. That way you can pinpoint the rewards that work best with each employee. Such information is particularly valuable, because in most instances you'll have to pick from a number of different rewards to use at any given need level of the Maslow hierarchy.

Also, continue to observe your subordinates even *after* you have ascertained their needs and the rewards they value most. This is crucial because workers' needs can change over time, and so can their attitudes toward particular rewards. For example, some workers get bored with certain rewards if they're used too often, causing them to lose their effectiveness. If you continue to observe your subordinates, you will be alerted to these changes and be able to take corrective action. Otherwise, you might miss such changes entirely and wonder why you suddenly wind up with a disgruntled, unproductive employee.

Remember, the best way to see if a reward "works" is to administer it to an employee and watch the results. If the rewarded behavior is maintained or increases in frequency, chances are the reward is effective.

In observing Guideline 2, it will help to keep the following points in mind (in addition to those already mentioned):

1 Many employees have several different needs at the same time, thus allowing you to use several different kinds of rewards in such circumstances.

2 Certain rewards (such as money) can satisfy more than one human need, and certain needs can be satisfied by more than one reward. Choose the reward that works best for the individual worker in question.

3 Be on the lookout for boredom effects if you use the same reward frequently with a particular employee. Try not to overuse a reinforcement so that it loses its effectiveness. Using more than one kind of reward, or decreasing use of the same reward, will reduce the risk of "reward boredom."

4 Try to familiarize yourself with all fourteen rewards and how they can be used to best advantage. The more rewards you can utilize comfortably and effectively, the better manager you'll be.

Guideline 3 You don't have to reward a desired behavior everytime it occurs.

Many managers believe that the best way to keep employee performance high is to reinforce effective behavior everytime it occurs. In reality, quite the opposite can occur: rewarding specific actions everytime they occur can actually decrease performance levels in the long run.

Initially, when an employee is learning a new task, it helps to reward the employee frequently, so that the behavior becomes fixed in the person's response pattern. Once the behavior has become established, however, it is appropriate to *gradually* cut back the frequency of rewards and move toward *intermittent* ("variable") reinforcement of effective performance. By rewarding behavior intermittently (rather than everytime it occurs) you gain three benefits:

1 You don't need as much of the reward (for instance, if you're using money as a reinforcement, it will last longer if administered intermittently rather than continuously).

2 The chance that the worker becomes bored with the reward through overuse will be reduced.

3 Intermittent reinforcement sustains higher levels of performance over longer periods of time. Employees keep working with the expectation that their reward is "right around the corner." This type of thinking keeps gamblers frantically pumping coins into slot machines. On one-armed bandits, "reinforcement in the form of winning is not dispensed each time nor on a regular basis, but on a random or intermittent basis. Therefore, the player is highly motivated to continue playing; the next play may be a winner."[1]

Now comes an interesting question. How intermittent should your intermittent reinforcement be? In other words, how often should you reward your employees for work well done? The answer is, often enough to sustain quality job performance. When you use reinforcement, observe the impact of your rewards on your employees' behavior. If worker performance level remains high, chances are that your frequency of reinforcement is "on target." If performance drops, however, you might want to decrease or increase the amount of reinforcement until you reach a level that brings employee performance up to optimum levels. In doing so, the following points might help:

1 Too much as well as too little reinforcement can lead to a decline in job performance. Do not reinforce so frequently that the reward loses potency or so infrequently as to "extinguish" appropriate behaviors.
2 Different employees require different amounts of reinforcement to keep their performance levels high. By observing your workers, you will be able to determine the ideal intermittent schedule for any particular employee.

Guideline 4   Reward desired behaviors immediately after they occur.

The sooner you can reward an employee for superior job performance, the more effective that reinforcement will be. Conversely, the longer the delay between the desired behavior and the ensuing reward, the less effective the reinforcement becomes. This timing-of-reinforcement effect is clearly documented in the behavioral science

[1]R. Beatty and C. Schneier, "A Case for Positive Reinforcement," *Business Horizons,* April 1975, p. 61.

literature and says, in effect, that you must act quickly once you become aware of reinforceable behavior.

Of course, sometimes it is not possible for a manager to reinforce an employee immediately for desired work behavior. For example, two weeks may pass before a manager learns that a salesperson has closed a big deal; or a manager may be away from the office when an employee does something outstanding. What then? Fortunately, reinforcement is still possible, but under these circumstances it is vitally important that the manager clearly state what the reward is for. It is not enough to say, "This bonus is for good work on the job." The work behavior in question must be specifically identified by saying, for example, "This bonus is to recognize your achievement in closing the Johnson account." It is necessary that the worker establish a bond between a specific reward and a specific behavior—otherwise behavior modification won't work. And it's up to you as manager to reinforce in a manner that makes such bonding possible.

Guideline 5 Whenever possible use reward rather than punishment in the workplace.

Perhaps you've wondered why I spent a whole chapter discussing workplace rewards and not a single page examining punishments. It is because I believe that rewards are more effective in establishing desired behaviors and avoiding undesirable ones. Professor Thomas Rotondi has this to say:

> . . . punishment tends to suppress rather than eliminate undesirable behavior. When the punishment ends, the undesirable behavior may be repeated. What's more, applying punishment to individuals may also create such undesirable side effects as fears, anxieties, erratic behavior, vindictiveness, or subtle sabotage.[2]

Much of my thinking about reward versus punishment is reflected in the fable of the old man and his coat. It seems the old gent was spotted by the spirits of Winter and Summer as he walked along a path in an enchanted forest. The two spirits were in a competitive mood that afternoon, and suddenly the spirit of Winter said, "I'll bet you I

[2]T. Rotondi, "Behavior Modification on the Job," *Supervisory Management,* February 1976, p. 26.

can strip that man of the coat he's wearing faster than you can." "It's a bet," the spirit of Summer replied, "you can go first."

The spirit of Winter took a deep breath and blew up a raging arctic storm that whipped through the forest and buffeted the old man about like a leaf. He gathered his tattered coat around him and hung on for dear life. The wind threatened to tear the coat right off his body. Every button was ripped away, and still the old man hung on gamely. Finally, the spirit of Winter tired and the storm dissipated. The old man brushed the debris off what was left of his coat and took a few tentative steps.

"It's my turn now," said the spirit of Summer, and with a nod sent the clouds scurrying across the sky and turned the sun's full radiance on the forest. The old man turned his face to the sun and felt the welcome, penetrating heat. It felt good. He took off his coat and continued on his way.

The moral? It is better if an employee wants to do something than if he has to do it. This is the spirit and essence of the human use of human resources; the cornerstone of the ++ relationship in the worthplace.

Does this mean I'm against all punishment in the workplace? No. There will be times when, having exhausted all avenues of positive reinforcement, your only recourse will be punitive action. Yet, even then, punishment can be administered in a constructive fashion—not for revenge but to get the worker back "on track." And, of course, punishment should always be done in private, as your goal is to educate, not humiliate, an employee.

Administered in the proper spirit—as a form of constructive criticism—even punishment can play a meaningful role in the worthplace. Before you opt for using it, however, it might be instructive to consider the words of management authority Bernard Rosenbaum: "When it comes to supervising people, rarely is there too much positive reinforcement. Managers who encounter undesirable behavior should ask themselves when and in what way the desired behavior was last reinforced."[3]

Guideline 6   Give rewards only when they are deserved.

---

[3]B. Rosenbaum, "Understanding and Using Motivation," *Supervisory Management,* January 1979, p. 12.

In other words, reinforcement should be sincere and earned. If an employee doesn't deserve praise, then don't give it; it is better to withhold a compliment than give one dishonestly. Not only is such behavior unethical, it is bad management. Employees are quick to detect your motives; they see such reinforcement as cheap manipulation—which it is. Don't behave in such a manner; it is not humane and it doesn't work.

Chapter 9

A Personal View of Effective Leadership

The lack of leadership in industry and government is the chief difficulty in this country.

William McCleery

I love to browse through bookstores. On a recent visit I noticed that an entire shelf was set aside for books on sexual techniques. Above the shelf someone had written a note claiming, "These techniques can make *you* a better lover." While I was mulling over that bit of advertising, a student walked up and showed me an armload of business books she had just purchased. "I want to make it big in my job," she explained, "and these books have the techniques I'll need to know to become an effective leader."

Do you find all this lamentable? I do. It is a sad commentary on the human condition that people believe effective loving or leading can be reduced to a series of techniques.

Please don't misunderstand me. I'm not saying that techniques are unimportant—they just aren't the whole story or, for that matter, the most important part of it. Take leadership, for example. There are literally dozens of techniques you can use to become a more effective supervisor, but those techniques by themselves won't make you a true leader. There is an ingredient missing, something else that has to be there. It's like trying to bake bread without yeast. You can still do it, but you'll never get the dough to rise past a certain point. As a manager you can use the various techniques to sharpen your supervisory skills, but you'll never *rise* to great leadership without adding the missing ingredient—the ingredient I call the "human component" of leadership.

What, exactly, is this human component so crucial for effective leadership? It is actually three things: *love, enthusiasm, and dedication.* It is no wonder that the first letters of these four words add up to another word:

L ove + E nthusiasm + A nd + D edication = L.E.A.D.

The manager who knows how to L.E.A.D. becomes a L.E.A.D.E.R., because L ove, E nthusiasm, A nd D edication E arn R espect—and that is basic to a meaningful bond between manager and employee.

Love, Enthusiasm, and Dedication Defined

These words have special meanings when utilized in the workplace, so it is best that we define them now.

Love   Another word for this term is "caring." What I am referring to here is the capacity of managers to love (in a caring sense) their employees, to sincerely care for them as human beings. This sense of caring is something which can be learned but can't be faked. Workers are quick to sense whether their managers truly care for them. If employees feel this caring is present, it can contribute mightily to their productivity and satisfaction in the workplace. If, on the other hand, they feel a manager lacks this capacity, then no amount of techniques—however well executed—will ever make that manager a great leader.

Let me illustrate the importance of love/caring with an example from where I work. In my department I have a colleague who is an outstanding scholar and a dedicated academician. I took it for granted he was also a topnotch teacher: after all, he knows his subject matter better than anyone else at the university, and I have seen him spend many hours preparing his lectures. You can imagine my surprise, then, when several students stopped by my office to complain about my colleague's poor teaching performance.

"What's wrong with him," I wanted to know, "Is he a boring speaker?"

"No," they responded.

"Is he unprepared for class?"

"No," again.

"Are his tests unfair?"

"No," again.

"Does he miss classes?"

"No," a fourth time.

"Well, what *is* it then?"

Silence. Finally a student came up with this response: "I guess it's not really his teaching that's the problem . . . it's a feeling I get that he doesn't really *care* about me as a person, that I'm somebody to be tolerated as part of the job."

"That's right," another student broke in. "The man is aloof and distant . . . he doesn't treat his students like human beings."

Love. It's a vital part of effective leadership.

Enthusiasm Enthusiastic managers are persons who put energy into their work, who bring a sense of spirit and excitement to the workplace. Enthusiasm is contagious. If managers have it, chances are better that their workers will have it, too. Lethargy, unfortunately, is also contagious. When managers walk into the office looking disinterested and bored, is it any wonder their employees become listless and unmotivated as well? As a manager you set a mood tone for your employees, and it is important that the mood be a positive one. But, in being enthusiastic, two points are worth remembering:

1 To be enthusiastic you don't have to be "rah rah" or "gung ho." A quiet enthusiasm is just as potent as animated enthusiasm—just so long as employees can sense your positive, interested attitude toward work.

2 As a manager you don't have to be enthusiastic about your work every moment of every working day. Nobody expects you to like your job all the time! There will be days when you come to work in a sour mood; there will also be times when your work gets you down. In these circumstances, it is perfectly all right to act "down in the dumps." Employees don't expect you to feign enthusiasm when you feel like hell. In fact, if you are usually enthusiastic in the workplace, a few "off" days will tend to reinforce that general enthusiasm.

Enthusiasm. It's an important part of the charisma generated by effective leaders.

Dedication Another word for dedication can be "commitment." Dedicated managers are committed to their work, and they pass along this sense of dedication to their employees.

Many managers ask me how they can be sure they're dedicated to their work. This is not a silly question, as being immersed in a job day after day sometimes limits our ability to judge work effectively. There are two ways you can take a reading of your job dedication level.

1 *Monitor your enthusiasm:* Keep tabs on your level of job enthusiasm over time. Dedication and enthusiasm are intimately linked: people who are dedicated to their jobs are almost always enthusiastic about them. Thus if you sense your enthusiasm for work is waning, it might be a sign of eroding dedication as well.

2 *Ask yourself two questions upon awakening in the morning:* (1) Am I looking forward to today? (2) Would I rather be doing something else than the work I'm in? If you find yourself *consistently* answering no to the first question and yes to the second question, it is doubtful you are generating much dedication to your job. And if that's the way *you* feel about your work, how can you expect your employees to feel any differently about theirs.

Dedication. It's a vital source of strength for effective leaders.

A Personal Request

Leadership is more than a series of techniques to be mastered. It is first and foremost a human being *being human.* It is a manager who understands the human component in the leadership equation—who cares about employees and is enthusiastic about and dedicated to the job. It is a manager who uses behavioral science techniques to establish a ++ relationship on the job, a *worthplace* where employees can satisfy their needs and be productive at the same time.

Of course, by my definition, there are not many managers who qualify as leaders in the contemporary business world. For that matter there are not many leaders among parents, teachers, and politicians either. That is because most of us have not learned to L.E.A.D. in a humane way.

Which brings me to my request: Just because there are so many inhumane managers in the work world doesn't mean you have to further populate their ranks. *If you feel you cannot or will not inject the human component into your leadership behavior, don't become a manager in the first place—at least not the kind of manager who has to consistently interact with subordinates.* It just won't be fair to you, and it certainly won't be fair to your employees. If your subordinate wants to be uncaring, unenthusiastic, and undedicated on the job, that is bad enough; but if you as a manager feel that way, then you are setting an example that can affect many other lives (as well as your own) in a negative way.

Some of you might not agree with, or honor, this request. That is your choice. As the chapter title suggests, this is my personal view of leadership, and you might not share it. But I do believe it is a correct view, and I, for one, certainly wouldn't want to work under a manager who disagreed with it. Think about it, would you?

Section Three

How to Succeed in Business without Really Dying

Chapter 10

How to Keep Physically and Mentally Alert on the Job

You can't help others if you can't help yourself.

Transportation industry manager

Our family physician is a busy man. I stopped by his office one morning for a routine physical exam and marveled at the sheer number of patients being shuffled in and out of doors as the doctor moved briskly from one examination room to the next.

When it came time for my appointment, I didn't wait for the physician to speak as he barreled through the door. "How are you feeling today, Doctor," I asked, smiling a hello.

The question stopped him in his tracks. He groped for words and then just gave up, his mouth half open.

"What's the matter?" I inquired.

"It's just . . . that . . . well, nobody ever asked me how *I* felt before."

As a manager you're going to be in basically the same predicament as my family physician. Your employees are going to expect you to listen to their everyday gripes and problems, without considering that you, too, have your hassles and difficulties.

This is unfortunate because you're a human being with human needs just like your subordinates. And it is important that you recognize and deal with these needs, even if your employees don't. It would be bitter irony indeed if, as an expert in human resource management, you couldn't manage the most important human resource of all—yourself.

Up to this point we have concentrated on what you can do to help others meet their needs and be more productive in the workplace; this final chapter focuses on what you can do to increase *your* satisfaction and productivity on the job. My concern here will be with showing you how to succeed in business without really dying—how you can be healthy, happy, *and* successful in the workplace.

A PINK SLIP NOBODY WANTS

Here's a brainteaser for you. Steve Johnson is a dynamic, aggressive executive with a Fortune 500 company. For the past 15 years he's risen steadily through the corporate ranks, gaining respect and recognition in the business community. Yet, a few months short of his forty-fifth birthday, Steve Johnson suddenly loses his job. Why?

Because Steve Johnson dropped dead—irrevocably cut down at the height of a promising career. Unusual? Unfortunately not. It has been estimated that loss of production due to premature deaths costs American business in excess of $20 billion yearly—and that figure doesn't even start to approach the billions more lost through health-related absenteeism.

Yet the real tragedy of Steve Johnson goes beyond economic profit and loss—even beyond the personal loss of those who loved him. *The real tragedy of Steve Johnson is that he died unnecessarily.* When a young man like Steve Johnson succumbs to a stroke or coronary seizure, we are grimly reminded of our own mortality; yet in most cases it didn't have to happen (at least at such a young age). It was preventable. By making certain medically recommended changes in his personal behavior—*changes that in no way would have dimin-*

ished his chances of succeeding in the business world—Steve Johnson could have dramatically increased his chances of living to full life expectancy, free from many of the medical problems that prematurely dull, cripple, and kill so many Americans.

Which brings me to you—who can still do something about your life. You don't have to go the way of a Steve Johnson. Nobody, of course, can live forever; but medical science has given us new insights to greatly increase our chances for living full, alert, healthy lives. I will share those insights with you. I can show you "how to succeed in business without really dying"—but the effectiveness of what I have to say will depend on *you* and your willingness to implement the recommendations of medical science in your own life. As you read further, keep in mind what Dr. John Knowles, president of the Rockefeller Foundation, has said: "The next major advance in the health of the American people will result only from what the individual is willing to do for himself."[1]

DOING BATTLE WITH EXCESSIVE STRESS

To help you help yourself toward better health, mental alertness, and longevity, medical science has identified many of the factors that can raise havoc with a person's well-being. None seems so culpable and widespread as *stress*. It has been called the disease of our time—the scourge of modern civilizations.

Just what is stress? It is a condition we all experience. It can be caused by many things, such as frustrations, time binds, overwork, frightening experiences, emotional conflicts, and even pleasant events like marriage or an outstanding personal achievement.

Please understand that normal amounts of stress never hurt anybody; in fact, moderate amounts of stress can actually enhance performance and make for a more meaningful, exciting life. Stress becomes dangerous only when it becomes *excessive*—forcing the body to run like a car with the accelerator stuck to the floor. When we become stressed, our bodies shift into a state of high physical arousal preparing us for the so-called "fight-or-flight" response. If we experi-

[1]From B. Kramer, "Wiser Way of Living, Not Dramatic 'Cures,' Seen as Key to Health," *The Wall Street Journal,* Mar. 22, 1976, p. 1.

ence this state too often, or stay in it too long, we will eventually break down like any overworked machine.

The word "stress" was borrowed from the language of physics and engineering, where it refers to a "force that tends to deform a body." How apt! For that is exactly what excessive stress does to the human body in ugly, crippling ways. To compile a list of stress-related diseases is like thumbing through a medical dictionary. High blood pressure, heart attack, strokes, headaches, ulcers, allergies, infections, insomnia, asthma, diabetes, cancer, even accidents—all can be triggered and made more severe by excessive stress.

How do you know if you are under stress? One way is to visit your doctor for various tests—blood pressure, hormone levels, brain activity, and so forth. This is the preferred method, but it is not always possible on a day-to-day basis. But, as Dr. Hans Selye, an international authority on stress, points out:

> There are other indices that anyone can judge. No two people react the same way, but the usual responses are . . . you will become more irritable and will sometimes suffer insomnia, even long after the stressor agent is gone. You will usually become less capable of concentrating, and you will have an increased desire to move about. I was talking with a businessman this morning who asked if he could walk back and forth because he couldn't think well sitting down. That is a stress symptom everyone will know.[2]

Dr. Selye also points out that an increase in pulse rate and an increased tendency to sweat is common in persons undergoing stress.

DEVELOPING THE PROPER PSYCHOLOGICAL ATTITUDE TOWARD EXCESSIVE STRESS

Knowing when you are stressed is important—but it's only half the battle. It is also necessary to *do* something about it, and it is here the typical manager confronts awesome difficulties. Most supervisors readily admit they experience stress on the job. One business manager put it bluntly: "Stress is as much a part of corporate life as the annual meeting and the balance sheet." Yet many managers are hesitant to—even refuse to—reduce excessive job stress in their own lives.

[2]H. Selye (interview), "Secret of Coping with Stress," *U.S. News & World Report,* Mar. 21, 1977, p. 52.

Victimized by the stressful world they have helped create, they accept stress as a necessary component of their existence. They accept constant business stress as "immutable," a force beyond the scope of change. Then there are those who go so far as to extol the virtues of excessive stress, like the executive who, informed he had an ulcer, bragged, "I'm not concerned about it . . . don't you know that only successful people get ulcers." It is these managers, who see their stress-related miseries as "red badges of courage," proof of their business worth, who are most unwilling to do anything about excessive stress in their life. No wonder. They believe that being good in business and excessive stress go hand in hand. Unfortunately, they are wrong, and unless they change their attitude and their behavior, they may end up *dead* wrong.

To put it bluntly, there is no room for excessive stress in the American workplace. If you want to succeed in business without really dying, your main hope lies in keeping your own stress under control. I'll present the techniques to help you do this. But no techniques, however powerful, will work unless you have the proper psychological attitude toward stress in the first place. Thus, if you want to conquer excessive stress, you first must fully believe in these three statements:

1 Excessive stress does *not* have to be an immutable force in your life. It can be overcome, and I'll show you how.

2 The quickest way to succumb to an enemy is to underestimate its strength. Learn to respect stress as a formidable opponent; realize what excessive stress can do to you and decide you want to do something about it. Remember this statement: "Stress may be the corporate executive's single most powerful and pervasive enemy."[3]

3 Realize that excessive stress does *not* improve business performance. To the contrary, it has been shown to mentally and physically debilitate the manager—causing lapses in judgment, unnecessary effort, loss of concentration, reduction of creativity, interpersonal difficulties, and, in severe cases, nervous breakdowns, disease, and even death. You will *want* to overcome the "stress oppressor" when you find that it dulls rather than sharpens your managerial acuity.

Now you've taken the first big step. You realize that excessive

[3]"Can You Cope with Stress?" *Dun's Review,* November 1975, p. 89.

stress isn't good for you and you want to do something about it. Good. Thus you're in the proper frame of mind to launch your own stress-reduction campaign and I'm going to give you a few stress-fighting "weapons" for your arsenal. These weapons, or stress-fighting techniques, can be used alone or in combination; but remember that each one, used conscientiously, can help turn the tide in your struggle against excessive stress. Try out the various weapons and choose the best one(s) for you.

The Relaxation Response⁴

The first weapon, or technique, seems so simple that many managers dismiss it out of hand. Don't let its simplicity fool you—it works, and it works well. Furthermore, it is a weapon against stress which *all* of us possess—an innate gladiator waiting to do battle with excessive stress *at our command.*

In the words of Harvard physician Herbert Benson: "Each of us possesses a natural and innate protective mechanism against 'overstress,' which allows us to turn off harmful bodily effects, to counter the effects of the fight-or-flight response."⁵ The name Dr. Benson has attached to this protective mechanism is the "relaxation response," and by using it he believes we can reduce the risk of stress-related illnesses such as heart attacks and related conditions—diseases that will cause the deaths of over 50 percent of the present population of the United States.

Just what is the relaxation response? Basically, it is a form of meditation. In calling forth the relaxation response, the meditator strives to achieve a state of "restful alertness" by spending two 20-minute periods each day in "comfortable isolation," letting the mind empty of all thoughts and distractions.

By employing the relaxation response, a person reaps many physiological benefits: decreased oxygen consumption, diminishing heart rate, lower respiratory rate, and increasing skin resistance, which is inversely related to stress. The relaxation response has also been found to increase overall memory, reduce anxiety, decrease blood pressure in hypertensive individuals, heighten perceptual ability, relieve asthma, and even alleviate dependence on certain drugs, alcohol, and tobacco.

⁴Adapted from pp. 112–113 and 114–115 in *The Relaxation Response* by Herbert Benson, M.D., with Miriam Z. Klipper. Copyright © 1975 by William Morrow and Company, Inc. By permission of the publishers.
⁵H. Benson, *The Relaxation Response,* Avon, New York, 1976, p. 25.

A real elixir, this relaxation response! Your body's natural defense against the stress spiral. Yet, as healthful as this technique is, many hardnosed managers will shun it because, as a form of meditation, they see it as "faddish hocus-pocus." Well, here is the good news. You don't need a guru, long flowing robe, or a mountaintop to practice the relaxation response. You don't even need a special "mantra" given to you in some secret ceremony. All you need is 40 minutes a day and the willingness to follow the instructions of Dr. Benson.

First, says Dr. Benson, you will need to find a *quiet, calm environment* with as few distractions as possible. Sound, even background noise, may prevent elicitation of the response. Choose a convenient, suitable place—for example, at an office desk in a quiet room or a silent area of the house.

Second, you must choose a *mental device* to focus on—for example, a single-syllable sound or word. This sound or word is repeated silently or in a low, gentle tone. The purpose of the repetition is to free oneself from logical, externally oriented thought by focusing solely on the sound or word, as repetition helps break the train of distracting thoughts. Many different words and sounds have been used in traditional practice. Because of its simplicity and neutrality, the one-syllable word "one" is suggested.

Third, you must maintain a *passive attitude*. This is very important. The purpose of the relaxation response is to help one rest and relax, and this requires a completely passive attitude. When distracting thoughts occur, they are to be disregarded and attention redirected to the single-syllable sound or word. You should not worry about how well you are performing the technique, because this may well prevent the relaxation response from occurring. Do not try to force the response, adopt a let-it-happen attitude.

Fourth, you must meditate in a *comfortable position* (comfortable for *you*). You should sit in a comfortable chair in as restful a position as possible. Your goal is to reduce any undue muscular tension. The head may be supported; the arms should be balanced or supported as well. The shoes may be removed and the feet propped up several inches, if desired. Loosen all tight-fitting clothes before beginning.[6]

Observing these four guidelines of Dr. Benson, you should be able to elicit your own relaxation response. Here is the way Dr. Benson suggests you actually conduct a session:

[6]H. Benson, "Your Innate Asset for Combating Stress," *Harvard Business Review,* July–August 1974, p. 54.

1 Sit quietly in a comfortable position.

2 Close your eyes.

3 Deeply relax all your muscles, beginning at your feet and progressing up to your face. Keep them relaxed.

4 Breathe through your nose (or mouth, if this is more comfortable). Become aware of your breathing. As you breathe out, say "One" silently to yourself. For example, breathe in . . . out, "One"; in . . . out, "One"; and so forth. Breathe easily and naturally.

5 Continue this practice for 20 minutes. You may open your eyes to check the time, but do not use an alarm. When you finish, sit quietly for several minutes, at first with your eyes closed and later with your eyes open. Do not stand up for a few minutes.

6 Remember not to worry about whether you are successful in achieving a deep level of relaxation. Maintain a passive attitude and permit relaxation to occur at its own pace. When distracting thoughts occur, try to ignore them by not dwelling upon them and return to repeating "One." With practice the response should come with little effort. Practice the technique once or twice daily, but not within 2 hours after any meal, since the digestive processes seem to interfere with elicitation of the relaxation response.[7]

There you have it. Your own innate weapon in the war on excessive stress. Use it wisely, and an equilibrium between tension and relaxation can be attained. "But," some of you may be worrying, "might the relaxation response upset my work effectiveness and make me a zombie?"

To the contrary, the relaxation response will not only combat excessive stress but will also enhance your alertness and job performance. Testimonials to that are rife in the business community. William Milton, general manager of Sprague Electric Company, refers to meditation as a "real battery charger"; Pamela Grant, director of a British printing machinery firm, says it helped her "concentrate properly for the first time in my life"; and J. Paul Chambers, president of First American Life Insurance Company claims it "helps me accomplish more with less work and effort." Dozens of American corporations, recognizing the value of the relaxation response, have initiated meditation programs at work—an idea Dr. Benson highly supports. He thinks employees should be given relaxation-response breaks instead of coffee breaks.

[7]Ibid.

The next time you want to make a really great investment in 20 minutes, why don't you take a relaxation-response break? As you do, remember the words of psychologist Daniel Goleman: "Meditators become more relaxed the longer they have been at it. At the same time they become more alert, something other ways to relax fail to bring about because they do not train the ability to pay attention. The combination of relaxation and concentration allows us to do better at whatever we try."[8]

Effective Exercise

When I ask you to practice the relaxation response, do not think I am recommending a less energetic existence—only a less stressful one. As a matter of fact, one of the best ways to beat the excessive stress syndrome is to live an active life, and our second stress-fighting weapon, exercise, will help you do just that.

"I don't know of a person who is highly regarded in medicine today who doesn't advocate exercise as an essential part of the lifestyle for healthful living."[9] So observed C. Carson Conrad while executive director of the President's Council on Physical Fitness. If you are willing to undertake an effective exercise program, you will most likely find it the *single most important* contribution you can make to your job performance and good health.

The key word here is "effective." To explain what I mean by effective, it is necessary to distinguish between two forms of exercise. One form, called aerobics, involves *sustained* activities that stimulate heart and lungs long enough to produce beneficial changes in the body. Such activities typically include walking (briskly), jogging, swimming, cycling and skipping rope. A second form of exercise does *not* require sustained action and includes sports like bowling and baseball, plus body-building activities such as weight lifting and isometrics. These undertakings can be fun, and some can give you an attractive physique, but they will *not* produce the health benefits of aerobic exercises. As science writer C. P. Gilmore notes:

> Sports such as tennis and touch football may be strenuous but they generally call for intermittent rather than prolonged effort. Golf may be

[8]D. Goleman, "Meditation Helps Break the Stress Spiral," *Psychology Today,* February 1976, p. 93.
[9]From P. Stephano, "Fitness, Health, and the National Pulse," *Action,* no. 1, 1976, p. 6.

pleasant but it does not raise the pulse rate. Calisthenics make the muscles stronger and more flexible and help keep the joints limber, but are not usually indulged in vigorously enough or long enough. And, of course, the machines that jiggle and bounce the flesh may be fun, but they do nothing for the heart.[10]

To put it bluntly, if you want to reap the health benefits from exercise, then you must be prepared to "get into" aerobics on a regular basis. This means that 4 to 6 days a week you will be expected to spend part of your time undertaking sustained, brisk physical activity. Dr. Kenneth Cooper, a noted authority on exercise and author of the informative book *The New Aerobics,* points out that you can achieve total aerobic fitness by running 1½ miles in from 12 to just under 15 minutes five times a week. This means you can achieve top physical fitness with a time investment of under 15 minutes a day; a little over an hour a week. As there are 1440 minutes in every day, spending 15 minutes on exercise seems like a worthwhile investment for better job performance, alertness, and health.

Of course, running that fast might not be your cup of tea. Do not despair! You can enjoy full aerobic fitness at a more leisurely pace—you'll just have to spend more time at the activity you choose. For example, instead of running the mile and a half in the 12- to 15-minute range, you may choose to walk it instead; then you will have to do so twice daily, five times a week, in 21½ minutes—which isn't exactly a marathon distance in jackrabbit time. What this means, best of all, is that the health benefits of aerobic fitness are within the reach of almost everyone—young and old. You don't need to be a young person or a "jock" to become aerobically fit—you don't even have to run. All you need is a little motivation, training, and perseverance, and you can walk your way to better health.

Just what *are* the benefits of regular, sustained, brisk exercise? One of the best ways to find out is to ask people involved in aerobics. Chances are their missionary zeal will send you scurrying for your sneakers. Most veteran exercisers agree that once you get into aerobics, you'll wonder how you ever got along without it. The benefits they (myself included) have experienced first hand are documented by scientific research.

[10]C. Gilmore, "And the Beat Goes On," *St. Petersburg Times,* Apr. 1, 1977, p. 1–D.

Would you be willing to spend some time, 4 to 6 days a week, to gain the advantages associated with lower blood pressure, substantial and permanent weight loss, healthier blood chemistry, and increased strength and efficiency of the heart? Regular aerobic exercise produces these beneficial physiological changes and more. It also helps those with diabetes and insomnia; and many doctors believe it can aid in the battle against the number one killer: heart disease. Some medical authorities question the preventive value of sustained exercise but support the notion that it can be very useful in rehabilitating heart victims. Others, like Dr. Cooper, believe that aerobics, properly followed, will lessen a person's chances of prematurely developing coronary heart disease or related vascular ailments. One physician, Dr. Thomas Bassler, goes so far as to claim that anyone in physical condition to run and finish a marathon will be permanently immune to heart attacks. Although his argument is controversial, it is interesting to note that Dr. Bassler heads a 1000-member group of running MD's called the American Medical Joggers Association. It is my belief that when doctors start "running for their lives," it might be the better part of wisdom to keep pretty close behind.

Regular aerobic exercise has also improved the psychological well-being of many participants.[11] A better self-image and more self-confidence are reported by many exercising managers, along with increased alertness and ability to concentrate. These individuals report they work with more energy and need less sleep when following an exercise regimen. A large study by the National Aeronautics and Space Administration is interesting in this respect. Among NASA employees who closely followed a fitness program, more than 90 percent reported a feeling of better health and stamina, and about 50 percent said they had a more positive work attitude with less strain and tension.

This brings us to the last major benefit of aerobic exercise. It helps reduce the manager's major enemy: excessive stress. Simply put, exercise is a kind of pressure-release valve that provides an outlet for stored-up tensions. It allows us to express our aggressive drives in physical action rather than keep them pent up inside where they can produce excessive stress effects. Also, a physically fit person's body is toned to a point where it can withstand stress more effectively. As

[11] A. Ismail and L. Trachtman, "Jogging the Imagination," *Psychology Today,* March 1973, pp. 79–82.

writers Walter McQuade and Ann Aikman have noted, "A person who is in good physical condition will withstand the assault of a virus, or a spell of overwork—or even a quarrel with the foreman—better than someone who isn't."[12]

So much for the benefits of exercise. The human body wasn't built to sit still, so it shouldn't come as a surprise to discover that aerobic exercise is good for us. Yet some of you may be worrying about the possible *dangers* of sustained exercise—you may have heard stories about joggers dying or injuring themselves. Many of these stories turn out to be greatly exaggerated; but it is true that aerobic exercise is demanding and can be potentially dangerous for people who ignore simple basic safety precautions. For those who *do* observe these precautions, sustained exercise is both safe and beneficial. In your own exercise program you should observe these rules:

1 See your doctor for a complete medical examination *before* you begin exercising. This is very important. The vast majority of managers will be able to undertake aerobic exercise with no difficulty; however, a small number of individuals might have hidden problems—like an unknown heart condition—that could make sustained exercise risky. Tell your doctor you intend to begin an aerobic program, so that he can advise you of any possible problems. Most exercise physiologists recommend that the checkup include a cardiopulmonary stress test.

2 Start slowly and gradually work your way up to good aerobic fitness. If you've spent 30 years getting out of shape, don't expect youthful vigor to return as soon as you pull on your sweat socks. If you have any questions, Dr. Cooper's *The New Aerobics* gives detailed instructions on how you can progress safely to physical fitness and what you have to do to maintain it. Each person follows a program based on age and current physical condition.[13]

3 Exercise regularly—at least three times a week—or do not exercise at all.

4 If you experience discomfort or pain while exercising, stop and check with your physician before you exercise again.

5 Prior to exercise, it is helpful to do a few calisthenics to limber up and get your body toned for action. After finishing aerobic

[12]W. McQuade and A. Aikman, *Stress,* Bantam, New York, 1975, p. 130.
[13]K. Cooper, *The New Aerobics,* Bantam, New York, 1970.

exercise, it is recommended that you let your body readjust by doing some slow walking or a similar "warming down" activity.

6 Do not overexert yourself during exercise. A good guideline for determining if you exercise too vigorously is your pulse rate. Five minutes after you exercise it should be under 120, according to Dr. Cooper. Ten minutes after exercise it should be back to below 100. Dr. Cooper also suggests you watch for these symptoms of overexertion during exercise: "Tightness or pain in the chest, severe breathlessness, light-headedness, dizziness, loss of muscle control and nausea. Should you experience any of these symptoms," he cautions, "stop exercising immediately."[14]

There you have six rules for making your exercise program medically sound and worthwhile. Remember you are exercising to achieve better health. You defeat that purpose if you don't exercise safely.

The value of aerobic exercise for managers is becoming more evident everyday. I hope that you will consider using this weapon in your fight against excessive stress. After all, company after company is instituting aerobic exercise programs (see Box 10–1); don't you think it's time you did, too?

[14]Ibid., p. 42.

BOX 10-1

A COMPANY WITH A TRACK RECORD*

If you asked an executive of Tyler Corporation about the company's track record, you might get an answer in terms of times and distances rather than profits and loss. This is because Tyler is one of the growing number of American corporations actively supporting jogging programs as a way to assure aerobic fitness in company management.

*Material and quotes for this box were taken from an article by R. Rowan, "The Company That Just Runs and Runs," *Fortune,* Dec. 4, 1978, pp. 94–97. Other articles of interest on the same topic include: D. Norfolk, "Keeping Fit to Manage," *Management Today,* March 1976, pp. 101ff.; and K. Moore, "A Run for Their Money," *Sports Illustrated,* November 4, 1974, pp. 68ff.

> Says Tyler's chairman and president, Joseph F. McKinney: "Running, like business, is full of drudgery. But inherent in our philosophy is the belief that physical fitness gives us a headstart over a less fit competitor."
>
> All that running must be doing something right. In the past decade Tyler Corporation sales "have sextupled (to $365 million) and net income has increased almost nine times (to $21 million)."
>
> McKinney's enthusiasm for aerobic fitness has stretched beyond the boundaries of his own company. One result: the Tyler Cup race for corporation executives. And not just "small time" executives, either! In fact, in a recent race 170 executives representing ". . . seventy-two companies with a total of 1.5 million employees and $90 billion in assets" lined up in the starting blocks.

The relaxation response and aerobic exercise are two weapons *all of us* can employ in the war on excessive stress. I have two other weapons left to present, each for combating a specific difficulty that creates excessive stress. If you don't have these difficulties, then you won't have to deploy these weapons against them. I hope you'll never have to use them. Unfortunately, scientific evidence suggests that the majority of people in business are experiencing one or both of these difficulties—and should be doing something about it.

Dealing with Job Dissatisfaction

The first of these difficulties involves job dissatisfaction. As we already saw in Section 1 of this book, many workers are unhappy with their jobs—and among them are managers. According to Dr. Harry Johnson, recently retired chairman of the medical board of the Life Extension Institute, "being in the wrong job accounts for a major percentage of stress problems in executives."[15]

It is important to note that the cause of medical problems is *not* work itself but, rather, the mismatch between the worker and the work performed. Put another way, we might say that one person's job is another person's poison. In this context, I'd like to share with you the insights of Dr. Selye, the stress authority mentioned earlier in the chapter.

[15]F. Stone, "A Sound Mind . . . ," *Management Review,* January 1975, p. 7.

Dr. Selye has spent a lifetime studying the relationship between stress and work and has developed an interesting theory. Work, to him, is a basic need in all of us—it is *not* to be avoided. He claims that "to function normally, man needs work as he needs air, food, sleep, social contacts, and sex." Further, stress is associated with every kind of work—*but,* if you like your work and are successful at it, this kind of stress won't harm you. Trouble occurs when workers don't like what they are doing or see a discrepancy between their job and their goals in life. This leads to *distress,* which can cause a whole host of miseries.

Dr. Selye's message is clear as a bell. Work is not harmful; a person's not enjoying work is. By the way, at the age of 18, Selye began his study of medicine—work he dearly loved. He worked from 4 A.M. till 6 P.M. At age 67, he still loved his work and kept exactly the same hours.

Are you one of those people who enjoy their work? Do you awaken in the morning looking forward to your job? If so, you are fortunate. But if you are seriously dissatisfied with your job, then you have three alternatives. You can stay at the job—spend at least 8 hours a day being unhappy—and risk the medical dangers associated with excessive stress; or you can try to maintain your present position but alter what you do to make it more interesting and in line with your life goals; if this is not possible, you can attempt to change jobs or careers.

Obviously, changing careers is not something to be taken lightly. But, then, neither is a lifetime spent at "distressful" labor. Dr. David Fink recognizes the importance of changing directions in life. He recommends making a fresh start "if your life has led you into a detour that is taking you where you do not want to go." And he goes on to say:

> It may be tough; tomorrow it will be tougher, because you will be that much farther away from your destination. . . . To many, this advice to redirect your own life will sound somehow subversive, radical, and dangerous. Nothing could be farther from the truth. If you want to subvert your life, to undermine it radically, live it against the direction of the flow of your real personality. If your job makes you sick, quit it. What difference does it make how good it is if it isn't good for you?[16]

[16]D. Fink, *Release from Nervous Tension,* Pocket Books, New York, 1973, pp. 200–201.

No job is going to be joyous and fulfilling all the time; and the decision to make a change should not be based on petty annoyances or momentary fits of pique. There is a line between the "trials and tribulations" of management and the tragedy of unfulfilling work. If you feel you have crossed over that line, Dr. Fink suggests you take five steps:

1 Make a list of your talents and skills.

2 Ask yourself what kind of work would give you an opportunity to exercise those talents and skills.

3 Pick that vocation within your scope which will furnish the most satisfactions.

4 Make a decision, and get started. If you need further training, that is priority number one.

5 All of your old activities and habits that do not fit in with your new purpose are out for the duration.[17]

Our third stress-fighting weapon involves making modifications in the work you do. I realize that current realities—the job market, the problem of credentials, financial considerations—might discourage use of such a weapon. Yet, a manager should also assess the realities of an unsatisfying job—the high potential for poor health and unfulfilled needs—and weigh these against the risks of job or even career modifications.

Should you use such a weapon? Take stock of where you are, carefully analyzing your own particular circumstances, and you should be able to determine which course of action to take. One manager put it this way: "Work to your heart's content; but if your heart isn't in your work, then your heart may very well put you out of work."

Eliminating Type A Behavior

Speaking of your heart brings us to our final weapon for combating excessive stress—a weapon designed to break you out of the dangerous stress spiral and help you combat America's number one killer: heart disease. What is this weapon? A change in diet? A new drug? No. The weapon is the elimination of Type A behavior from your personality.

[17]Ibid., p. 209.

Type A is a term created by two heart specialists, Drs. Meyer Friedman and Ray Rosenman, to describe a behavior pattern they think is the *major* cause of premature coronary heart disease. They sound a very strong warning: "In the absence of Type A Behavior Pattern, coronary heart disease almost never occurs before seventy years of age. . . . But when this behavior pattern is present, coronary heart disease can easily erupt in one's thirties or forties."[18]

How many American business managers exhibit the Type A behavior? If current estimates are correct, about 50 percent of the men and a growing number of the women in managerial positions possess the deadly Type A personality. It is those individuals who must alter their behavior, according to Drs. Friedman and Rosenman, if they want to reduce their risk of heart disease.

Just what *is* Type A behavior? Some describe it as "hurry sickness." Others label it "compulsive striving." Here is how Drs. Friedman and Rosenman define it:

> . . . a style of living characterized by excesses or competitiveness, striving for achievement, aggressiveness (sometimes stringently repressed), time urgency, acceleration of common activities, restlessness, hostility, hyper-alertness, explosiveness of speech amplitude, tenseness of facial musculature and feelings of struggle against the limitations of time and the insensitivity of the environment. This torrent of life is usually, but not always, channeled into a vocation or profession with such dedication that Type A persons often neglect other aspects of their life, such as family and recreation.[19]

Sound familiar? I suspect so. In the business world where racing against the clock is as American as apple pie, one should not be surprised at the number of Type A personalities around. The question is, How *long* will they be around? This is what worries Drs. Friedman and Rosenman, who want business managers to develop a "Type B" personality. In most ways, the Type B behavior pattern is the exact opposite of Type A. The Type B person isn't locked in a constant struggle to "beat the clock." Such an individual can also be ambitious,

---

[18]M. Friedman and R. Rosenman, *Type A Behavior and Your Heart,* Fawcett-Crest, New York, 1974, p. 9.

[19]Quoted in J. Howard, P. Rechnitzer, and D. Cunningham, "Coping with Job Tension—Effective and Ineffective Methods," *Public Personnel Management,* September–October, 1975, p. 318.

but feels more confident and secure than the Type A person and is able to be more relaxed. Most important, Type B persons are just as successful as their Type A counterparts; they just handle themselves differently. They also live long enough to enjoy the fruits of their labor.

To help determine what kind of personality *you* have—Type A or Type B—Drs. Friedman and Rosenman developed a Type A self-identification test. An adapted version is included in Box 10-2. Take a moment to read the instructions carefully; then take the test.

BOX 10-2

TYPE A SELF-IDENTIFICATION TEST*

INSTRUCTIONS

Here is a test to help you determine whether you are a Type A or Type B personality. If you are honest in your self-appraisal . . . we believe you will not have too much trouble accomplishing this. . . . Incidentally, we have found that Type A persons are by and large more common, and that if you are not quite sure about yourself, chances are that you, too, are Type A—not fully developed, perhaps, but bad enough to think about changing. And after you have assessed yourself, ask a friend or your spouse whether your self-assessment was accurate. If you disagree, *they* are probably right.

YOU POSSESS TYPE A BEHAVIOR PATTERN

　　1　If you have (a) a habit of explosively accentuating various key words in your ordinary speech even when there is no real need for such accentuation, and (b) a tendency to utter the last few words of your sentences far more rapidly than the opening words.

　　2　If you *always* move, walk, and eat rapidly.

　　3　If you feel (particularly if you openly exhibit to others) an impatience with the rate at which most events take place. Here are some examples of this sort of impatience: if you become *unduly* irritated or even enraged when a car ahead of you in your lane runs at a pace you consider too slow; if you find it anguishing to wait in a line or to wait your turn to be seated at a restaurant; if you find it intolerable

　　*Adapted from M. Friedman & R. Rosenman, *Type A Behavior and Your Heart,* Knopf, New York, 1974.

to watch others perform tasks you know you can do faster; if you find it difficult to restrain yourself from hurrying the speech of others.

4 If you indulge in *polyphasic* thought or performance, frequently striving to think of or do two or more things simultaneously. Some examples: while trying to listen to another person's speech you persist in continuing to think about an irrelevant subject; while golfing or fishing you continue to ponder your business or professional problems; while using an electric razor you attempt also to eat your breakfast or drive your car; or while driving your car you attempt to dictate letters for your secretary. This is one of the commonest traits in the Type A person.

5 If you find it *always* difficult to refrain from talking about or bringing the theme of any conversation around to those subjects which especially interest and intrigue you, and when unable to accomplish this maneuver, you pretend to listen but really remain preoccupied with your own thoughts.

6 If you almost always feel vaguely guilty when you relax and do absolutely nothing for several hours to several days.

7 If you no longer observe the more important or interesting or lovely objects that you encounter in your milieu. For example, if you enter a strange office, store, or home, and after leaving any of these places you cannot recall what was in them, you no longer are observing well—or for that matter enjoying life very much.

8 If you do not have any time to spare to become the things worth *being* because you are so preoccupied with getting the things worth *having*.

9 If you attempt to schedule more and more in less and less time, and in doing so make fewer and fewer allowances for unforeseen contingencies. A concomitant of this is a *chronic sense of time urgency,* one of the core components of the Type A behavior pattern.

10 If on meeting another severely afflicted Type A person, instead of feeling compassion for his affliction, you find yourself compelled to "challenge" him. This is a telltale trait because no one arouses the aggressive and/or hostile feelings of one Type A subject more quickly than another Type A subject.

11 If you resort to certain characteristic gestures or nervous tics. For example, if in conversation you frequently clench your fist, or bang your hand upon a table, or pound one fist into the palm of your other hand in order to emphasize a conversational point, you are exhibiting Type A gestures. Similarly, if the corners of your mouth spasmodically, in ticlike fashion, jerk backward slightly exposing your teeth, or if you habitually clench your jaw, or even grind your teeth, you are subject to muscular phenomena suggesting the presence of a continuous *struggle,* which is, of course, the kernel of the Type A behavior pattern.

12   If you believe that whatever success you have enjoyed has been due in good part to your ability to get things done faster than other people, and if you are afraid to stop doing everything faster and faster.

13   If you find yourself increasingly and ineluctably committed to translating and evaluating not only your own but also the activities of others in terms of numbers.

YOU POSSESS THE TYPE B BEHAVIOR PATTERN

1   If you are completely free of *all* the habits and exhibit none of the traits we have listed that harass the severely afflicted Type A person.

2   If you never suffer from a sense of time urgency with its accompanying impatience.

3   If you harbor no free-floating hostility, and you feel no need to display or discuss either your achievements or accomplishments unless such exposure is demanded by the situation.

4   If when you play, you do so to find fun and relaxation, not to exhibit your superiority at any cost.

5   If you can relax without guilt, just as you can work without agitation.

How did you do? Of course, nobody is a pure Type A or Type B person—but, in general, which behavior pattern seems to fit you best? If you possess many of the characteristics of the Type A personality, you should take steps *now* to try and do something about it. As Drs. Friedman and Rosenman point out, ". . . in the majority of cases, Type A Behavior Patterns can be altered and altered drastically; and it is a terribly dangerous delusion to believe otherwise."[20]

Regretfully, there is no simple formula that can transform you from a Type A into a Type B personality overnight. Changing behavior

---

[20]Friedman and Rosenman, op. cit., p. 209.

patterns, particularly ones as socially acceptable and deeply ingrained as Type A behavior patterns, will take a lot of time and conscientious effort. In extreme cases, moving away from destructive Type A behavior will require significant changes in your basic lifestyle. But the changes *can* be made, and they *will* be worth it. To help you, Drs. Friedman and Rosenman offer some good suggestions. Here are a few of them, along with some of my own.

1 Realize that you can be just as successful in business by being Type B as by being Type A. Drs. Friedman and Rosenman see Type A behavior as actually detrimental to long-term success, and they tell Type A business people: "If you have been successful, it is not *because* of your Type A Behavior Pattern, but *despite* it."

2 Do not think you'll be lucky enough to escape the medical consequences of long-term Type A behavior. Many Type A persons delude themselves in such a manner, and therefore don't try to modify their potentially dangerous actions.

3 During each day, set some time aside for rest and relaxation.

4 Allow yourself enough time to get things done, so that you won't have to feel pressured and rushed. For example, leave ample time between your appointments.

5 Quit trying to think of or do more than one thing at a time. Concentrate on one task at a time.

6 Live by the calendar, not the stopwatch.

7 Learn to take breaks when doing work that can cause you stress.

8 Try to work in a setting that promotes peace of mind. Constant interruptions, messy desks, and drab surroundings do not help soothe the ragged mind.

9 Remind yourself once a day that no enterprise ever failed because it was executed too slowly, too well.

10 Acquire a taste for reading.

11 Spend some time with just yourself.

12 When facing a task, ask yourself two questions: Will this matter be important 5 years from now? Must I do this right now, or do I have enough time to think about the *best* way to accomplish it?

13 Don't think you have to finish all your work by 5 P.M. every day. The world will still be around when you wake up the next morning.

14 Avoid irritating, overcompetitive people.

15 Learn to slow down and be patient with the rate at which events take place. When you act rushed, you will feel pressured. Eat slower; walk slower; don't drive as if you were in the Indianapolis 500; try to talk slower; quit rushing the conversation of others; learn to wait in line without getting the jitters.[21]

I hope you will find these suggestions helpful in battling Type A behavior in your life. Drs. Friedman and Rosenman recommend these and others in their book if you would like further methods for combating the Type A syndrome. The two doctors also emphasize that it's never too late to begin a Type A prevention program—even if you're in your sixties and a victim of one or more heart attacks. One MD began just such a program after a heart attack in 1967. His name is Meyer Friedman.

The Bottom Line

Heart attacks, excessive stress, relaxation, exercise—I've deluged you with a lot of information; tendered some suggestions; sounded some warnings; and, I hope, sparked your enthusiasm for practicing preventive medicine in your own life.

Social historians tell us we are living in an age of ecology. We speak of the need to reduce waste, to save precious resources. Do you know of any greater waste than the needless waste of human life? Do you know of any resource more precious than the human resource? Practice a little personal ecology: take the steps necessary to enhance your chances for living a healthier, happier, and more active and productive life. You *can* succeed in business without really dying. Make it your business to do so.

[21]Ibid., pp. 207–271.

BIBLIOGRAPHY

Andrews, L., and M. Karlins: *Requiem for Democracy?*, Holt, New York; 1971.

"Are You a Candidate for Heart Disease?" *Supervisory Management,* October 1974, pp. 39–42.

Beatty, R., and C. Schneier: "A Case for Positive Reinforcement," *Business Horizons,* April 1975, pp. 57–66.

Benson, H.: "Your Innate Asset for Combating Stress," *Harvard Business Review,* July-August 1974, pp. 49–60.

————: *The Relaxation Response,* Avon, New York, 1976.

"Big Firms Start to Talk Job Enrichment," *Industry Week,* July 9, 1973, pp. 42–46.

Boxx, W., and J. Chambless: "Preventive Health Maintenance for Executives," *California Management Review,* Fall 1975, pp. 49–54.

Cangemi, J., and J. Claypool: "Complimentary Interviews: A System for Rewarding Outstanding Employees," *Personnel Journal,* February 1978, pp. 87–90.

"Can You Cope with Stress?" *Dun's Review,* November 1975, pp. 89–90.

Cecil-Wright, J.: "How to Use Incentives," *Management Today,* January 1978, pp. 76ff.

Clutterbuck, D.: "Motivation Programme Is a Give-Away," *International Management,* August 1977, pp. 40–41.

"Commuter Stress," *Science Digest,* August 1975, pp. 18–19.

Cooper, K.: *The New Aerobics,* M. Evans, New York; 1970; paperback ed., Bantam, New York, 1970.

"Coping with Stress," *Industrial Management,* November 1975, pp. 32–36.

"Cracking under Stress," *U.S. News & World Report,* May 10, 1976, pp. 59–61.

Curley, D.: "Employee Sounding Boards: Answering the Participative Need," *Personnel Administrator,* May 1978, pp. 69ff.

"Deep Sensing: A Pipeline to Employee Morale," *Business Week,* Jan. 29, 1979, pp. 124ff.

Donnelly, J.: "Participative Management at Work," *Harvard Business Review,* January-February 1977, pp. 117–127.

Dowling, W.: "At General Motors: System 4 Builds Performance and Profits," *Organizational Dynamics,* Winter 1975, pp. 23–38.

Dreyfack, R.: "Dismal Disincentives," *Management Review,* December 1976, pp. 48–51.

Dutton, R.: "The Executive and Physical Fitness," *Personnel Administration,* March-April 1966, pp. 13–18.

Dyson, B.: "Leading to Satisfaction," *Management Today,* April 1975, pp. 76ff.

"Executive's Guide to Living with Stress," *Business Week,* Aug. 23, 1976, pp. 75–80.

Field, R.: "Scorecard for Heart Attacks," *Science Digest,* May 1976, pp. 87–88.

"Fighting Stress," *Dun's Review,* January 1977, pp. 59–61.

Fink, D.: *Release from Nervous Tension,* Pocket Books, New York, 1973.

"Flying High on an Idea," *Nation's Business,* August 1978, pp. 41–48 (interview with M. Ash).

Friedman, M., and R. Rosenman: *Type A Behavior and Your Heart,* Fawcett-Crest Books, New York, 1974.

Friis, R.: "Job Dissatisfaction and Coronary Heart Disease," *Intellect,* May-June 1976, pp. 594–596.

Galambos, A.: "There Is an Alternative to 'Shape Up or Ship Out'!" *Supervisory Management,* November 1977, pp. 16–21.

Giblin, E.: "Motivating Employees: A Closer Look," *Personnel Journal,* February 1976, pp. 68–72.

Gilmore, C.: "And the Beat Goes On," *St. Petersburg Times,* Apr. 1, 1977, p. 1-D.

————: "Does Exercise Really Prolong Life?" *Reader's Digest,* July 1977, pp. 140–143.

Glass, D.: "Stress, Competition and Heart Attacks," *Psychology Today,* December 1976, pp. 54ff.

Goleman, D.: "Meditation Helps Break the Stress Spiral," *Psychology Today,* February 1976, pp. 82ff.

Gullett, R., and R. Reisen: "Behavior Modification: A Contingency Approach to Employee Performance," *Personnel Journal,* April 1975, pp. 206–211.

Hekimian, J., and C. Jones: "Put People on Your Balance Sheet," *Harvard Business Review,* January-February 1967, pp. 105ff.

Homans, G.: "The Western Electric Researches," in S. Hoslett (ed.), *Human Factors in Management,* Harper, New York, 1951.

"How to Survive in Business," *Newsweek,* July 14, 1975, p. 64.

Howard, J., P. Rechnitzer, and D. Cunningham: "Coping with Job Tension—Effective and Ineffective Methods," *Public Personnel Management,* September-October 1975, pp. 317–326.

Huebner, H., and A. Johnson: "Behavior Modification: An Aid in Solving Personnel Problems," *Personnel Administrator,* October 1974, pp. 31–34.

Ismail, A., and L. Trachtman: "Jogging the Imagination," *Psychology Today,* March 1973, pp. 79–82.

Janis, I., D. Kaye, and P. Kirschner: "Facilitating Effects of 'Eating-While-Reading' on Responsiveness to Persuasive Communications," *Journal of Personality and Social Psychology,* vol. 1, 1965, pp. 181–186.

Jenkins, D.: "Democracy in the Factory," *The Atlantic,* April 1973, pp. 78–83.

Jewett, M.: "Employee Benefits: The Need to Know," *Personnel Journal,* January 1976, pp. 18–22.

Kafka, V., and J. Schaefer: "What's Your Motivational Rating?" *Training and Development Journal,* October 1977, pp. 38–40.

Kane M.: "Scorecard," *Sports Illustrated,* July 24, 1972, pp. 6–7.

Karlins, M., and H. Abelson: *Persuasion,* Springer, New York, 1970.

——— and L. Andrews: *Biofeedback,* Lippincott, New York, 1972.

——— and ———: *Psychology: What's In It for Us?"* Random House, New York, 1973.

Kenton, L.: "Management's Toughest Course," *Industrial Management,* November 1976, pp. 10–14.

Kirby, P.: "Productivity Increases through Feedback Systems," *Personnel Journal,* October 1977, pp. 512–515.

Kotulak, R.: "Stress: A Small Reward of the Good Life," *Miami Herald,* June 1, 1976, Sec. F.

Kovach, K.: "Improving Employee Motivation in Today's Business Environment," *MSU Business Topics,* Autumn 1976, pp. 5–12.

Kramer, B.: "Wiser Way of Living, Not Dramatic 'Cures,' Seen as Key to Health," *The Wall Street Journal,* Mar. 22, 1976, p. 1.

Kreitner, R.: "People Are Systems, Too: Filling the Feedback Vacuum," *Business Horizons,* November 1977, pp. 54–58.

Lamott, K.: "What to Do When Stress Signs Say You're Killing Yourself," *Today's Health,* January 1975, pp. 30ff.

Lawler, E.: "Workers Can Set Their Own Wages Responsibly," *Psychology Today,* February 1977, pp. 109ff.

———: "Developing a Motivating Work Climate," *Management Review,* July 1977, pp. 25ff.

Lazer, R.: "Behavior Modification as a Managerial Technique," *The Conference Board Record,* January 1975, pp. 22–25.

Leavitt, H.: *Managerial Psychology,* rev. ed., University of Chicago Press, Chicago, 1964.

Loving, R.: "W. T. Grant's Last Days—as Seen from Store 1192," *Fortune,* April 1976, pp. 126–130.

Maccoby, M.: "The Corporate Climber," *Fortune,* December 1976, pp. 98–108.

McQuade, W., and A. Aikman: *Stress,* Bantam, New York, 1975.

Markin, R., and C. Lillis: "Sales Managers Get What They Expect," *Business Horizons,* June 1975, pp. 51–58.

Martin, R.: "Five Principles of Corrective Disciplinary Action," *Supervisory Management,* January 1978, pp. 24ff.

Maslow, A.: *Motivation and Personality,* Harper, New York, 1954.

Mayer, A., and M. Ruby: "One Firm's Family," *Newsweek,* Nov. 21, 1977, pp. 82–88.

Mayo, E., F. Roethlisberger, and W. Dickson: *Management and the Worker,* Harvard, Cambridge, Mass.; 1939.

Mayr, O.: "The Origins of Feedback Control," *Scientific American,* no. 223, 1970, pp. 110–118.

Mealiea, L.: "The TA Approach to Employee Development," *Supervisory Management,* August 1977, pp. 11–19.

Mee, J. (interview): "Understanding the Attitudes of Today's Employees," *Nation's Business,* August 1976, pp. 22–28.

Meyer, P.: "If Hitler Asked You to Electrocute a Stranger, Would You? Probably," *Esquire,* February 1970, pp. 130ff.

Milgram, S.: "Behavioral Study of Obedience," *Journal of Abnormal and Social Psychology,* vol. 67, 1963, pp. 371–378.

———: "Some Conditions of Obedience and Disobedience to Authority," *Human Relations,* vol. 18, 1965, pp. 57–76.

Moore, K.: "A Run for Their Money," *Sports Illustrated,* Nov. 4, 1974, pp. 68–78.

Moore, L.: "Motivation through Positive Reinforcement," *Supervisory Management,* October 1976, pp. 2–9.

"New Tool: Reinforcement for Good Work," *Psychology Today,* April 1972, pp. 67–69.

Norfolk, D.: "Keeping Fit to Manage," *Management Today,* March 1976, pp. 101–103.

Northrup, B.: "Working Happier . . . ," *The Wall Street Journal,* Oct. 25, 1974, pp. 1ff.

Oberle, R.: "Administering Disciplinary Actions," *Personnel Journal,* January 1978, pp. 29–31.

Page, R.: *How to Lick Executive Stress,* Prentice-Hall, Englewood Cliffs, N.J., 1977.

"Participative Management, Bonuses Boost Productivity for Michigan Firm," *Commerce Today,* Nov. 11, 1974, pp. 12–13.

Pascarella, P.: "What Makes a Good Manager?" *Industry Week,* Sept. 1, 1975, pp. 33–42.

Piers, P., *Alive,* Lippincott, New York, 1974.

"Productivity Gains from a Pat on the Back," *Business Week,* Jan. 23, 1978, pp. 56ff.

"Quality of Work Life," *The Wall Street Journal,* Feb. 3, 1976, p. 1.

Rabkin, J., and E. Struening: "Life Events, Stress, and Illness," *Science,* Dec. 3, 1976, pp. 1013–1020.

"Recognizing Merit at Xerox," *Management Review,* June 1978, p. 44.

Repp, W.: "Motivating the NOW Generation," *Personnel Journal,* July 1971, pp. 540ff.

Roach, J.: "Managing Psychological Man," *Management Review,* June 1977, pp. 27ff.

Robins, J.: "Firms Try Newer Way to Slash Absenteeism as Carrot and Stick Fail . . . ," *The Wall Street Journal,* Mar. 14, 1979, pp. 1ff.

Rosenbaum, B.: "Understanding and Using Motivation," *Supervisory Management,* January 1979, pp. 9–13.

Rosow, J.: "Solving the Human Equation in the Productivity Puzzle," *Management Review,* August 1977, pp. 40–43.

Rossiter, A.: "Cholesterol from Jogging Seems to Be Good for You, New Research Indicates," *St. Petersburg Times,* Jan. 28, 1977, pp. 2-Dff.

Rotondi, T.: "Behavior Modification on the Job," *Supervisory Management,* February 1976, pp. 23–28.

Rowan, R.: "The Company That Runs and Runs," *Fortune,* Dec. 4, 1978, pp. 94–97.

Salpukas, A.: "Work Democracy Tested at Scandinavian Plants," *The New York Times,* Nov. 11, 1974.

————: "Swedish Auto Plant Drops Assembly Line," *The New York Times,* Nov. 12, 1974.

————: "Plant is Experimenting with Changing Work on Line," *The New York Times,* Apr. 9, 1975, p. 24.

Sawyer, K.: "Work Habits in U.S. Changing," *St. Petersburg Times,* Jan. 1, 1978, pp. 1ff.

Schrank, R.: "How to Relieve Worker Boredom," *Psychology Today,* July 1978, pp. 79–80.

Schroder, H., M. Karlins, and J. Phares: *Education for Freedom,* Wiley, New York, 1973.

Scott, E.: "Motivation, Productivity and the American Worker," unpublished manuscript, 1978.

Selye, H.: *Stress Without Distress,* Lippincott, New York, 1974.

———— (interview): "Secret of Coping with Stress," *U.S. News & World Report,* Mar. 21, 1977, pp. 51–53.

Shelton, B.: "'Team Spirit' Results in Higher Productivity, Job Satisfaction," *Commerce Today,* Sept. 30, 1974, pp. 5–6.

Sherif, M., and C Sherif: *Social Psychology,* Harper, New York, 1969.

Skinner, B.: *Walden Two,* Macmillan, New York, 1948.

Spiegel, D.: "How Not to Motivate," *Supervisory Management,* November 1977, pp. 11–15.

Steinbrink, J.: "How to Pay Your Sales Force," *Harvard Business Review,* July-August 1978, pp. 94–122.

Stephano, P.: "Fitness, Health, and the National Pulse," *Action,* no. 1, 1976, pp. 6–7.

Stone, F.: "A Sound Mind . . . ," *Management Review,* January 1975, pp. 4–11.

Student, K.: "Changing Values and Management Stress," *Personnel,* January–February 1977, pp. 48–55.

"Stunning Turnaround at Tarrytown," *Time,* May 5, 1980, p. 87.

Suinn, R.: "How to Break the Vicious Cycle of Stress," *Psychology Today,* December 1976, pp. 59ff.

Swengros, G. (interview): ". . . A Sound Body," *Management Review,* January 1975, pp. 12–21.

Tarkenton, F.: "Productivity and Job Satisfaction," *American Express Newsletter,* April 1980, pp. 1ff.

"'Team Spirit' Results in Higher Productivity, Job Satisfaction," *Commerce Today,* Sept. 30, 1974, pp. 5–6.

"The Growing Disaffection with 'Workaholism,'" *Business Week,* Feb. 27, 1978, p. 97.

Townsend, R.: *Up the Organization,* Fawcett-Crest, New York, 1970.

Truell, G.: "Core Managerial Strategies Culled from Behavioral Research," *Supervisory Management,* January 1977, pp. 10–17.

Twain, M.: *The Adventures of Tom Sawyer,* Heritage Press, New York, 1936.

Velghe, J., and G. Cockrell: "What Makes Johnny Mop?" *Personnel Journal,* June 1975, pp. 324ff.

Walsh, R.: "You Can Deal with Stress," *Supervisory Management,* October 1975, pp. 16–21.

Watson, J.: *Behaviorism,* People's Institute, New York, 1924.

—— and R. Rayner: "Conditioned Emotional Reactions," *Journal of Experimental Psychology,* 3, 1920, 1–14.

Ways, M.: "The American Kind of Worker Participation," *Fortune,* October 1976, pp. 168–182.

Whitehill, A.: "Maintenance Factors: The Neglected Side of Worker Motivation," *Personnel Journal,* October 1976, pp. 516–526.

Whyte, W.: *Money and Motivation,* Harper, New York, 1955.

Wilbur, L.: "But Do You Inspire Your Employees? *Supervision,* November 1976, pp. 4–5.

Witkin, A. (interview): "How Bosses Get People to Work Harder," *U.S. News & World Report,* Jan. 29, 1979, pp. 63–64.

Index

OCEAN ACOUSTICS

THEORY AND EXPERIMENT IN UNDERWATER SOUND

Ivan Tolstoy and C. S. Clay
HUDSON LABORATORIES, COLUMBIA UNIVERSITY

McGRAW-HILL BOOK COMPANY

NEW YORK ST. LOUIS SAN FRANCISCO TORONTO
LONDON SYDNEY

103400

534.23
T 654

OCEAN ACOUSTICS:
THEORY AND EXPERIMENT IN UNDERWATER SOUND

Library of Congress Catalog Card Number 65-28830

64941

1234567890 MP 7321069876

PREFACE

This book deals primarily with the theory of sound propagation in the oceans and with comparisons of theory with experiment when such comparisons are possible.

Perhaps the chief difficulty in writing such a book is to decide what type of reader one hopes to interest. Very few, if any, of the people doing research in this field have had any special training prior to their beginning work on some specific problem in underwater acoustics. Most of the current workers are drawn from a remarkably varied range of technical and academic backgrounds. Theoretical physicists, applied mathematicians, geophysicists, oceanographers, a sprinkling of professional acousticians, electrical engineers, spectroscopists, and many other backgrounds are represented. In the future, underwater acoustics will continue to depend, for its progress, upon people of these varied qualifications, since the subject is hardly ever taught as a field in its own right. Because those who might have an interest in this book will have an unusually diversified assortment of technical backgrounds, it did not seem likely that we could write something satisfying, or even accessible, to all. We have therefore aimed at those graduates who, one would assume, have had a graduate course in theoretical mechanics and one in partial differential equations. This should include most budding and seasoned physicists, mathematicians, geophysicists, and engineering scientists (today's classical physicists).

Concerning the subject matter, we must immediately make a number of points clear, if only to forestall part of the criticism to which this book may be vulnerable. Over the last twenty-five years, underwater acoustics has grown into a somewhat untidy subject; a good deal of it is "systems oriented" in the sense that it developed, inevitably, under the pressure of practical problems. As a result, there exists a large body of data that has not been, and probably cannot be, compared with theory and that has gone into constructing empirical rules of the handbook variety, with heavy reliance on the usual smoothing paraphernalia. Although this type of empirical information does have a certain limited practical utility, it is of no interest to us here. We have limited ourselves exclusively to the use of published data that have been successfully compared with theory. We have likewise concentrated on those aspects of the theory that have some experimental confirmation or, at least, some fairly immediate and obvious uses. This has considerably reduced both the volume of data and the body of theory that have gone into this book. Thus we have set ourselves a relatively modest goal. But, even within these rather narrow limits, we make no claims at completeness. For instance, we have omitted a number of theoretical concepts and methods, such as Keller's[1] interesting generalization of ray theory, the classic Laplace transform method[2,3] (i.e., the Cagniard-Pekeris-Heaviside approach), a number of promising numerical techniques, such as Longman's integration procedure for oscillating integrands,[4] etc. We felt that we should write a book that would be as systematic and as direct as we could make it and that multiplying unnecessarily the number of techniques to be used on the same problem, or exploring interesting theoretical sidelines that we did not subsequently apply, would make for a turgid and indigestible end product. It may be that the result still strikes the reader as muddy; let him be assured, nevertheless, that we did our best to spare him much unnecessary material. Future writers may not be so kind.

The plan of the book is simple. In the first chapters we treat the field as a problem in linear, undamped acoustics. This enables us to formulate the main outlines of the problem in uncluttered terms. Later, we introduce more realistic models with attenuation, scattering, and fluctuations as perturbations. It is fortunately possible to cover most of the significant material in this manner. Thus, Chap. 1 gives a brief introduction to the pertinent acoustical properties of the ocean, sufficient, we hope, to explain the use of some approximations and idealizations made in the next two chapters. Chapter 2 outlines the basic properties of plane waves in the absence of attenuation and the major physical concepts of rays, reflection, waveguides, characteristic equations, dispersion, and certain approximations. Chapter 3 explains the use of normal coordinates, or modes, and establishes the basic solutions which will be needed in subsequent developments—especially in the next two chapters. In Chap. 4 we examine the application of these results to the propagation of sound in shallow water when the wavelength and water depth are of the same order. We show why and how attenuation must be introduced as a perturbation of the undamped theory and how model experiments conducted at Brown University show quantitatively the effect and importance of specific mechanisms of attenuation. In Chap. 5 we apply the results of Chaps. 2 and 3 to deep-water propagation, i.e., to problems involving wavelengths that are small in comparison with the water depth. Factors which, in practice, often perturb our idealized models are considered in Chap. 6. In particular, we give an account of the effects of boundary roughness. Chapter 7 supplies the reader with the basics of information processing and linear filter theory useful in handling the uncontrollable and unpredictable fluctuations typical of so many geophysical field measurements. In Chap. 8 we review the preceding chapters and conclude, perhaps unwisely, with some guesses about the future of this field.

We have used both ray and mode concepts throughout this book. But, whenever possible, emphasis has been on the normal-mode point of view. This provides a flexible and general formulation for all pertinent problems. It has perhaps not been sufficiently appreciated by workers in this and in allied fields of geophysics (e.g., seismology) that the concept of modes is both general and rigorous, embracing in principle *all* isentropic linear propagation processes in bounded and unbounded media.

Ocean acoustics began largely as a branch of acoustics and has inherited some of the practices of that field. Frequently data are reported in decibels (dB), i.e., $20 \log_{10}$ (acoustic pressure/constant). Unfortunately there has been little agreement concerning the choice of the constant, and both 1 dyne/cm^2 and 0.0002 dyne/cm^2 are widely used. Geophysicists usually report pressures in dyne/cm^2 or μbar. We have generally followed this practice, since we see no compelling reason to express geophysical measurements in units that were chosen for physiological reasons.

For those wishing to pursue further the subject of acoustic and elastic wave propagation in natural or artificial media, a number of books have appeared in the last decade.[2,3,5-7] Insofar as underwater acoustics specifically is concerned, the number of even moderately up-to-date sources in book form is small indeed.[8-11] For thorough treatments of quite similar problems encountered in the study of electromagnetic wave propagation in the earth's atmosphere, there is a somewhat broader choice of references, of which we give three[12-14] at the end of this preface. A more general account of mechanical radiation theory is given in Lindsay's book.[15]

We are very grateful to Professor A. O. Williams, Jr., of Brown University, whose careful and critical comments on our manuscript we greatly appreciated.

Most of our research reported in this book was originally supported by the Office of Naval Research and has already appeared elsewhere, primarily in the Journal of the Acoustical Society of America. But the writing of this book has been a private undertaking, carried out entirely at our own expense.

IVAN TOLSTOY

C. S. CLAY

REFERENCES

1. J. B. Keller: "Symposia in Applied Mathematics. Proceedings," vol. 8, p. 27, McGraw-Hill Book Company, New York, 1958.
2. W. M. Ewing, W. S. Jardetzky, and F. Press: "Elastic Waves in Layered Media," McGraw-Hill Book Company, New York, 1957.
3. L. Cagniard: "Reflection and Refraction of Progressive Seismic Waves," McGraw-Hill Book Company, New York, 1962.
4. I. M. Longman: *Proc. Cambridge Phil. Soc.,* **52**:764–768 (1956).
5. L. M. Brekhovskih: "Waves in Layered Media," Academic Press, Inc., New York, 1960.
6. M. Redwood: "Mechanical Waveguides," Pergamon Press, New York, 1960.
7. K. G. Budden: "The Wave Guide Mode Theory of Wave Propagation," Prentice-Hall, Inc., Englewood Cliffs, N.J., 1962.
8. V. M. Albers (ed.): "Underwater Acoustics" (a Symposium), Plenum Press, New York, 1963.
9. J. W. Horton: "Fundamentals of Sonar," 2d ed., U.S. Naval Institute Press, Annapolis, 1959.
10. B. F. Officer: "Introduction to the Theory of Sound Transmission," McGraw-Hill Book Company, New York, 1958.
11. V. M. Albers: "Handbook of Underwater Acoustics," The Pennsylvania State University Press, University Park, Pa, 1960.
12. J. R. Wait: "Electromagnetic Waves in Stratified Media," The Macmillan Company, New York, 1962.
13. H. Bremmer: "Terrestrial Radio Waves," American Elsevier Publishing Company, New York, 1949.
14. D. E. Kerr (ed.): "Propagation of Short Radio Waves," McGraw-Hill Book Company, New York, 1951.
15. R. B. Lindsay: "Mechanical Radiation," McGraw-Hill Book Company, New York, 1960.

CONTENTS

CHAPTER ONE

INTRODUCTION

In ocean acoustics most authors restrict themselves, tacitly or explicitly, to a vaguely defined band of frequencies f lying somewhere between 1 cps and, say, 100 kcps. At the high-frequency end, sound absorption by seawater is very high. Except for a small number of very special applications, such as acoustic image makers and side-looking sonars, which are used for very short-range studies, applications of sound transmission are limited to frequencies less than a few tens of kilocycles. At the low end, below 1 cps, one has great difficulty in generating sound (except with earthquakes and very large explosions). Most acousticians happily concede this field to the student of microseismic and seismic phenomena.

We have therefore restricted ourselves in this book to frequencies between 1 cps and a few tens of kilocycles. In this band, sound waves are not measurably affected by the density gradients encountered in ocean waters, nor are they sensitive to gravity.[1,2] The possible effects of ocean currents are, as a rule, neglected. The sound amplitude is treated as small, even for explosive sources (this is still a good approximation for ranges greater than a few hundred meters and charge sizes of up to several tons). Although the attenuation of sound by seawater is, for these frequencies, small enough to allow sound to propagate over ranges of practical interest, it is, nevertheless, a sufficiently important effect to have to be taken into account in many cases. Actually, at medium and low frequencies ($f < 1$ kcps) sound is scattered and effectively attenuated by random inhomogeneities and by interaction with the bottom and subbottom (see Chap. 6). It is only for the higher frequencies that, strictly speaking, attenuation is due to the properties of the water itself and materials dissolved in it.

Acoustical propagation experiments have shown that high-frequency signals have an attenuation constant proportional to f^2.[3] Since this is expected for an approximate solution to the Stokes equation, it is assumed that part of the intrinsic absorption is due to the shear and dilatational viscous losses.[4] Attenuation caused by heat conduction in water is negligible.[5] Attenuation measurements in seawater reveal that salts dissolved in the water are an additional cause of absorption.[6,7] Measurements on artificial seawater have shown that $MgSO_4$ is the principal cause. (In seawater, $MgSO_4$ salts constitute only about 4.7 percent of the mass of dissolved salts.) The absorption due to chemical effects is a relaxation-type mechanism and has a characteristic frequency and magnitude. Absorption depends upon pressure, temperature, and the electrolyte.[6-9] Various effects have been combined in the equation for the sound absorption in seawater. The plane-wave amplitude attenuation constant according to Shulkin and Marsh[10] is

$$\delta = \left(\frac{2.34 \times 10^{-6} S f_T f^2}{f_T{}^2 + f^2} + \frac{3.38 \times 10^{-6} f^2}{f_T} \right) (1 - 6.54 \times 10^{-4} P)$$

$$\text{nepers m} \qquad (1.1)$$

where S = salinity, parts per thousand

$f_T = 21.9 \times 10^{6-1,520/(T+273)}$, kcps

T = temperature, °C

f = frequency, kcps

P = pressure, kg/cm² or atm

(To convert to db, 1 neper is 8.686 db.)

A plot of Eq. (1.1) together with experimental data is shown on Fig. 1.1. Detailed descriptions of absorption and dispersion of high-frequency sound waves are discussed in a review paper by Markham et al.[11] and in a text by Herzfeld and Litovitz.[5] Other causes of absorption and dispersion are air bubbles and biological materials.[12,13] In any particular set of conditions at sea the attenuation of sound with range is best measured experimentally. It can subsequently be tacked on (with or without an explanation of its mechanism) to theories based on zero attenuation. This is permissible in view of the (normally) demonstrable smallness of this effect in the frequency range of interest to us here.

Thus, the essence of underwater acoustical theory is contained in the simple scalar wave equation:

$$\nabla^2 \Phi = \frac{1}{c^2} \frac{\partial^2 \Phi}{\partial t^2} \qquad (1.2)$$

where Φ is a potential or a pressure perturbation and c is the speed of sound, which can be a function of one or several coordinates. Therefore, apart from boundary effects, propagation depends upon the single parameter c.

A complete discussion of the various direct and indirect methods of measuring c, of the observed $c(x,y,z)$ variations, and of their causes is beyond the scope of this book. But we shall, nevertheless, give a brief outline in order to provide the necessary background for the idealized models of the ocean used in the theoretical developments of the next few chapters.

Until rather recently, most of our knowledge concerning the dependence of c upon depth had been *indirect*, and was based upon experimentally measured values of the temperature T, pressure P, and salinity S. Of these three parameters, S is usually the least important and is defined as "the total amount of solid material in grammes contained in 1 kg of salt water when all the bromine and iodine have been replaced by the equivalent amount of chlorine, all the carbonate converted to oxide and all organic matter has been completely oxidized."[14]   For our purposes it is sufficient to remember that S is approximately a measure of the solid salts dissolved, that it is of the order of 35 g, that is, 35 parts per thousand, and that it is a quantity which is routinely measured by oceanographers.

Accurate determinations of T require the use of special highly sensitive thermometers.[14]   A common, very convenient instrument is the bathythermograph, which, when allowed to sink, gives a continuous record of T vs. P, which is accurate enough for most purposes.   Relative temperatures can be read to almost $\pm 0.05°C$, corresponding to changes in c of the order of ± 0.3 m/sec.   As a rule its use is limited to the top few hundred meters.

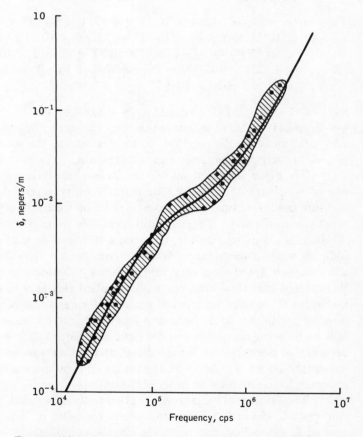

Fig. 1.1 High-frequency sound attenuation in seawater. The curve is calculated with (1.1) for $T = 20°C$ and $S = 35$ parts per thousand.   The shaded part indicates the extent of experimental data.   (1 neper is 8.686 db.)

Given T, P, and S, the best equation for calculating c appears to be Wilson's:[15]

$$c = 1{,}449.14 \text{ msec}^{-1} + V_T + V_P + V_S + V_{STP} \qquad (1.3)$$

where

$$V_T = 4.5721T - 4.4532 \times 10^{-2}T^2 - 2.6045 \times 10^{-4}T^3 \\ + 7.9851 \times 10^{-6}T^4$$

$$V_P = 1.60272 \times 10^{-1}P + 1.0268 \times 10^{-5}P^2 + 3.5216 \times 10^{-9}P^3 \\ - 3.3603 \times 10^{-12}P^4$$

$$V_S = 1.39799 \times (S - 35) + 1.69202 \times 10^{-3} \times (S - 35)^2$$

$$V_{STP} = (S - 35)(-1.1244 \times 10^{-2}T + 7.7711 \times 10^{-7}T^2 + 7.7016 \\ \times 10^{-5}P - 1.2943 \times 10^{-7}P^2 + 3.1580 \times 10^{-8}PT + 1.5790 \\ \times 10^{-9}PT^2) + P(-1.8607 \times 10^{-4}T + 7.4812 \times 10^{-6}T^2 \\ + 4.5283 \times 10^{-8}T^3) + P^2(-2.5294 \times 10^{-7}T + 1.8563 \times 10^{-9}T^2) \\ - P^3 \times 1.9646 \times 10^{-10}T$$

for $-4°\text{C} < T < 30°\text{C}; 1 \text{ kg/cm}^2 < P < 1{,}000 \text{ kg/cm}^2; 0 < S < 37$ parts per thousand. This equation fits the experimentally determined values of c to ± 0.3 m/sec. We see that, to the first order, the sound velocity increases linearly with pressure and temperature.

The *direct* measurement of c *in situ* can now be accomplished by the use of *velocimeters*. These instruments, a fairly recent development,[16] measure the travel time of an acoustic pulse between two crystals spaced a short distance apart. Commercially available units provide an accuracy of about ± 0.3 m/sec, that is, essentially the same as that of the lengthy indirect method based upon Wilson's equation (1.3). They have great advantages in speed, flexibility, and continuity of measurement, and it may be expected that they will eventually supplant the more laborious indirect methods. However, much of our general information concerning the variations of c with depth, latitude, and longitude will, for some time to come, still be based upon oceanographic data and Eq. (1.3). As of today the accuracy of measurement by the direct and indirect methods is about the same, that is, ± 0.3 m/sec. In the future one may expect the velocimeter accuracy to improve by an order of magnitude.

The horizontal variations of c are usually quite weak compared with the vertical changes. Thus, the sound velocity in Eq. (1.2) is often treated as depending only upon the vertical coordinate z. This is a good approximation in many cases and greatly simplifies the theory. The effect of actual departures and fluctuations about these idealized mean models will be discussed in Chaps. 5 and 6.

Typical mean $c(z)$ curves for deep water fall into several categories, depending upon the latitude and the ocean. Figure 1.2 shows a series of typical $c(z)$ curves for the North Atlantic Ocean. The most interesting profiles are those of equatorial and moderate latitudes, displaying a prominent $c(z)$ minimum at a depth of about 1,270 m for moderate latitudes and

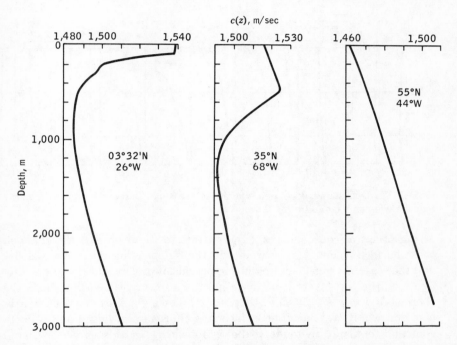

Fig. 1.2   Acoustical velocity as a function of depth. The curves are based on winter temperature data.

a little nearer to the surface for equatorial latitudes. This type of profile is due to the opposing effects of pressure and temperature. At first the temperature effect dominates; the decreasing temperature results in a decreasing c. After a certain depth, however, the increase in hydrostatic pressure gives an increasing c. Similar profiles characterize the South Atlantic and the Pacific but, in the latter case especially, the minimum c is closer to the surface than in the North Atlantic. In polar latitudes the minimum c value is at the surface.

It is obvious, from elementary considerations, that sound may be trapped in such zones of minimum velocity, i.e., that these are acoustic waveguides or *sound channels*. They allow the propagation of sound to very great distances with relatively little loss. The classic sound channel was named the SOFAR† channel by its discoverers, M. Ewing and J. L. Worzel.[17]

The common occurrence of *surface sound channels*, i.e., of relative minima of c at or near the ocean surface (Fig. 1.3), has a number of inter-

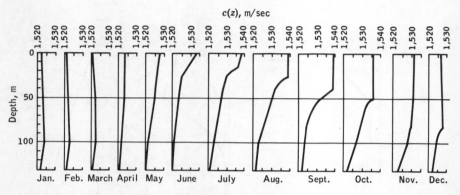

Fig. 1.3 Surface sound duct as a function of season. Based on average monthly temperature-depth curves in the Bermuda area.

esting practical consequences. In contrast to the deep SOFAR channel, these surface channels are variable in time, depending upon the weather and the season. For instance, during periods of prolonged calm and sunny weather, the top layers heat up, c increases toward the surface, and the channel disappears. On the other hand, following a storm or consistently cool and windy weather, the surface gets churned and mixed and a fairly constant temperature tends to be established. In this case, the sound velocity will increase with depth because of the pressure effect (Fig. 1.3, December, January, February, March). At greater depth the nonseasonal, permanent T structure takes over.

In *shallow coastal waters*, the water layer is frequently quite homogeneous. For wavelengths of the order of magnitude of the water thickness it is expedient and reasonably accurate to consider the layer as being characterized by some constant average value of c.

The *ocean bottom* is often significant in determining the properties of sound transmission. This is particularly true of shallow-water transmission at low frequencies, when water depth and wavelength are of the same order (Chap. 4). In this case, the bottom properties are of paramount importance. Deep-water propagation to short and intermediate ranges (out to 100 km or so) is also sensitive to bottom parameters (Chap. 5).

Most sediment densities vary between 1.5 and 2.5.[18] On the whole,

† Sound Fixing And Ranging.

our knowledge of bottom sound-velocity structure is based on seismic, i.e., essentially acoustic, studies. In the shallow, continental shelf areas, there is often additional confirmation from holes drilled on land, and the structure is known to be usually layered. Some regions, such as parts of the continental seaboard of the eastern United States, are reasonably well understood from the acoustical point of view. But there is usually enough local variation from the average to require careful redetermination of the bottom parameters whenever precise interpretation of acoustical experiments is required. In deep waters, such as the abyssal plains of the Atlantic and Pacific, recent investigations are beginning to clarify the sedimentary structure.[18-20]

In the ocean, the essential parameter c is a complicated function of depth. Because of this, one often has to deal extensively with the inverse problem of determining the appropriate model by acoustical measurements. Many acoustical experiments exhibit thus a dual nature: part of the experiment is designed to decide upon a model, and another part makes use of this model to interpret some characteristics of the sound field. As a rule, one should try to use the relatively well-understood, standard properties of sound to determine the model (e.g., travel times of short pulses, as in the seismic method). Sometimes, however, it is found that the standard methods are not accurate enough, and then the experiment itself becomes a test of the model. Actually, since the essential validity of Eq. (1.2) is unquestionable, one may adopt the attitude that a complete, scientifically acceptable interpretation of propagation measurements is but a highly accurate, sophisticated method of determining the structure of the medium and, in particular, the variations of c!

Another important acoustical parameter of the ocean medium is the ambient noise. Although its presence in no way affects any of the preceding conclusions, it is of great practical significance in all problems involving signal detection and processing. This art, upon which a great deal of ingenuity has been lavished, requires some knowledge of the properties of the noise background.

The spectrum and characteristics of the background noise are complicated because this noise is partly man-made and partly natural. It depends upon location, position of the receiver, direction, nearby weather, and distant weather conditions. In addition to acoustical noise, the noise signal at the output of the receiver terminals includes nonacoustical pressure fluctuations, flow noise, vibration, and thermal noise.

The frequency spectrum of the ambient noise was studied by Knudsen, Alford, and Emling in 1948.[21] They showed that the noise level increased with the wind force or sea state. The mean-square noise pressure in a 1-cps band was higher at low frequencies than at high frequencies. In the range 100 to 10,000 cps, their average curves had a slope of 5 ± 1 db/octave. The frequency range has been extended in more recent studies.[22,23] The average curves of Wenz and other data are shown on Fig. 1.4.[23]

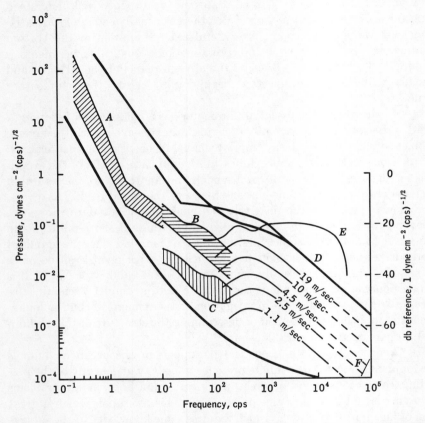

Fig. 1.4 Ambient noise. (*A*) Pacific Ocean bottom seismic data. (After Schneider, Farrell, and Brannian.[24]) (*B*) Tyrrhenian Sea—bathyscaphe. (After Lomask and Frassetto.[25]) (*C*) Lake Pend Oreille, Idaho. (After Lomask and Saenger.[26]) (*D*) Wenz-average curves. The original curves were specified on the Beaufort wind-force scale. (After Wenz[23]) (*E*) Rain. (After Heidsmann et al.[27]) (*F*) Thermal agitation. (After Mellen[30] and Ezrow.[31])

The shaded area *A* shows the limits of the low-frequency noise data taken with a seismograph on the bottom at several locations in the Pacific Ocean.[24] Observations made during dives of the bathyscaphe *Trieste* are indicated in the shaded area *B*.[25] Shaded area *C* indicates the range of noise level observed in a deep inland lake.[26] The data of

Wenz are the curves D.[23] Curve E indicates the noise produced by rain.[27] Other noises associated with rain noise are cavitation and breaking waves.[28,29] The thermal noise limit is indicated by F.[30,31]

Extensive studies of ambient noise levels as a function of wind speed have been made in shallow water. Since the attenuation of signals is much larger in shallow water than deep water, one would expect shallow-water ambient noise to be closely related to local conditions. Studies of spectrum level were made in Narragansett Bay, Rhode Island.[32] The hydrophone was 300 m offshore in 12 m of water. The center frequency of the filter was 630 cps. The spectrum level was found to correlate 90 percent with wind speed and 90 percent with wave height under steady wind conditions. Under variable wind conditions the correlation of spectrum level with wind speed was higher than with wave height. Similar studies were made at 36 m and 50 m water depth in the shallow water of the Scotian Shelf.[33] Piggot found that above a limiting background level, the spectrum level increased linearly with the log of wind speed. This relation held from 8 to 3,200 cps.

This survey of the outstanding acoustic properties of an ocean is admittedly very brief. Anything approaching completeness would simply require too much space. We have merely tried to show the reader how, in face of the very real complexities of the problem, one reduces it, in a first approximation, to the study of relatively simple equations—in particular, Eq. (1.2). The next two chapters will be devoted to developing the solutions needed to describe in detail the acoustical behavior of a few typical, important, but highly idealized models.

REFERENCES

1. C. Eckart: "Hydrodynamics of Oceans and Atmospheres," Pergamon Press, New York, 1960.
2. I. Tolstoy: *Rev. Mod. Phys.*, **35**:1, 207 (1963).
3. "Physics of Sound in the Sea," pt. I, Transmission, pp. 27–28, 105, National Research Council, Research Analysis Group (1946).
4. L. N. Liebermann: *J. Acoust. Soc. Am.*, **20**:868 (1948).
5. K. F. Herzfeld and T. A. Litovitz: "Absorption and Dispersion of Ultrasonic Waves," Academic Press Inc., New York, 1959.
6. L. N. Liebermann: *Phys. Rev.*, **76**:1520 (1949).
7. G. Kurtze and K. Tamm: *Acustica*, **3**:34 (1953).
8. F. H. Fisher: *J. Acoust. Soc. Am.*, **30**:442 (1958).
9. O. B. Wilson and R. W. Leonard: *J. Acoust. Soc. Am.*, **26**:223 (1954).
10. M. Shulkin and H. W. Marsh: *J. Brit. IRE*, **25**:493 (1963).

11. J. J. Markham, R. T. Beyer, and R. B. Lindsay: *Rev. Mod. Phys.*, **23**:353 (1951).
12. W. R. Turner: *J. Acoust. Soc. Am.*, **33**:1223 (1961).
13. J. D. Watson and R. Meister: *J. Acoust. Soc. Am.*, **35**:1584 (1963).
14. A. Defant: "Physical Oceanography," Pergamon Press, New York, 1961.
15. W. D. Wilson: *J. Acoust. Soc. Am.*, **23**:10, 1357 (1960).
16. M. Greenspan and C. E. Tschiegg: A Sing-around Velocimeter for Measuring the Speed of Sound in the Sea, in V. M. Albers (ed.), "Underwater Acoustics," Proceedings of an Institute sponsored by the Scientific Affairs Committee of NATO, Plenum Press, New York, 1963.
17. M. Ewing and J. L. Worzel: *Geol. Soc. Am.*, *Mem.* 27, 1948.
18. J. E. Nafe and C. L. Drake: Physical Properties of Marine Sediments, in M. N. Hill (ed.), "The Sea," vol. 3, pp. 794–815, Interscience Publishers (Division of John Wiley & Sons, Inc.), New York, 1963.
19. J. B. Hersey: Continuous Reflection Profiling, in M. N. Hill (ed.), "The Sea," vol. 3, pp. 47–71, Interscience Publishers (Division of John Wiley & Sons, Inc.), New York, 1963.
20. M. Ewing, J. Ewing, and M. Talwani: *Geol. Soc. Am.*, **75**:17–36 (1964).
21. V. O. Knudsen, R. S. Alford, and J. W. Emling: *J. Marine Res.*, **7**:410–429 (1948).
22. A. Berman and A. J. Saur: *J. Acoust. Soc. Am.*, **32**:915 (1960).
23. G. M. Wenz: *J. Acoust. Soc. Am.*, **34**:1936–1956 (1962).
24. W. A. Schneider, P. J. Farrell, and R. E. Brannian: *Geophysics*, **29**:745–771 (1964).
25. M. R. Lomask and R. Frassetto: *J. Acoust. Soc. Am.*, **32**:1028–1033 (1960).
26. M. R. Lomask and R. A. Saenger: *J. Acoust. Soc. Am.*, **32**:878–883 (1960).
27. T. Heidsmann, R. Smith, and A. Arneson: *J. Acoust. Soc. Am.*, **27**:378–379 (1955).
28. G. Franz: *J. Acoust. Soc. Am.*, **31**:1080 (1959).
29. M. Strasberg: *J. Acoust. Soc. Am.*, **28**:20 (1956).
30. R. Mellen: *J. Acoust. Soc. Am.*, **24**:478–480 (1952).
31. D. Ezrow: *J. Acoust. Soc. Am.*, **34**:550–554 (1962).
32. W. S. Penhallow and F. T. Dietz: *J. Acoust. Soc. Am.*, **36**:2149 (1964).
33. C. L. Piggot: *J. Acoust. Soc. Am.*, **36**:2152 (1964).

CHAPTER TWO

BASIC WAVE THEORY: PULSES AND DISPERSION

2.1 EQUATIONS OF MOTION

As pointed out in Chap. 1, we are primarily concerned with small-amplitude sound waves in the frequency range 1 cps $< f < 20$ kcps or so for which the linear, undamped scalar wave equation (1.2) is a good first approximation:

$$\nabla^2 \Phi = \frac{1}{c^2} \frac{\partial^2 \Phi}{\partial t^2} \tag{2.1}$$

The sound velocity c is related to the bulk modulus λ by the equation

$$\lambda = \rho c^2 \tag{2.2}$$

It can be shown that for the range of frequencies treated in this book, the density ρ may be considered constant within the water layer (refs. 1, 2 of preceding chapter). Thus the propagation of sound in the body of water is, for our purposes, a function of the single parameter $c(x,y,z)$.

It is true that whenever sound waves propagate over long distances a certain amount of attenuation is observed. However, even when this attenuation is appreciable from a practical standpoint, it still corresponds only to a minor perturbation of Eq. (2.1). The highest attenuations are observed in shallow water whenever the sound waves suffer many reflections from the bottom and the surface, and are mainly a result of imperfect reflectivity of the boundaries. Equation (2.1) still gives a valid description of the behavior of sound in the water layer.

We shall see in Chap. 4 how the measured attenuations can be accounted for and included in the analysis.

In Eq. (2.1) Φ may be used to represent pressure, velocity, or displacement potentials. We shall adopt the latter definition, so that

$$\mathbf{d} = \nabla \Phi \tag{2.3}$$

is the displacement of a particle from its equilibrium position, and by Hooke's law

$$p = -\lambda \nabla \cdot \mathbf{d} = -\lambda \nabla^2 \Phi \tag{2.4}$$

is the incremental pressure due to the wave. In view of (2.1) it may also be written as

$$p = -\rho \frac{\partial^2 \Phi}{\partial t^2} \tag{2.5}$$

The ocean bottom materials may behave either as liquids or as elastic solids, depending upon circumstances. We shall thus have occasion to use the equations of small motion in solids. For homogeneous, isotropic solids, they reduce to two simultaneous wave equations:

$$\nabla^2 \Phi = \frac{1}{c_p{}^2} \frac{\partial^2 \Phi}{\partial t^2} \tag{2.6}$$

$$\nabla^2 \Psi = \frac{1}{c_s{}^2} \frac{\partial^2 \Psi}{\partial t^2} \tag{2.7}$$

c_p and c_s being the propagation velocities of pure compressional and pure shear waves, respectively, and Φ and Ψ the scalar and vector potentials such that the particle displacement is

$$\mathbf{d} = \nabla \Phi + \text{curl } \Psi \tag{2.8}$$

In two dimensions (x,z), Ψ is normal to the x,z plane. The component of tension normal to a plane $z = $ constant is

$$\sigma_{zz} = \lambda \nabla^2 \Phi + 2\mu \left(\frac{\partial^2 \Phi}{\partial z^2} - \frac{\partial^2 \Psi}{\partial z\, \partial x} \right) \tag{2.9}$$

The component of shear stress in this plane is

$$\sigma_{zx} = \mu \left(\frac{\partial^2 \Psi}{\partial z^2} - \frac{\partial^2 \Psi}{\partial x^2} + 2 \frac{\partial^2 \Phi}{\partial z\, \partial x} \right) \tag{2.10}$$

λ is Lamé's constant and μ the rigidity. They are related to c_p and c_s by

$$c_p{}^2 = \frac{\lambda + 2\mu}{\rho} \tag{2.11}$$

$$c_s{}^2 = \frac{\mu}{\rho} \tag{2.12}$$

Equations (2.6) and (2.7) are valid for constant c_p and c_s.

2.2 PLANE WAVES, CYLINDRICAL SYMMETRY, AND MODES

Equation (2.1) can often be solved exactly when the variables are separable in some suitably chosen system of coordinates.[1] In cartesian and cylindrical coordinates a separable model of considerable interest and utility corresponds to the so-called stratified medium, in which c is, at the most, a function of one coordinate (z). Additional assumptions, such as those of harmonic motion and plane (or cylindrical) waves, simplify the problem to the point where it is possible to illustrate many fundamental wave properties by means of simple solutions and equations.

Thus, we begin by assuming the problem to be two-dimensional:

$$\Phi(x,z,t) = \phi(z) e^{i(\pm \alpha x - \omega t)} \tag{2.13}$$

Equation (2.1) has the form

$$\frac{\partial^2 \Phi}{\partial x^2} + \frac{\partial^2 \Phi}{\partial z^2} + \frac{\omega^2}{c^2} \Phi = 0 \tag{2.14}$$

Equation (2.13) assumes waves propagating in the direction of increasing x ($+$ sign) or decreasing x ($-$ sign) with the *phase velocity*†

$$v = \frac{\omega}{\alpha} \tag{2.15}$$

Substituting (2.13) into (2.14) gives

$$\frac{d^2\phi}{dz^2} + \gamma^2\phi = 0 \tag{2.16}$$

where
$$\gamma^2 = \frac{\omega^2}{c^2} - \alpha^2 = \alpha^2\left(\frac{v^2}{c^2} - 1\right) \tag{2.17}$$

Equation (2.16) is the separated space-form of the wave equation and is familiar to all students of optics, acoustics, and quantum theory (time-independent Schrödinger equation).

In the special case of a homogeneous medium, c = constant and γ = constant, the elementary solutions of (2.16) are

$$\phi = Ae^{i\gamma z} + Be^{-i\gamma z} \tag{2.18}$$

A and B being constants of integration.

If (2.18) is combined with (2.13), we see that the first term corresponds to waves traveling in the direction of increasing z, that is, propagating downward in Fig. 2.1, and that the second term corresponds to up-going waves.

† α in Eqs. (2.15) ff. may be used interchangeably with the κ of cylindrical coordinates [Eqs. (2.33) ff.]—both represent the horizontal wave number.

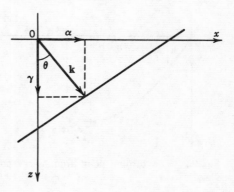

Fig. 2.1 Components of wave number k. The wave front is perpendicular to k.

Equation (2.17) is often written in the form

$$\frac{\omega^2}{c^2} = k^2 = \alpha^2 + \gamma^2 \tag{2.19}$$

where k, the wave number in the direction of propagation, is the magnitude of the vector $\mathbf{k}$ normal to the surfaces of constant phase or wave fronts. $\mathbf{k}$ defines the ray direction, and α and γ are its x and z components. If θ is the angle of $\mathbf{k}$ with respect to the vertical (Fig. 2.1), we have

$$\alpha = k \sin \theta \tag{2.20}$$

$$\gamma = k \cos \theta \tag{2.21}$$

In a homogeneous medium $\mathbf{k}$ is a constant.

The wavelength in the ray direction, i. e., that of $\mathbf{k}$, is

$$\lambda = \frac{2\pi}{k} \tag{2.22}$$

In *stratified media*, k, λ, and γ are functions of z, α remaining constant by Snell's law:

$$\frac{\sin \theta}{c} = \text{const} \tag{2.23}$$

When the rays are horizontal,

$$\alpha = k \tag{2.24}$$

and, by (2.19),

$$\gamma = 0 \tag{2.25}$$

with

$$v = c(z) \tag{2.26}$$

$$\theta = \pi/2 \tag{2.27}$$

The condition (2.25) defines a *turning point* of the differential equation (2.16) corresponding to a point at which the rays become horizontal (Fig. 2.2).

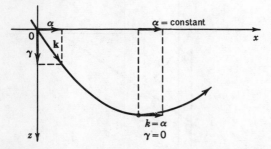

Fig. 2.2 The turning point from a ray point of view.

For z such that $v < c(z)$, $k < \alpha$ and γ^2 is negative. The character of the solutions of Eq. (2.16) is quite different in this region. Whereas for $\gamma^2 > 0$, ϕ is an oscillatory function of z, for $\gamma^2 < 0$, its behavior is exponential or hyperbolic. We shall have occasion to illustrate this point further.

The superposition of waves traveling in opposite directions and having equal amplitudes results in *standing waves*. Thus, for a homogeneous medium,

$$\phi = \frac{A}{2}\left(e^{i\gamma z} + e^{-i\gamma z}\right) = A \cos \gamma z \tag{2.28}$$

is a standing-wave system obtained by superposing up- and down-going waves.

More generally

$$\Phi = \phi(z)e^{i(\alpha x - \omega t)} \tag{2.29}$$

where ϕ is a real (or imaginary) function, represents a wave pattern which is standing insofar as the z coordinate is concerned, but is traveling in the x direction with the phase velocity v [Eq. (2.15)].

Standing-wave solutions are often called *modes*, as in vibration theory, since they represent motions for which the whole medium is vibrating at a single frequency ω. This concept is a fruitful one and will be developed in Chap. 3.

One may, conversely, obtain traveling waves by superposing modes, e.g., in one dimension:

$$A \cos \alpha x \cos \omega t + A \sin \alpha x \sin \omega t = A \cos(\alpha x - \omega t) \tag{2.30}$$

In many problems of interest to us we shall have *cylindrical symmetry* about the z axis. In this case, we have, for harmonic waves

$$\frac{\partial^2 \Phi}{\partial r^2} + \frac{1}{r}\frac{\partial \Phi}{\partial r} + \frac{\partial^2 \Phi}{\partial z^2} + k^2\Phi = 0 \tag{2.31}$$

$$r = (x^2 + y^2)^{1/2} \tag{2.32}$$

and it is easily verified that

$$\Phi = \phi(z)H_0^{(1,2)}(\kappa r)e^{-i\omega t} \tag{2.33}$$

where κ is the horizontal component of the wave number, and $H_0^{(1,2)}$ are Hankel functions of the first and second kind. These are progressive cylindrical waves. It is important to notice that the $\phi(z)$ used in this equation is identical to that of Eq. (2.29) or (2.16) for the plane-wave case. Furthermore, Eqs. (2.15) to (2.29) remain valid providing α is replaced by κ.

The asymptotic approximation

$$H_0^{(1,2)}(\kappa r) \simeq \sqrt{\frac{2}{\pi \kappa r}}\, e^{\pm i(\kappa r - \pi/4)} \tag{2.34}$$

is valid for $\kappa r \gg 1$. From this we see by analogy with (2.13) that $H_0^{(2)}(\kappa r)$ corresponds to waves converging to the axis $r = 0$, whereas $H_0^{(1)}(\kappa r)$ is an outgoing wave train. Standing waves, or r modes, are obtained by superposing the two:

$$\Phi = \phi(z)J_0(\kappa r)e^{-i\omega t} \tag{2.35}$$

In infinite homogeneous media, situations involving *spherical symmetry* occur for point sources. Equation (2.1) is then

$$\frac{\partial^2 \Phi}{\partial R^2} + \frac{2}{R}\frac{\partial \Phi}{\partial R} = \frac{1}{c^2}\frac{\partial^2 \Phi}{\partial t^2} \tag{2.36}$$

$$R = (x^2 + y^2 + z^2)^{1/2}$$

a general solution of which is, for waves diverging from $R = 0$

$$\Phi = \frac{1}{R}f(R - ct) \tag{2.37}$$

Equations (2.6) and (2.7) are of the same form as (2.1) for $c = $ constant, and for the homogeneous solid we have similar results for elastic compression or shear waves. But important differences arise in the presence of boundaries (Sec. 2.4).

2.3 ENERGY, ENERGY FLUX, AND RATE OF TRANSPORT

In a fluid, the local value of the potential (elastic) energy density is

$$\mathcal{U} = \tfrac{1}{2}\rho c^2 (\nabla \cdot \mathbf{d})^2 = \tfrac{1}{2}\rho c^2 (\nabla^2 \Phi)^2 \tag{2.38}$$

and the kinetic energy density is

$$\mathfrak{J} = \tfrac{1}{2}\rho \dot{\mathbf{d}}^2 = \tfrac{1}{2}\rho (\nabla \dot{\Phi})^2 \tag{2.39}$$

where the dot represents the differentiation $\partial/\partial t$ with respect to time. Thus, the energy density e is

$$e = \mathfrak{J} + \mathcal{U} = \tfrac{1}{2}\rho(\nabla \dot{\Phi})^2 + \tfrac{1}{2}\rho c^2 (\nabla^2 \Phi)^2 \tag{2.40}$$

The rate of change of the total energy E contained in a volume τ is then

$$\dot{E} = \int_\tau \dot{e}\, d\tau = -\int_s \mathbf{f} \cdot \mathbf{ds} \tag{2.41}$$

where $\mathbf{f}$ is the *energy flux*, s the surface bounding the volume τ, and, by Gauss' theorem,

$$\nabla \cdot \mathbf{f} = -\dot{e} \tag{2.42}$$

But, by (2.40) and (2.1),

$$\dot{e} = \rho(\nabla\dot{\Phi}\cdot\nabla\dot{\Phi} + \dot{\Phi}\,\nabla^2\dot{\Phi}) = \rho\nabla\cdot(\dot{\Phi}\,\nabla\dot{\Phi}) \tag{2.43}$$

and therefore, using (2.3) and (2.5),

$$\mathbf{f} = -\rho\dot{\Phi}\,\nabla\dot{\Phi} = p\mathbf{v} \tag{2.44}$$

where

$$\mathbf{v} = \dot{\mathbf{d}} \tag{2.45}$$

This result states that the energy flux is a vector pointing in the direction of particle motion and is the rate at which work is being done per unit surface.

Consider the case of harmonic spherical waves in a homogeneous medium, diverging from a source at $R = 0$. By (2.37) we may represent these as

$$\Phi = A\,\frac{1}{R}\cos k(R - ct) = A\,\frac{1}{R}\cos(kR - \omega t) \tag{2.46}$$

From (2.44) we obtain

$$\mathbf{f} = \mathbf{1}_R\left[A^2\frac{\omega^4}{c}\rho\frac{1}{R^2}\cos^2(kR - \omega t) - A^2\omega^3\rho\frac{1}{R^3}\frac{1}{2}\sin 2(kR - \omega t)\right] \tag{2.47}$$

where $\mathbf{1}_R$ is a unit vector in the radial direction.

The *power output* Π of the source must be equal to the mean energy flux per cycle through any sphere of radius R centered at the source, i.e.,

$$\Pi = 4\pi R^2\frac{\omega}{2\pi}\int_0^{2\pi/\omega} f\,dt \tag{2.48}$$

where f is the term in brackets in (2.47). Upon integration, the term in $\sin 2(kR - \omega t)$ vanishes and one obtains

$$\Pi = 2\pi\rho\frac{\omega^4}{c}A^2 \tag{2.49}$$

Conversely, if one has a harmonic point source of power output Π in a homogeneous space of density ρ and sound velocity c, the coefficient A in Eq. (2.46) is

$$A = \frac{1}{\omega^2}\left(\Pi\frac{c}{2\pi\rho}\right)^{1/2} \tag{2.50}$$

A very useful quantity is the *rate of energy transport* in a particular direction. This concept is valuable in dealing with harmonic mode systems of the type (2.29), and may be defined for the x direction as the ratio of the mean energy flux $\bar{f}$ through a vertical section $x =$ constant to the mean energy density $\bar{E}$ between two such planes one x wavelength $2\pi/\alpha$ apart. We call it U:

$$U = \frac{\bar{f}}{\bar{E}} \tag{2.51}$$

Now, for harmonic waves the potential energy V in a volume τ is

$$V = \frac{1}{2}\int_\tau \rho c^2 (\nabla^2\Phi)^2 \, d\tau = \frac{1}{2}\int_\tau \frac{\omega^4}{c^2}\rho\Phi^2 \, d\tau \tag{2.52}$$

The kinetic energy

$$T = \frac{1}{2}\int_\tau \rho(\nabla\dot{\Phi})^2 \, d\tau \tag{2.53}$$

is, by Green's theorem

$$T = -\frac{1}{2}\int_s \rho\dot{\Phi}\,\nabla\dot{\Phi}\cdot\mathbf{ds} - \frac{1}{2}\int_\tau \rho\dot{\Phi}\,\nabla^2\dot{\Phi} \, d\tau \tag{2.54}$$

s being the surface bounding the volume τ. This surface may be so chosen that the corresponding integral vanishes, e.g., in the case of plane waves or modes such as (2.29), if two planes one wavelength apart are considered, $\nabla\dot{\Phi}\cdot\mathbf{ds}$ has opposite signs on the two planes (the positive normals are in opposite directions), and their contributions to the surface integral cancel. The other bounding surfaces may be chosen so that $\dot{\Phi}$ or $\nabla\dot{\Phi}$ vanish. In such cases then, for harmonic waves

$$T = \frac{1}{2}\int_\tau \rho\frac{\omega^2}{c^2}\dot{\Phi}^2 \, d\tau \tag{2.55}$$

For modes of the type (2.29) $V = T$, and

$$\bar{E} = 2\bar{T} = \frac{\alpha}{2\pi}\int_0^{2\pi/\alpha} dx \int_{-\infty}^{+\infty} \rho\frac{\omega^4}{c^2}\Phi^2 \, dz \tag{2.56}$$

where the integral with respect to z is taken over a complete section of the medium. Integrating,

$$\bar{E} = \frac{1}{2}\omega^4\int_{-\infty}^{+\infty}\frac{\rho}{c^2}\Phi^2 \, dz \tag{2.57}$$

The mean energy flux per cycle through such a section is

$$\bar{f} = \frac{\omega}{2\pi} \int_0^{2\pi/\omega} dt \int_{-\infty}^{+\infty} p \frac{\partial \Phi}{\partial x} \, dz \tag{2.58}$$

This becomes, by virtue of Eqs. (2.4) and (2.13),

$$\bar{f} = \frac{1}{2} \omega^3 \alpha \int_{-\infty}^{+\infty} \rho \Phi^2 \, dz \tag{2.59}$$

and using (2.29),

$$U = \frac{\bar{f}}{\bar{E}} = \frac{\alpha}{\omega} \frac{\int_{-\infty}^{+\infty} \rho \phi^2 \, dz}{\int_{-\infty}^{+\infty} \frac{\rho}{c^2} \phi^2 \, dz} \tag{2.60}$$

or, if

$$\int_{-\infty}^{+\infty} \rho \phi^2 \, dz = \nu$$

$$\int_{-\infty}^{+\infty} \frac{\rho}{c^2} \phi^2 \, dz = \sigma \tag{2.61}$$

Using the definition of phase velocity v in Eq. (2.15),

$$Uv = \frac{\nu}{\sigma} \tag{2.62}$$

Analogous results can be derived for elastic solids.[2]

2.4 BOUNDARIES: REFLECTIONS AND BOUNDARY WAVES

Since in most problems the media are of finite extent, boundary conditions are required to complete the solution of Eqs. (2.1) or (2.6) and (2.7).

At a *free surface*, the stresses must vanish, e.g., in the two-dimensional case, at a $z = $ constant surface, this implies for an elastic solid

$$\sigma_{zz} = 0 \tag{2.63}$$

$$\sigma_{zx} = 0 \tag{2.64}$$

For the free surface of a fluid, this reduces to

$$\phi = 0 \tag{2.65}$$

Conditions of this type are approximated by water-air and rock-air boundaries.

At an *infinitely rigid wall*, one has, for an elastic solid, the condition of no relative motion:

$$\mathbf{d} = 0 \qquad (2.66)$$

For an ideal fluid (no viscosity), there can be slippage parallel to the wall. It is only the normal component that vanishes:

$$\frac{\partial \phi}{\partial n} = 0 \qquad (2.67)$$

For the case of two media in contact, we assume the boundary to be $z =$ constant and the problem to be two-dimensional, and $\partial\phi/\partial n$ becomes $\partial\phi/\partial z$.

If two elastic solids are in welded contact, it is required that the stresses (2.9) and (2.10) and the vertical and horizontal displacements be continuous.

If a fluid (1) is in contact with a solid (2), one must have continuity of vertical displacement and of normal stress, as well as vanishing of the tangential stress, i.e., the three conditions

$$\frac{\partial \phi_1}{\partial z} = \frac{\partial \phi_2}{\partial z} + \frac{\partial \psi_2}{\partial x} \qquad (2.68)$$

$$p_1 = -\sigma_{zz} \qquad (2.69)$$

$$\sigma_{zx} = 0 \qquad (2.70)$$

If both media (1) and (2) are fluids, these reduce to

$$\rho_1\phi_1 = \rho_2\phi_2 \qquad (2.71)$$

$$\frac{\partial \phi_1}{\partial z} = \frac{\partial \phi_2}{\partial z} \qquad (2.72)$$

The standard procedure for deriving reflection and transmission coefficients at boundaries is to assume an incident wave of unit amplitude and reflected and transmitted waves of amplitudes $\mathfrak{R}$ and $\mathfrak{I}$, and to determine these by substitution into the boundary conditions.

Thus, consider a fluid (1) in contact with a solid (2) at $z = 0$ (Fig. 2.3). Assume an incident wave in the fluid:

$$\Phi_1 = e^{i(\alpha x + \gamma_1 z - \omega t)} \qquad (2.73)$$

Part of the energy is reflected, giving an up-going wave:

$$\Phi_R = \mathfrak{R}_{12} e^{i(\alpha x - \gamma_1 z - \omega t)} \qquad (2.74)$$

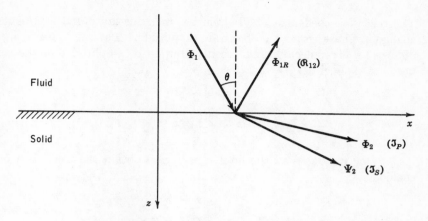

Fig. 2.3 Reflected and transmitted waves at a liquid-solid interface.

In addition, there will be transmitted compression and shear waves obeying Eqs. (2.6) and (2.7), that is,

$$\Phi_2 = \mathfrak{I}_p e^{i(\alpha x + \gamma_2 z - \omega t)} \tag{2.75}$$

$$\Psi_2 = \mathfrak{I}_s e^{i(\alpha x + \delta_2 z - \omega t)} \tag{2.76}$$

where

$$\gamma_2 = \left(\frac{\omega^2}{c_{p_2}{}^2} - \alpha^2\right)^{1/2} = \alpha \left(\frac{v^2}{c_{p_2}{}^2} - 1\right)^{1/2} \tag{2.77}$$

$$\delta_2 = \left(\frac{\omega^2}{c_{s_2}{}^2} - \alpha^2\right)^{1/2} = \alpha \left(\frac{v^2}{c_{s_2}{}^2} - 1\right)^{1/2} \tag{2.78}$$

Assuming the phase velocity v to be

$$v > c_{p_2} \tag{2.79}$$

and substituting (2.68) to (2.70), one finds

$$\mathfrak{R}_{12} = \frac{4\gamma_2\delta_2\alpha^2 + (\delta_2{}^2 - \alpha^2)^2 - (\rho_1/\rho_2)(\gamma_2/\gamma_1)(\omega^4/c_{s_2}{}^4)}{4\gamma_2\delta_2\alpha^2 + (\delta_2{}^2 - \alpha^2)^2 + (\rho_1/\rho_2)(\gamma_2/\gamma_1)(\omega^4/c_{s_2}{}^4)} \tag{2.80}$$

Expressions for $\mathfrak{I}_p$ and $\mathfrak{I}_s$ are also easily derived. For these formulas and for numerical examples we refer the reader to Ewing et al.[3]

In the case

$$c_{p_2} > c_{s_1} > v \tag{2.81}$$

γ_2 and δ_2 become imaginary:

$$\gamma_2 = ig_2 \tag{2.82}$$

$$\delta_2 = id_2 \tag{2.83}$$

The reflection coefficient (2.80) then has modulus unity and represents a change in phase without a change in amplitude. The sound wave in the fluid is totally reflected, and the distribution of amplitudes in the solid becomes exponential:

$$\mathcal{R}_{12} = -e^{2i\eta} \tag{2.84}$$

$$\eta = \text{Arctan}\left\{\frac{\rho_2}{\rho_1}\frac{\gamma_1}{g_2}\frac{c_{s_2}{}^4}{\omega^4}[-4g_2d_2\alpha^2 + (d_2{}^2 + \alpha^2)^2]\right\} \tag{2.85}$$

One may pass to the limit $c_{s_2} \to 0$ and obtain the usual Rayleigh coefficients:

$$\mathcal{R}_{12} = \frac{\rho_2\gamma_1 - \rho_1\gamma_2}{\rho_2\gamma_1 + \rho_1\gamma_2} \tag{2.86}$$

$$\mathfrak{I}_{12} = \frac{2\rho_1\gamma_1}{\rho_2\gamma_1 + \rho_1\gamma_2} \tag{2.87}$$

Here, if $c_1 < c_2$ and $v < c_2$, that is, for angles of incidence greater than the critical angle

$$\theta = \text{Arcsin}\frac{c_1}{c_2} \tag{2.88}$$

one has total reflection with

$$\mathcal{R}_{12} = -e^{2ix} \tag{2.89}$$

$$\chi = \text{Arctan}\left(\frac{\rho_2}{\rho_1}\frac{\gamma_1}{g_2}\right) \tag{2.90}$$

Condition (2.65) for a *free surface* is satisfied by taking $\rho_2 = 0$ (2.86), giving $\mathcal{R} = -1$. Thus, insofar as the pressure perturbation is concerned, there is a change of polarity upon reflection. This is equivalent to taking $\chi = 0$ in (2.89).

In the case of solid boundaries, examination of the equations of motion and boundary conditions shows the existence of *boundary waves*.

Thus, consider once more the plane liquid-solid interface of Fig. 2.3. If v is assumed to be less than c_1 and c_{s_2}, the equations of wave motion have exponential solutions only. In order that the energy densities at infinity converge, these must be of the form

$$\Phi_1 = Ae^{g_{1z}z}e^{i(\alpha x - \omega t)} \qquad z < 0 \tag{2.91}$$

$$\Phi_2 = Be^{-g_{2z}z}e^{i(\alpha x - \omega t)} \qquad z > 0 \tag{2.92}$$

$$\Psi_2 = Ce^{-d_{2z}z}e^{i(\alpha x - \omega t)} \qquad z > 0 \tag{2.93}$$

and the boundary conditions (2.68) to (2.70) give

$$Ag_1 + Bg_2 - i\alpha C = 0 \tag{2.94}$$

$$A\omega^2 + B\frac{\rho_2}{\rho_1} c_{s_2}^2(d_2^2 + \alpha^2) + iC2\frac{\rho_2}{\rho_1} c_{s_2}^2\alpha d_2 = 0 \tag{2.95}$$

$$-iB\, 2\alpha g_2 + C(d_2^2 + \alpha^2) = 0 \tag{2.96}$$

In order for these equations to be compatible, the determinant of the coefficients must vanish. Writing out this condition, one has, after some simple algebra,

$$-(d_2^2 + \alpha^2)^2 + 4g_2 d_2\alpha^2 - \frac{\rho_1}{\rho_2}\frac{g_2}{g_1}\frac{\omega^4}{c_{s_2}^4} = 0 \tag{2.97}$$

or

$$-\left(2 - \frac{v^2}{c_{s_2}^2}\right)^2 + 4\left(1 - \frac{v^2}{c_{p_2}^2}\right)^{1/2}\left(1 - \frac{v^2}{c_{s_2}^2}\right)^{1/2}$$

$$-\frac{\rho_1}{\rho_2}\frac{v^4}{c_{s_2}^4}\left(1 - \frac{v^2}{c_{p_2}^2}\right)^{1/2}\left(1 - \frac{v^2}{c_1^2}\right)^{-1/2} = 0 \tag{2.98}$$

This equation always has one real root $v_s < c_1$, $v_s < c_{s_2}$. Therefore, at a liquid-solid interface there exists a boundary or interface wave, the amplitudes of which die off exponentially in both directions $z \to \pm\infty$, having a characteristic (frequency-independent) velocity of propagation when the two media are of infinite extent. Curves giving v_s as a function of ρ_1/ρ_2, c_1/c_{p_2}, and c_{s_2}/c_{p_2} have been computed by Ginzbarg and Strick.[4]

This wave has received the name of Stoneley wave, after R. Stoneley who discovered a similar effect for the case of two solids in contact.[5] In the liquid-solid case it was discovered by Biot,[6] who pointed out that if we make $\rho_2 \to 0$ and $c_1 \to \infty$ (incompressible liquid over massless solid), Eq. (2.98) still has a root:

$$v_s = \left(\frac{2\mu_2}{\rho_1}\frac{\lambda_2 + \mu_2}{\lambda_2 + 2\mu_2}\right)^{1/2} \tag{2.99}$$

Since in this case neither of the two media can propagate body waves of any kind, this shows that the Stoneley wave is an entirely distinct mode of propagation characteristic of the interface; it is a *boundary wave* in the true sense of the word. In the extreme case, $\rho_2 \to 0$ and $c_1 \to \infty$, energy propagates by being stored alternately on each side of the boundary (as kinetic energy in the liquid, then as potential energy in the solid, etc.).

Another boundary-wave characteristic of solid media occurs when the solid has a free surface; this is the well-known *Rayleigh wave*, the velocity equation for which may be simply obtained from (2.98) by replacing the liquid by a vacuum, i.e., making $\rho_1 = 0$:

$$\left(2 - \frac{v^2}{c_s^2}\right)^2 - 4\left(1 - \frac{v^2}{c_p^2}\right)^{1/2}\left(1 - \frac{v^2}{c_s^2}\right)^{1/2} = 0 \tag{2.100}$$

This has always one real root $v = v_R < c_s < c_p$. The amplitudes decrease exponentially with distance from the surface.

We will encounter both Stoneley and Rayleigh waves as limiting cases in Chap. 4, when we study the propagation of sound in a liquid layer over a solid elastic bottom.

2.5 REFLECTION COEFFICIENTS IN STRATIFIED MEDIA

The concept of plane-wave reflection coefficients in continuously stratified sections requires definition. In a stratified medium, rays and wave fronts are curved, and it is no longer quite proper to talk of plane waves. However, this difficulty is obviated, and the definition of $\mathfrak{R}$ is clarified, by the following subterfuge: Consider, in a stratified medium, a specific level $z = 0$, characterized by a sound velocity c_1. Remove the overlying $z < 0$ region and replace it by a homogeneous medium of sound velocity c_1. The concept of reflection coefficient acquires its usual meaning as the ratio of the amplitudes between an up-going and a down-going incident plane wave (Fig. 2.4).

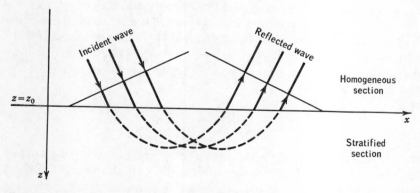

Fig. 2.4   Illustrating the meaning of $\mathfrak{R}$ at $z = z_0$. In this schematic drawing we have chosen the special case of a $c(z)$ which increases with depth.

Thus, assuming unit amplitude for the incident wave, the total sound field resulting from it and the reflection is

$$\phi = e^{i\gamma_1 z} + \mathfrak{R}e^{-i\gamma_1 z} \tag{2.101}$$

By this process we may define a plane-wave reflection coefficient $\mathcal{R}(z)$ for any z.

$\mathcal{R}(z)$ obeys a differential equation which we now derive, following Shelkunoff.[7]

The vertical displacement associated with (2.101) is

$$\frac{d\phi}{dz} = \phi_z = i\gamma_1(e^{i\gamma_1 z} - \mathcal{R}e^{-i\gamma_1 z}) \tag{2.102}$$

One may define the impedance at $z = 0$ as

$$Z = \frac{\rho_1 \phi}{\phi_z} = \frac{\rho_1}{i\gamma_1} \frac{1 + \mathcal{R}}{1 - \mathcal{R}} \tag{2.103}$$

In view of (2.71) and (2.72), it is clear that Z is continuous even in the presence of c and ρ jumps. Thus, if c and ρ change at $z = 0$ from c_1 and ρ_1 ($z < 0$) to c_2 and ρ_2 ($z > 0$),

$$\frac{\rho_1}{i\gamma_1} \frac{1 + \mathcal{R}(-\epsilon)}{1 - \mathcal{R}(-\epsilon)} = \frac{\rho_2}{i\gamma_2} \frac{1 + \mathcal{R}(\epsilon)}{1 - \mathcal{R}(\epsilon)} \qquad \text{as } \epsilon \to 0 \tag{2.104}$$

If the half-space $z > 0$ is infinite and homogeneous, $\mathcal{R}(\epsilon) = 0$, $\mathcal{R}(-\epsilon) \to \mathcal{R}_{12}$ as $\epsilon \to 0$, and (2.104) gives the result (2.86). Assuming the medium to be continuously stratified, but of constant density, Eq. (2.103) gives

$$\frac{d}{dz} \log \phi = i\gamma \frac{1 - \mathcal{R}}{1 + \mathcal{R}} \tag{2.105}$$

The fundamental equation (2.16) may be rewritten as

$$\frac{d^2}{dz^2} \log \phi = -\gamma^2 - \left(\frac{d}{dz} \log \phi\right)^2 \tag{2.106}$$

Differentiating (2.105) and eliminating ϕ gives

$$\frac{d\mathcal{R}}{dz} - \frac{1}{2}(1 - \mathcal{R}^2)\frac{d}{dz} \log \gamma + 2i\gamma\mathcal{R} = 0 \tag{2.107}$$

i.e., a first-order, nonlinear differential equation of the Riccati type.

If
$$\frac{1}{\gamma}\frac{d}{dz} \log \gamma \ll 1 \tag{2.108}$$

then
$$\frac{d\mathcal{R}}{dz} \approx -2i\gamma\mathcal{R} \tag{2.109}$$

and
$$\mathcal{R} = \mathcal{R}(z_0) \exp\left(-2i \int_{z_0}^{z} \gamma \, dz\right) \tag{2.110}$$

The exponent is simply a phase shift due to the ray path from z to z_0 and back; this approximation assumes that the only effect of a smoothly varying $c(z)$ is to bend the rays.

We shall see in Sec. 2.9 that Eq. (2.108) is the criterion for validity of the W.K.B. and ray approximations, and we therefore call (2.110) the ray-approximation reflection coefficient.

In a homogeneous half-space, Eq. (2.110) is exact and γ is a constant. We then have the reflection coefficient, referred to some level h above the boundary:

$$\Re = \Re(z_0)e^{-2i\gamma(z-z_0)} = \Re(z_0)e^{2i\gamma h} \tag{2.111}$$

It is not difficult to obtain an exact expression for the reflection coefficient from a homogeneous layer or any number of such layers. Suppose the upper boundary of the layer (of thickness h_2, sound velocity c_2, density ρ_2) to be in contact at $z = 0$ with a half-space c_1, ρ_1 (Fig. 2.5).

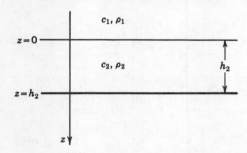

Fig. 2.5   Homogeneous layer c_2, ρ_2, h_2.

Then, by (2.111)

$$\lim_{\epsilon\to 0}\Re(\epsilon) = \Re(h_2)e^{2i\gamma_2 h_2} \tag{2.112}$$

and, from (2.104)

$$\frac{1+\Re}{1-\Re} = \frac{\rho_2}{\rho_1}\frac{\gamma_1}{\gamma_2}\frac{1+\Re(h_2)e^{2i\gamma_2 h_2}}{1-\Re(h_2)e^{2i\gamma_2 h_2}} \tag{2.113}$$

or

$$\Re = \frac{\Re_{12}+\Re(h_2)e^{2i\gamma_2 h_2}}{1+\Re_{12}\Re(h_2)e^{2i\gamma_2 h_2}} \tag{2.114}$$

If we now suppose $\Re(h_2)$ to be the reflection coefficient from a third layer c_3, ρ_3, h_3, we easily get a series of recursive equations giving $\Re$ for any number n of underlying layers.

For the general case $c = c(z)$ one must usually resort to numerical integration of Eq. (2.107). Exact solutions may be obtained whenever (2.16) can be solved in terms of known functions, by inverting Eq. (2.105):

$$\Re = \frac{i\gamma - d(\log\phi)/dz}{i\gamma + d(\log\phi)/dz} \tag{2.115}$$

Insofar as *total reflection* is concerned we note first of all that if ϕ in (2.115) is a real or imaginary function this implies that an incident, plane, progressive wave sets up a standing-wave pattern; i.e., the amplitudes of incident and reflected waves are equal, and there is only a phase difference between the two:

$$\mathfrak{R} = -e^{2i\theta} \tag{2.116}$$

$$\theta = \operatorname{Arctan}\left[-\frac{\gamma}{d(\log \phi)/dz} \right] \tag{2.117}$$

This will be the case when the condition of total reflection is met at the lower boundary of the stratified section or, if this is of infinite extent, whenever $\omega/\alpha = v < \lim_{z\to\infty} c(z)$. We may, from (2.117) and (2.107) obtain a differential equation for θ as

$$\frac{d\theta}{dz} - \frac{1}{2}\left(\frac{d}{dz}\log\gamma\right)\sin 2\theta + \gamma = 0 \tag{2.118}$$

From this equation, or from (2.116) and (2.110), it is clear that if (2.108) holds, one has

$$\theta \approx -\int_{z_0}^{z}\gamma\,dz + \theta_0 \tag{2.119}$$

When the stratified section is of infinite extent, total reflection occurs by the bending back of rays, which become horizontal at the turning point $z = z_T$:

$$\frac{\omega}{\alpha} = v = c(z_T) \tag{2.120}$$

$$\gamma(z_T) = 0 \tag{2.121}$$

Near $z = z_T$, condition (2.108) is never satisfied, since

$$\frac{1}{\gamma}\frac{d}{dz}\log\gamma \to \infty$$

as $\qquad\qquad z \to z_T \tag{2.122}$

If (2.108) is satisfied everywhere except in a narrow region near $\gamma = 0$, a good approximation to θ is given by (2.119) with

$$\theta_0 = \frac{\pi}{4} \tag{2.123}$$

a result which is justified in particular cases by examining the asymptotic behavior of ϕ for large z (see Appendix 1).

For a medium consisting of homogeneous layers of various velocities and densities, simple recursion equations may be derived for θ for total reflection. Thus, assuming that at $z = h_2$ (in Fig. 2.5),

$$\Re(h_2) = -e^{2i\theta(h_2)} \tag{2.124}$$

We have from (2.111) ($z_0 = h_2$) and (2.116), the condition that as $z \to 0$ from larger values of z,

$$\theta(\epsilon) \underset{\epsilon \to 0}{\longrightarrow} \gamma_2 h_2 + \theta(h_2) \tag{2.125}$$

But, since Z [Eq. (2.103)] is continuous through a boundary of discontinuity of ρ and c, it follows that

$$-\frac{\rho\phi}{\phi_z} = \frac{\rho}{\gamma} \tan\theta \tag{2.126}$$

must also be continuous, and

$$\theta(-\epsilon) \underset{\epsilon \to 0}{\longrightarrow} \arctan\left\{ \frac{\gamma_1}{\gamma_2}\frac{\rho_2}{\rho_1} \tan\left[\gamma_2 h_2 + \theta(h_2)\right] \right\} \tag{2.127}$$

where $\theta(-\epsilon)$ is in the same quadrant as $\gamma_2 h_2 + \theta(h_2)$.

This leads immediately to recursive relations for n layers. Thus, let θ_1 be the value of θ at a height h_1 above the 1–2 boundary, θ_2 being $\theta(\epsilon)$, etc.:

$$\theta_1 = \gamma_1 h_1 + \operatorname{Arctan}\left(\frac{\gamma_1}{\gamma_2}\frac{\rho_2}{\rho_1} \tan\theta_2\right)$$
$$\theta_2 = \gamma_2 h_2 + \operatorname{Arctan}\left(\frac{\gamma_2}{\gamma_3}\frac{\rho_3}{\rho_2} \tan\theta_3\right) \tag{2.128}$$

$$\cdots\cdots\cdots\cdots\cdots\cdots\cdots\cdots$$

If the nth layer is underlaid by a homogeneous half-space,

$$\theta_n = \gamma_n h_n + \chi_{n,n+1} \tag{2.129}$$

where $\chi_{n,n+1}$ has the form (2.85) or (2.90) depending upon whether the half-space is a solid or a liquid, and providing the subscripts 1 and 2 are replaced by n and $n+1$ respectively.

Note that the condition of total reflection (that is, $v < c_{n+1}$ for the liquid half-space and $v < c_{s_{n+1}}$ for the solid case) must be obeyed. For intermediate layers one may have $v > c_j$ or $v < c_j$. In the latter case one needs only to replace γ_j by ig_j in Eq. (2.128). It is easily seen that θ remains real; for example, $\theta_j \to i\theta_j$, $\gamma_j \to ig_j$, and one has $\theta_{j-1} = \gamma_{j-1}h_{j-1} + \operatorname{Arctan}\left[(\gamma_{j-1}/g_j)(\rho_j/\rho_{j-1}) \tanh\theta_j\right]$ for $v > c_{j-1}$.

θ is a well-behaved, monotonic function. This behavior must be contrasted to that of $\mathcal{R}$, which oscillates, or that of Z in Eq. (2.103), which not only oscillates but also has poles.

2.6 TYPES OF SOLUTION: DISCRETE VS. CONTINUOUS MODES. WAVEGUIDES

The modes (Sec. 2.2) of an acoustic or elastic system may be classified into two types, corresponding physically to cases for which the energy of the wave system is or is not contained in a finite region.

The prototype of the first possibility is the perfect acoustic waveguide, e.g., a homogeneous layer of fluid between perfectly reflecting boundaries $z = 0$ and $z = h$. Let both these surfaces be free. Condition (2.65) at $z = 0$ requires that ϕ be of the form

$$\phi = q \sin \gamma z \tag{2.130}$$

The same condition at $z = h$ can be satisfied only if

$$\gamma h = m\pi \qquad m = 1, 2, \ldots \tag{2.131}$$

Thus, the presence of the second boundary limits the permissible values of γ, or eigenvalues, to a discrete set γ_m corresponding to integral values of m (mode numbers). One says that *the γ spectrum is discrete.*

Equation (2.130) describes a standing-wave system resulting from the total reflection of harmonic waves, and Eq. (2.131) implies that only certain angles of incidence are allowed for these component waves once the frequency is fixed. In terms of the wavelength λ along a ray, Eq. (2.131) reads

$$\gamma_m h = kh \cos \theta_m = 2\pi \frac{h}{\lambda} \cos \theta_m = m\pi \tag{2.132}$$

or

$$2h \cos \theta_m = m\lambda \tag{2.133}$$

One recognizes the diffraction-grating equation, or Bragg's law, where m defines the order of the spectrum. Its significance in the present context is simply this: since the surfaces $z = 0$ and $z = h$ are perfect reflectors, a point source in the fluid is equivalent to an infinite array of images (Fig. 2.6). At very long ranges, the spherical waves radiated by each image become essentially plane, and Eq. (2.133) says that the contributions from all images are in phase for certain angles θ_m only. Thus, in a very real sense, a waveguide is equivalent to a diffraction grating or an infinite array of sources.

If there is no boundary at $z = h$, Eq. (2.130) is still the solution of the problem; i.e., it represents also the modes of an infinite homogeneous

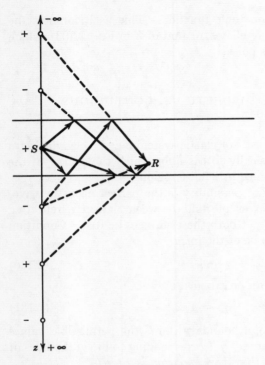

Fig. 2.6 The perfect waveguide as an infinite array of images. The signs indicate polarity of images when both boundaries are free.

half-space, but now, without limitations on the value of γ: *The γ spectrum is continuous.* This state of affairs can be obtained from the waveguide case by making $h \to \infty$, that is, by removing the lower boundary to very great distances. It is then seen that the increment between neighboring values of γ_m becomes infinitesimal:

$$\Delta\gamma = \gamma_{m+1} - \gamma_m = \frac{\pi}{h} \to 0 \qquad (2.134)$$

From the energy standpoint we may say that the two types of spectrum correspond, on one hand, to confining the energy within a region of finite width (discrete spectrum), and, on the other, to its distribution over an infinite region. Clearly, in the discrete case, the integral (2.57) converges, whereas it diverges for the continuous spectrum. In other words, the energy contained in a complete vertical slice of the medium is finite in one case and infinite in the other. This, as we shall see, is the general distinction between guided or trapped modes and the free modes of an infinite section.

Strictly speaking, of course, there are no infinite acoustic or elastic systems in nature. The ocean waters, the earth's crust, and the earth itself are of finite size so that all acoustic and elastic modes of propagation will have discrete spectra. But when the dimensions become very large compared with a wavelength, the spacing between neighboring eigenvalues is small, and it is often more convenient to treat such a spectrum as if it were continuous.

From the standpoint of the theory of differential equations [Eq. (2.16)], there are too few integration constants to satisfy all the boundary conditions in the waveguide case. Thus (2.130) cannot be made to satisfy the remaining condition at $z = h$ through choice of the integration constant. One thus has to select the wave numbers for which this condition is obeyed. This is done by means of the *characteristic equation*, e.g., Eq. (2.131). This selection is typical of all waveguide problems and discrete spectra: one is led to a characteristic equation with discrete roots defining a *spectrum of eigenvalues*.

A completely general form of the characteristic equation for stratified waveguides is easily defined in terms of the variable θ obeying Eq. (2.118).

We suppose first a medium with a free surface $z = 0$ in which guided waves may exist. This means that a "plane" wave starting near the surface $z = 0$ will be totally reflected, giving a standing-wave pattern at $z = 0$:

$$\phi = 1 - e^{2i\theta} \tag{2.135}$$

by (2.101) and (2.116). At the free surface, both real and imaginary parts of (2.135) must vanish, that is,

$$\theta = m\pi \tag{2.136}$$

This is the characteristic equation, expressed in terms of the value of θ at $z = 0$.

If we suppose next that the nature of the boundaries, if any, is not specified, we look for a more general form. First, we choose arbitrarily a plane $z = 0$ dividing the medium into two sections. A down-traveling "plane" wave sets up a standing-wave field at $z = 0$:

$$\phi \downarrow = 1 - e^{2i\theta \downarrow} \tag{2.137}$$

An up-traveling system similarly would give

$$\phi \uparrow = 1 - e^{2i\theta \uparrow} \tag{2.138}$$

These standing-wave patterns must be matched at $z = 0$, according to the conditions (2.71) and (2.72), with $\rho_1 = \rho_2$. But, by (2.101) and (2.116), we have for the real parts

$$\frac{d\phi \downarrow}{dz}\bigg|_{z=0} = \left(2\,\frac{d\theta \downarrow}{dz} - \gamma\right)\sin 2\theta \downarrow \qquad (2.139)$$

$$\frac{d\phi \uparrow}{dz}\bigg|_{z=0} = \left(2\,\frac{d\theta \uparrow}{dz} + \gamma\right)\sin 2\theta \uparrow \qquad (2.140)$$

And, it is clear that the only way in which the real parts of both ϕ and $d\phi/dz$ will be continuous through $z = 0$ is to have

$$\theta \downarrow = -\theta \uparrow + m\pi \qquad (2.141)$$

or $$\theta \downarrow + \theta \uparrow = m\pi \qquad (2.142)$$

This is the general form of the characteristic equation for stratified acoustic waveguides.

2.7 DISPERSION IN WAVEGUIDES. GROUP VELOCITY

The characteristic equation for discrete spectra is the key relationship for describing and understanding guided waves in stratified media. Unfortunately, it is almost never possible to obtain exact, explicit solutions and one must be satisfied with approximations or numerical solutions. For the proper interpretation of such results it is essential to have a good grasp of the properties of guided waves and, in particular, of the important phenomenon of *dispersion*.

In the special case of the perfect, homogeneous waveguide of Sec. 2.6, the characteristic equation has the simple form (2.131) which, in view of (2.17), may be rewritten as

$$\omega = (\omega_{0m}{}^2 + \alpha^2 c^2)^{1/2} \qquad (2.143)$$

where $$\omega_{0m} = \frac{c}{h}\,m\pi \qquad (2.144)$$

is, clearly, the mth-mode low-frequency cutoff; it is a natural frequency of an acoustic pipe with open ends.

Note that α may be imaginary $(m > h\omega/\pi c)$. These attenuated solutions are known as *evanescent modes* (see for example K. G. Budden in ref. 6 of Foreword). They correspond to modes whose cutoff ω_{0m} is higher than the source frequency. They are of little, if any, practical significance in underwater acoustics.

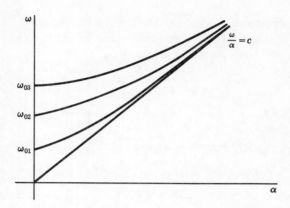

Fig. 2.7 Characteristic $\omega(\alpha)$ curves of a perfect waveguide.

The $\omega_m(\alpha)$ curves for each mode give a family of hyperbolas (Fig. 2.7) having the line $\omega = \alpha c$ as a common asymptote. The phase velocity in the x direction

$$v_m = \frac{\omega}{\alpha_m} = c\left(1 - \frac{\omega_{0m}{}^2}{\omega^2}\right)^{-1/2} \tag{2.145}$$

is, therefore, a function of the frequency, and one says that the propagation is *dispersive*. The cause of this dispersion is clear from the remarks made in Sec. 2.6. The waveguide is equivalent to an infinite array or diffraction grating, and the characteristic equation (2.131) or its alternate forms (2.143) and (2.145) simply state that only certain privileged directions allow propagation to occur without destructive interference effects, i.e.,

$$\sin\theta_m = \frac{c}{v_m} = \left(1 - \frac{\omega_{0m}{}^2}{\omega^2}\right)^{1/2} \tag{2.146}$$

The phase velocity $v_m(\omega)$ is simply the horizontal velocity of a point of constant phase, corresponding to one of these permissible directions of propagation of a harmonic wave train. This sort of dispersion has thus a geometric character and is referred to as *geometric dispersion*. It is to be contrasted with intrinsic dispersion, occurring for instance in the "anomalous" dispersion of light in dielectrics. This is due to the microscopic structure of the medium, which can be visualized as a continuous distribution of ionic and atomic resonators having their characteristic proper frequencies.

Consider now two harmonic wave trains, of slightly different frequencies $\omega + \Delta\omega$ and $\omega - \Delta\omega$, propagating in the same direction through a dispersive medium. They will have different wave numbers $\alpha + \Delta\alpha$ and $\alpha - \Delta\alpha$. In view of the dispersion, their phase velocities are different:

$$\frac{\omega + \Delta\omega}{\alpha + \Delta\alpha} \neq \frac{\omega - \Delta\omega}{\alpha - \Delta\alpha} \tag{2.147}$$

and

$$\frac{\Delta\omega}{\Delta\alpha} \neq \frac{\omega}{\alpha} \tag{2.148}$$

Let both wave trains have unit amplitude. Then

$$\Phi = \cos\left[(\alpha + \Delta\alpha)x - (\omega + \Delta\omega)t\right] + \cos\left[(\alpha - \Delta\alpha)x - (\omega - \Delta\omega)t\right] \tag{2.149}$$

or

$$\Phi = 2\cos(\alpha x - \omega t)\cos(x\,\Delta\alpha - t\,\Delta\omega) \tag{2.150}$$

The resultant pattern (Fig. 2.8) is thus a series of beats or groups traveling with the velocity

$$U = \frac{\Delta\omega}{\Delta\alpha} \tag{2.151}$$

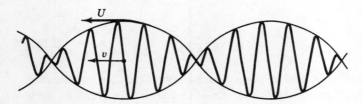

Fig. 2.8   The envelope of the beats travels with the group velocity U, and the points of constant phase, with phase velocity v.

Within each group, points of constant phase travel with the speed

$$v = \frac{\omega}{\alpha} \tag{2.152}$$

In view of (2.148) one sees the necessity of introducing the quantity U measuring the velocity of the groups; this is the *group velocity*.

In this simple example it is clear that the points of maximum amplitude of the envelope correspond to the condition

$$x\,\Delta\alpha - t\,\Delta\omega = n\pi \tag{2.153}$$

for which the individual wave trains interfere constructively.

At the nodes, which are similarly spaced, there is cancellation. In a coordinate system $x' = x - Ut$, these nodes are at rest; there is no net energy transfer between groups; i.e., the energy travels with the group velocity.

This reasoning is easily extended to a superposition of waves clustered about a mean frequency

$$\Phi = \int_{\omega_0-\epsilon}^{\omega_0+\epsilon} G(\omega)e^{i(\alpha x - \omega t)}\, d\omega \tag{2.154}$$

In general, this is a series of groups of variable amplitude (Fig. 2.9). A group maximum corresponds to a point where all neighboring components

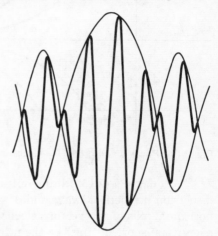

Fig. 2.9 Envelope of the superposition of waves clustered about a mean frequency.

are in phase. Since the change in phase of any wave as it travels is $\alpha\, dx - \omega\, dt$, the condition that all neighboring components *stay* in phase is

$$d\alpha\, dx - d\omega\, dt = 0 \tag{2.155}$$

that is,

$$\frac{dx}{dt} = \frac{d\omega}{d\alpha} = U \tag{2.156}$$

is the velocity of a group maximum.

Thus, we say that, in dispersive systems, the energy in a narrow bandwidth centered upon a frequency ω_0 travels with the group velocity (2.156), whereas, within any group of waves, a given phase, such as a wave crest, moves with the phase velocity v. This obviously imposes limitations on U; for example, it may never exceed the speed of light. There is no such limit for v. Thus in the perfect waveguide, v is infinite at cutoff.

Here:

$$U_m v_m = c^2 \tag{2.157}$$

$$U_m = c \sin \theta_m$$
$$v_m = \frac{c}{\sin \theta_m} \tag{2.158}$$

Figure 2.10 shows U_m and v_m plotted against ω for $m = 1, 2, 3$.

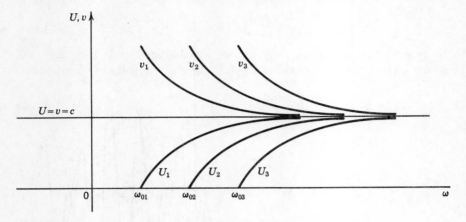

Fig. 2.10 Phase v and group U velocities vs. ω for a perfect waveguide.

Equations (2.158) bring out once more the geometrical character of dispersion in perfect waveguides. U is simply the projection on the horizontal axis of the vector velocity $\mathbf{c}$ along a ray. Since $\mathbf{c}$ is the rate of energy transport, U must be the rate of energy transport in the horizontal direction, and it would seem that U, as defined by (2.156), also has meaning in the context of harmonic waves. Since the concept of bandwidth $d\omega$ has no place here, the physically meaningful quantity is rate of energy transport. It is easy to check, in the case of the perfect waveguide, that the two Eqs. (2.156) and (2.60) define the same function $U(\omega)$. This is actually a general theorem, valid for all isentropic wave processes, as has been shown by Biot.[2] Although we shall appeal to this theorem elsewhere, lack of space does not permit us to reproduce Biot's elegant proof.

2.8 PROPAGATION OF PULSES IN DISPERSIVE MEDIA

A traveling pulse is usually represented by integrals of the form

$$\Phi = \int_{-\infty}^{+\infty} F(\alpha) e^{i(\alpha x - \omega t)} \, d\alpha \tag{2.159}$$

If the medium is not dispersive, $\omega = \alpha c$ where c is a constant, and $\Phi = \Phi(x - ct)$ so that the pulse does not change shape as it travels. If there is dispersion, $c = c(\omega)$, and the pulse shape changes with x and t. The discussion in Sec. 2.7 indicates that the energy in a narrow band $\omega \pm \frac{1}{2} d\omega$ travels with the group velocity $U(\omega)$. Since U is not constant and is always finite, there will be both a largest and a smallest value of U, and the pulse (2.159) will spread out in space and time as x increases. In order to describe the changes in shape of the traveling pulse, it is necessary to integrate (2.159). Unfortunately, it is usually quite impossible to do this exactly, and one must resort to approximations or numerical methods. A lot of mathematical ingenuity has been devoted to this problem. Today it appears possible to integrate (2.159) numerically in most cases, thanks in part to some methods suggested by Longman[8] and, in part, to the availability of fast electronic computers. However, this is not a book on methods and for our purposes an old method of approximation due to Lord Kelvin[9] is very useful, enlightening, and surprisingly accurate. It is based upon the observation that if $F(\alpha)$ is a relatively slowly varying function, the oscillations of the integrand effectively cancel each other upon integration, except near stationary values of $\alpha x - \omega t$ where

$$\frac{d}{d\alpha}(\alpha x - \omega t) = x - tU = 0 \tag{2.160}$$

It is known, for this reason, as the *method of stationary phase*,† and is, in the present context, but a restatement of the principle that energy travels with the group velocity.

Expand the exponent in (2.159) into Taylor series:

$$\alpha x - \omega t = \alpha_0 x - \omega_0 t + (\alpha - \alpha_0)(x - tU_0) - \tfrac{1}{2}(\alpha - \alpha_0)^2 \frac{dU_0}{d\alpha} t$$
$$- (\alpha - \alpha_0)^3 \frac{d^2 U_0}{d\alpha^2} t + \cdots \tag{2.161}$$

Assuming (2.160) to hold exactly and limiting ourselves to second-order terms,

$$\Phi = e^{i(\alpha_0 x - \omega_0 t)} F(\alpha_0) \int_{\alpha_0 - \epsilon}^{\alpha_0 + \epsilon} e^{-\frac{1}{2} it(\alpha - \alpha_0)^2 dU_0/d\alpha} d\alpha \tag{2.162}$$

If we make the change of variable,

$$\tfrac{1}{2} t (\alpha - \alpha_0)^2 \left| \frac{dU_0}{d\alpha} \right| = \sigma^2 \tag{2.163}$$

if $t|dU_0/d\alpha|$ is large, and since the contribution of the α's far removed from α_0 is negligible, the limits of integration in (2.162) may, without appreciable error, be extended to $\pm \infty$:

$$\Phi = e^{i(\alpha_0 x - \omega_0 t)} F(\alpha_0) \left[\frac{2}{t|dU_0/d\alpha|} \right]^{1/2} \int_{-\infty}^{+\infty} e^{\mp i\sigma^2} d\sigma \tag{2.164}$$

† The saddle-point method [cf. for example Brekhovskikh[10]] is the generalization of this to complex ω and α.

where the $\mp$ signs correspond to $dU_0/d\alpha > 0$ or <0, respectively. The infinite integral in (2.164) is well known, giving

$$\Phi = F(\alpha_0) \left[\frac{2\pi}{t|dU_0/d\alpha|} \right]^{1/2} e^{i(\alpha_0 x - \omega_0 t \mp \pi/4)} \tag{2.165}$$

If one knows $\omega(\alpha)$ and $U(\alpha)$ explicitly, ω_0 and α_0 can be expressed as functions of x and t by virtue of (2.160). This result is valid asymptotically for large t, providing we are not too close to a stationary value of U.

As an illustration, consider the following example: Let $F(\alpha) = (2\pi)^{-1}$ and take only the real part of (2.159). The pulse at $t = 0$ is then a Dirac delta function at $t = 0$:

$$\Phi = \frac{1}{2\pi} \int_{-\infty}^{+\infty} \cos(\alpha x - \omega t)\, d\alpha \tag{2.166}$$

Assume a dispersion law of the type (2.143):

$$\omega = (\nu^2 + \alpha^2 c^2)^{1/2} \tag{2.167}$$

Thus ω is an even function of α and (2.166) reduces to

$$\Phi = \frac{1}{\pi} \int_0^\infty \cos \alpha x \, \cos\left[ct\left(\frac{\nu^2}{c^2} + \alpha^2\right)^{1/2} \right] d\alpha \tag{2.168}$$

This is a known integral† and we have the exact result:

$$\Phi = \begin{cases} -\tfrac{1}{2}\nu t (c^2 t^2 - x^2)^{-1/2} J_1\left[\frac{\nu}{c}(c^2 t^2 - x^2)^{1/2} \right] & ct > x \\ 0 & ct < x \end{cases} \tag{2.169}$$

For $ct \gg x$ we use the asymptotic formula for J_1, giving

$$J_1\left[\frac{\nu}{c}(c^2 t^2 - x^2)^{1/2} \right] \approx \left(\frac{2c}{\pi\nu} \right)^{1/2} (c^2 t^2 - x^2)^{-1/4} \cos\left[\frac{\nu}{c}(c^2 t^2 - x^2)^{1/2} - \frac{3\pi}{4} \right] \tag{2.170}$$

and $\quad \Phi \approx (2\pi)^{-1/2} (\nu c)^{1/2} t(c^2 t^2 - x^2)^{-3/4} \cos\left[\frac{\nu}{c}(c^2 t^2 - x^2)^{1/2} + \frac{\pi}{4} \right]$ (2.171)

We now apply the approximation (2.165), noting that by (2.167)

$$\frac{x}{t} = U_0 = \frac{\alpha_0}{\omega_0} c^2 \tag{2.172}$$

---

† See "Tables of Integral Transforms," Erdélyi (ed.).(11)   The result (2.169) is actually obtained by differentiating the transform 1.7(30) in Vol. 1.

and
$$\alpha_0 = \frac{\nu}{c} x (c^2 t^2 - x^2)^{-1/2} \tag{2.173}$$

$$\omega_0 = \frac{\nu}{c} c^2 t (c^2 t^2 - x^2)^{-1/2} \tag{2.174}$$

Also, from (2.167) and (2.172)

$$\frac{dU_0}{d\alpha} = \frac{c^2}{\omega_0} \left(1 - \frac{\alpha_0{}^2 c^2}{\omega_0{}^2}\right) = \frac{1}{\nu c} t^{-3} (c^2 t^2 - x^2)^{3/2} \tag{2.175}$$

This quantity is always positive. Substituting (2.173) to (2.175) in (2.165) gives (2.171), showing the asymptotic nature of the approximation (2.165).

Near stationary values of the group velocity, $dU_0/d\alpha \to 0$ and (2.165) breaks down. It is found[12] that a sufficient degree of accuracy can usually be secured here by following the same type of procedure, including the third-order term in (2.161). However, we no longer assume the phase to be exactly stationary. The values ω_0 and α_0 correspond to the value U_0 for which

$$\frac{dU_0}{d\alpha} = 0 \tag{2.176}$$

but we allow for a spread of values in x and t. Thus we use the expansion

$$\alpha x - \omega t = \alpha_0 x - \omega_0 t + (\alpha - \alpha_0)(x - t U_0) - \tfrac{1}{6}(\alpha - \alpha_0)^3 \frac{d^2 U_0}{d\alpha^2} t + \cdots \tag{2.177}$$

and
$$\Phi = F(\alpha_0) e^{i(\alpha_0 x - \omega_0 t)} \int_{-\infty}^{+\infty} e^{i(a\xi - b\xi^3)} d\xi \tag{2.178}$$

with
$$a = x - U_0 t \tag{2.179}$$

$$b = \tfrac{1}{6} t \frac{d^2 U_0}{d\alpha^2} \tag{2.180}$$

In other words, (2.178) and (2.176) define an amplitude-modulated wave, whereas (2.165) and (2.160) define a frequency-modulated disturbance. This amplitude modulation implies a finite bandwidth, i.e., arrivals of frequency $\omega \neq \omega_0$ at times $t \neq t_0$, implicitly included in (2.178).

The validity of the approximation (2.178) may be explored by including higher-order terms in (2.177) and evaluating the size of the corrections thus obtained. This has been done, in particular, by Pekeris[12] in connection with a problem of special interest to us (Chap. 4). He shows that (2.178) is valid as long as $t - t_0$ is not too great. In that case, it also appears that as soon as (2.178) becomes inaccurate, (2.165) takes over quite satisfactorily. Nevertheless, caution must be used when applying the method, and the errors should be investigated in each particular case. A really general, thorough study of these questions is lacking.

In Eq. (2.178) one recognizes the Airy integral, which is discussed in Watson's book.[13] Applying a classic formula,[12,13] *the Airy phase* is

$$\Phi = F(\alpha_0) \cos (\alpha_0 x - \omega_0 t) \frac{2\pi}{3|2b|^{1/3}} E(v) \tag{2.181}$$

with $$v = 2(3)^{-3/2}|a|^{3/2}|b|^{-1/2} \tag{2.182}$$

and $$E(v) = v^{1/3} [J_{1/3}(v) + J_{-1/3}(v)] \qquad ab > 0 \tag{2.183}$$

$$E(v) = v^{1/3} [I_{1/3}(v) - I_{-1/3}(v)] \qquad ab < 0 \tag{2.184}$$

These formulas bring out a number of interesting points.

Equation (2.181) defines a wave packet with a pronounced amplitude maximum near $v = 0.7$ (Fig. 2.11). Thus, corresponding to stationary values of the group velocity, one sees conspicuous large-amplitude wave groups [provided, of course, that $F(\alpha)$ does not happen to have a strong minimum at $\alpha = \alpha_0$ as would be the case in stop-band filtering]. In addition, since $E(v)$ is a function of v only, the amplitude of the group is propor-

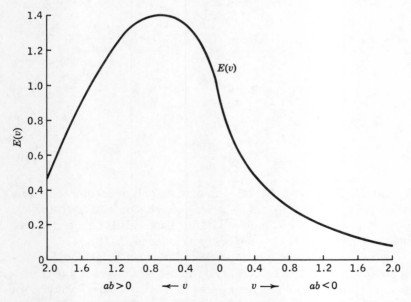

Fig. 2.11   The Airy-phase envelope $E(v)$ [Eqs. (2.183) and (2.184)]: $ab > 0$ corresponds to arrivals following a group velocity maximum or preceding a group velocity minimum.

tional to $b^{-1/3}$, that is, to $x_0^{-1/3}U_0^{1/3}$ approximately.   At other frequencies the amplitudes are, by Eq. (2.165), proportional to $x_0^{-1/2}U_0^{1/2}$.   Therefore, as a dispersive wave train travels outward from its source, not only will there appear prominent wave groups corresponding to frequencies for which (2.176) holds, but also the relative importance of these groups will increase with range like $x^{1/6}$.   This is an important result since it enables one, from a cursory examination of the $\omega(\alpha)$ or $U(\alpha)$ curves, to predict the arrival times and approximate frequencies of the major wave packets due to a transient source.   Conversely, experimental records may be used to infer the stationary values of the group velocity.

Next we see that, for given $x = x_0$

$$a = x_0 - U_0t = U_0(t_0 - t) \tag{2.185}$$

t_0 being the arrival time of the frequency ω_0 for which (2.176) holds.   Thus, for $U_0 = U_{max}$, times $t > t_0$, that is, $a < 0$, correspond to arrivals later than the one traveling with maximum group velocity.   For $U_0 = U_{min}$, times $t < t_0$, that is, $a > 0$, are arrivals preceding the group-velocity minimum. On the other hand, the sign of b [Eq. (2.180)] is that of $d^2U/d\alpha^2$; it is $-$ for U_{max} and $+$ for U_{min}.   Therefore, in Eq. (2.183) the condition $ab > 0$ implies arrivals preceding the "last arrival" or following the "first arrival" (assuming only one maximum and one minimum U).   But $ab < 0$ in Eq. (2.184) describes the tail end or *coda* of the last arrival at times $t > x_0/U_{min}$, or a *precursor* of the first arrival $t < x_0/U_{max}$.   Clearly, these arrivals do not fit into our scheme of things.   In particular, the existence of a precursor, with no sharp beginning, is troublesome as a matter of general principle.†   For large v, a well-known asymptotic result[13] is

$$I_{-1/3}(v) - I_{1/3}(v) \approx 3^{1/2}\pi^{-1/2}2^{-1/2}v^{-1/2}e^{-v} \tag{2.186}$$

so that actually $E(v)$ vanishes quite rapidly in this region.

Another observation concerns the effective bandwidth of the wave packet (2.181).   From Eqs. (2.185), (2.182), and (2.180) we see that, for given $v = v_M$

$$|t - t_0| = \Delta t = v_M^{2/3}2^{-1}3^{2/3}U_0^{-2/3}x_0^{1/3}\left|\frac{d^2U}{d\omega^2}\right|^{1/3} \tag{2.187}$$

This is a measure, for a given x_0, of the actual time interval corresponding to a range of values $0 \leq v \leq v_M$.

On the other hand, a Taylor series expansion of $U(\omega)$ near $\omega = \omega_0$ is

$$U = U_0 + \tfrac{1}{2}(\Delta\omega)^2\frac{d^2U}{d\omega^2} + \cdots \tag{2.188}$$

† This difficulty is due to the neglect of a large part of the spectrum in evaluating (2.159).   It will probably be encountered in any approximate evaluation.

using
$$t_0 = \frac{x_0}{U_0}$$

$$t = t_0 + \Delta t = \frac{x_0}{U} \tag{2.189}$$

and solving (2.188) for $\Delta\omega$ gives

$$\Delta\omega \simeq 2^{1/2} U_0 x_0^{-1/2} \left| \frac{d^2 U}{d\omega^2} \right|^{-1/2} |\Delta t|^{1/2} \tag{2.190}$$

that is, from (2.187)

$$\Delta\omega \simeq v_M^{1/3} 3^{1/3} U^{2/3} x^{-1/3} \left| \frac{d^2 U}{d\omega^2} \right|^{-1/3} \tag{2.191}$$

and, therefore,

$$\Delta\omega\, \Delta t \simeq \tfrac{3}{2} v_M \tag{2.192}$$

We thus have an approximate relationship between the bandwidth and the duration of a wave packet traveling past $x = x_0$, depending upon our choice of v_M. Figure (2.11) shows that for $v_M \approx 2$, the amplitude is about e^{-1} of its maximum value. We may, therefore, choose $v_M = 2$ as defining the effective time width of the packet [since, in the exponential region, Eq. (2.184), the amplitude dies off fast] and

$$\Delta\omega\, \Delta t \simeq 3 \tag{2.193}$$

This simply states that for a wave packet of long duration the bandwidth is small, and vice versa. Equations (2.187) and (2.191) show that for large $|d^2 U/d\omega^2|$, $\Delta\omega$ is small and Δt large; for a sharply peaked group-velocity curve one observes a ringing effect, i.e., a long, almost harmonic wave train. Conversely, for small $|d^2 U/d\omega^2|$, that is, for a broad, flat $U(\omega)$ curve, one has a concentrated wave packet with few oscillations. This is, of course, in agreement with the *classical uncertainity principle* for pulses which states that the effective bandwidth and duration must satisfy the inequality†

$$\Delta\omega\, \Delta t \geq 1 \tag{2.194}$$

† This rule, which has long been familiar to electrical engineers, is simply a well-known qualitative law in Fourier analysis.[14] It does *not* have the definiteness of Heisenberg's principle for quantum theory because the latter involves observables whose averages and statistical dispersion can be unambiguously defined in view of the statistical meaning of the Schrödinger wave function; the quantum uncertainty relations then follow from Schwartz's theorem.[15] It is not possible to pursue an analogous reasoning to derive (2.194) without introducing some *ad hoc* averaging procedure, so that this relationship does not acquire the absolute significance it has in quantum theory.

The distortion of a pulse upon total reflection is also essentially a dispersion phenomenon. Thus, if total reflection occurs, and the reflection coefficient is

$$\mathcal{R} = -e^{2i\chi} = e^{i\varphi} \tag{2.195}$$

$$\varphi = 2\chi \pm \pi \tag{2.196}$$

where χ is given by Eq. (2.90) and depends only upon the angle of incidence. The reflected plane wave can be written as

$$\Phi_{\text{refl}} = e^{i[\alpha x - \gamma z - \omega(t-\tau)]} \tag{2.197}$$

where

$$\tau = \frac{\varphi}{\omega} \tag{2.198}$$

represents a delay. Since φ is frequency independent, it follows that this delay varies inversely with the frequency, and one may expect the pulse to be deformed or dispersed upon total reflection. As an example, consider a plane delta-function pulse:

$$\Phi_{\text{inc}} = \delta(c_1 t - r) = \frac{1}{\pi} \int_0^\infty \cos k(c_1 t - r)\, dk \tag{2.199}$$

where r is the distance along the ray, counted from some arbitrary origin. The reflection is then

$$\Phi_{\text{refl}} = \frac{1}{\pi} \int_0^\infty \cos\,[k(c_1 t - r) + \varphi]\, dk \tag{2.200}$$

Since φ does not depend upon k, we have

$$\Phi_{\text{refl}} = \frac{1}{\pi} \cos\varphi \int_0^\infty \cos k(c_1 t - r)\, dk - \frac{1}{\pi} \sin\varphi \int_0^\infty \sin k(c_1 t - r)\, dk \tag{2.201}$$

$$\Phi_{\text{refl}} = \cos\varphi[\delta(c_1 t - r)] - \sin\varphi \cdot P\left(\frac{1}{c_1 t - r}\right) \tag{2.202}$$

where P stands for principal part of, and is a function encountered in radiation theory [cf. Heitler[16]]. Thus $P(1/x)$ is a function which becomes very large for small x and tends to zero like $1/x$ as $x \to \infty$. The pulse has, upon total reflection, acquired an infinitely long "tail."

However $P(1/x)$ is defined for $x > 0$ and $x < 0$, and equation (2.202) implies a precursor disturbance starting at $t = -\infty$! There is a physical reason for this. Consider a spherical wave front emitted by a point source in medium (1) $c = c_1$, overlying medium (2) $c = c_2 > c_1$ (Fig. 2.12). If the receiver is relatively close, the reflected arrival corresponds to angles of incidence less than critical and one observes a direct arrival followed by a

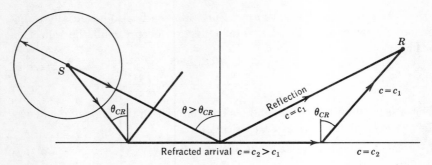

Fig. 2.12 For large source-receiver distances, the refracted arrival leads the reflection by a large amount. If S is removed to infinity in the direction of the light arrow, all wave fronts become plane and the refracted arrival becomes the precursor of Eq. (2.202), leading the reflection by an infinite amount.

reflection. But if the receiver is sufficiently distant, the reflection corresponds to angles of incidence greater than critical and one sees a precursor arrival. This arrival corresponds to a narrow beam incident at the critical angle and diffracted along a grazing path with the velocity c_2. For large source-receiver spacing, this so-called *refracted arrival* leads all other arrivals by a large amount—indeed the lead is obviously proportional to the source-receiver distance. This picture is somewhat oversimplified, but gives the correct answer for the travel time of the leading edge of the first arrival.[3] We see, therefore, that as the source is removed to infinity and the wave fronts become plane, the refracted precursor acquires an infinite advance over all other arrivals; this explains the precursor of infinite duration given by the second term in Eq. (2.202). Nevertheless it is still correct to consider the reflected pulse proper as being proportional only to $P(1/r - c_1 t)$, $t \geq r/c_1$ (Fig. 2.13). One may even ignore the precursor entirely by assuming a narrow beam rather than a plane wave front. This effect has been confirmed experimentally by Arons and Yennie.[17]

2.9 THE W.K.B. APPROXIMATION

This method is useful in dealing with stratified media whenever c varies slowly enough [criterion: Eq. (2.213)]. Starting from the separated equation (2.16), we write

$$\phi = \rho e^{is} \tag{2.203}$$

Substituting into (2.16), and separating real and imaginary parts,

$$\rho_{zz} - \rho(s_z{}^2 - \gamma^2) = 0 \tag{2.204}$$

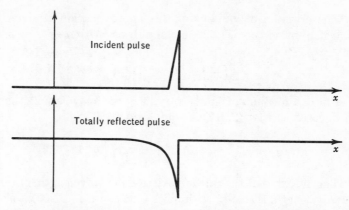

Incident pulse

Totally reflected pulse

Fig. 2.13 Schematic of total reflection of narrow pulse approximating a delta function.

$$\rho s_{zz} + 2\rho_z s_z = 0 \qquad (2.205)$$

where subscripts indicate differentiation.

Equation (2.205) gives

$$\rho = A s_z^{-1/2} \qquad (2.206)$$

A being a constant of integration. So far, we have made no approximations.

The standard approximation consists in assuming that the first term in (2.204) is negligible, i.e., that

$$\left| \frac{1}{\gamma^2} \frac{\rho_{zz}}{\rho} \right| \ll 1 \qquad (2.207)$$

We examine the meaning of this inequality below, but first we shall look at its consequences. By (2.204),

$$s_z{}^2 = \gamma^2 \qquad (2.208)$$

and

$$s = \pm \int_{z_0}^{z} \gamma \, dz + s_0 \qquad (2.209)$$

Equation (2.203) represents a progressive "plane" wave solution, in the sense defined in Sec. 2.4.

$$\phi = A\gamma^{-1/2} e^{is} \qquad (2.210)$$

is the corresponding *W.K.B. approximation*, also known as the *plane-wave ray solution*, since in this context they coincide (Sec. 2.10).

The corresponding modes are the standing waves obtained by superposing up- and down-going waves, e.g.,

$$\phi = A\gamma^{-1/2} \sin s \qquad (2.211)$$

The criterion of validity of this approximation is given by Eq. (2.207), which, by virtue of (2.206), can also be written as

$$\left| \frac{1}{\gamma^2} \frac{d^2}{dz^2} \log \gamma - \frac{1}{\gamma^2} \left(\frac{d}{dz} \log \gamma \right)^2 \right| \ll 1 \tag{2.212}$$

But in a medium of slowly varying γ, one may assume that locally γ varies linearly, so that (2.212) is equivalent to

$$\frac{1}{\gamma} \left| \frac{d}{dz} \log \gamma \right| \ll 1 \tag{2.213}$$

This means that the rate of variation per wavelength, of the z component of wavelength, is small. It implies that ρ in Eq. (2.203) is slowly varying.

For *steep rays and high frequencies* $k = \omega/c \gg \alpha$ and $\gamma \simeq \omega/c$. Then (2.213) becomes

$$\frac{1}{\omega} \frac{dc}{dz} = \frac{1}{2\pi} \frac{\lambda}{c} \frac{dc}{dz} \ll 1 \tag{2.214}$$

where λ is the wavelength along the ray. This illustrates the high-frequency, low-gradient nature of the approximation.

In some texts and manuals one may find (2.214) as the criterion of validity of the W.K.B. and ray approximations. This is incorrect. Condition (2.214) is necessary but not sufficient. For example, it may hold near *a turning point* $\gamma = 0$, at which (2.213) fails since as $\gamma \to 0, \frac{1}{\gamma} |(d/dz) \log \gamma| \to \infty$. Here the W.K.B. and ray approximations break down.† There is a perfectly obvious physical interpretation to this breakdown. Thus we saw, in Sec. 2.5, that when (2.213) is satisfied, the plane-wave reflection coefficient referred to some level z is $\Re(z_0)e^{2is}$; that is, the effect of a continuously variable c is assumed to be simply a change in phase along a curved ray path. In this approximation, one takes account of the ray curvature but not of the continuous process of reflection occurring along the ray. One may view a continuous c law as a superposition of a great many infinitesimal layers with sound velocities $c_0 + dc, c_0 + 2dc$, etc. At each boundary there is a reflection; in the W.K.B.-ray approximation this is assumed to be negligible. But near a turning point, the ray is almost horizontal, and, no matter how small the contrast dc in velocities, this partial reflection tends to become total as grazing angles are approached. Therefore, near $\gamma = 0$ it is no longer proper to consider this partial reflec-

---

† The exact wave function and its derivatives are perfectly well-behaved at turning points. Only the W.K.B. and ray approximations behave pathologically near $\gamma = 0$ owing to their being specifically designed to hold good at points far removed from $\gamma = 0$.

tion process as negligible; there is an appreciable smearing out of the energy originally contained in a narrow beam of rays.

However, this phenomenon is primarily of importance in calculating amplitudes near a turning point. As has been pointed out in Sec. 2.5, its effect upon the *phase* of a wave thus totally reflected at a turning point may be included quite accurately by taking $s_0 = \pi/4$ in (2.209), that is, by assuming that the net effect is to introduce the equivalent of a $\pi/2$ change in phase upon total reflection. With this assumption, the characteristic equation (2.142) for guided waves takes on a simple form even when turning points are present. Thus, for a turning point at $z = z_T$, we have approximately from (2.119)

$$\theta \downarrow = -\int_{z_T}^{0} \gamma \, dz + \frac{\pi}{4} \tag{2.215}$$

if there is also one at $z = -z'_T$,

$$\theta \uparrow = -\int_{0}^{-z'_T} \gamma \, dz + \frac{\pi}{4} \tag{2.216}$$

and (2.142) is
$$\int_{-z'_T}^{z_T} \gamma \, dz + \frac{\pi}{2} = m\pi \tag{2.217}$$

in which we recognize the Bohr-Sommerfeld[1] approximation for the eigenvalues of a potential well.

Equation (2.217) turns out to be surprisingly accurate in practice; but unfortunately, there is no method for estimating in advance the errors incurred in its use. For the range of frequencies involved here, and for typical oceanic sound channels, it gives results accurate to five significant figures or better. There are even cases, such as the symmetric channel

$$c = (az^2 + b)^{-1/2} \tag{2.218}$$

for which (2.217) gives exact answers—a fact well known to quantum physicists (the quantized oscillator).

Note that Eq. (2.217) allows a spread of values for α_m; that is, $\omega/c_{max} \leq \alpha \leq \omega/c_{min}$ is small in the case of the weak channels encountered in practice. For high frequencies, moreover, the total number of modes M may still be quite large. Thus, the interval between neighboring eigenvalues is small; α_m becomes an almost continuous function of m. Taking (2.217) and differentiating with respect to m, keeping ω constant, one has

$$\alpha_m \, \Delta\alpha_{m-1,m} \int_{-z'_T}^{z_T} \frac{dz}{\gamma} \simeq \pi \tag{2.219}$$

$$\frac{2\pi}{\Delta\alpha_{m-1,m}} \simeq 2\alpha_m \int_{-z'_T}^{z_T} \frac{dz}{\gamma} = 2\int_{-z'_T}^{z_T} \tan\theta \, dz \tag{2.220}$$

a result which we will find useful later.

2.10 RAY OPTICS

In Sec. 2.8 we indicated that in the case of "plane" waves (in the sense of Sec. 2.4) in stratified media, the ray solution and W.K.B. approximation are the same thing.   However, the ray method has a broader meaning in general, since its usefulness is by no means confined to stratified media.   It also differs from the W.K.B. approach in the method of calculating the field of a source.

In the general case, the transition from wave theory to ray optics is effected as follows: In the harmonic case,

$$\nabla^2\Phi = -k^2\Phi \tag{2.221}$$

One defines

$$\Phi = Ae^{iS} \tag{2.222}$$

where S is the *eikonal*. Substituting into (2.221) and collecting real and imaginary terms,

$$\nabla^2 A - (S_x{}^2 + S_y{}^2 + S_z{}^2)A + k^2 A = 0 \tag{2.223}$$

$$2\,\nabla A \cdot \nabla S + A\,\nabla^2 S = 0 \tag{2.224}$$

These equations are exact and are generalizations of Eq. (2.204) and (2.205) to three dimensions.

The first assumption usually made in ray optics is

$$\frac{\nabla^2 A}{A} \ll k^2 \tag{2.225}$$

which is simply the generalization of (2.207).   This condition can usually be met if one is far enough from turning points and if the frequency is high enough.   Equation (2.223) then becomes

$$S_x{}^2 + S_y{}^2 + S_z{}^2 = k^2 \tag{2.226}$$

which is known as the *eikonal equation*.

The surfaces of constant phase, $S = $ constant, are the *wave fronts* and the normals to these, of direction cosines S_x, S_y, and S_z, are the *rays*. In this sense the concepts of wave front and ray are exact when used in the context of Eqs. (2.223) and (2.224).   It is only when the approximate equation (2.226) is used that they acquire an approximate character.

If we take a new system of coordinates ξ, η, and ζ,

$$d\xi = k\,dx$$
$$d\eta = k\,dy \tag{2.227}$$
$$d\zeta = k\,dz$$

The eikonal equation becomes

$$S_\xi{}^2 + S_\eta{}^2 + S_\zeta{}^2 = 1 \tag{2.228}$$

that is, in the ξ, η, and ζ space the rays are straight lines; these are geodesics in the ξ, η, and ζ space. Thus, if

$$d\sigma^2 = d\xi^2 + d\eta^2 + d\zeta^2 \tag{2.229}$$

it follows that

$$\delta \int d\sigma = 0 \tag{2.230}$$

where the variation δ is performed with fixed end points.

But by (2.227) and (2.229),

$$d\sigma^2 = k^2\,d\ell^2 \tag{2.231}$$

where

$$d\ell^2 = dx^2 + dy^2 + dz^2 \tag{2.232}$$

and (2.230) is

$$\delta \int k\,d\ell = \delta \int \frac{d\ell}{c} = 0 \tag{2.233}$$

where the integral obviously measures the travel time along a ray. In other words, the rays are, in real physical space, paths of stationary time; this is *Fermat's principle*. It allows one to construct the rays for any law $c(x,y,z)$, a process known as *ray tracing*. Actually, ray tracing is a difficult procedure whenever c varies appreciably in all three directions x, y, and z. The oceans are, fortunately enough, mostly stratified in the vertical direction, and most useful results are obtained from ray tracing in two dimensions with c a function of z only. In this case Fermat's principle reads

$$\delta \int \frac{d\ell}{c} = \delta \int \frac{1}{c} (1 + x_z{}^2)^{1/2}\,dz = 0 \tag{2.234}$$

and, applying the Euler-Lagrange equations,

$$\frac{1}{c} \frac{x_z}{(1 + x_z{}^2)^{1/2}} = a \tag{2.235}$$

a being a constant. But $x_z = \tan\theta$ and (2.235) is simply Snell's law:

$$\frac{\sin\theta}{c} = a \tag{2.236}$$

Integrating (2.235) gives the equation for the rays:

$$x = \pm a \int_0^z \frac{c\, dz}{(1 - a^2 c^2)^{1/2}} = \pm \int_0^z \tan \theta \, dz \tag{2.237}$$

For a cycling ray, with turning points at $z = z_T$ and $z = -z_T'$, (2.237) gives the horizontal distance between turning points (Fig. 2.14):

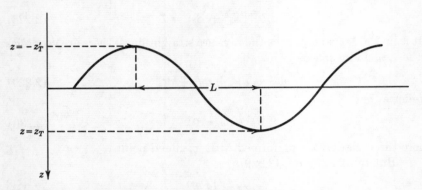

Fig. 2.14   Horizontal distance L between turning points of cycling ray.

$$L = \int_{-z'_T}^{z_T} \tan \theta \, dz \tag{2.238}$$

One of the simplest and commonly used $c(z)$ laws is

$$c = pz \tag{2.239}$$

Equation (2.237) then integrates as

$$x = \text{const} \pm \frac{1}{ap} (1 - a^2 p^2 z^2)^{1/2} \tag{2.240}$$

and the choice constant $= 0$ gives

$$x^2 + z^2 = \frac{1}{a^2 p^2} = R^2 \tag{2.241}$$

i.e., the rays are circles of radius $1/ap$ centered on the line $c = 0$. This makes the construction of the rays a very simple matter. The integration constant a is given by (2.236) and defines the particular ray in terms of its angle of incidence θ at some reference depth (Fig. 2.15).

The integral in Fermat's principle represents the time of the leading edge of a pulse. Thus, if we wish to calculate the time τ_{01} taken by the signal to go from z_0 to z_1 along a simple arc of the circular ray (2.241)

$$\tau_{01} = \int_{z_0}^{z_1} \frac{1}{pz} (1 + x_z^2)^{1/2} \, dz \tag{2.242}$$

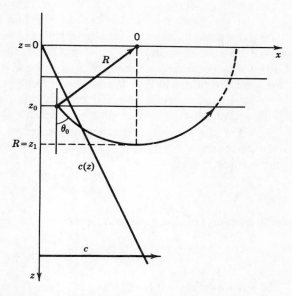

Fig. 2.15 Circular ray centered at $z = 0$ for case $c = pz$.

where, by (2.241)

$$x_z{}^2 = \frac{z^2}{R^2 - z^2} \tag{2.243}$$

Substituting in (2.242), and integrating,

$$\tau_{01} = -\frac{1}{p} \log \left(\frac{z_0}{z_1} \frac{1 + \sqrt{1 - z_1{}^2/R^2}}{1 + \sqrt{1 - z_0{}^2/R^2}} \right) \tag{2.244}$$

If $z = z_1$ is a turning point (Fig. 2.15),

$$z_1 = z_T = R \tag{2.245}$$

$$\frac{z_0}{R} = \sin \theta_0 \tag{2.246}$$

and

$$\tau_{0T} = -\frac{1}{p} \log \left(\frac{z_0}{R} \frac{1}{1 + \sqrt{1 - z_0{}^2/R^2}} \right) \tag{2.247}$$

$$\tau_{0T} = -\frac{1}{p} \log \frac{\sin \theta_0}{1 + \cos \theta_0} \tag{2.248}$$

The travel time for a full cycle (Fig. 2.15) is just $2\tau_{0T}$.

These times refer to the leading edge of a pulse, i.e., to first arrivals. The pulse actually changes form as it travels along these curved ray paths. If the rays are steep and the gradients weak, the change in shape is slight. But it may become appreciable when dealing with rays with turning points, for we have noted in Sec. 2.9 that a turning point is equivalent to total reflection with a change in phase of $\pi/2$. As pointed out in Sec. 2.8, this implies that a delta-function pulse $\delta(x)$ acquires a tail of the type $P(1/x)$.

For the harmonic case, the above travel times are easily converted to phase changes S. Thus, if the angular frequency is ω, for a path without turning points

$$S_{01} = \int_{z_0}^{z_1} 2\pi \frac{d\ell}{\lambda} = \omega\tau_{01} \qquad (2.249)$$

with turning point, e.g., a complete cycle, we write

$$2S_{0T} = 2\omega\tau_{0T} + \frac{\pi}{2} \qquad (2.250)$$

Thus, if we consider a plane wave in a homogeneous medium incident upon a stratified half-space with linearly increasing $c(z)$ (Fig. 2.4), the wave is totally reflected with reflection coefficient

$$R = e^{i\varphi} \qquad (2.251)$$

$$\varphi = 2S_{0T} = 2\omega\tau_{0T} + \frac{\pi}{2} \qquad (2.252)$$

and the delay upon total reflection, in the sense of Sec. 2.8, is, as one would expect, composed of two terms:

$$\tau = \frac{\varphi}{\omega} = 2\tau_{0T} + \frac{\pi}{2\omega} \qquad (2.253)$$

The first term corresponds simply to the travel time along the curved ray (frequency independent) from point of entry to emergence. The second term is inversely proportional to the frequency; it is the "delay upon total reflection" due to the turning point and produces a smearing out of the pulse.

The calculation of *field amplitudes* due to a source, i.e., of A, is in principle very simple. In the general case of an arbitrary $c(x,y,z)$ law, one may use the law of conservation of energy flux. By Eqs. (2.43) to (2.45) the energy flux is the vector

$$\mathbf{f} = -\rho\dot{\Phi}\nabla\Phi \qquad (2.254)$$

In the harmonic case,

$$\mathbf{f} = \rho\omega^3\Phi^2\mathbf{k} \qquad (2.255)$$

Consider a tube of rays (Fig. 2.16). The energy flowing in through $d\sigma_0$ must equal that flowing out through $d\sigma_1$:

$$\rho_0 \frac{\omega^4}{c_0} A_0{}^2 \, d\sigma_0 = \rho_1 \frac{\omega^4}{c_1} A_1{}^2 \, d\sigma_1$$

thus

$$A_1 = \left(\frac{\rho_0}{\rho_1} \frac{c_1}{c_0} \frac{d\sigma_0}{d\sigma_1}\right)^{1/2} A_0 \tag{2.256}$$

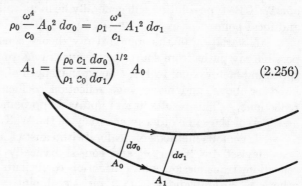

Fig. 2.16 Tube of rays. Conservation of energy flux through variable cross section $d\sigma$ gives law of amplitudes A.

Various schemes can then be applied for point-by-point calculation, e.g., in terms of the original point-source amplitude A, and $d\sigma_0/d\sigma_1$ is calculated as $\Delta\sigma_0/\Delta\sigma_1$ where $\Delta\sigma_0$ corresponds to a small solid angle of the initial spherical wave. The result (2.256) is, of course, also applicable to plane-wave calculations, the concept of plane wave being defined as in Sec. 2.5.

Clearly, the method fails in the vicinity of caustics and focal points, at which $d\sigma_1 \to 0$ (Fig. 2.17). Also, in stratified media, it breaks down at turning points (which are essentially plane-wave caustics) for the reasons shown in Sec. 2.9. Indeed, the whole question of the validity of the ray theory in stratified media has, to a considerable degree, been investigated in Sec. 2.9 in the context of the plane-wave W.K.B. approximation. In stratified media, the W.K.B. wave theory and the ray approximation start out with the same approximation; it is only in their methods of amplitude calculation that they differ substantially. Thus, as we shall see, the W.K.B. approximation is used in conjunction with exact point-source solutions, so that the only errors introduced into the calculation of fields are those accumulated through small discrepancies due to condition (2.213) not being exactly verified. In the usual ray theories, these errors are also present; but an additional source of error is found in Eq. (2.256) which becomes unmanageable near caustics and focal points. In W.K.B. wave theory, these errors are absent, and the calculation of acoustic fields near caustics and focal points presents no particular difficulties of principle. It is at the turning points that both the ray and W.K.B. methods break down, for the reasons explored in Sec. 2.9. Thus, ray methods are less accurate than

W.K.B. wave methods, although in cases for which *both* can be applied, there will be no really significant difference (see Chap. 5). The superiority of a W.K.B.-type solution will generally lie in its validity at caustic surfaces and focal points.

A variation of the standard ray theory consists in constructing all possible ray paths from source to receiver, weighting each with a spherical spreading factor equal to $1/\ell$, ℓ being the length of the path, a phase calculated as above, and plane-wave reflection coefficients (in case of sizable reflections). This results in an improved approximation, valid at caustics and foci, of the same order of accuracy as the W.K.B. wave solution.

Ingenious methods of dealing with caustics and turning points have been devised by Keller,[18] and consist basically in defining plane-wave reflection, transmission, and diffraction coefficients for cases which would otherwise be ambiguous from a ray standpoint. Thus the transmission through, and reflection by, a high-velocity "barrier" can be described in ray optics by means of suitable plane-wave coefficients,[18] which are not too difficult to derive.

A very useful *modified ray theory* has been systematically developed by Brekhovskikh[10] in his discussions of stratified media, caustics, and waveguides. It consists of the following steps:

One begins by recognizing the fact that the field of a harmonic point source radiating *spherical waves* into a homogeneous medium may be represented by a double summation of *plane waves* over all azimuths and angles of incidence. This equivalence is made obvious by the well-known integral transforms[10,13]

$$\frac{e^{ikR}}{R} = i \int_0^\infty \frac{e^{\mp i\gamma z}}{\gamma} J_0(\kappa r)\kappa \, d\kappa \qquad z \lessgtr 0 \tag{2.257}$$

$$J_0(\kappa r) = \int_0^\pi e^{i\kappa r \cos \vartheta} \, d\vartheta \tag{2.258}$$

$$R = (x^2 + y^2 + z^2)^{1/2} = (r^2 + z^2)^{1/2} \tag{2.259}$$

One notes, of course, that in view of (2.20) integration with respect to κ from 0 to ∞ or from 0 to k and k to ∞ is equivalent to integrating with respect to θ from 0 to $\pi/2$ and $\pi/2$ to $\pi/2 + i\infty$. Thus complex angles of incidence are included—this is a mathematical device, void of physical significance. But these also satisfy the boundary conditions, and Van der Pol and Bremmer[19] recognized that it is a simple matter to obtain an integral representation of the reflected spherical wave; one needs only to multiply each plane wave by the corresponding plane-wave coefficient. This simply means multiplying the integrand in (2.257) by this coefficient, expressed as a function of κ. Thus, consider Fig. 2.17. If the source is

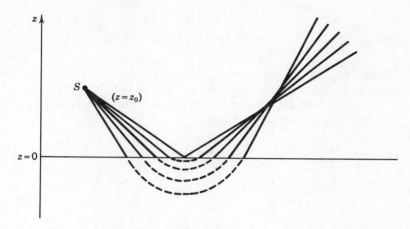

Fig. 2.17 Caustic produced by reflection of spherical wave from half-space with increasing sound velocity. S is the source.

located at $z = z_0$, z in (2.257) and (2.259) must be replaced by $z - z_0$. The reflection coefficient, referred to the level $z = z_0$, is, as explained in Sec. 2.5,

$$\Re = e^{2i\gamma z_0} \Re_0 \qquad (2.260)$$

where $\Re_0$ is the reflection coefficient at $z = z_0$. Thus the reflected field of the point source is

$$\Phi_{\text{refl}} = i \int_0^\infty \Re_0 \frac{e^{i\gamma(z+z_0)}}{\gamma} J_0(\kappa r)\kappa \, d\kappa \qquad (2.261)$$

In general, in order to obtain useful results one must now resort to approximation. Thus, one may assume first of all that $\kappa r \gg 1$, and in

$$J_0(\kappa r) = \frac{1}{2}[H_0^{(1)}(\kappa r) + H_0^{(2)}(\kappa r)] \qquad (2.262)$$

keep $H_0^{(1)}(\kappa r)$ only [as giving an outgoing wave in combination with $e^{-i\omega t}$ in (2.257)], with

$$H_0^{(1)}(\kappa r) = \sqrt{\frac{2}{\pi \kappa r}} \, e^{i(\kappa r - \pi/4)} \qquad (2.263)$$

If we then use the W.K.B. (or plane-ray) approximation for $\Re_0$, we have in the case of total reflection

$$\Re_0 = -e^{i(2s+\pi/2)} \qquad (2.264)$$

Equation (2.261) gives what Brekhovskikh[10] calls a ray approximation to the reflected field:

$$\Phi_{\text{refl}} = \frac{1}{\sqrt{2\pi r}} \, e^{i\pi/4} \int_0^\infty \frac{\kappa^{1/2}}{\gamma} e^{iW} \, d\kappa \qquad (2.265)$$

where
$$W = 2s + \kappa r + \gamma(z + z_0) - \frac{\pi}{2} \qquad (2.266)$$

This integral can be evaluated approximately by the method of stationary phase to give a description of the field at and near a caustic.

If, for example, we assume that the stratified half-space $z < 0$ in Fig. 2.17 is characterized by the law

$$\frac{1}{c^2} = \frac{1}{c_0{}^2} + pz \qquad z < 0 \qquad (2.267)$$

it follows from (2.209) that

$$s = \frac{2}{3\omega^2 p} \gamma^3 \qquad (2.268)$$

The equation

$$\frac{\partial W}{\partial \kappa} = -\frac{4}{\omega^2 p} \kappa\gamma - \frac{\kappa}{\gamma}(z + z_0) + r = 0 \qquad (2.269)$$

is simply a statement of the geometry of the ray paths (Fig. 2.18), and by virtue of (2.20) and (2.21)

$$r = (z + z_0) \tan\theta_0 + \frac{2}{pc_0{}^2} \sin 2\theta_0 \qquad (2.270)$$

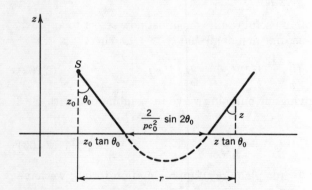

Fig. 2.18   Elements of ray-path geometry [Eqs. (2.269) and (2.270)].

the last term being, as in Eqs. (2.238) and (2.237),

$$2 \int_0^{z_T} \tan\theta \, dz = 2a \int_0^{z_T} \frac{dz}{(1/c^2 - a^2)^{1/2}} = \frac{2}{pc_0{}^2} \sin 2\theta_0 \qquad (2.271)$$

i.e., the distance between the points of entry and emergence of the ray in the stratified $z < 0$ section. The fact that we are dealing with a caustic would be stated by the equation

$$\frac{\partial^2 W}{\partial \kappa^2} = \frac{4}{\omega^2 p \gamma} (2\kappa^2 - k^2) - \frac{k^2}{\gamma^3} (z + z_0) = 0 \tag{2.272}$$

Eliminating κ from (2.269) and (2.272) gives the equation of the caustic.

Using (2.272) and $\partial k/\partial \kappa = \sin \theta_0$, one obtains

$$\frac{\partial^3 W}{\partial \kappa^3} = \frac{16}{\omega^2 p} \tan^2 \theta_0 \cotan 2\theta_0 \tag{2.273}$$

If we want a representation of the field as we go through the caustic region, we assume (2.272) to hold and $\partial W/\partial \kappa = \Delta r$ in

$$W = W_0 + (\kappa - \kappa_0) \frac{\partial W}{\partial \kappa} + \frac{1}{6} (\kappa - \kappa_0)^3 \frac{\partial^3 W}{\partial \kappa^3} + \cdots \tag{2.274}$$

where κ_0 is a function of z determined by (2.272). Substituting (2.274) into (2.265) we see that we get an Airy integral of the type (2.178). A little algebra gives for the end result[10]

$$\Phi_{\text{refl}} =$$

$$2^{-11/6} \pi^{1/2} 3^{-2/3} k^{1/6} p^{1/3} c_0^{2/3} r^{-1/2} \cos^{-1/3} \theta_0 \sin^{-1/6} \theta_0 \tan^{1/3} 2\theta_0 e^{i(W_0 + \pi/4)} E(v) \tag{2.275}$$

where
$$v = \tfrac{2}{3} |t|^{3/2}$$
$$t = \tfrac{1}{2} \Delta r (pc^2 k^2 \cot^2 \theta_0 \tan 2\theta_0)^{1/3}$$

for
$$\theta_0 > \pi/4 \,, \, t < 0$$

Δr being counted from the caustic positively toward the right. $E(v)$ has the same meaning as in Sec. 2.8, where (2.183) corresponds to $t < 0$ and (2.184) to $t > 0$. Thus, approaching a caustic from the illuminated side, one will observe oscillations of the field ($t > 0$). The field dies off exponentially into the shadow side (see Sec. 5.2, Figs. 5.17 and 5.18). Note that Eq. (2.275) gives $\Phi = \infty$ at $\theta_0 = \pi/4$. This is due to a somewhat unrealistic feature of Eq. (2.267), which not only gives $c = \infty$ for a finite negative value of z, but also produces a stationary value at $\theta_0 = \pi/4$ for the distance $(2/pc_0^2) \sin 2\theta_0$ between points of entry and emergence of a ray in the stratified section $z < 0$. This implies that the ray $\theta_0 = \pi/4$ is the asymptote of the caustic. Equation (2.273) shows furthermore that $\partial^3 W/\partial k^3$ vanishes when θ_0 approaches $\pi/4$, so that (2.275) is no longer valid. In practice this need not worry us, since caustic effects of this type in the ocean will be limited to the range $\theta_0 > \pi/4$.

REFERENCES

1. P. M. Morse and H. Feshbach: "Methods of Theoretical Physics," McGraw-Hill Book Company, New York, 1953.
2. M. A. Biot: *Phys. Rev.*, **105**:1129 (1957).
3. W. M. Ewing, W. S. Jardetzky, and F. Press: "Elastic Waves in Layered Media," McGraw-Hill Book Company, New York, 1957.
4. A. S. Ginzbarg and E. Strick: *Bull. Seism. Soc. Am.*, **48**:51 (1958).
5. R. Stoneley: *Proc. Roy. Soc. (London), Ser. A*, **160**:416 (1924).
6. M. A. Biot: *Bull. Seism. Soc. Am.*, **42**:81 (1952).
7. S. A. Shelkunoff: *Commun. Pure Appl. Math.*, **4**:117 (1951).
8. I. M. Longman: *Proc. Cambridge Phil. Soc.*, **52**:764 (1956).
9. H. Lamb: "Hydrodynamics," Dover Publications, Inc., New York, 1932.
10. L. M. Brekhovskikh: "Waves in Layered Media," Academic Press Inc., New York, 1960.
11. A. Erdélyi (ed.): "Tables of Integral Transforms," McGraw-Hill Book Company, New York, 1954.
12. C. L. Pekeris: *Geol. Soc. Am., Mem.* 27, 1948.
13. G. N. Watson: "Theory of Bessel Functions," Cambridge University Press, New York, 1922.
14. L. Brillouin: "Science and Information Theory," Academic Press Inc., New York, 1956.
15. H. Margenau and G. Murphy: "The Mathematics of Physics and Chemistry," D. Van Nostrand Company, Inc., Princeton, N.J., 1953.
16. W. Heitler: "The Quantum Theory of Radiation," Clarendon Press, Oxford, 1954.
17. A. B. Arons and D. R. Yennie: *J. Acoust. Soc. Am.*, **22** (2):231 (1950).
18. J. B. Keller: *Proc. Symp. Microwave Optics*, McGill University, Montreal, 1953; also, B. D. Seckler and J. B. Keller: *J. Acoust. Soc. Am.*, **31**:192 (1959).
19. Van der Pol and H. Bremmer: *Phil. Mag.*, **24**:825 (1937); and *Phil. Mag.*, **25**:817 (1938).

CHAPTER THREE

NORMAL MODES

3.1 GENERAL CONSIDERATIONS

Physicists and engineers in diverse fields have long been familiar with normal modes of vibration. As a rule, the concept is first introduced in the context of finite, discrete systems of masses and springs, vibrating molecules, etc. In this case it is shown that the motion of any conservative mechanical system near a configuration of stable equilibrium can be compounded of a finite number of harmonic vibrations of definite frequencies (eigenfrequencies).[1] These ideas are extended easily enough to bounded continua, examples of which are the acoustic modes of a room,[2] the characteristic modes of a crystal, the modes of oscillation of the earth, etc. In these cases there are infinitely many eigenfrequencies, but these are discrete (discrete spectrum). Somewhat more subtle, perhaps, is the application of normal mode concepts to unbounded continua. A well-known illustration is the treatment of the electromagnetic modes of infinite space used in the quantum theory of fields.[3] Here the frequencies may be dense and form a continuous spectrum. Biot and Tolstoy[4] have generalized the procedure to conservative, unbounded, mechanical media of any type, so that the normal mode concept may, in principle, be used to provide a unified point of view on the theory of all types of mechanical, electromagnetic, and electromechanical waves. In particular, it also gives us a method for the treatment of problems in underwater acoustics, one that emphasizes the intimate ties of this somewhat special field to other branches of physical theory.

In this chapter we shall review a few fundamental concepts and examine the meaning of normal modes and normal coordinates in acoustics. We shall formulate the general point-source problem and the excitation of acoustic modes in a number of simple cases, including some idealized ocean models.†

3.2 NORMAL MODES AND COORDINATES IN DISCRETE, FINITE SYSTEMS

Consider a conservative mechanical system in stable equilibrium having n degrees of freedom. If it is perturbed, it acquires a potential energy V which is, to the second order of small quantities, a positive definite quadratic form of the displacements η_i:

$$V = \tfrac{1}{2} \sum_{i,j} \eta_i V_{ij} \eta_j \tag{3.1}$$

† There exist other methods of treating the source problem. With one exception, they have been omitted from this text. Our purpose here is not to present a complete discussion of methods for the solution of problems, but to provide as much as possible a homogeneous account of acoustic wave propagation in the ocean.

The kinetic energy is

$$T = \tfrac{1}{2} \sum_{i,j} \dot{\eta}_i T_{ij} \dot{\eta}_j \tag{3.2}$$

The coefficients V_{ij} and T_{ij} define symmetric matrices.

Lagrange's equations for the system are

$$\sum_j T_{ij}\ddot{\eta}_j + \sum_j V_{ij}\eta_j = 0 \tag{3.3}$$

Assuming solutions of the form $e^{\pm i\omega t}$ we have

$$\sum_j (V_{ij}\eta_j - \omega^2 T_{ij}\eta_j) = 0 \tag{3.4}$$

This is a system of n linear, homogeneous equations in the η_i, the compatibility of which requires that the determinant of the coefficients vanish:

$$|V_{ij} - \omega^2 T_{ij}| = 0 \tag{3.5}$$

that is, an nth-degree algebraic equation in ω^2 having n real, positive roots.†
Let these roots, or eigenvalues, be $\omega_1{}^2, \ldots, \omega_m{}^2, \ldots$. One may then, for given ω_m, solve Eq. (3.4) to within an arbitrary multiplying constant. These solutions can be written in the form

$$\eta_{im} = q_m a_{im} \tag{3.6}$$

As the roots of Eq. (3.5) define the permissible frequencies of vibration of the system, so Eq. (3.6) describes its configurations at these frequencies.

The a_{im} form a fixed eigenvector in n space and the q_m are functions of time only.

It is not difficult to show that[1]

$$\sum_{i,j} T_{ij} a_{im} a_{jn} \delta_{mn} = \mu_m \delta_{mn} \tag{3.7}$$

δ_{mn} being the Kronecker delta. This is the orthogonality condition which states that in a space of metric tensor T_{ij} the vectors $\mathbf{a}_m$ are orthogonal. In this equation no choice of the multiplying constants inherent to the solution (3.6) has been made. These constants could be so chosen as to make the $\mathbf{a}_m$ unit vectors, in which case the μ_m in (3.7) would be unity (normalization). But we shall find it convenient to retain the μ_m explicitly. Since we are dealing with harmonic vibrations, we note that, to within a multiplying factor, μ_m is the *kinetic energy* of the vibration for $\omega = \omega_m$.

Using Eqs. (3.7), (3.6), and (3.4) one shows that[1]

$$\sum_{i,j} V_{ij} a_{im} a_{jn} = \mu_m \omega_m{}^2 \delta_{mn} = \pi_m \delta_{mn} \tag{3.8}$$

† For proofs of this and other statements see Goldstein.[1] The question of multiple roots (degeneracy) need not concern us here.

Equation (3.6) defines a change in coordinates from the η to the a systems. Equations (3.7) and (3.8) show that this is an orthogonal transformation which diagonalizes both T_{ij} and V_{ij} matrices.

In this new frame of reference the q_m represent the amplitudes of motion. Substituting (3.6) into (3.1) and (3.2) gives, by virtue of (3.7) and (3.8),

$$V = \tfrac{1}{2} \sum_m \pi_m q_m{}^2 \tag{3.9}$$

$$T = \tfrac{1}{2} \sum_m \mu_m \dot{q}_m{}^2 \tag{3.10}$$

And, in the absence of external forces, Lagrange's equations become

$$\mu_m \ddot{q}_m + \pi_m q_m = 0 \tag{3.11}$$

These are simple harmonic vibrations of angular frequency ω_m out of which all motions of our linear system can be compounded by superposition. These are the *normal modes* of the system, the q_m being the *normal coordinates*.

If a force $\mathbf{F}$ is acting on the system, the components Q_m of the generalized force in normal coordinate space are obtained from the principle of virtual work, which is equivalent to the statement that the scalar-vector product is invariant:

$$\mathbf{F} \cdot \delta \boldsymbol{\eta}_m = \mathbf{F} \cdot \mathbf{a}_m \delta q_m = Q_m \delta q_m \tag{3.12}$$

or

$$Q_m = \mathbf{F} \cdot \mathbf{a}_m \tag{3.13}$$

The equations of motion are then

$$\mu_m \ddot{q}_m + \pi_m q_m = Q_m \tag{3.14}$$

or, by (3.8)

$$\ddot{q}_m + \omega_m{}^2 q_m = \frac{Q_m}{\mu_m} \tag{3.15}$$

These equations are easy to solve for any form of the function $Q_m(t)$. Equation (3.6) then gives the complete solution in terms of the displacements η_i, in the form

$$\eta_i = \sum_m \eta_{im} = \sum_m q_m a_{im}$$

$$\tag{3.16}$$

and

$$\Phi = \sum_m \Phi_m$$

where Φ is any quantity linearly related to η, e.g., a displacement potential.

3.3 CONTINUOUS SYSTEMS. ONE-DIMENSIONAL FINITE ROD

An illuminating illustration of the transition from discrete systems to continua is provided by the longitudinal motions of mass points m located at intervals a along a spring of constant K.[1]   In the absence of end conditions the Lagrangian for such a system is

$$L = \tfrac{1}{2} \sum_i \left[m_i \dot{\eta}_i{}^2 - K(\eta_{i+1} - \eta_i)^2 \right] \tag{3.17}$$

η_i being the longitudinal displacement from equilibrium of the ith mass. One may factor out an a in Eq. (3.17), make $a \to dx \to 0$, $(\eta_{i+1} - \eta_i)/a \to \partial\eta/\partial x$, $m/a \to \rho$, and $Ka \to \lambda$. L becomes

$$L = \frac{1}{2} \int \left[\rho \dot{\eta}^2 - \lambda \left(\frac{\partial\eta}{\partial x} \right)^2 \right] dx \tag{3.18}$$

the integration extending over the complete system.   The term in brackets is the Lagrangian density.   The discontinuous index i is replaced by the coordinate x and the summation in (3.17) becomes an integral.   Application of the Euler-Lagrange equations gives

$$\rho \frac{\partial^2\eta}{\partial t^2} = \lambda \frac{\partial^2\eta}{\partial x^2} \tag{3.19}$$

This is the equation of longitudinal waves in a rod if we interpret λ as Young's modulus, or of acoustic waves in a tube if λ is the bulk modulus (2.2).

In the simple harmonic case, the independent solutions of (3.19) are the modes of the system:

$$\eta = q \sin \alpha x \tag{3.20}$$

or
$$\eta = q \cos \alpha x \tag{3.21}$$

with
$$\omega = \alpha c \tag{3.22}$$

It is not difficult to verify that if the kinetic- and potential-energy coefficients used in Eq. (3.17) are substituted into Eq. (3.5), the eigenvalues ω_m become dense as $a \to 0$, $m/a \to \rho$, and $Ka \to \lambda$, providing there are no end conditions.   In the limit, then, there are no limitations on ω.   Equations (3.21) and (3.20) are the modes of an infinite rod or acoustic tube.

Although in principle the transition of a finite discrete system with end constraints to a bounded continuum can also be performed, it is more difficult to carry out because, in physical systems, such constraints are not simply limited to the end particle but are distributed.   This difficulty is avoided by first passing to the limit $a \to 0$ with an infinite discrete system, as above, and then imposing the boundary conditions on the solutions for the continuum.

For the elastic rod or acoustic tube with rigidly held ends at $x = \pm l$, these conditions are that η vanish at $x = \pm l$. Thus, for the symmetric modes (3.21) one has

$$\alpha_m = (2m + 1)\,\frac{\pi}{2l} \tag{3.23}$$

$$\omega_m = \alpha_m c \tag{3.24}$$

These eigenvalues are the limits of the roots of the eigenvalue equation for the discrete system with rigidly held ends, as $a \to 0$. *The summations over the discrete indices i, j such as (3.13) and (3.7) are now replaced by integrations* with respect to the appropriate variable.

This completes the analogy between the discrete and continuous cases. We may now apply the techniques of Sec. 3.2, suitably modified, to the case of a continuous rod of finite length.

Suppose that a concentrated force is acting at the midpoint. We then need only the symmetric modes

$$\eta_m = q_m \cos \alpha_m x \tag{3.25}$$

The orthogonality condition (3.7) has the form

$$\mu_m = \rho \int_{-l}^{+l} \cos^2 \alpha_m x \, dx = \rho l \tag{3.26}$$

If the force is

$$F = \delta(x)\, \delta'(t) \tag{3.27}$$

$\delta'(t)$ being the derivative of the Dirac delta function, then

$$Q_m = \delta'(t) \int_{-l}^{+l} \cos \alpha_m x \, \delta(x)\, dx = \delta'(t) \tag{3.28}$$

The solution of Eq. (3.15) is[10]

$$q_m = \frac{1}{\rho l} \cos \omega_m t \tag{3.29}$$

Therefore, by (3.16)

$$\eta = \sum_{m=0}^{\infty} \eta_m = \frac{1}{\rho l} \sum_{m=0}^{\infty} \cos \alpha_m x \cos \alpha_m c t \tag{3.30}$$

$$\eta = \frac{1}{2}\frac{1}{\rho l} \sum_{m=0}^{\infty} [\cos \alpha_m (x - ct) + \cos \alpha_m (x + ct)] \tag{3.31}$$

This is easily recognized as the sum of two delta functions of arguments $x - ct$ and $x + ct$ and of period $2l$:

$$\eta = \frac{1}{2}\frac{1}{\rho}\sum_{n=0}^{\infty}[\delta(x - ct + n2l) + \delta(x + ct - n2l)] \tag{3.32}$$

i.e., we have obtained the complete solution as a sum of progressive transient arrivals corresponding to the direct arrival ($n = 0$) and an infinity of reflections ($n = 1, 2, \ldots$).

We have thus shown, by means of a one-dimensional example, the complete analogy between the normal modes of a continuum and those of a discrete case. Both represent the configurations of the permissible states of harmonic vibration of a system into which its motion can be analyzed. We saw how in the continuous case the equations of motion would reduce to a single partial differential equation, which we recognized as the wave equation. One could thus expect that if a disturbance were set up in the medium, it would create traveling waves. This we verified explicitly in the case of a finite bar; the solution (3.32) gives a succession of arrivals reflected back and forth between the boundaries. Equation (3.30) actually represents this progressive wave solution in terms of standing modes. Conversely, it may be noted that a normal mode of vibration may be considered as the superposition of traveling waves [Eq. (2.28)].

3.4 ACOUSTICAL SOURCES AND ENCLOSURES

In three dimensions the situation remains analogous, except that the mode indices, summations, or integrations may have to be double or triple. A good example is that of the acoustic modes of a room. But before we examine this problem, we must formulate the generalized forces associated with sources of sound. In the example of a one-dimensional rod in Sec. 3.3, we simply assumed an expression for the physical force without inquiring more closely into its character. In acoustic problems, the formulation of forces describing a sound source requires a little more attention.

We assume a three-dimensional mode system:

$$\eta_{mnp} = q_{mnp}a_{mnp} \tag{3.33}$$

In the case of a distribution of forces $\mathbf{f}$ over a surface s, Eq. (3.13) becomes

$$Q_{mnp} = \int_s \mathbf{f} \cdot \mathbf{a}_{mnp}\, ds \tag{3.34}$$

Consider a spherical volume V centered at some point x_0, y_0, z_0 (Fig. 3.1) which has been kept compressed from time $t = -\infty$ to $t = 0$. At $t = 0$

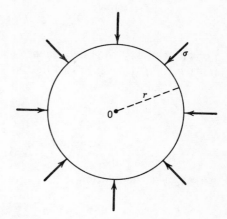

Fig. 3.1 Acoustical source. As $r \to 0$, this becomes a point source.

the constraining forces are removed. This assumes a surface stress σ on the sphere:

$$\mathbf{f} = -\sigma 1(-t) \tag{3.35}$$

with

$$1(-t) = \begin{cases} 1 & t < 0 \\ 0 & t > 0 \end{cases} \tag{3.36}$$

Equation (3.34) and Gauss' theorem give

$$Q_{mnp} = -1(-t)\int_s \sigma \mathbf{a}_{mnp} \cdot \mathbf{ds} = -1(-t)\sigma \int_V \nabla \cdot \mathbf{a}_{mnp}\, dV \tag{3.37}$$

For vanishing V this becomes

$$Q_{mnp} = -\sigma V 1(-t)(\nabla \cdot \mathbf{a}_{mnp})_0 \tag{3.38}$$

where the subscript 0 indicates that the divergence of $\mathbf{a}_{mnp}$ is to be taken at the point x_0, y_0, z_0.

Now, if ϵ is the volume change per unit volume and λ is the bulk modulus, Hooke's law states that

$$\sigma = \lambda \epsilon \tag{3.39}$$

Substituting in Eq. (3.38), we have the factor $\lambda \epsilon V$. But ϵV is simply the total increment of volume, so that this source corresponds to a sudden injection of volume ϵV. This simulates an instantaneous explosion at $t = 0$; at the instant of detonation, matter that had been previously constrained in a negligible volume is suddenly made to expand. A "unit" explosive point source, corresponding to the injection of a unit volume, is thus†

† As a consequence all formulas obtained in this chapter and describing the field of this source will carry an implicit factor of unity and of dimensionality V.

$$Q_{mnp} = -\lambda 1(-t)(\nabla \cdot \mathbf{a}_{mnp})_0 \tag{3.40}$$

For an arbitrary time dependence $g(t)$ of the decompression we need only replace $1(-t)$ by $g(t)$ in (3.40).

If we write

$$\Phi = q\Psi \tag{3.41}$$

$$\boldsymbol{\eta} = \nabla\Phi \tag{3.42}$$

$$\mathbf{a} = \nabla\Psi \tag{3.43}$$

we may use the relation

$$\nabla \cdot \mathbf{a} = \nabla^2\Psi = -\frac{\omega^2}{c^2}\Psi \tag{3.44}$$

to conclude that

$$Q_{mnp} = \lambda_0 1(-t) \frac{\omega^2}{c_0^2} (\Psi_{mnp})_0 \tag{3.45}$$

where the subscript 0 indicates that the corresponding quantities must be evaluated at the source point.   Equation (3.15) is

$$\ddot{q}_{mnp} + \omega_{mnp}^2 q_{mnp} = \mu_{mnp}^{-1} \lambda_0 \frac{\omega_{mnp}^2}{c_0^2} (\Psi_{mnp})_0 1(-t) \tag{3.46}$$

The solution of this equation is, to within an additive constant,[10]

$$q_{mnp} = \begin{cases} \mu_{mnp}^{-1}\lambda_0 \dfrac{\omega_{mnp}^2}{c_0^2} (\Psi_{mnp})_0 \dfrac{\cos \omega_{mnp}t}{\omega_{mnp}^2} & t \geq 0 \\ 0 & t < 0 \end{cases} \tag{3.47}$$

Also (using Green's theorem with the boundary conditions as in Sec. 2.3), the orthogonality integral is, by virtue of (3.7), (3.43), and (3.44),

$$\mu_{mnp} = \int_V \rho(\nabla\Psi_{mnp})^2 \, dV = \int_V \rho \frac{\omega_{mnp}^2}{c^2} \Psi^2_{mnp} \, dV \tag{3.48}$$

As pointed out in Sec. 3.2, this quantity is a measure of the kinetic energy of the mnp mode.

Consider the case of a room with rigid walls of lengths $2a$, $2b$, and $2h$ in the x, y, and z directions, with a source of the type (3.45) located at the center $x = y = z = 0$.   Clearly, only the modes giving symmetric pressures are excited:

$$\Phi_{mnp} = q_{mnp}\Psi_{mnp} = q_{mnp} \cos \alpha_m x \cos \beta_n y \cos \gamma_p z \tag{3.49}$$

with

$$\alpha_m = \frac{m\pi}{a}$$

$$\beta_n = \frac{n\pi}{b} \tag{3.50}$$

$$\gamma_p = \frac{p\pi}{h}$$

and

$$\omega_{mnp}{}^2 = c^2(\alpha_m{}^2 + \beta_n{}^2 + \gamma_p{}^2) \tag{3.51}$$

The normal modes (3.49) represent standing waves of frequency ω_{mnp} resulting from the interference of harmonic plane-wave trains reflected back and forth between the walls.

We have

$$\mu_{mnp} = \rho \frac{\omega_{mnp}{}^2}{c^2} \int_{-a}^{+a} dx \int_{-b}^{+b} dy \int_{-h}^{+h} \Psi_{mnp}{}^2 \, dz = \frac{\omega_{mnp}{}^2}{c^2} \rho abh \tag{3.52}$$

and it follows from (3.47) that

$$q_{mnp} = \frac{\lambda}{\rho abh} \frac{\cos \omega_{mnp} t}{\omega_{mnp}{}^2} \qquad t \geq 0 \tag{3.53}$$

and from (3.16)

$$\Phi = \sum_{m,n,p} \Phi_{mnp} = \frac{c^2}{abh} \sum_{m,n,p} \cos \alpha_m x \, \cos \beta_n y \, \cos \gamma_p z \, \frac{\cos \omega_{mnp} t}{\omega_{mnp}{}^2} \tag{3.54}$$

This is a classic result, reducing to†

$$\Phi = -\frac{1}{4\pi} \sum_n \frac{1}{R_n} 1\left(t - \frac{R_n}{c}\right) \tag{3.55}$$

where the R_n are simply distances from the field point x, y, z to the successive images of the source in the walls.

The corresponding pressure arrivals are a succession of pressure doublets:

$$p = \frac{\rho}{4\pi} \sum_n \frac{1}{R_n} \delta'\left(t - \frac{R_n}{c}\right) \tag{3.56}$$

This simple example shows how the normal mode methods are applied to a typical acoustic problem.

† Note the $1/4\pi$ factor.   For a harmonic time dependence $Be^{i\omega t}$ of the source, the solution is $(B/4\pi)(1/R)e^{-i(kR - \omega t)}$.   Thus, for a power output Π of a harmonic source, we use Eq. (2.50) with $A = B/4\pi$; that is, $B = (4\pi/\omega^2)(\Pi c/2\pi\rho)^{1/2}$.

3.5 UNBOUNDED CONTINUA. THE INFINITE SPACE

If all the walls of the room in Sec. 3.4 are removed to infinity, we obtain an infinite medium without boundaries. If only some of the walls are removed, we have a medium with boundaries, but extending indefinitely in some directions (rectangular waveguides, plane parallel waveguides, half-spaces, etc.).

For example, let us think of the length $2a$ as tending to infinity. We see from Eq. (3.50) that the difference between neighboring eigenvalues is

$$\Delta\alpha = \alpha_{m+1} - \alpha_m = \frac{\pi}{a} \tag{3.57}$$

This tends to zero continuously as $a \to \infty$, and one has in the limit a continuous set of eigenvalues α.† We may also express Eq. (3.57) as

$$a \to \frac{\pi}{d\alpha} \qquad \text{as } a \to \infty \tag{3.58}$$

In the process of removing the boundaries $x = \pm a$ to infinity, the orthogonality integral (3.52) diverges; i.e., the kinetic energy of a mode is no longer finite since a medium of infinite extent is being set into vibration. The kinetic energy per x wavelength, however, remains finite; i.e., the integrations with respect to y and z in (3.52) still converge. From the mathematical standpoint the divergence of the integral with respect to x is awkward, but it can be handled satisfactorily in a number of ways. For example, we may recall the analogy of Eq. (3.52) with the "box normalization" of quantum theory and we know[5] that the walls of the box can be expanded by using a delta-function technique due to Weyl. We prefer to use here the symbolic limiting procedure, often found in textbooks, in passing from orthogonal series expansions to the corresponding integral transforms.[6] In the present case this simply means using Eq. (3.58) at face value, i.e., saying that

$$\lim_{a \to \infty} \int_{-a}^{+a} \cos^2 \frac{m\pi}{a} x \, dx = \int_{-\infty}^{+\infty} \cos^2 \alpha x \, dx = \frac{\pi}{d\alpha} \tag{3.59}$$

If, for example, we also expand the other walls, we obtain from (3.52), (3.53), and (3.54)

---

† Note that equation (3.51) then becomes the eigenvalue equation for the rectangular waveguide with rigid walls, describing its geometrical dispersion.

$$\mu_{mnp} \rightarrow \mu = \frac{\omega^2}{c^2} \rho \frac{\pi^3}{d\alpha \, d\beta \, d\gamma} \tag{3.60}$$

$$q_{mnp} \rightarrow q = \frac{1}{\pi^3 \rho} \frac{\lambda \cos \omega t}{\omega^2} \, d\alpha \, d\beta \, d\gamma \tag{3.61}$$

and $\quad \Phi = \frac{c^2}{\pi^3} \int_0^\infty d\alpha \int_0^\infty d\beta \int_0^\infty \cos \alpha x \cos \beta y \cos \gamma z \frac{\cos \omega t}{\omega^2} d\gamma \tag{3.62}$

This is a well-known transform,[7] giving

$$\Phi = -\frac{1}{4\pi R} 1\left(t - \frac{R}{c}\right) \tag{3.63}$$

$$R = (x^2 + y^2 + z^2)^{1/2} \tag{3.64}$$

that is, the pressure wave is

$$p = \frac{\rho}{4\pi R} \delta'\left(t - \frac{R}{c}\right) \tag{3.65}$$

that is, a diverging spherical wave having a "doublet" time dependence. In practice, one would apply the result (3.59) directly to the modes of an infinite space:

$$\Phi = q \cos \alpha x \cos \beta y \cos \gamma z \tag{3.66}$$

$$\omega^2 = c^2(\alpha^2 + \beta^2 + \gamma^2) \tag{3.67}$$

and thus obtain Eq. (3.62).

Limiting formulas similar to Eq. (3.59) can be obtained for other coordinate systems. Thus, many problems in underwater acoustics have cylindrical symmetry and it is convenient to use cylindrical coordinates. One may then use the symbolic result

$$\int_0^\infty J_0^2(\kappa r) r \, dr = \int_0^\infty J_1^2(\kappa r) r \, dr = \frac{1}{\kappa \, d\kappa} \tag{3.68}$$

which can be justified by considering the radial modes of a circular membrane or cylinder which is expanded radially to infinity. Assuming symmetry and a source at the origin, the modes of an infinite medium expressed in cylindrical coordinates are

$$\Phi = q J_0(\kappa r) \cos \gamma z \tag{3.69}$$

$$\omega^2 = c^2(\kappa^2 + \gamma^2) \tag{3.70}$$

and
$$\mu = \rho \int_0^{2\pi} d\theta \int_{-\infty}^{+\infty} dz \int_0^{\infty} \frac{\omega^2}{c^2} J_0{}^2(\kappa r) \cos^2 \gamma z \, r dr \qquad (3.71)$$

using Eq. (3.68) and (3.59) this is

$$\mu = \rho \frac{\omega^2}{c^2} \frac{2\pi^2}{\kappa \, d\kappa \, d\gamma} \qquad (3.72)$$

and
$$q = \frac{c^2}{2\pi^2} \frac{\cos \omega t}{\omega^2} \kappa \, d\kappa \, d\gamma \qquad (3.73)$$

We thus find an alternative representation of Eq. (3.62):

$$\Phi = \frac{c^2}{2\pi^2} \int_0^{\infty} \cos \gamma z \, d\gamma \int_0^{\infty} J_0(\kappa r) \frac{\cos \omega t}{\omega^2} \kappa \, d\kappa \qquad (3.74)$$

Well-known transforms[7] enable us to verify that this result is identical to (3.62) and leads, therefore, to the spherical pressure wave (3.65).

3.6 PARTIALLY BOUNDED CONTINUA WITH CONTINUOUS AND DISCRETE SPECTRA

When, in the rectangular box of Sec. 3.4, we make $a \to \infty$ and $b \to \infty$ we obtain the perfect waveguide of Sec. 2.6 with walls at $z = \pm h$. If we change the z coordinates so that the boundaries are at $z = 0$ and $z = h$ and if we assume now that these are free surfaces, the modes are, in cylindrical coordinates,

$$\Phi_m = q_m J_0(\kappa r) \sin \gamma_m z \qquad (3.75)$$

$$\gamma_m = \frac{m\pi}{h} \qquad (3.76)$$

The orthogonality condition, Eq. (3.48), is

$$\mu_m = 2\pi\rho \int_0^h dz \int_0^{\infty} \frac{\omega_m{}^2}{c^2} \sin^2 \gamma_m z \, J_0{}^2(\kappa r) r \, dr \qquad (3.77)$$

This gives, by virtue of (3.68) and (3.76),

$$\mu_m = \pi\rho h \frac{\omega_m{}^2}{c^2} \frac{1}{\kappa \, d\kappa} \qquad (3.78)$$

If the source (3.45) is at $r = 0$, $z = z_0$ it follows that

$$q_m = \frac{c^2}{\pi h} \sin \gamma_m z_0 \frac{\cos \omega_m t}{\omega_m{}^2} \kappa \, d\kappa \qquad (3.79)$$

and, by (3.16)

$$\Phi = \frac{c^2}{\pi h} \sum_{m=1}^{\infty} \sin \gamma_m z \, \sin \gamma_m z_0 \int_0^{\infty} \frac{\cos \omega_m t}{\omega_m{}^2} J_0(\kappa r) \kappa \, d\kappa \qquad (3.80)$$

This is more easily evaluated by first differentiating:

$$\frac{\partial \Phi}{\partial t} = -\frac{c^2}{\pi h} \sum_{m=1}^{\infty} \sin \gamma_m z \, \sin \gamma_m z_0 \int_0^{\infty} \frac{\sin \omega_m t}{\omega_m} J_0(\kappa r) \kappa \, d\kappa \qquad (3.81)$$

The integral is a well-known transform,[7] giving

$$\frac{\partial \Phi}{\partial t} = -\frac{c}{\pi h} \sum_{m=1}^{\infty} \sin \gamma_m z \, \sin \gamma_m z_0 \frac{\cos \gamma_m \sqrt{c^2 t^2 - r^2}}{\sqrt{c^2 t^2 - r^2}} \qquad ct > r \quad (3.82)$$

This is an exact solution in terms of the modes. One sees that an alternate representation may be obtained by summing this series and noting that it is periodic in z, with period $2h$ as in the simpler example of Sec. 3.3 (see Appendix 2). The result is

$$\frac{\partial \Phi}{\partial t} = -\frac{1}{4\pi} \sum_n \left[\frac{1}{R_n} \delta \left(t - \frac{R_n}{c} \right) - \frac{1}{R'_n} \delta \left(t - \frac{R'_n}{c} \right) \right] \qquad (3.83)$$

$$R_n = [(z - z_0 + 2nh)^2 + r^2]^{1/2}$$
$$R'_n = [(z + z_0 + 2nh)^2 + r^2]^{1/2} \qquad (3.84)$$

Equation (3.83) represents the solution in terms of an infinite string of images, and will be discussed further in Chap. 4.

We see that in this problem the κ spectrum is continuous, whereas the γ spectrum is discrete; i.e., in Eq. (3.77) the integration with respect to r diverges, whereas it converges with respect to z. This fact has an obvious meaning in the light of our interpretation of μ as a kinetic energy. The waveguide traps the energy between two parallel walls $z = 0$ and $z = h$, and therefore the kinetic energy in a vertical slice is finite, corresponding to a discrete γ spectrum. The κ spectrum, on the other hand, is continuous, because any horizontal slice of the medium has infinite energy in the simple harmonic case. Clearly, this is a general feature of all propagation problems; finite energies correspond to discrete wave-number spectra, infinite energies to continuous spectra. This distinction is encountered in even more striking form in the following example, in which γ will have a continuous spectrum for certain ranges of ω and κ and a discontinuous one for others.

Consider a two-layered half-space with a free surface at $z = 0$. The boundary between the two fluids is at $z = h$. The sound velocities and densities of the two fluids are c_1, ρ_1 and c_2, ρ_2 (Fig. 3.2) [this model was first treated in detail by Pekeris[(8)]]. Suppose that $c_1 < c_2$. It is clear that plane waves in the top layer may be either totally reflected at $z = h$

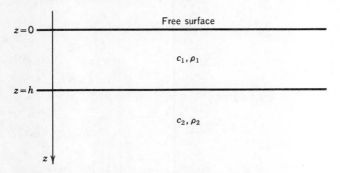

Fig. 3.2   For $c_2 > c_1$, this is the "Pekeris waveguide" for totally reflected waves.

$(\omega/\kappa < c_2)$ or partly transmitted $(\omega/\kappa > c_2)$. Thus, two distinct types of standing-wave patterns, or families of modes, can coexist:—

1.   Modes with amplitudes decreasing exponentially in the half-space $z > h$, but varying sinusoidally in the top layer. This corresponds to total reflection and trapping of energy in this layer (waveguide behavior). The energy in a vertical slice of the medium is finite and the γ spectrum is discrete.

2.   Modes with amplitudes varying sinusoidally throughout the medium, corresponding to partial reflection and transmission of energy at the interface $z = h$. The integral for the energy in a vertical slice of the model will not converge and the γ spectrum is continuous.

The first system, or *guided modes*, may be formulated thus:

$$\Phi_m = q_m \sin \gamma_{1m} z \, J_0(\kappa r) \qquad 0 \le z \le h \tag{3.85}$$

$$\Phi_m = q_m a \sin \gamma_{1m} h e^{-g_{2m}(z-h)} J_0(\kappa r) \qquad h \le z \tag{3.86}$$

where

$$a = \frac{\rho_1}{\rho_2} \tag{3.87}$$

and γ_1 and g have their usual meanings [Eqs. (2.17) and (2.82)]. m is the mode number, corresponding to the roots of the characteristic equation (2.136), where θ has the form (2.129) with $n = 1$:

$$\gamma_1 h + \text{Arctan} \, \frac{1}{a} \frac{\gamma_1}{g_2} = m\pi \tag{3.88}$$

As has been explained in Sec. 2.6, this is the condition that must be obeyed by ω, κ in order that (3.85) and (3.86) verify the boundary conditions (2.71) and (2.72) at $z = h$.

The orthogonality integral is

$$\mu_m = \omega^2 \int_0^{2\pi} d\theta \int_0^{\infty} J_0{}^2(\kappa r) r \, dr \left(\int_0^h \frac{\rho_1}{c_1{}^2} \sin^2 \gamma_{1m}z \, dz \right.$$
$$\left. + \int_h^{\infty} \frac{\rho_2}{c_2{}^2} a^2 \sin^2 \gamma_{1m}h \, e^{-2g_{2m}(z-h)} dz \right) \quad (3.89)$$

Equation (3.68) and an elementary integration give

$$\mu_m = \omega^2 \frac{\rho_1}{c_1{}^2} \frac{\pi}{\kappa d\kappa} \frac{1}{\gamma_{1m}} \left[\gamma_{1m}h - \cos \gamma_{1m}h \sin \gamma_{1m}h - \frac{c_1{}^2}{c_2{}^2} a^2 \tan \gamma_{1m} h \sin^2 \gamma_{1m}h \right] \quad (3.90)$$

and thus, for a source (3.45) at $z = z_0 < h$ and a receiver at $z < h$, we have, by (3.47) and (3.16)

$$\Phi = \frac{c_1{}^2}{\pi h} \sum_{m=0}^{\infty} \int_0^{\infty} \frac{\cos \omega_m t}{\omega_m{}^2} \frac{\gamma_{1m}h \sin \gamma_{1m}z_0 \sin \gamma_{1m}z \, J_0(\kappa r)\kappa \, d\kappa}{\gamma_{1m}h - \cos \gamma_{1m}h \sin \gamma_{1m}h - \dfrac{c_1{}^2}{c_2{}^2} a^2 \tan \gamma_{1m}h \sin^2\gamma_{1m}h} \quad (3.91)$$

for the guided waves in the upper layer excited by an "instantaneous explosion."

The second system, or *continuous-spectrum modes*, is easily seen to be

$$\Phi = q \sin \gamma_1 z \, J_0(\kappa r) \qquad 0 \le z \le h \quad (3.92)$$

$$\Phi = q \left[a \sin \gamma_1 h \cos \gamma_2(z - h) + \frac{\gamma_1}{\gamma_2} \cos \gamma_1 h \sin \gamma_2(z - h) \right] J_0(\kappa r)$$
$$z \ge h \quad (3.93)$$

This is the only other possible system of free modes obeying the boundary conditions (2.71) and (2.72) at $z = h$ and the free surface condition at $z = 0$.

Equation (3.48) gives

$$\mu = \rho_1 \frac{\omega^2}{c_1{}^2} 2\pi \int_0^{\infty} J_0{}^2(\kappa r) r \, dr \int_0^h \sin^2 \gamma_1 z \, dz$$

$$+ \rho_2 \frac{\omega^2}{c_2{}^2} 2\pi \int_0^{\infty} J_0{}^2(\kappa r) r \, dr \int_0^{\infty} \left[a \sin \gamma_1 h \cos \gamma_2(z - h) \right.$$
$$\left. + \frac{\gamma_1}{\gamma_2} \cos \gamma_1 h \sin \gamma_2(z - h) \right]^2 dz \quad (3.94)$$

In the first term on the right-hand side the integration from 0 to h converges. In the second term, the integral over z diverges. Therefore, we neglect the first term. In addition, we note that the cross-product term in the second integrand may also be dropped, since, if one considers $\int_h^\infty$ as $\lim\limits_{M\to\infty} \int_h^M$, we see that the contribution of this term oscillates between finite limits as M increases and it is therefore negligible in comparison with the divergent terms. Thus,

$$\mu = \rho_2 \frac{\omega^2}{c_2{}^2} 2\pi \int_0^\infty J_0{}^2(\kappa r) r \, dr \int_0^\infty \left[a^2 \sin^2 \gamma_1 h \cos^2 \gamma_2(z-h) \right. $$
$$\left. + \frac{\gamma_1{}^2}{\gamma_2{}^2} \cos^2 \gamma_1 h \sin^2 \gamma_2(z-h) \right] dz \quad (3.95)$$

and, using Eqs. (3.59) and (3.68),

$$\mu = 2\pi^2 \rho_2 \frac{\omega^2}{c_2{}^2} \frac{1}{\kappa \, d\kappa \, d\gamma_2} \left(a^2 \sin^2 \gamma_1 h + \frac{\gamma_1{}^2}{\gamma_2{}^2} \cos^2 \gamma_1 h \right) \quad (3.96)$$

and thus, by (3.47)

$$\Phi = \frac{ac_2{}^2}{2\pi^2} \int_0^\infty J_0(\kappa r) \kappa \, d\kappa \int_0^\infty \frac{\sin \gamma_1 z \sin \gamma_1 z_0}{a^2 \sin^2 \gamma_1 h + \dfrac{\gamma_1{}^2}{\gamma_2{}^2} \cos^2 \gamma_1 h} \frac{\cos \omega t}{\omega^2} d\gamma_2 \quad (3.97)$$

represents the excitation of the continuous-spectrum modes by the instantaneous explosion.

Similar expressions may be immediately written for $z_0 \lessgtr h$ and $z \geq h$ by simply replacing $\sin \gamma_1 z \sin \gamma_1 z_0$ in the integrands by the suitable form of the eigenfunctions.†

These results illustrate the physical and mathematical differences between discrete and continuous wave-number spectra. Discrete spectra correspond to waveguide phenomena, in which mode energy is trapped by total reflection. As long as there is no leakage of energy, the mode amplitudes tend to zero exponentially at infinity, the integration with respect to z converges, and the γ spectrum is discrete. On the other hand, if there is leakage or, more generally, if the mode amplitudes do not fall off sufficiently fast (e.g., sinusoidal modes), the corresponding spectrum will be continuous. From the mode standpoint this is the essential distinction between trapped waves on one hand and unconfined modes on the other. One is, of course, reminded of the analogous situation in quantum theory (discrete states for the stable case of a particle trapped in a potential well and continuous states for the metastable case and for scattering problems).

† The equivalence of our results to those of Pekeris will be taken up in Chap. 4 and in Appendix 3.

3.7 THE SIMPLE HARMONIC SOURCE

This type of source is often approximated in underwater acoustical devices and is extensively used for experimental purposes.

The problem may be formulated in various ways. For example, we know that for a time dependence $1(-t)$ of a compressional source (Sec. 3.4) concentrated at a point, the solution has a certain form. One may then, by Duhamel's theorem, obtain the solution for a harmonic source which is turned on at $t = t_0$. In this solution $\Phi(t,t_0)$, one could make $t_0 \to -\infty$. This would lead us to the solution for the "usual" sort of harmonic source which is assumed to have acted for all time. In this manner some very real difficulties of principle are bypassed; e.g., it would no longer be necessary to introduce additional *ad hoc* conditions to eliminate the incoming waves. One obtains a progressive divergent wave train.[4] But unfortunately this method is not very useful, because the integrals for $\Phi(t)$ cannot usually be evaluated in closed form, even for the simple explosive source in Sec. 3.4.

However, there is a standard procedure which, although physically unsatisfying, does lead to a correct and very general result. It consists in taking

$$Q = \lambda_0 \frac{\omega^2}{c_0^2} \Psi_0 g(t) \tag{3.98}$$

$$g(t) = A e^{i\omega_0 t} \tag{3.99}$$

Solving Eq. (3.15), one has

$$q = A\mu^{-1}\lambda_0 \frac{\omega^2}{c_0^2} \Psi_0 \frac{e^{i\omega_0 t}}{\omega^2 - \omega_0^2} \tag{3.100}$$

Assuming modes

$$\Phi = q\Psi = qJ_0(\kappa r)\phi(z) \tag{3.101}$$

and a source located at $r = 0$, $z = z_0$, one obtains when the z spectrum is discrete

$$\Phi = A \sum_m \int_0^\infty \lambda_0 \frac{\omega^2}{c_0^2} \frac{1}{\mu_m} \frac{e^{i\omega_0 t}}{\omega_m^2 - \omega_0^2} \varphi(z)\varphi(z_0)J_0(\kappa r)\kappa \, d\kappa \tag{3.102}$$

If the z spectrum is continuous, the solution will be of the form

$$\Phi = B \int_0^\infty d\gamma \int_0^\infty \lambda_0 \frac{\omega^2}{c_0^2} \frac{1}{\mu_m} \frac{e^{i\omega_0 t}}{\omega_m^2 - \omega_0^2} \varphi(z)\varphi(z_0)J_0(\kappa r)\kappa \, d\kappa \tag{3.103}$$

Note that $1/\kappa \, d\kappa$ has been factored out of the μ, so that in (3.102) and (3.103),

$$\mu_m = \omega^2 \int_{-\infty}^{+\infty} \frac{\rho}{c^2} \phi^2 \, dz \tag{3.104}$$

Equations (3.102) and (3.103) contain an improper integral which is dealt with by the following subterfuge:

Consider the integral

$$I = \int_0^\infty J_0(\kappa r) \frac{G}{\omega^2 - \omega_0^2} \kappa \, d\kappa \qquad (3.105)$$

Write

$$I = \frac{1}{2}\left[I_1 + I_2\right] = \frac{1}{2}\int_0^\infty \left[H_0^{(1)}(\kappa r) + H_0^{(2)}(\kappa r)\right]\frac{G}{\omega^2 - \omega_0^2} \kappa \, d\kappa \qquad (3.106)$$

and examine the behavior of I_1 and I_2 in the complex plane. Assume the propagation to be ever so slightly damped; the pole $\kappa = \kappa_0$ corresponding to $\omega = \omega_0$ becomes $\kappa = \kappa_0 - i\epsilon$, $\epsilon > 0$; that is, it is displaced off the real axis into the fourth quadrant. Since for $x = iu$, $H_0^{(1)}(x)$ vanishes like $u^{-1/2}e^{-u}$ as $u \to \infty$ and since $H_0^{(2)}(x)$ does the same for $x \to -i\infty$, we may group the contours of integration as indicated in Fig. 3.3, with convergent integrals along the imaginary axis. Referring to this figure, we see that

$$I_1 = -J_1 = \int_0^{i\infty} H_0^{(1)}(\kappa r) \frac{G}{\omega^2 - \omega_0^2} \kappa \, d\kappa$$

$$= -\int_0^\infty H_0^{(1)}(iur) \frac{G}{\omega^2 - \omega_0^2} u \, du \qquad (3.107)$$

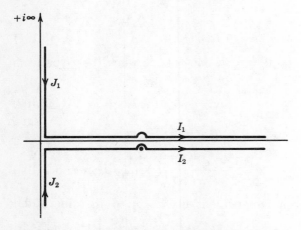

Fig. 3.3   Contours for evaluating Eq. (3.106).

and that

$$I_2 = -2\pi iR - J_2 = -2\pi iR + \int_0^{-i\infty} H_0^{(2)}(\kappa r)\frac{G}{\omega^2 - \omega_0^2}\kappa\, d\kappa$$

$$= -2\pi iR - \int_0^\infty H_0^{(2)}(-iur)\frac{G}{\omega^2 - \omega_0^2}u\, du \tag{3.108}$$

where R is the residue at the pole (or a sum of residues if there are several poles).

Since it is true that

$$H_0^{(2)}(-iur) = -H_0^{(1)}(iur) \tag{3.109}$$

the integrals in (3.107) and (3.108) cancel upon substitution into (3.106), and we obtain

$$I = -\pi iR \tag{3.110}$$

where, from the theory of residues, R is given by

$$R = H_0^{(2)}(\kappa_0 r)\frac{G(\omega_0,\kappa_0)\kappa_0}{2\omega_0(\partial\omega/\partial\kappa)_0} \tag{3.111}$$

Using the usual definitions of phase and group velocity [Eqs. (2.15) and (2.156)], this gives

$$I = -\frac{\pi i}{2}H_0^{(2)}(\kappa_0 r)\frac{G(\omega_0,\kappa_0)}{v_0 U_0} \tag{3.112}$$

When there are several poles, as in the case of a discrete spectrum, the result is

$$\Phi = A\sum_m I_m = -\frac{\pi i}{2}A\sum_m H_0^{(2)}(\kappa_m r)\,\lambda_0\,\frac{\omega^2}{c_0^2}\frac{1}{\mu_m}\frac{\varphi_m(z)\varphi_m(z_0)}{v_m U_m}e^{i\omega t} \tag{3.113}$$

where the κ_m are roots of the characteristic equation for $\omega = \omega_0$, and U_m and v_m the corresponding values of U and v.

But by (2.62) we know that

$$\sigma_m\, U_m v_m = \nu_m \tag{3.114}$$

where, by (3.104) and (2.61),

$$\sigma_m = \frac{\mu_m}{\omega^2}$$

and

$$\nu_m = \int_{-\infty}^{+\infty}\rho\varphi_m^2\, dz \tag{3.115}$$

ν_m being a measure of the mean energy flux per cycle. Thus we have

$$\Phi = -\frac{\pi i}{2}e^{i\omega t}\rho A\sum_m H_0^{(2)}(\kappa_m r)\frac{1}{\nu_m}\varphi_m(z)\varphi_m(z_0) \tag{3.116}$$

This is a very useful, classic result.[9] Our derivation brings out clearly the significance of the denominator in Eq. (3.116); the excitation of each mode by a harmonic source of frequency ω_0 is inversely proportional to the mean energy flux per cycle characteristic of that mode at that frequency.

For a given power rating Π of the source we multiply this solution by 4π (see Footnote, p. 73) and use the A given by Eq. (2.50). Using the asymptotic form

$$H_0^{(2)}(x) \simeq \sqrt{\frac{2}{\pi x}}\, e^{-i(x-\pi/4)} \tag{3.117}$$

we have, for large ranges $(\kappa r \gg 1)$,

$$\Phi = -i\,\frac{1}{\sqrt{r}}\frac{1}{\omega^2}\sum_m P_m e^{-i(\kappa_m r - \omega t - \pi/4)} \tag{3.118}$$

where
$$P_m = p_m\,\frac{1}{\rho_s}\,\varphi_m(z)\,\varphi_m(z_0)$$

$$\tag{3.119}$$

$$p_m = 2\pi(\rho_0 c_0 \Pi)^{1/2}\,\frac{\rho_s}{v_m\sqrt{\kappa_m}}$$

Here ρ_s is the layer density at the source depth and p_m is defined as the *excitation function*.

Keeping only the real part, one has

$$\Phi = \frac{\sin(\omega t + \phi)}{\omega^2 \sqrt{r}}\left\{\left[\sum_m P_m \cos\left(\kappa_m r - \frac{\pi}{4}\right)\right]^2 + \left[\sum_m P_m \sin\left(\kappa_m r - \frac{\pi}{4}\right)\right]^2\right\}^{1/2} \tag{3.120}$$

where
$$\phi = \operatorname{Arctan}\left[\frac{\sum P_m \sin(\kappa_m r - \pi/4)}{\sum P_m \cos(\kappa_m r - \pi/4)}\right] \tag{3.121}$$

The solution (3.118) represents M interfering wave trains having the same frequency ω_0, but different wave numbers κ_m. These interferences produce large pressure fluctuations, which we shall have occasion to study in some detail in later chapters. The pressure amplitude for long ranges will have the general form

$$p_a = \frac{\rho}{\sqrt{r}}\left\{\left[\sum P_m \cos\left(\kappa_m r - \frac{\pi}{4}\right)\right]^2 + \left[\sum P_m \sin\left(\kappa_m r - \frac{\pi}{4}\right)\right]^2\right\}^{1/2} \tag{3.122}$$

In the case of layered structures, ρ may be different for the source and receiver positions. In such a case, ρ_0 in (3.119) refers to the source position and ρ in (3.122) to the receiver position.

Note that (3.122) can be written

$$p_a = \frac{\rho}{\sqrt{r}} \sum_{n \neq m} \sum_m \left(P_m{}^2 + P_n{}^2 + 2P_n P_m \cos r \, \Delta\kappa_{mn} \right)^{1/2} \qquad (3.123)$$

a form which emphasizes the individual mode interferences, with

$$\Delta\kappa_{mn} = \kappa_m - \kappa_n \qquad (3.124)$$

When many modes m are excited, Eq. (3.123) may represent an extremely complex distribution of amplitudes (for examples, see Chap. 5). On the other hand, if the number of modes is small, the field has clearly identifiable wavelengths of oscillation $2\pi/\Delta\kappa_{mn}$, as we shall see in our discussions of shallow-water propagation (Chap. 4).

3.8 NORMAL MODES AND APPROXIMATIONS

In describing the propagation of sound in the oceans, one is always confronted with the necessity of making reasonable approximations. These may, generally speaking, be divided into two kinds.

Approximations of the *first kind* consist in idealizing the physical model, i.e., giving it properties which simplify the theoretical or numerical analysis of the problem. For example, one may neglect surface or bottom roughness, rigidity and viscosity of the bottom, etc. Approximations of the *second kind* are those made in the mathematical solutions for these idealized models, as in W.K.B. or ray-type methods. Thus, in Eqs. (3.91) and (3.97) used as solutions for the *shallow-water* propagation problem, only approximations of the first kind have been made; the model here is sufficiently simple so that approximations of the second kind are unnecessary.

But in describing the behavior of radiation from a point source in *deep water*, it is often necessary to appeal to both kinds of approximation. Thus, one first assumes a constant water depth. Second, all boundaries are taken to be smooth, horizontal planes. Third, the bottom sediment is treated as a liquid, preferably unstratified. Fourth and finally, the actual $c(z)$ ocean stratification is replaced by a manageable approximation in the sense that it leads to reasonably simple analytical or numerical formulas.

For example, a typical $c(z)$ profile such as that in Fig. 1.2 may be replaced by a layered section such as those in Figs. 3.4 and 3.5. In Fig. 3.4 each layer has a linear velocity $c = az + b$, whereas in Fig. 3.5 $1/c^2 = pz + q$. The first case is particularly well-adapted to ray techniques; as we have seen in Sec. 2.10, the rays are arcs of circles centered on the level $c = 0$ when c is a linear function of z. The exact solutions of the wave

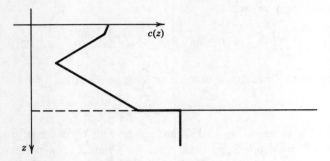

Fig. 3.4   Schematic linear-segment fit.

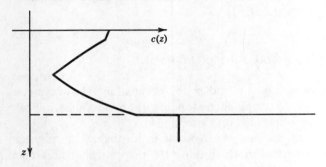

Fig. 3.5   Schematic fit by Eq. (3.125).

equation are linear combinations of Bessel functions whose order is a function of the frequency, and they are not easy to use.

The second case is more convenient for mode techniques, since the modes are expressible in terms of Bessel functions of constant order ($\pm\frac{1}{3}$). In such a model, one has in each layer,

$$c_i(z) = (p_i z + q_i)^{-1/2} \qquad z_i \geq z \geq z_{i-1} \tag{3.125}$$

and, if

$$\gamma_i = [\omega^2(p_i z + q_i) - \kappa^2]^{1/2} \tag{3.126}$$

$$\zeta_i = \frac{2}{3\omega^2 p_i}\gamma_i^3 \tag{3.127}$$

Eq. (2.16) becomes

$$\varphi_{\zeta\zeta} + \zeta\varphi = 0 \tag{3.128}$$

This is Stokes' differential equation, which has solutions of the type

$$\varphi_i = A_i\gamma_i J_{1/3}(\zeta_i) + B_i\gamma_i J_{-1/3}(\zeta_i)$$

$$\frac{\partial \varphi_i}{\partial z} = A_i\gamma_i^2 J_{-2/3}(\zeta_i) - B_i\gamma_i^2 J_{2/3}(\zeta_i) \tag{3.129}$$

for the illuminated (or insonified) region corresponding to real rays.

In the hyperbolic regions, we write

$$\eta_i = \frac{2}{3\omega^2 p_i} g_i^3 \tag{3.130}$$

where

$$g_i = [\kappa^2 - \omega^2(p_i z + q_i)]^{1/2} \tag{3.131}$$

and

$$\varphi_i = -A_i g_i I_{1/3}(\eta_i) + B_i g_i I_{-1/3}(\eta_i)$$

$$\frac{\partial \varphi_i}{\partial z} = A_i g_i^2 I_{2/3}(\eta_i) - B_i g_i^2 I_{2/3}(\eta_i) \tag{3.132}$$

J_ν and I_ν are Bessel functions of real and imaginary argument respectively. The A_i and B_i in each layer are easily deduced from each other by the conditions of continuity of φ_i and $\partial\varphi_i/\partial z$. We use the matrices

$$M_i = \begin{bmatrix} J_{1/3}(\zeta_i) & J_{-1/3}(\zeta_i) \\ J_{-2/3}(\zeta_i) & -J_{2/3}(\zeta_i) \end{bmatrix} \tag{3.133}$$

and

$$(M_i)\begin{pmatrix} A_i \\ B_i \end{pmatrix} = (M_{i+1})\begin{pmatrix} A_{i+1} \\ B_{i+1} \end{pmatrix} \qquad \text{at } z = z_i \tag{3.134}$$

etc.

All the quantities necessary for the normal mode formulation [Eqs. (3.119) to (3.123)] are easily found.

For instance, to compute ν in (3.115) and (3.119)

$$\int \varphi^2 \, dz = \frac{1}{\omega^2 p}\left[\gamma^2\varphi^2 + \left(\frac{\partial\varphi}{\partial z}\right)^2\right] \tag{3.135}$$

a result which is proved by differentiating both sides and using (2.16) and (3.126). Thus, for a model consisting of an arbitrary number of layers (3.125),

$$\nu = \sum_i \nu_i = \sum_i \frac{1}{\omega^2 p_i}\left\{\left[\gamma_i^2\varphi_i^2 + \left(\frac{\partial\varphi_i}{\partial z}\right)^2\right]_{z=z_i}\right.$$
$$\left. - \left[\gamma_i^2\varphi_i^2 + \left(\frac{\partial\varphi_i}{\partial z}\right)^2\right]_{z=z_{i-1}}\right\} \tag{3.136}$$

In this case, the variable s of the W.K.B. method [Eq. 2.209] is simply

$$s = -\zeta + s_0 \tag{3.137}$$

It is easily verified that the W.K.B. approximation corresponds to the use of the first term in the asymptotic expansion of the Bessel functions in Eqs. (3.129) and (3.132).

Both the exact solution and the W.K.B. approximation take on particularly simple forms for the case of the *symmetric wave duct*

$$c(z) = (p|z| + q)^{-1/2} \tag{3.138}$$

corresponding to the profile in Fig. 3.6. It is true that $c \to \infty$ as $|z| \to -q/p$ ($p < 0$ if c increases with $|z|$). But if one is interested in the relatively weak gradients encountered in practice, $q/|p|$ is very large indeed; the actual boundaries of the medium enclose a much narrower region, and one has no need to worry about this effect. For example, consider the

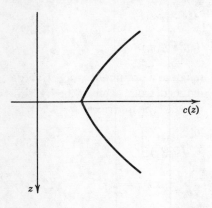

Fig. 3.6 Symmetric wave duct [Eq. (3.138)].

model shown in Fig. 3.7. It has M discrete modes of propagation. We may, to a sufficient degree of accuracy, treat this as an indefinite medium (or as a medium extending on both sides to $z = \pm q/p$) keeping only those modes for which the phase velocity v is less than the sound velocity c_1 at the edge of the duct. This means that we consider modes $m \le M$ of the indefinite case for which energy is trapped by total reflection within the region $c < c_1$ and $|z| < z_1$. The errors involved are largest for mode numbers near $m = M$ and, in cases considered here, amount to no more than a few digits in the sixth significant figure of κ. This would be equivalent, in practice, to a perturbation of the fine structure of the acoustic field which is quite trivial and undetectable in comparison with those that can be

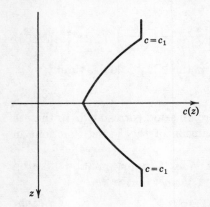

Fig. 3.7 Symmetric wave duct with non-reflecting boundaries. $c_1 = 1539$ m/sec, $c(0) = 1524$ m/sec, $z_1 = \pm 914.4$ m.

expected in nature.   Thus, quite satisfactory results are obtained from the model of Fig. 3.7, using only modes such that $v_m < c_1$. The "exact solutions," for the discrete spectrum, pertinent to the symmetric case of *source and receiver both on the channel axis* are

$$\varphi_m = q_m \gamma_m [J_{1/3}(\zeta_m) + J_{-1/3}(\zeta_m)] \tag{3.139}$$

for the illuminated region, and

$$\varphi_m = q_m g_m [-I_{1/3}(\eta_m) + I_{-1/3}(\eta_m)] \tag{3.140}$$

in the shadow beyond the turning point.

The eigenvalue condition for the pressure *symmetric* modes is simply:

At $z = 0$
$$\frac{\partial \varphi}{\partial z} = 0 \tag{3.141}$$

or
$$J_{-2/3}(\zeta_m) - J_{2/3}(\zeta_m) = 0 \tag{3.142}$$

having infinitely many roots, of which we need only M such that $v_M < c_1 < v_{M+1}$. Referring back to (3.115), (3.135),

$$\nu_m = 2\rho \int_0^z \varphi_m{}^2 \, dz = -\frac{2\rho}{\omega^2 p} \gamma_m{}^2 \varphi_m{}^2(0) \tag{3.143}$$

So that the solution for the acoustical pressure amplitude is (3.122), with

$$P_m = -\pi \omega^2 p \sqrt{\rho c \Pi} \, \frac{1}{\rho \gamma_m{}^2 \sqrt{\kappa_m}} \tag{3.144}$$

In the W.K.B. approximation we have exactly the same result; (3.144) still holds except for the numerical value of κ_m, which is now deduced from the approximate (Bohr-Sommerfeld) equation

$$-2\zeta_m + \frac{\pi}{2} = m\pi \tag{3.145}$$

This is simply the asymptotic form of (3.142) providing $m = 2n - 1$, $n = 1, 2, \ldots$, that is, providing we confine ourselves to the roots

$$-2\zeta_n + \frac{\pi}{2} = (2n - 1)\pi \tag{3.146}$$

corresponding to the symmetric modes.   Here again we limit ourselves to the first M roots such that $v_m = \omega/\kappa_m < c_1$. Typical errors of approximation and their practical significance will be discussed in Chap. 5.   Here we simply note the difference between exact and approximate values of κ_m.

Thus, for the numerical values of $c(z)$ at $z = 0$ and $z = \pm 914.4\,m$, shown in Fig. 3.7, one calculates for $m = 1, 9$, and 19, in units of m^{-1},

$$m = 1 \quad \begin{cases} \kappa_m = 1.64862 & \text{(W.K.B.) error: } 5 \times 10^{-5} \\ \kappa_m = 1.64867 & \text{(exact)} \end{cases}$$

$$m = 9 \quad \begin{cases} \kappa_m = 1.64387 & \text{(W.K.B.) error: } 1 \times 10^{-5} \\ \kappa_m = 1.64388 & \text{(exact)} \end{cases}$$

$$m = 19 \quad \begin{cases} \kappa_m = 1.640194 & \text{(W.K.B.) error: } 3 \times 10^{-6} \\ \kappa_m = 1.640197 & \text{(exact)} \end{cases}$$

Another interesting example of a symmetric waveguide corresponds to

$$\frac{1}{c^2} = \frac{1}{c_0^2} - a^2 z^2 \tag{3.147}$$

The sound velocity and its derivatives are continuous at $z = 0$, in contrast to the previous example. The solution for the unlimited medium can be obtained in closed form; here, as before, the behavior of the lower modes approximates very closely that of a symmetric waveguide with nonreflecting boundaries (Fig. 3.8). We briefly sketch the solution of (2.16) with (3.147). We have

$$\gamma^2 = \frac{\omega^2}{c_0^2} - \kappa^2 - \omega^2 a^2 z^2 = \gamma_0^2 - \omega^2 a^2 z^2 \tag{3.148}$$

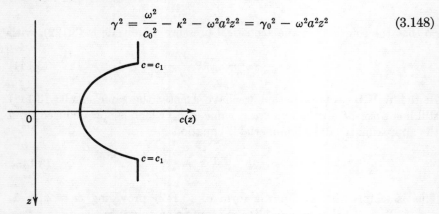

Fig. 3.8   Symmetric wave duct [Eq. (3.147)] with nonreflecting boundaries.

where γ_0 is the value of γ on the sound-channel axis. The change of variable

$$\xi = \omega^{1/2} a^{1/2} z \tag{3.149}$$

with

$$\lambda = \frac{\gamma_0^2}{\omega a} \tag{3.150}$$

gives
$$\varphi_{\xi\xi} + (\lambda - \xi^2)\varphi = 0 \tag{3.151}$$

which is a well-studied equation [for example, see Schiff[5]]. The transformation

$$\varphi = e^{-\frac{1}{2}\xi^2}H \tag{3.152}$$

gives
$$H_{\xi\xi} - 2\xi H_\xi + (\lambda - 1)H = 0 \tag{3.153}$$

i.e., Hermite's differential equation. It is then not too difficult to show, e.g., by power series expansions,[5] that the only way to secure a solution (3.152) that vanishes for $\xi \to \pm\infty$ is to take

$$\lambda = 2m + 1 \qquad m = 0, 1, \ldots \tag{3.154}$$

where m is an integer. This is the eigenvalue equation, corresponding to the eigenfunctions

$$\varphi_m = e^{-\frac{1}{2}\xi^2}H_m(\xi) \tag{3.155}$$

H_m being the Hermite polynomial of order m.

The eigenvalue equation (3.154) implies

$$\gamma_0^2 = \frac{\omega^2}{c_0^2} - \kappa^2 = \omega a(2m + 1) \tag{3.156}$$

or
$$\kappa_m = \left[\frac{\omega^2}{c_0^2} - \omega a(2m + 1)\right]^{1/2} \tag{3.157}$$

The Bohr-Sommerfeld condition is, on the other hand,

$$2s = \left(n - \frac{1}{2}\right)\pi \tag{3.158}$$

with
$$s = \int_0^{\lambda^{1/2}(\omega a)^{-1}} \gamma \, dz = \int_0^{\lambda^{1/2}} (\lambda - \xi^2)^{1/2} \, d\xi \tag{3.159}$$

Integrating and substituting the limits gives

$$\lambda\frac{\pi}{2} = \left(n - \frac{1}{2}\right)\pi$$

or
$$\lambda = 2n - 1 \qquad n = 1, 2, \ldots \tag{3.160}$$

This is the same result as in (3.154). Thus, in this case, the Bohr-Sommerfeld condition gives exact answers for the eigenvalues. In order to apply the formulas of Sec. 3.7, we still need

$$\nu_m = \frac{\rho}{\sqrt{a\omega}} \int_{-\infty}^{+\infty} e^{-\xi^2}[H_m(\xi)]^2 \, d\xi \tag{3.161}$$

and, using a well-known result, [5]

$$\nu_m = \frac{\rho}{\sqrt{a\omega}} \sqrt{\pi} 2^m(m!) \tag{3.162}$$

We thus have the sound field (3.122) where P_m is defined by

$$P_m = \frac{2}{\rho\sqrt{\kappa_m}} \left[\pi a\omega\rho c\Pi \right]^{1/2} e^{-(\xi_R^2+\xi_s^2)/2} \frac{H_m(\xi_R)H_m(\xi_s)}{2^m(m!)} \tag{3.163}$$

where ξ_R and ξ_S are values of ξ corresponding to receiver and source depths z_R and z_S. Typical behavior of $P_m(\xi)$ for $\xi_R = \xi_S = \xi$ is shown in Fig. 3.9 for $m = 0$, 1, and 5.

In the special case of source and receiver both on axis, only the

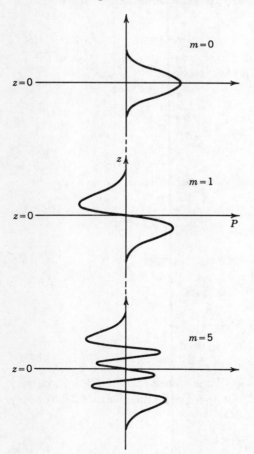

Fig. 3.9   Mode amplitudes vs. z for wave duct of Fig. 3.8.

symmetric (even m) modes are retained.   Then, in view of the property

$$H_m(0) = (-1)^{m/2}2^{m/2}(m - 1)(m - 3) \cdots 3 \cdot 1 \qquad (3.164)$$

one has

$$P_m = \frac{2}{\rho\sqrt{\kappa_m}}\left[\pi a\omega\rho c\Pi\right]^{1/2}\frac{m!}{2^m[(m/2)!]^2} \qquad (3.165)$$

which tends to zero for large m like $1/\sqrt{2m}$.

REFERENCES

1. H. Goldstein: "Classical Mechanics," Addison-Wesley Publishing Company, Inc., Reading, Mass., 1953.
2. Lord Rayleigh: "Theory of Sound," Macmillan & Co., Ltd., London, 1878.
3. W. Heitler: "The Quantum Theory of Radiation," Clarendon Press, Oxford, 1954.
4. M. A. Biot and I. Tolstoy: *J. Acoust. Soc. Am.*, **29**:381 (1957).
5. L. I. Schiff: "Quantum Mechanics," 2d ed., McGraw-Hill Book Company, New York, 1955.
6. A. Sommerfeld: "Partial Differential Equations," Academic Press Inc., New York, 1949.
7. A. Erdélyi (ed.): "Tables of Integral Transforms," McGraw-Hill Book Company, New York, 1954.
8. C. L. Pekeris: *Geol. Soc. Am., Mem.* 27, 1948.
9. J. E. Freehafer: in D. E. Kerr (ed.), "Propagation of Short Radio Waves," pp. 58 ff., McGraw-Hill Book Company, New York, 1951.
10. Th. v. Kármán and M. A. Biot: "Mathematical Methods in Engineering," McGraw-Hill Book Company, New York, 1940.

CHAPTER FOUR

PROPAGATION OF SOUND IN SHALLOW WATER

4.1 INTRODUCTION

The distinction between shallow- and deep-water propagation is a matter of scale, and depends chiefly upon the value of the dimensionless parameter κh, h being the water depth and κ the horizontal wave number. In practice, small to moderate κh values (for example, $\kappa h \leq 10$) are chiefly encountered in coastal or continental shelf waters, whereas large κh values will occur mostly in deep water. Although there *are* differences in the behavior of sound at small and large κh values so that this distinction is useful, any sharp numerical definition would be quite arbitrary and rather meaningless; it is just not possible to define an exact criterion. It suffices to say that in shallow-water propagation one deals *mostly* with κh values less than 10 or so. But one must also keep in mind that the use of very high frequencies (e.g., high-frequency sonar) in coastal waters leads to a "deep-water" type of problem, and conversely, the study of very low frequencies in deep water (submarine earthquakes and very large explosions) conforms to "shallow-water" theory.

This chapter describes some of the basic theoretical and experimental work pertaining to small and moderate κh values.

Idealized models of varying complexity have been used in attempts to understand observed propagation effects in shallow water. The simplest correspond to perfect homogeneous waveguides of the type discussed in Secs. 2.6 and 3.6. Models of this type were used by Ide, Post, and Fry,[1] who were the first to use a waveguide theory in interpreting their observations in the Potomac River. A little later, Pekeris[2] made a wide use of a partial or imperfect waveguide consisting of a homogeneous layer of water of sound velocity c_1 over a fluid half-space of sound velocity $c_2 > c_1$ in which the surface layer acted as a waveguide for totally reflected waves incident at an angle $\theta > \theta_c$ (see Sec. 3.6). Pekeris' detailed analysis of this problem met with considerable success and explained the chief properties, observed by Worzel and Ewing,[3] of explosion-generated sound in coastal waters. More recently, the interpretation of continuous-wave (c-w) sound-field experiments by Tolstoy[4] and Clay[5] has required the use of waveguide models consisting of several layers. Experiments by Kriazhev,[6] using similar models, have given results well in accord with theory. Laboratory scale models have also met with considerable success.[7]

Theoretical studies of a fluid layer over a homogeneous, elastic, solid half-space have been performed by various investigators,[8-10] and are in reasonably good agreement with the observed behavior of seismic and low-frequency acoustic signals in the deep ocean, for the 0.1- to 10-cps frequency range.[11-13] In principle, such studies would also be relevant to higher frequencies in coastal waters with hard rock bottoms.

Although in special situations more complex models could be invoked, it is, we think, proper to consider the theory of shallow-water propagation as involving primarily a number of homogeneous layers of different sound velocities, densities, and thicknesses, overlying a half-space (or a very thick layer) of high sound velocity. Such models will exhibit both the effects of partially reflected and totally reflected (guided) waves. In other words, one must distinguish between modes having continuous and discrete γ spectra (see Secs. 2.6 and 3.6), corresponding to important differences in behavior of the sound field at short and long ranges from the source. Thus, for source and receiver both situated in a low-velocity surface layer, the contribution of partial reflections (continuous spectrum) may be important or even dominant at short ranges, whereas at great distances the guided waves (discrete spectrum) alone contribute significantly to the field. The continuous spectrum and the discrete spectrum may have to be combined in the near-field; this region has been discussed by Pekeris,[2] Brekhovskikh,[14] and others. The theory has been successfully applied by Weinstein[15] to some model experiments. But by far the biggest theoretical and experimental effort has been concerned with the waveguide effects which become dominant at ranges exceeding 10 water depths or so. In the present state of the art, the theory of layered waveguides constitutes the principal body of acoustics relevant to shallow-water propagation. At the very least, we shall endeavor to show in this chapter that it provides a convincing framework against which to gauge one's experimental results and a convenient starting point for further refinements of the theory.[16] Although the theory is built around extremely idealized models and highly simplified assumptions, it predicts a surprising number of observed features. It also brings out the great importance of bottom parameters such as sound velocity and layering.

4.2 THE PERFECT HOMOGENEOUS WAVEGUIDE

In view of the importance of waveguide theory in shallow-water acoustics, it is worthwhile to make a few more comments on the perfect waveguide.

Let us summarize some pertinent results from Chaps. 2 and 3. If both boundaries are free, the modes are

$$\Phi_m = q_m J_0(\kappa_m r) \sin \gamma_m z \tag{4.1}$$

The characteristic equation is

$$\gamma_m h = m\pi \tag{4.2}$$

where γ_m is the vertical wave number for the mth mode. It is related to the wave number k along the ray (normal to a wave front) and the horizontal component κ by Eq. (2.19):

$$\gamma^2 + \kappa^2 = \frac{\omega^2}{c^2} = k^2$$

where ω is the angular frequency.

Thus Eq. (4.2) gives the dispersion equations for each mode m

$$\omega_m = (\omega_{0m}{}^2 + \kappa^2 c^2)^{1/2} \tag{4.3}$$

where ω_{0m}, the cutoff frequency of the mth mode, is given by Eq. (2.144):

$$\omega_{0m} = \frac{c}{h}\, m\pi \tag{2.144}$$

The $\omega_m(\kappa)$ curves are, by Eq. (4.3), a family of hyperbolas (Fig. 2.7).

The group and phase velocities U and v are related to the plane-wave angle of incidence θ as follows:

$$U_m = c \sin \theta_m = c \sqrt{1 - \frac{\omega_{0m}{}^2}{\omega^2}} \tag{4.4}$$

$$v_m = \frac{c}{\sin \theta_m} = \frac{c}{\sqrt{1 - \omega_{0m}{}^2/\omega^2}} \tag{4.5}$$

At cutoff, $v_m = \infty$ and $U_m = 0$, corresponding to normal incidence $\theta_m = 0$. Equations (4.4) and (4.5) admit of a straightforward vector interpretation corresponding to the purely geometric character of the dispersion (Sec. 2.7).

For an "instantaneous explosion" (Sec. 3.4) at a depth $z = z_0$, $t = 0$, we found two convenient forms of the solution (Sec. 3.6):

$$\frac{\partial \Phi}{\partial t} = -\frac{c}{\pi h} \sum_{m=1}^{\infty} \sin \gamma_m z \, \sin \gamma_m z_0 \frac{\cos \gamma_m \sqrt{c^2 t^2 - r^2}}{\sqrt{c^2 t^2 - r^2}} \qquad t \geq \frac{r}{c} \tag{4.6}$$

or

$$\frac{\partial \Phi}{\partial t} = -\frac{1}{4\pi} \sum_{n=0}^{\infty} \left[\frac{1}{R_n} \delta\left(t - \frac{R_n}{c}\right) - \frac{1}{R'_n} \delta\left(t - \frac{R'_n}{c}\right) \right] \tag{4.7}$$

where the meaning of R_n and R'_n is shown in Fig. 4.1 [Eq. 3.84].

These two forms, (4.6) and (4.7), correspond to two essentially different and complementary points of view. Here they are illustrated most clearly; this is one of the few nontrivial problems having *exact* solutions in both forms.

Equation (4.7) typifies the *ray* or *image* approach, which represents the sound field as a superposition of discrete arrivals due to 0, 1, 2, . . . reflections from both surfaces, i.e., of contributions from the infinite array of images in both boundaries (Fig. 4.1).

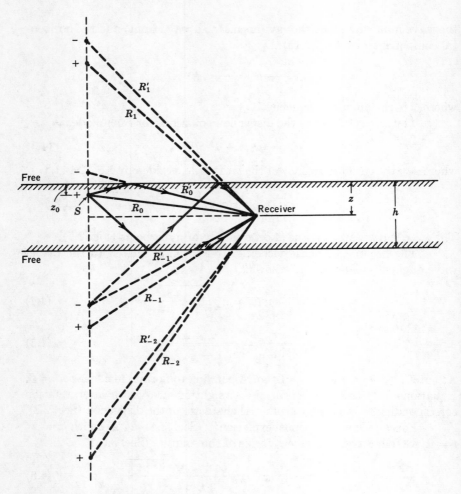

Fig. 4.1   Perfect waveguide.

Equation (4.6) illustrates the *mode* point of view, representing the field as a superposition of discrete dispersive modes. It can be obtained by expanding (4.7) in Fourier series and regrouping terms. The mode solution (4.6) shows that for each m the earliest arrivals are at $t_0 = r/c$ and correspond to high rates of oscillation (asymptotic end of the dispersion curves $\omega \to \infty$ and $U_m \to v_m \to c$). Thus let τ be the time elapsed after t_0, that is,

$$t = t_0 + \tau$$

$$\tau \ll t_0 = \frac{r}{c}$$

(4.8)

Then, $$c^2t^2 - r^2 \approx 2rc\tau \qquad (4.9)$$

and $$\cos \gamma_m \sqrt{c^2t^2 - r^2} \approx \cos (\gamma_m\sqrt{2rc\tau}) \qquad (4.10)$$

For $r \to \infty$ the rate of oscillation also becomes infinite.

The latest arrivals for $t \to \infty$ have vanishing amplitude. Their frequency is defined by observing that in this case,

$$c^2t^2 - r^2 \approx c^2t^2 \qquad (4.11)$$

and $$\cos \gamma_m \sqrt{c^2t^2 - r^2} \approx \cos \gamma_m ct = \cos \omega_{0m}t \qquad (4.12)$$

Thus, as $t \to \infty$ the arrival frequency tends to the cutoff value ω_{0m}, corresponding to vanishing group velocity.

Since in practice one always has finite bandwidth receivers and since each mode has a low-frequency cutoff ω_{0m}, only a finite number of terms in (4.6) will be used. Thus the mode point of view leads to a finite number of terms; this number is independent of range.

The ray optical solution (4.7) contains at all times an infinity of terms. But at short ranges, $R_n \gg R_0$ for large n; the higher-order images can be neglected. At long ranges, the number of terms that must be considered is very large and (4.7) becomes cumbersome. Note that for more realistic time dependence of the source, and/or filtering, there may be interferences between images and, under certain conditions, some cancellation and perhaps simplification of the numerical work. However, the usefulness of this feature is hard to gauge in advance.

Broadly speaking, the ray solution is at its best for short ranges and broad bandwidths, whereas the mode solution is advantageous for long ranges and finite bandwidths.

The extreme case of a line filter brings us to the pure *harmonic source*. The image solution is, of course,

$$\Phi = A \sum_{n=0}^{\infty} \left[\frac{e^{i(\omega t - kR_n)}}{R_n} - \frac{e^{i(\omega t - kR_n')}}{R_n'} \right] \qquad (4.13)$$

The mode solution is given by Eq. (3.116). Since

$$\nu_m = \rho \int_0^h \sin^2 \gamma_m z \, dz = \frac{1}{2}\rho h \qquad (4.14)$$

one has

$$\Phi = -A \frac{\pi i}{h} e^{i\omega t} \sum_{m=1}^{M} H_0^{(2)}(\kappa_m r) \sin \gamma_m z \sin \gamma_m z_0 \qquad (4.15)$$

where M is determined by

$$\omega_{0M} < \omega < \omega_{0M+1} \qquad (4.16)$$

Proceeding as in Sec. 3.7, we have for long ranges the pressure field described by Eqs. (3.119) to (3.123). We may define the *excitation function* for each mode as

$$p_m = \frac{4\pi}{h} \sqrt{\Pi\rho c} \, \frac{1}{\sqrt{\kappa_m}} \qquad (4.17)$$

giving the pressure amplitude as a function of source frequency, assuming that both source and receiver are at an antinode (Fig. 4.2).

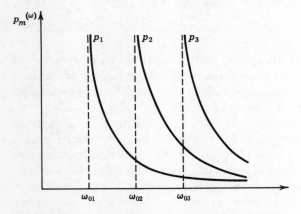

Fig. 4.2   Excitation functions for perfect waveguide.

Since $\kappa_m = 0$ here at $\omega = \omega_{0m}$, (4.17) is, strictly speaking, not valid at cutoff (except asymptotically for $r \to \infty$) because the asymptotic form of $H_0^{(2)}(\kappa_m r)$ is not applicable. In practice, however, this is not important since for very long ranges it is sufficient to take $\omega = \omega_{0m} + \epsilon$, $\epsilon \ll 1$.

The ray solution contains an infinity of terms, corresponding to angles of incidence

$$\theta_n = \operatorname{Arcsin} \frac{r}{R_n} \qquad (4.18)$$

The mode solution defines a *finite* number of angles

$$\theta_m = \operatorname{Arcsin} \frac{c}{v_m} \qquad (4.19)$$

This simply means that in the use of modes, we used Eq. (4.2) to keep only those directions of travel for which the individual array elements reinforce each other. It implies that in a ray calculation the only images that contribute to any extent to the field, at any frequency, are those whose angles of incidence are close to those specified by (4.2).

Conversely, whenever the chief contributions to the acoustic field come from certain ray angles, the modes of phase velocities v_m, Eq. (4.5), corresponding to neighboring angles, will dominate. Thus, in the waveguide of this section, high modes are *relatively* more important at short ranges and become less so as r increases. This becomes clear if one notices that steep rays play a more important role at short ranges, for which low-order images may correspond to steep rays, i.e., large horizontal phase velocities v. At longer ranges, steep rays correspond to high-order images and to large spherical spreading (small $R_m{}^{-1}$) (Fig. 4.1).

The transition between mode and ray points of view may be illustrated as follows:

Consider first the case in which only two modes are excited. Then, by Eq. (3.123),

$$p_a = \frac{\rho}{\sqrt{r}}\left(P_1{}^2 + P_2{}^2 + 2P_1P_2 \cos r\, \Delta\kappa_{12}\right)^{1/2} \tag{4.20}$$

giving a typical two-mode interference pattern (Fig. 4.3) in which successive minima and maxima are spaced one *interference wavelength* apart:

$$\Lambda_{12} = \frac{2\pi}{\Delta\kappa_{12}} = \frac{2\pi}{\kappa_1 - \kappa_2} \tag{4.21}$$

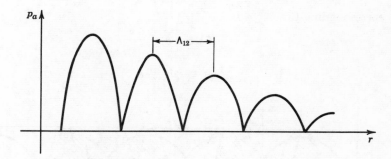

Fig. 4.3   Mode-interference pattern for two equally excited modes.

We have also,

$$P_1 = p_1 \sin \gamma_1 z_0 \sin \gamma_1 z$$
$$P_2 = p_2 \sin \gamma_2 z_0 \sin \gamma_2 z \tag{4.22}$$

where p_1 and p_2 are given by (4.17) and are of the same order as long as ω is not too close to ω_{02}. P_1 and P_2 have the shapes shown in Fig. 4.4, and the product P_1P_2 is positive or negative, depending upon z. Thus the pressure field amplitudes $p_a(r)$ near the surface and near the bottom are displaced horizontally with respect to each other by approximately $\frac{1}{2}\Lambda_{12}$ as in Fig. 4.5.

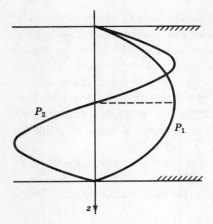

Fig. 4.4   Excitation as function of z.

If we now consider the low-amplitude regions as dark and high-amplitude zones as illuminated (cross-hatching in Fig. 4.5), we obtain, broadly speaking, a sinusoidally shaped belt—this is a beam or rather fuzzy sort of ray, of average angle of incidence

$$\tan \theta = \frac{1}{2}\frac{\Lambda_{12}}{h} \tag{4.23}$$

corresponding to

$$2h \tan \theta = \frac{2\pi}{\Delta\kappa_{12}} \tag{4.24}$$

or

$$h(\kappa_1 - \kappa_2)\tan \theta = \pi \tag{4.25}$$

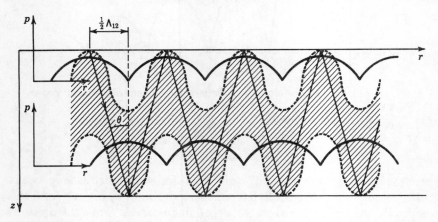

Fig. 4.5   Mode-interference maxima as function of z and r.   Shaded area shows more strongly insonified region.

This relationship is only approximate. It is a poor approximation for low modes, but a good one for high modes, as we now proceed to show.

By (4.2) and (2.21)

$$\kappa h \cot \theta = m\pi \tag{4.26}$$

Assuming m large enough so that $\Delta m = 1$ will correspond to small increments in κ and θ,

$$\Delta\kappa_{m+1,m} h \cot \theta - \kappa h \, \Delta\theta_{m+1,m} \frac{1}{\sin^2 \theta} = \pi \tag{4.27}$$

But for the harmonic case, a change in θ corresponds also to a change in κ since, from Eq. (2.20),

$$\kappa = k \sin \theta \tag{4.28}$$

$$\Delta\theta_{m+1,m} = \frac{\Delta\kappa_{m+1,m}}{k \cos \theta} = \frac{\Delta\kappa_{m+1,m}}{\kappa} \tan \theta \tag{4.29}$$

and by (4.27)

$$\Delta\kappa_{m+1,m} h \tan \theta = -\pi \tag{4.30}$$

where

$$\Delta\kappa_{m+1,m} = \kappa_{m+1} - \kappa_m \tag{4.31}$$

i.e., strictly speaking, (4.25) is too coarse an approximation, but

$$h(\kappa_m - \kappa_{m+1}) \tan \theta = \pi \tag{4.32}$$

holds for $m \gg 1$.

4.3 TWO-LAYERED HALF-SPACE: GUIDED MODES AND DISPERSION

In this model (Fig. 4.6), when $c_2 > c_1$, there are two families of modes in the sense defined in Chaps. 2 and 3.

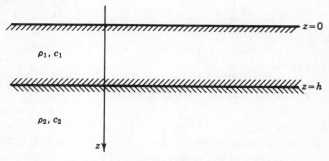

Fig. 4.6 Two-layered half-space.

One is a family with *continuous γ spectrum* corresponding to phase velocities $v \geq c_2$, that is, to partial reflection at the boundary $z = h$. These modes have the form given in Eqs. (3.92) and (3.93). Their excitation by an impulsive source is given by Eq. (3.97). We shall not discuss them in this section. At long ranges, they become relatively unimportant in comparison with the totally trapped energy (discrete spectrum), the amplitude of which falls off more slowly. In Sec. 4.7 it will be necessary to include them for short-range studies, but we shall then find it more convenient to use a different approach, which considers both families simultaneously.

The other family has a *discrete γ spectrum*, $v \leq c_2$, and its energy is concentrated in the surface layer by total reflection at $z = h$ (waveguide modes). It is given by Eqs. (3.85) and (3.86), which we reproduce here:

$$\Phi_m = q_m \sin \gamma_{1m}z, \, J_0(\kappa r) \qquad 0 \leq z \leq h \tag{4.33}$$

$$\Phi_m = q_m a \sin \gamma_{1m} h e^{-g_{2m}(z-h)} J_0(\kappa r) \qquad z \geq h \tag{4.34}$$

The characteristic equation is Eq. (3.88):

$$\gamma_1 h + \text{Arctan} \frac{1}{a} \frac{\gamma_1}{g_2} = m\pi \tag{4.35}$$

By virtue of Eqs. (2.17) and (2.82),

$$\gamma_1 = \left(\frac{\omega^2}{c_1{}^2} - \kappa^2\right)^{1/2} = \kappa \left(\frac{v^2}{c_1{}^2} - 1\right)^{1/2}$$

$$g_2 = \left(\kappa^2 - \frac{\omega^2}{c_2{}^2}\right)^{1/2} = \kappa \left(1 - \frac{v^2}{c_2{}^2}\right)^{1/2} \tag{4.36}$$

Thus Eq. (4.35) is simply

$$\kappa h \left(\frac{v^2}{c_1{}^2} - 1\right)^{1/2} = m\pi - \text{Arctan} \frac{1}{a}\left(\frac{v^2/c_1{}^2 - 1}{1 - v^2/c_2{}^2}\right)^{1/2} \tag{4.37}$$

In other words, we may solve Eq. (4.35) explicitly for κ as a function of the phase velocity v:

$$\kappa_m = \left(\frac{v^2}{c_1{}^2} - 1\right)^{-1/2}\left[\frac{m\pi}{h} - \frac{1}{h} \text{Arctan} \frac{1}{a}\left(\frac{v^2/c_1{}^2 - 1}{1 - v^2/c_2{}^2}\right)^{1/2}\right] \tag{4.38}$$

This equation gives real κ_m for $c_1 \leq v \leq c_2$, and Eq. (2.15) gives ω_m.

If $v \rightarrow c_1$, the second term in brackets tends to zero and Eq. (4.38) becomes equivalent to Eq. (4.2) for the perfect waveguide with two free surfaces. If $v \to c_2$, this term tends to $\pi/2h$, corresponding to the mth mode low-frequency cutoff,

$$\omega_{0m} = \kappa_m c_2 = \frac{c_2 \pi}{h} \left(\frac{c_2^2}{c_1^2} - 1 \right)^{-1/2} \left(m - \frac{1}{2} \right) \tag{4.39}$$

Typical $\omega_m(\kappa)$ curves are shown in Fig. 4.7. For given ω, it is seen from this figure that κ_m decreases as m increases; i.e., high modes correspond to larger phase velocities v_m and steeper rays:

$$\theta_m = \text{Arcsin} \frac{c_1}{v_m} = \text{Arcsin} \frac{c_1 \kappa_m}{\omega} \tag{4.40}$$

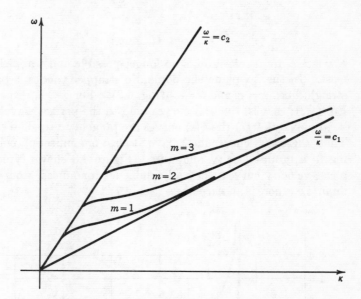

Fig. 4.7 Characteristic curves for layered waveguide.

As indicated in Sec. 2.7, the group velocity U may be calculated from Eq. (2.62):

$$\nu_m = \rho_1 \int_0^h \sin^2 \gamma_{1m} z \, dz + \rho_2 a^2 \sin^2 \gamma_{1m} h \int_h^\infty e^{-2g_{2m}(z-h)} dz$$

$$= \frac{\rho_1}{2\gamma_{1m}} \left(\gamma_{1m} h - \cos \gamma_{1m} h \sin \gamma_{1m} h - a^2 \tan \gamma_{1m} h \sin^2 \gamma_{1m} h \right) \tag{4.41}$$

and

$$\sigma_m = \frac{1}{c_1^2} \frac{\rho_1}{2\gamma_{1m}} \left(\gamma_{1m} h - \cos \gamma_{1m} h \sin \gamma_{1m} h - \frac{c_1^2}{c_2^2} a^2 \tan \gamma_{1m} h \sin^2 \gamma_{1m} h \right) \tag{4.42}$$

and, by virtue of (4.35),

$$U_m v_m = \frac{v_m}{\sigma_m} = c_1^2 \frac{g_{2m}h(\gamma_{1m}^2 + a^2 g_{2m}^2) + a(g_{2m}^2 + \gamma_{1m}^2)}{g_{2m}h(\gamma_{1m}^2 + a^2 g_{2m}^2) + a[g_{2m}^2 + (c_1^2/c_2^2)\gamma_{1m}^2]} \tag{4.43}$$

We are thus in a position to calculate $\omega_m(\kappa)$, $v_m(\omega)$, and $U_m(\omega)$. Note that all modes cut off at

$$v = c_2 \tag{4.44}$$

at which point

$$g_2 = 0 \tag{4.45}$$

$$\kappa_{0m} = \frac{\omega_{0m}}{c_2} \tag{4.46}$$

$$U_m = c_2 \tag{4.47}$$

For $v > c_2$ total reflection is no longer possible and trapped modes do not exist. In the ω,κ plane the domain of trapped modes is bounded by the straight lines $v = c_1$ and $v = c_2$ (Fig. 4.7). For $v \to c_1$, Eq. (4.35) tends to Eq. (4.2); that is, the $\omega(\kappa)$ curves tend to the perfect waveguide curves as $\omega \to \infty$. By (4.47) the $\omega(\kappa)$ curves are tangent to the line $v = c_2$ at cutoff. Thus, these $\omega(\kappa)$ curves must have at least one inflection point corresponding to a group-velocity minimum. Figure 4.8 shows typical group- and phase-velocity curves; they all exhibit a pronounced group-velocity minimum; i.e., there is an *Airy phase* (Sec. 2.7).

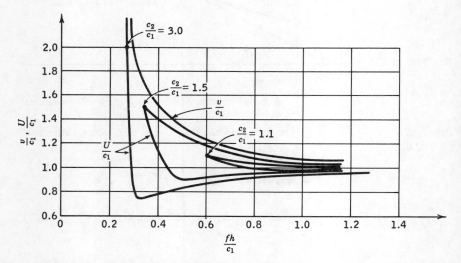

Fig. 4.8 Dispersion curves v/c_1 and U/c_1 for two-layered (Pekeris) half-space, for various values of c_2/c_1 in model of Fig. 4.6.

Insofar as the mechanism of dispersion is concerned, these results imply that we do not have a case of pure geometric dispersion. The simple vector relationships between c, v, and U for perfect waveguides are no longer valid except in the high-frequency, asymptotic limit of each mode. It can be shown that this is due to a resonant condition characteristic of the layered structure.[17]

Under conditions of transient excitation, the shape of the $U(\omega)$ curve implies, for each mode, the following sequence: the first arrival recorded at some point r,z appears at time $t = r/c_2$, the corresponding frequency being ω_{0m}. As time increases, the frequency increases. At time $t = r/c_1$ a high-frequency "rider" or "water" wave arrives and is superimposed upon the lower frequency corresponding to the point $U = c_1$ on the left-hand part of the curve (Fig. 4.8). As time increases further, the frequencies of these two superimposed trains of waves tend to become equal. At $t_{max} = r/U_{min}$ they are the same; the two wave trains interfere constructively and merge into a single prominent wave group, i.e., the Airy phase. For $t > t_{max}$ the disturbance vanishes exponentially (Sec. 2.7). A typical series of $p(t)$ curves for modes $m = 1, 2, 3$ is shown in Fig. 4.14. Usually several modes will be excited simultaneously, giving a quite complicated trace (Sec. 4.4, Fig. 4.15). But whenever the individual modes can be isolated by some form of dispersion analysis, each is found to obey the above-mentioned time history. In underwater acoustics a good deal of attention has been given to shallow-water waveguides since the early 1940s. Their dispersive properties were first studied and understood by Ewing, Worzel, and Pekeris.[2,3] These investigators showed, in a systematic and classic series of measurements, that the behavior of explosively generated sound in the shallow seas of the Eastern seaboard conformed closely to theory. Figure 4.9 shows one of their comparisons between theory and experiment; we see that for short wavelengths the agreement is excellent. For longer wavelengths, the experimental points drift consistently toward curves for models with higher c_2/c_1 ratios. This may be accounted for by introducing the effect of additional, deeper, high-velocity layers in the sediment.[2,4]

These early dispersion analyses were performed by reading frequency and time from oscillograph records of an explosion, i.e., essentially by eye. The advent of sound spectrographs has greatly simplified the process. One needs only to record the sound pressure on magnetic tape. This is played into a spectrograph, the output of which will display frequency vs. time on spark-sensitized facsimile paper. In other words, one obtains a direct display of r/U vs. ω. Since, further, the spark strength is a function of arrival intensity, a certain amount of amplitude information is also provided. Figure 4.10 shows a typical shallow-water explosion spectrograph analysis obtained by J. B. Hersey, at the Woods Hole Oceanographic Institution

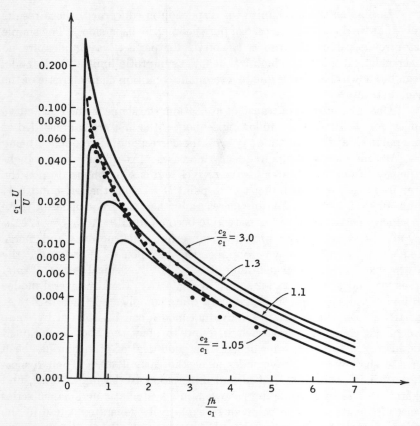

Fig. 4.9 A comparison of calculated $(c_1 - U)/U$ with experimental points from a number of shots in the Virgin Islands Shoal. The solid curves correspond to various values of c_2/c_1. The dashed curve shows the better fit obtained with a three-layer model with $h_2 = \frac{1}{2}h_1$, $c_2/c_1 = 1.05$, and $c_3/c_1 = 1.3$. (After Worzel and Ewing.[3])

who was the first to propose this method. Three modes are clearly visible. Figure 4.11 gives a comparison of the curves of Fig. 4.10 with calculations based upon a model with $c_2 = 1.1c_1$, $h_1 = 30$ m, and $\rho_2 = 2\rho_1$.[18] A well-documented discussion of the spectrograph method has been given by Ewing, Mueller, Landisman, and Sato[18] in 1959.

One should add that the experience of many investigators, in dealing with hundreds or even thousands of shot records of this kind, is invariably in agreement with the theory, at least to the extent that attenuation and layering can be known and used in the theory. In particular, the Airy-phase frequencies and group velocities can be correctly predicted once the bottom properties have been established by independent means. A number of typical shallow-water spectrographs is given by Barakos.[34]

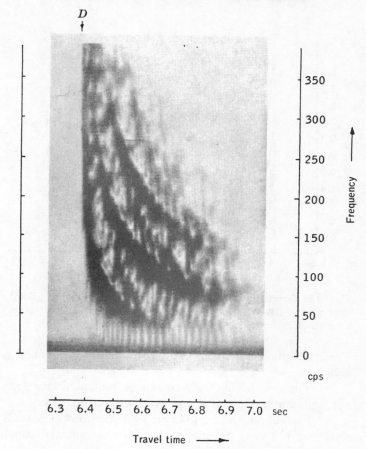

Fig. 4.10 Group-velocity curves displayed by a spectrum analyzer for typical shallow-water shot: 12 kg of TNT at 9.7 km distance in 30 m of water. (Courtesy of J. B. Hersey, Woods Hole Oceanographic Institution.)

4.4 TRANSIENT EXCITATION OF TWO-LAYERED WAVEGUIDE MODES

Here again we limit ourselves to the discrete γ spectrum. In Sec. 3.6 we showed that its excitation by an "instantaneous explosion" was

$$\Phi_1 = \sum_{m=1}^{\infty} \Phi_{1m} \tag{4.48}$$

$$\Phi_{1m} = \frac{c_1^2}{\pi h} \int_0^{\infty} \frac{\cos \omega_m t}{\omega_m^2} \frac{\gamma_{1m} h \sin \gamma_{1m} z \sin \gamma_{1m} z_0 J_0(\kappa r) \kappa \, d\kappa}{\gamma_{1m} h - \sin \gamma_{1m} h \cos \gamma_{1m} h - (c_1^2/c_2^2) a^2 \tan \gamma_{1m} h \sin^2 \gamma_{1m} h} \tag{4.49}$$

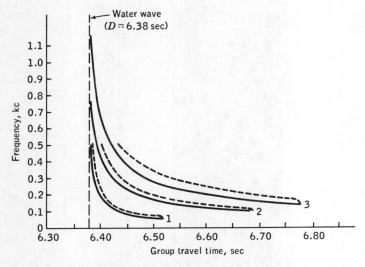

Fig. 4.11 Comparison of shot data of Fig. 4.10 with theory. Solid lines are the observed and dashed lines are the calculated group velocities for a model $c_2/c_1 = 1.1$, $\rho_2/\rho_1 = 2.0$, and $h_1 = 30$ m.

This result holds for a source and receiver at depths z and z_0 in the surface layer.

The integral in (4.49) cannot be evaluated exactly. However, the approximations of Sec. 2.8 are here quite satisfactory.

First of all, the group of arrivals described in Sec. 4.3 as the rider or water wave, i.e., the contribution of the asymptotic branches in Fig. 4.8, may be dealt with as follows:

If, for given m, $\omega \to \infty$, $\kappa \to \infty$, and $v \to U \to c_1$, it was shown in Sec. 4.3 that the perfect waveguide equations of Sec. 4.2 become approximately valid, i.e.,

$$\gamma_{1m}h = m\pi - \epsilon \tag{4.50}$$

where ϵ vanishes like $(v^2/c_1^2 - 1)^{1/2}$. Then $\sin \gamma_{1m}h \approx \tan \gamma_{1m}h \approx \epsilon$ and, in Eq. (4.49),

$$\Phi_{1m} = \frac{c_1^2}{\pi h} \sin \gamma_{1m}z \sin \gamma_{1m}z_0 \int_0^\infty \frac{\cos \omega_m t}{\omega_m^2} J_0(\kappa r)\kappa \, d\kappa \tag{4.51}$$

We recognize the perfect waveguide solution of Eq. (3.80). Thus, for times $t = r/c_1 + \Delta t$ where Δt is small, $\partial \Phi_{1m}/\partial t$ is equivalent to (4.6). This, of course, corresponds to the fact that as $v \to c_1$, that is, for angles of incidence approaching $\pi/2$, the change in phase upon total reflection at the bottom [Eq. (2.90)] tends to zero, as for a free boundary.

The other arrivals preceding, following, or coincident with the rider wave cannot be dealt with quite so simply. In order to obtain useful approximations, one must assume that r is large and apply the stationary phase method of Sec. 2.8. We begin by writing

$$\cos \omega t \, J_0(\kappa r) \approx \sqrt{\frac{2}{\pi \kappa r}} \, \cos \left(\kappa r - \frac{\pi}{4} \right) \cos \omega t$$

$$= \sqrt{\frac{1}{2\pi \kappa r}} \left[\cos \left(\kappa r + \omega t - \frac{\pi}{4} \right) + \cos \left(\kappa r - \omega t - \frac{\pi}{4} \right) \right] \quad (4.52)$$

The principle of stationary phase assumes that the only important contributions to the integral (4.49) come from the neighborhood of the values κ_0 and ω_0 which make $\kappa r \pm \omega t$ stationary [Eq. (2.160)]. In this problem all modes cut off at κ_{0m}, specified by Eqs. (4.39) and (4.46). Therefore there are no contributions to the integral near $\kappa = 0$. The smallest possible stationary value would be $\kappa = \kappa_{01}$ and the asymptotic approximation (4.52) is valid for all modes, providing

$$\kappa_{01} r = \frac{\pi}{2} \left(\frac{c_2^2}{c_1^2} - 1 \right)^{-1/2} \frac{r}{h} \gg 1 \quad (4.53)$$

The first term in brackets in (4.52) can be dropped. Since it corresponds to waves converging toward the source, it cannot have a stationary phase for positive group velocity.

The problem is now reduced to the evaluation of

$$\Phi_{1m} = \frac{c_1^2}{\pi h} \frac{1}{\sqrt{2\pi r}} \, \Re e \int_0^\infty \frac{\kappa_m^{1/2}}{\omega_m^2} \, S_m e^{i(\kappa_m r - \omega t - \pi/4)} \, d\kappa \quad (4.54)$$

where $\Re e$ means "the real part of," and

$$S_m = \frac{\gamma_{1m} h \sin \gamma_{1m} z \sin \gamma_{1m} z_0}{\gamma_{1m} h - \cos \gamma_{1m} h \sin \gamma_{1m} h - (c_1^2/c_2^2) a^2 \tan \gamma_{1m} h \sin^2 \gamma_{1m} h} \quad (4.55)$$

We first consider the case $\partial U/\partial \kappa \neq 0$, that is, arrivals preceding the Airy phase. Equation (2.165) gives

$$\Phi_{1m} = \frac{c_1^2}{\pi h} \frac{1}{\sqrt{r}} \frac{1}{\sqrt{t \, |\partial U/\partial \kappa|}} \, S_m \kappa_m^{1/2} \omega_m^{-2} \Re e \{ e^{i(\kappa_m r - \omega_m t - \pi/4)} e^{\pm i\pi/4} \} \quad (4.56)$$

where κ_m and ω_m are the mth mode κ and ω values for which

$$U_m = \frac{d\omega_m}{d\kappa} = \frac{r}{t} \quad (4.57)$$

and the $\pm$ signs in $e^{\pm i\pi/4}$ correspond to $\partial U/\partial \kappa < 0$ (frequencies lower than that of Airy phase) or $\partial U/\partial \kappa > 0$ (frequencies higher than Airy phase).

For $\partial U/\partial\kappa < 0$ then

$$\Phi_{1m} = \frac{c_1^2}{\pi h}\frac{1}{r}\frac{\kappa_m^{1/2}}{\omega_m^2}\frac{S_m}{|U_m^{-1}\partial U_m/\partial\kappa|^{1/2}}\cos(\kappa_m r - \omega_m t) \qquad (4.58)$$

Note that at cutoff, $\omega = \omega_{0m}$, $U = c_2$, $g_2 = 0$, and $\tan\gamma_{1m}h = \infty$. By Eq. (4.35), $S_m = 0$ and the first arrivals start out with zero amplitude.†
For $\partial U/\partial\kappa > 0$,

$$\Phi_m = \frac{c_1^2}{\pi h}\frac{1}{r}\frac{\kappa_m^{1/2}}{\omega_m^2}\frac{S_m}{|U_m^{-1}\partial U_m/\partial\kappa|^{1/2}}\sin(\kappa_m r - \omega_m t) \qquad (4.59)$$

Since U_m (Eq. 4.43) is of a form precluding explicit solution of (4.57), one must resort to numerical methods; given r and t, Eq. (4.57) determines U. Tables of $U_m(\omega)$ and $\omega_m(\kappa)$ give the appropriate values of ω and κ. Tables of $\partial U_m/\partial\kappa$ are then consulted. All these numerical values are substituted into (4.58) and (4.59)—or into these formulas multiplied by $\rho_1\omega^2$, giving pressure.

Near the Airy-phase arrival time we use Eqs. (2.181) to (2.186), in conjunction with (4.57), giving

$$\Phi_m = \frac{2c_1^2}{h3^{2/3}}\frac{1}{\sqrt{2\pi}}\frac{1}{r^{5/6}}\frac{\kappa_{0m}^{1/2}}{\omega_{0m}^2}\frac{E(v)}{|U_m^{-1/3}\partial^2 U_m/\partial\kappa^2|^{1/3}}S_{0m}\cos\left(\kappa_{0m}r - \omega_{0m}t - \frac{\pi}{4}\right)$$
$$(4.60)$$

where ω_{0m} and κ_{0m} are now the mth mode Airy-phase values of ω and κ, v is defined by (2.182), (2.179), and (2.180), and $E(v)$ by (2.183) and (2.184) (see Fig. 2.11).

All the remarks made in Sec. 2.8 apply here. For example, if the group-velocity minimum is deep and sharp (large c_2/c_1, see Fig. 4.8), the Airy phase is a long train of waves with many oscillations and a poorly defined arrival time. If the minimum is shallow and wide, $c_2/c_1 \approx 1$, it is a narrow packet of less ambiguous travel time and few oscillations.

Note also the $r^{-5/6}$ law for the Airy phase, as compared with r^{-1} for other frequency bands.

Very little quantitative work has been done in comparing experimental results with these formulas in natural surroundings. Although Eqs. (4.58) to (4.60) were derived, in slightly modified form, 20 years ago by Pekeris, investigators have shown an understandable reluctance to apply these results to actual problems in the field, because of the additional complications imposed by nature. For example, the frequent occurrence of layering in the bottom, the importance of frequency-dependent attenuation, and the scattering by irregularities of the surface and bottom all con-

† For comparison of these results with those of Pekeris, see Appendix 3.

spire to increase manyfold the already significant amount of numerical labor required for the use of these solutions.   However, with the current availability of high-speed computing machinery, progress in this direction may be expected.

In model work, where one has good control and knowledge of the parameters, some measure of success has been achieved along these lines.

Knudsen[7], using a 1- to 2-cm layer of oil over a thick saline solution and frequencies in the 10^5- to 10^6-cps range, has obtained accurate checks for the $r^{-5/6}$ law for the Airy phase (Fig. 4.12) and of the behavior of the solutions as a function of depth (Fig. 4.13).

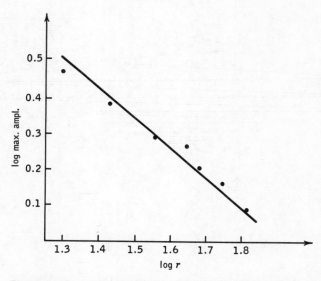

Fig. 4.12   Comparison of experimental points with theoretical straight line of slope $-5/6$ for Airy-phase amplitude vs. range (model experiments).   (After Knudsen.[7])

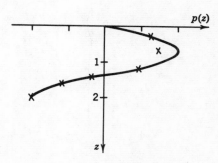

Fig. 4.13   Theory (solid curve) and experimental points for pressure law vs. depth.   (After Knudsen.[7])

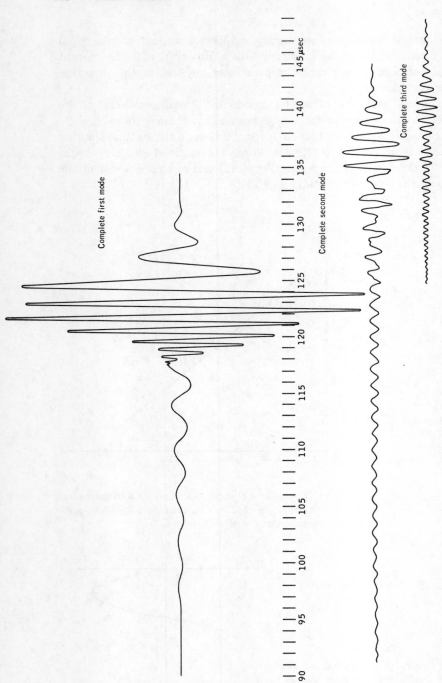

Fig. 4.14 Calculated excitation of three modes for the source of $Q(t) = Ate^{-\lambda t}\sin \alpha t,\ t \geq 0$, in the model experiment with two-layer waveguide (Sec. 4.4).

Another experiment was carried out in 1953 by Evans, Tolstoy, and Ritter.† The model consisted of a 2-mm layer of kerosene over a saline solution, frequencies of 3×10^5 to 3×10^6 cps being used. Source and receiver consisted of $LiSO_4$ crystals, 0.5 cm long. The source output was of the form

$$Q(t) = Ate^{-\lambda t} \sin \alpha t \qquad \lambda = 1.8 \times 10^6 \text{ sec}^{-1} \qquad \alpha = 3.5 \times 10^6 \text{ sec}^{-1}$$

The corresponding pressure (vs. time) wave forms for each mode were calculated for $r = 75h$ and are shown in Fig. 4.14. The properties discussed in this and previous sections are clearly visible (Sec. 4.3). In Fig. 4.15 the calculated contributions of the first three modes have been added, and the result is compared with experiment. The agreement is seen to be good, although discrepancies appear at the end of the record. Thus, one oscillation too many is predicted by the theory in the group of waves preceding the first-mode Airy phase. Also, the arrivals calculated for the second- and third-mode Airy phases hardly appear at all in the actual record. These differences may be plausibly ascribed to the treatment of the source as a point, whereas it was in fact big enough to be distributed through the top layer; the higher modes, in particular, would be very sensitive to this feature.

† Presented as a paper by D. Silverman at a symposium on elastic waves in Pasadena (1953).

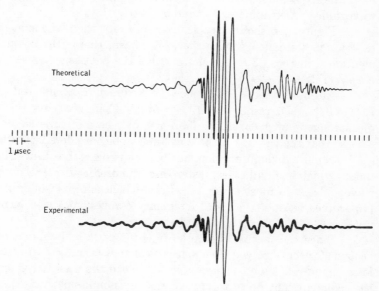

Fig. 4.15   Superposition of the three calculated modes of Fig. 4.14 (theoretical curve) compared with experiment for the two-layer waveguide model.

This experiment also substantiates our initial assumption that for source and receiver in the top layer, the contribution of the continuous κ spectrum is, for long ranges, negligible in comparison with the guided waves.

4.5 HARMONIC EXCITATION OF GUIDED MODES AND THEIR DAMPING

Equations (3.118) and (3.119) can be applied directly. With the help of the result (4.41), the excitation function for each mode defined as in Sec. 4.2 is for source and receiver in the top layer,

$$p_m = \frac{4\pi}{h} \sqrt{\Pi \rho_1 c_1} \frac{1}{\sqrt{\kappa_m}} \frac{\gamma_{1m} h}{\gamma_{1m} h - \cos \gamma_{1m} h \sin \gamma_{1m} n - a^2 \tan \gamma_{1m} h \sin^2 \gamma_{1m} h} \tag{4.61}$$

In view of (4.35) this may also be written as

$$p_m = \frac{4\pi}{h} \sqrt{\Pi \rho_1 c_1} \frac{1}{\sqrt{\kappa_m}} \left[\frac{g_{2m} h(\gamma_{1m}^2 + a^2 g_{2m}^2)}{g_{2m} h(\gamma_{1m}^2 + a^2 g_{2m}^2) + a(g_{2m}^2 + \gamma_{1m}^2)} \right] \tag{4.62}$$

For each mode, as $v \to c_1$, $\kappa \to \infty$, and $\omega \to \infty$ by (4.38), and $g_2 \to \kappa(1 - c_1^2/c_2^2)^{1/2}$ also tends to ∞ like κ. Therefore the term in brackets in (4.62) tends to unity and p_m tends asymptotically to (4.17) for the perfect waveguide. At cutoff, $g_{2m} = 0$ and $p_m = 0$.

Figure 4.16 shows a typical p_m curve for the first mode. It is seen to peak at a frequency near the Airy phase; this is the resonance effect mentioned in Sec. 4.3. The sharpness of the peak is enhanced by increasing c_2/c_1 ratios.

Although there have been no direct experimental checks of Eq. (4.62), good results have been obtained in verifying the theory by measurements of $p_m(\omega)$ in the more complex case of three layers (see Sec. 4.6), so that the validity of these results can be considered as established.

A more difficult problem has been to explain the observed amplitude falloff, which is, in all cases, faster than the predicted $r^{-1/2}$ law for lossless waveguides. In most cases this effect, which is of considerable practical importance, is due to a *small* imaginary component δ in a complex wave number $\kappa + i\delta$.

Since the specific absorption due to seawater is much too small to account for the observed effects, it is clear that we are confronted here with losses upon reflection. These may be due to the dissipative properties of the sediment, not quite total reflection by nondissipative sediments (i.e., partial reflection with $|\Re| = 1 - \epsilon$, $\epsilon \ll 1$), scattering by ocean waves at the surface, irregularities of the bottom topography, etc. Since, for a given

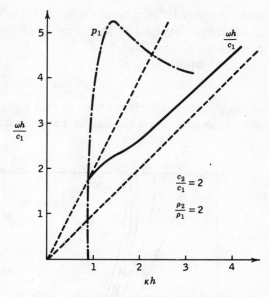

Fig. 4.16.   Excitation function p_1 of the first mode
and dimensionless $\omega - \kappa$ plot for the two-layer
(Pekeris) waveguide.

frequency, higher modes correspond to steeper rays and thus to a greater
number of reflections, they will in most cases be more strongly attenuated
as they travel along the waveguide.   An exception to this rule may be
furnished by solid bottoms, for which ϵ may go through a minimum for
increasing angle of incidence.[19, 20]   Clearly, attenuation measurements
which do not attempt to distinguish between modes will be meaningless.
Losses due to "total" reflection from a *dissipative liquid bottom* have been
taken into account by Kornhauser and Raney[21] by assuming

$$\frac{\omega}{c_2} = k_2 + il \tag{4.63}$$

$$l \ll k_2 \tag{4.64}$$

The inequality (4.64) appears to be verified in the majority of field experiments, so that the Kornhauser and Raney results are of considerable general
interest.   The basic results of the undamped mode theory are not appreciably perturbed, and $\kappa_m(\omega)$ and $p_m(\omega)$ may still be calculated by means of
Eqs. (4.35), (4.61), and (4.62) [the perturbations are easily shown to be of
the order of $(l/k_2)^2$].   Some straightforward algebra gives the horizontal
wave number κ'

$$\kappa'_m = \kappa_m + i\delta_m \tag{4.65}$$

where δ_m may be calculated explicitly by a formula given by Kornhauser and Raney. Figure 4.17 shows values of δ_m for the first five modes when $c_2 = 1.5c_1$ and $\rho_2 = 2\rho_1$.

At cutoff,

$$\delta_m = l \tag{4.66}$$

as one would expect, since at the critical angle one approaches the condition of a plane wave traveling horizontally through the bottom.

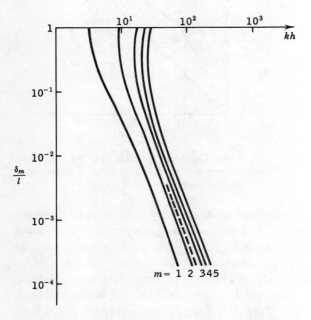

Fig. 4.17 The behavior of δ_m for $m = 1, 2, 3, 4$, and 5 vs. $k_1 h = (\omega/c_1)h$ for a two-layer half-space (Pekeris waveguide) with absorbing bottom [Eqs. (4.63) and (4.65)], according to Kornhauser and Raney.[21] The dashed line shows the values given for $m = 2$ by the asymptotic formula (4.67).

For frequencies $\omega \gg \omega_{0m}$ one has, asymptotically,

$$\delta_m \propto \frac{m^2}{h^3 \omega^3} \tag{4.67}$$

The mode attenuations due to *incomplete reflection* will depend upon the model assumed. However, the following reasoning provides the basis for calculations in this case: for some angle of incidence θ, the modulus of the reflection coefficient $\mathcal{R}$ is

$$|\mathcal{R}| = 1 - \epsilon \qquad \epsilon \ll 1 \tag{4.68}$$

where ϵ is the decrement in amplitude per single reflection of a plane wave. In a water layer of thickness h, the horizontal distance between successive bottom reflections is $2h \tan \theta$. Therefore, the decrement ΔA per unit horizontal distance is

$$\Delta A = -\frac{\epsilon}{2h \tan \theta} A \tag{4.69}$$

or

$$\frac{dA}{A} = -\frac{\epsilon}{2h \tan \theta} dr \tag{4.70}$$

and

$$A = A_0 e^{-\delta r} \tag{4.71}$$

$$\delta = \frac{\epsilon}{2h \tan \theta} \tag{4.72}$$

where, for any given case, ϵ is calculated from the reflection coefficient and (4.68).

Attenuations due to bottom or surface roughness are more difficult to calculate, and will depend upon the geometry or statistics of the irregularities (see Chap. 6).

Model and theoretical studies of these mechanisms of mode attenuation have been reported in interesting papers by Eby, Williams, Ryan, and Tamarkin[19] and Williams and Eby.[20] They used frequencies of 50 to 500 kcps in a 0.5- to 2.5-cm water layer over a thick hycar rubber bottom. The specific absorption of sound in hycar for this range of frequencies is sufficiently high to give observed δ_m/κ_m values for lower modes (2×10^{-2} to 5×10^{-4}) of the same order of magnitude as in many actual shallow-water experiments on the Eastern seaboard of the United States (1×10^{-3} to 4×10^{-3}, see Sec. 4.6). Thus, this is a good scale model in all respects.

For a smooth bottom, it was found that the observed attenuations were too large to be explained solely by the K.R. (Kornhauser and Raney) theory (Fig. 4.18). It was assumed, therefore, that there must also be a leakage of energy into the bottom; i.e., there was incomplete reflection above and beyond that due to bottom dissipation. This could occur because, although the liquid-liquid condition of total reflection $v < c_2$ was met, the hycar had an appreciable rigidity μ and could transmit shear waves of velocity $c_s = \sqrt{\mu/\rho} < c_1$. This energy was lost to the waveguide because of the considerable hycar thickness and its dissipative properties. Eby et al. measured the velocity c_s (which is somewhat frequency dependent), and could thus compute the reflection coefficient (2.80) and, there-

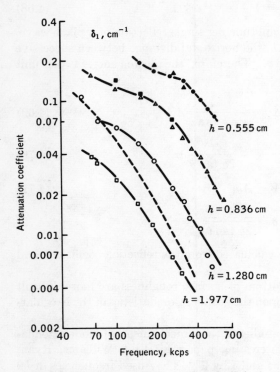

Fig. 4.18 The first-mode attenuation coefficient δ_1 (units cm^{-1}) vs. frequency for various depths of the water layer over a hycar rubber bottom. The dashed line is the δ_1 calculated from the K.R. formula for $h = 1.280$ cm. (After Eby, Williams, Ryan, and Tamarkin.[19])

fore, the small ϵ and δ by (4.68) and (4.72). The results of Eby et al., plotted against the difference between the observed and K.R. attenuations, are shown in Fig. 4.19. The agreement is quite good, and it would appear that the guided mode attenuation is almost completely explained here as a superposition of these two mechanisms. Somewhat better approximations were obtained subsequently by Williams and Eby.[20]

Other cases relevant to shallow-water acoustics, but involving much larger number of modes, have been studied by A. B. Wood[22] in some rather remarkable scale models having a layer of water over rubber or glass bottoms. He used a frequency of 560 kcps and water thicknesses of the order of several centimeters, with a scanning technique giving a two-dimensional (r,z) picture of the sound field. Thus, Fig. 4.20 shows one of Wood's sequences obtained by filming a cathode-ray spot given by the scanning

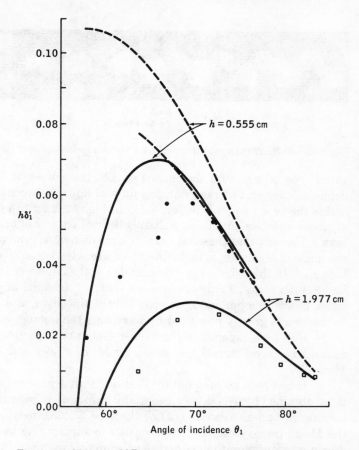

Fig. 4.19   After the K.R. attenuation is subtracted from the total observed attenuation (dashed lines), one obtains the experimental points shown here, which should correspond mostly to attenuation due to shear waves radiated into the hycar bottom.   The corresponding δ_1' coefficients calculated from Eqs. (4.72), (4.68), and (2.80) vary with the angle of incidence as shown by the solid curves.   We see that observation and theory are in quite good agreement.

transducer.   Here one sees predominantly two to three modes, all others having been almost entirely damped out at these ranges.   Figure 4.21 shows the case of a plate glass over steel bottom, in which the attenuation is less, and in which, therefore, a great number of modes will propagate to relatively large distances.   These two figures are good illustrations of the connection and overlap between the mode and ray points of view.[23]   Thus, Fig. 4.20 shows essentially an interference pattern of the type (4.20) for only two modes of well-defined interference wavelength Λ_{12}.   Its maxima are shifted with increasing depth, and the net result is the sinusoidal, corru-

$$h = 1.9 \text{ cm}$$
$$f = 560 \text{ kilocps}$$

Fig. 4.20   A. B. Wood's model experiment for shallow water and rubber bottom.

gated type of structure shown in Fig. 4.5; this corresponds to a vaguely defined, fuzzy sort of ray bouncing up and down between the boundaries and of the type predicted in Sec. 4.2.   In Fig. 4.21, a much greater number of modes interfere, producing a sharply defined pattern of multiply reflected rays.   The fact that these rays are, at large distances, primarily confined to one angle of incidence, is undoubtedly due to selective effects of the layered bottom.   In these figures one is reminded of the development of a function into Fourier series; if only the first few terms of the series are kept, the definition of the function is vague, especially at the edges, and, conversely, its delineation is greatly improved by increasing the number of terms.

Full-scale experiments involving similar or even greater numbers of modes have been carried out at sea by McKenzie[24] and by Bucker and Morris[35].

It has been pointed out by Weston,[25] that patterns quite similar to those obtained by Wood, i.e., essentially graphical representations of interferences in two dimensions (r,z) of the type (3.123), may be obtained by the Moiré fringe method.   This consists in superposing identical gratings drawn on transparent paper and photographing the resulting fringes.

4.6   MULTILAYERED WAVEGUIDES

Although the two-layered case discussed in Secs. 4.3 to 4.5 is a useful first approximation to natural models, typical geologic sections in coastal waters[26] will usually show a more complex structure.   Very often, pre-

$$h = 5.1 \text{ cm}$$
$$f = 560 \text{ kilocps}$$

Fig. 4.21   A. B. Wood's model experiment for a thicker layer and glass bottom.

liminary geophysical exploration shows one or more layers of sediment separating the water layer from a thick, high-velocity section. If the thickness of the latter is large enough compared with a wavelength it may be conveniently assumed to be infinite and homogeneous, and of sound velocity c_{n+1} and density ρ_{n+1}. Then, for phase velocities $v < c_{n+1}$, sound waves are trapped by total reflection in the upper layered section. One is thus led to consider the general problem of n homogeneous layers of sound velocities $c_1, c_2, \ldots, c_n$, densities $\rho_1, \rho_2, \ldots, \rho_n$, and thicknesses $h_1, h_2, \ldots, h_n$ overlying a homogeneous half-space c_{n+1}, ρ_{n+1} (Fig. 4.22). Whenever the half-space corresponds to a thick sedimentary column one may, as a first approximation, treat it as a liquid. However, it will often be a solid of relatively low shear velocity, and one may see a mode damping effect due to partial transmission of shear energy (as in the Eby et al. experiments described in Sec. 4.5).

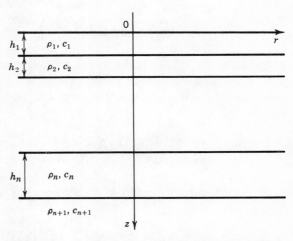

Fig. 4.22 n homogeneous layers overlying a homogeneous half-space ($n + 1$ layered model).

The characteristic equation for the guided modes follows immediately from the discussion of Sec. 2.6, Eq. (2.136):

$$\theta_1 = m\pi \tag{4.73}$$

where θ_1 is obtained from the recursive equations (2.128) and (2.129).

We shall now examine in some detail the particular case of two layers ($c_1 < c_2$) over a half-space $c_3 > c_2$ (Fig. 4.23). Here

$$\left. \begin{aligned} \theta_1 &= \gamma_1 h_1 + \arctan\left(\frac{\gamma_1 \rho_2}{\gamma_2 \rho_1} \tan \theta_2\right) \\ \theta_2 &= \gamma_2 h_2 + \arctan\left(\frac{\gamma_2 \, \rho_3}{g_3 \, \rho_2}\right) \end{aligned} \right\} \quad v > c_2 \tag{4.74}$$

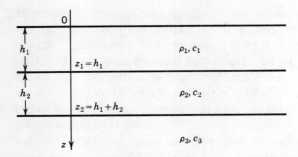

Fig. 4.23 The three-layered model.

or
$$\theta_1 = \gamma_1 h_1 + \arctan\left(\frac{\gamma_1}{g_2}\frac{\rho_2}{\rho_1}\tanh\theta_2\right)$$
$$\theta_2 = g_2 h_2 + \operatorname{arg}\tanh\left(\frac{g_2}{g_3}\frac{\rho_3}{\rho_2}\right) \Bigg\} \quad v < c_2 \qquad (4.75)$$

Equation (4.73) is then easily solved by numerical methods, giving dispersion curves for each mode of the type shown in Figs. 4.24 and 4.25. Explicit expressions for the modes are, when $c_3 > v > c_2$,

$$\begin{aligned}
\varphi_1 &= q \sin \gamma_1 z & z < z_1 \\
\varphi_2 &= q(A_2 \sin \gamma_2 z + B_2 \cos \gamma_2 z) & z_1 < z < z_2 \\
\varphi_3 &= q A_3 e^{-g_3(z-z_2)} & z_2 < z
\end{aligned} \qquad (4.76)$$

With
$$A_2 = \frac{\gamma_1}{\gamma_2}\cos \gamma_2 h_1 \cos \gamma_1 h_1 + \frac{\rho_1}{\rho_2}\sin \gamma_2 h_1 \sin \gamma_1 h_1$$

$$B_2 = -\frac{\gamma_1}{\gamma_2}\sin \gamma_2 h_1 \cos \gamma_1 h_1 + \frac{\rho_1}{\rho_2}\cos \gamma_2 h_1 \sin \gamma_1 h_1 \qquad (4.77)$$

$$A_3 = \frac{\rho_2}{\rho_3}(A_2 \sin \gamma_2 z_2 + B_2 \cos \gamma_2 z_2)$$

For $c_1 < v < c_2$ we need only replace γ_2 by ig_2 in (4.77) and (4.76). Equations (2.62) and (3.119) give explicit formulas for the group-velocity and excitation functions. Elementary integrations give

$$\sigma_m = \frac{1}{2}\frac{\rho_1}{c_1{}^2\gamma_1}\Bigg\{\gamma_1 h_1 - \cos \gamma_1 h_1 \sin \gamma_1 h_1 + \frac{\rho_2}{\rho_1}\frac{c_1{}^2}{c_2{}^2}\frac{\gamma_1}{\gamma_2}\left[\gamma_2 h_2(A_2{}^2 + B_2{}^2)\right.$$

$$+ (B_2{}^2 - A_2{}^2)\cos \gamma_2(z_1 + z_2)\sin \gamma_2 h_2 + 2A_2 B_2 \sin \gamma_2(z_1 + z_2)\sin \gamma_2 h_2]$$

$$+ \left.\frac{\rho_3}{\rho_1}\frac{c_1{}^2}{c_3{}^2}\frac{\gamma_1}{g_3}A_3{}^2\right\}_{\kappa=\kappa_m} \qquad (4.78)$$

$$\nu_m = \frac{1}{2}\frac{\rho_1}{\gamma_1}\left\{\gamma_1 h_1 - \cos\gamma_1 h_1 \sin\gamma_1 h_1 + \frac{\rho_2\,\gamma_1}{\rho_1\,\gamma_2}\left[\gamma_2 h_2(A_2{}^2 + B_2{}^2)\right.\right.$$
$$+ (B_2{}^2 - A_2{}^2)\cos\gamma_2(z_1 + z_2)\sin\gamma_2 h_2 + 2A_2 B_2 \sin\gamma_2(z_1 + z_2)\sin\gamma_2 h_2]$$
$$\left.\left. + \frac{\rho_3\,\gamma_1}{\rho_1\,g_3}A_3{}^2\right\}_{\kappa=\kappa_m} \right. \tag{4.79}$$

These expressions could be somewhat simplified, albeit laboriously, by using (4.77) and (4.73) to (4.75) and reducing ν_m and μ_m to algebraic functions of γ_1, γ_2, and g_3. However, there seems to be little to be gained by this. (For generalizations of these results to the case of n layers, see Ref. 27.)

The group velocity

$$U_m = \frac{1}{\nu_m}\frac{\nu_m}{\sigma_m} \tag{4.80}$$

and excitation functions for source and receiver in surface layer,

$$p_m = \frac{4\pi}{h_1}\sqrt{\Pi\rho_1 c_1}\,\frac{1}{\sqrt{\kappa_m}}\left(\frac{\rho_1 h_1}{2\nu_m}\right) \tag{4.81}$$

are shown for some representative cases in Figs. 4.24 and 4.25.

Note that as ω and κ become large, for $v < c_2$, $\gamma_2 = ig_2$ all the above results tend to those of the two-layer case of Secs. 4.3 to 4.5. Total reflection occurs at $z = z_1$, and for sufficiently short wavelengths the second layer acts as a half-space. This is most easily seen by examining the characteristic equation; as $g_2 \to \infty$, $\tanh\theta_2 \to 1$, and the first Eq. (4.75) tends to the left-hand side of (4.35) (corresponding roughly to $f > 600$ cps in Fig. 4.25).

In Figs. 4.24 and 4.25 it is seen that there may be several stationary values of the group velocity. For sufficiently large h_2 or for high modes, the first minimum on the right (high frequency) is, approximately, the Airy phase of the two-layer problem $h_2 = \infty$. It is separated from the next, lower frequency minimum by a maximum U which, for large h_2 and c_2/c_1 or high modes, tends to c_2; this gives the "refracted arrival" of the seismic refraction shooting method. It is seen that for low frequencies and low modes, it may be appreciably less than c_2. For high modes, the $U_m(\omega)$ curves are quite oscillatory, each higher mode displaying one more maximum and minimum than the one preceding it. This effect is explained by coupling effects between the top layer and the underlying section, and has been investigated in detail by Tolstoy.[27]

The behavior of p_m parallels that of U_m in the sense that its maxima are connected to U minima and vice versa, corresponding to resonant and antiresonant effects.

As usual, we may use Eqs. (3.120) and (4.81) to predict the shape of the c-w field of a point source. Comparison with experiments under actual field conditions have, on the whole, been quite successful. In particular,

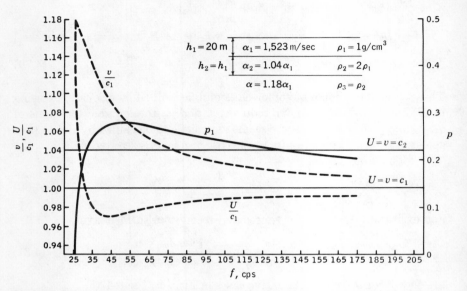

Fig. 4.24 Phase v and group U velocities with excitation functions for first mode. Model shown in upper right-hand insert.

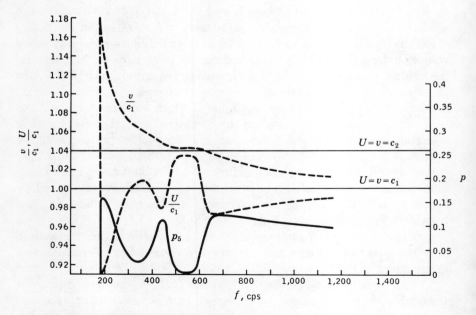

Fig. 4.25 Same as Fig. 4.24, for the fifth mode.

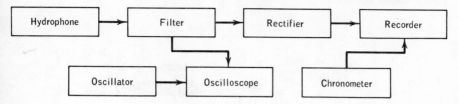

Fig. 4.26   Block diagram of recording equipment.

measurements by Tolstoy[4] and Clay[5] have yielded gratifying results. These writers used c-w sources of known power output, with calibrated hydrophones at a location about 3 km offshore from Fire Island, N.Y., in water 20 m deep.   In these experiments the c-w source was towed† at constant speed and depth ($\simeq$ 13 m), and the output from the fixed hydrophone was fed through a filter and rectifier onto moving chart paper (Fig. 4.26).

† From elementary physics we know that motion of the source at a velocity v toward or away from the receiver results in the latter seeing a frequency shifted by $\pm v/c_1$ (Doppler shift).   This effect is often present in ocean transmission experiments and is usually ignored.   For typical source speeds of the order of a few meters per second, the shift is very small and need only be taken into account for very narrow filters. [4] However, it *is* measurable and is exploited for a number of practical purposes.

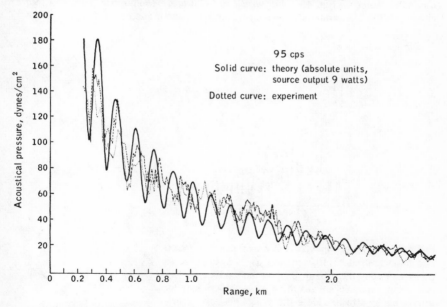

Fig. 4.27   Theory vs. experiment for c-w source (95 cps) in shallow water off the coast of Fire Island for three-layer model of the type shown in Fig. 4.23 with $h_1 = 22.6$ m, $h_2 = 0.9\ h_1$, $c_1 = 1.5 \times 10^3$ msec^{-1}, $c_2 = 1.12\ c_1$, $c_3 = 1.24\ c_1$, and $\rho_2 = \rho_3 = 2$.   All units were calibrated as described in Tolstoy.[4]   The hydrophone was fixed on bottom and the source was towed at a depth of 13.3 m.   Two modes primarily were excited. Attenuation has been taken into account as in Eq. (4.82).

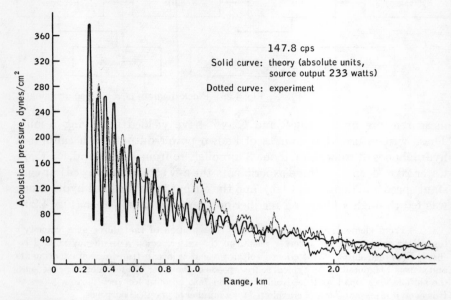

Fig. 4.28 Same as Fig. 4.27, but with $f = 147.8$ cps. Modes one, two, and four are chiefly visible. Attenuation has been taken into account as in Eq. (4.82).

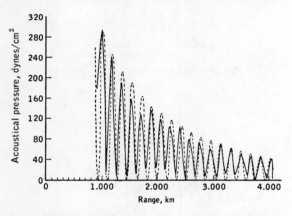

Fig. 4.29 Same as Fig. 4.28, but now the source depth has been shifted to 10.7 m and as a result, modes three and four have been suppressed and mode two has been emphasized resulting in a much simpler interference pattern. Here the solid lines are experimental and the dashed theoretical. Attenuation has been taken into account as in Eq. (4.82).

It was found that, if suitable care was exercised in (1) determining the velocities and thicknesses of the formations and (2) measuring the attenuation coefficients of each mode, one could predict absolute sound levels,

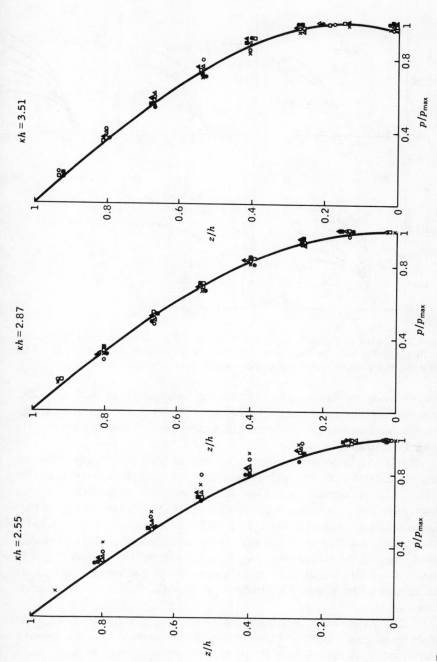

Fig. 4.30 Solid curves show the theoretical curves of $p(z)$ for a three-layer model corresponding to local conditions in the Caspian, for the first mode. (After Kriazhev.[6])

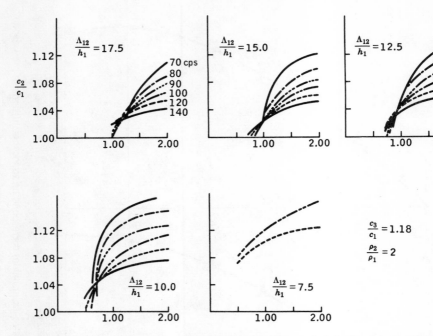

Fig. 4.31 Curves of constant Λ_{12}/h_1, which is the 1-2 mode-interference wavelength for 70 cps $\leq f \leq$ 140 cps, for three-layer models of variable c_2/c_1 and h_2/h_1. This illustrates the extreme sensitivity of the acoustic field to bottom parameters.

relative mode excitation, and interference patterns (Figs. 4.27 to 4.29). Very good results have been achieved by Kriazhev[6] for the vertical distribution of acoustic pressures for the water layer of the Caspian Sea, in water 11 m deep (Fig. 4.30).

In all of these measurements, agreement with theory depends critically on the use of correct values for h_i, c_i, and ρ_i in the equations of this section. In particular, in a three-layered section, propagation is very sensitive to the parameters h_2/h_1, c_2/c_1, and c_3/c_1. This sensitivity is best illustrated by numerical studies of Λ_{12} such as those shown in Fig. 4.31.[28] It is actually possible to use the experimental values of Λ_{12} vs. f as a tool in determining these parameters (Fig. 4.32). It is worth emphasizing here that in the Tolstoy and Clay experiments, the parameters h_i and c_i were not arrived at by guesswork but from systematic, successive approximations.[4]

The water-layer thickness h_1 and sound velocity c_1 were given accurately by echo soundings and temperature measurements. A first approximation for c_2, c_3, and h_2 was obtained from standard seismic exploration results. These values were then perturbed until adequate agreement between observed and calculated Λ_{12} was obtained for the full experimental frequency range of 88 to 150 cps (Fig. 4.32). Since these results are not very sensitive to ρ_i, the plausible assumption $\rho_2 = \rho_3 = 2$ was made. In this manner the layered waveguide shown as an insert in Fig. 4.32 was obtained, and calculations of the sound field by means of Eqs. (3.120) and (4.81) for a number of different frequencies and geometries produced the quite reasonable degree of agreement with observation shown in Figs. 4.27 to 4.29.

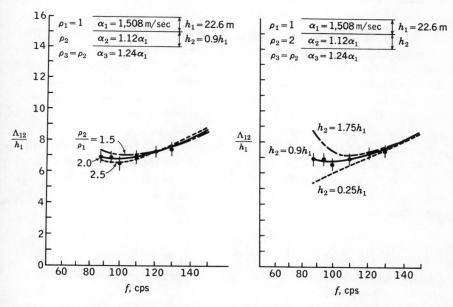

Fig. 4.32 The best fit of observed Λ_{12} vs. f in the Tolstoy[4] and Clay[5] experiments, illustrating the relative sensitivity to h_2/h_1 and insensitivity to density contrast: $\rho_2/\rho_1 = 1.5$, 2.0, and 2.5, and $\rho_2 = \rho_3$.

The attenuation of the individual modes must also be taken into account. The coefficients δ_m of each mode may be found from graphic analysis of the interference patterns and can then be substituted into the formula (3.122) corrected for small attenuations:

$$p_a = \frac{\rho}{\sqrt{r}} \left\{ \left[\sum_m P_m e^{-\delta_m r} \cos\left(\kappa_m r - \frac{\pi}{4} \right) \right]^2 + \left[\sum_m P_m e^{-\delta_m r} \sin\left(\kappa_m r - \frac{\pi}{4} \right) \right]^2 \right\}^{1/2}$$

(4.82)

In the following table we display some experimental values for δ_m, κ_m:

Numerical values of δ_m and κ_m obtained in the Tolstoy experiment (units m^{-1})

f, cps	κ_1	$\delta_1 \times 10^4$	κ_2	$\delta_2 \times 10^4$	κ_3	$\delta_3 \times 10^4$	κ_4	$\delta_4 \times 10^4$
88	0.34	5.9	0.30	10.0	0.28			
95	0.36	5.2	0.32	6.9	0.31			
121	0.47	4.6	0.43	7.2	0.41			
147.8	0.57	4.1	0.54	9.0	0.50	14.0	0.48	20.0

It is seen that the ratios δ_m/κ_m vary between 1×10^{-3} and 4×10^{-3}. Thus the Eby, Williams, Ryan, and Tamarkin model work[19] also provides good scaling for the attenuation laws (Sec. 4.5). It is clear from both their results and ours that attenuations must be specified for each mode individually. Unfortunately, this often is not the practice, and as a result, weird conclusions have been drawn at times concerning spreading power laws, transmission losses, etc.

In the Tolstoy and Clay experiments, the δ_m and the Λ_{12} are determined by the model. The actual experimental verification of the theory consists in the observed agreements of the relative excitations of the individual modes, the absolute levels of sound pressure, and interference patterns (or lack of them) for higher modes.

4.7 HOMOGENEOUS WAVEGUIDE WITH SOLID ELASTIC WALL

Underlying the sedimentary layers of the ocean there are high-velocity, crystalline rocks such as gneiss, granite, or basalt, which cannot be approximated by liquids. When the sediment is very thick or absorbs sound efficiently, it is necessary to take cognizance of these "basement" formations only for very low frequencies. But, occasionally, the sediments may be very thin or even absent, and the ocean floor must be treated as an elastic solid at all frequencies.

In this section we shall briefly sketch the theoretical implications of bottom elasticity for waveguide modes, in a homogeneous water layer over a solid half-space, in order to illustrate the type of effect to be expected. Comparisons with experiments are sorely needed, since they exist only for the very low frequencies observed in connection with submarine earthquakes[12] and, to some extent, mud slides or small tremors[30] and large underwater explosions.[13]

The characteristic equation is

$$\gamma_1 h_1 + \chi_{12} = m\pi \tag{4.83}$$

where χ_{12} now has the form (2.85), that is,

$$\chi_{12} = \text{Arctan} \left\{ \frac{\rho_2}{\rho^1} \frac{\gamma_1}{g_2} \frac{c_{s_2}^4}{\omega^4} [-4g_2 d_2 \kappa^2 + (d_2^2 + \kappa^2)^2] \right\} \tag{4.84}$$

Equation (4.83) can be solved explicitly for κ if the phase velocity is given, since, by (2.77) and (2.78) and (2.82) and (2.83),

$$\chi_{12} = \text{Arctan} \left\{ \frac{\rho_2}{\rho_1} \left(\frac{v^2/c_1^2 - 1}{1 - v^2/c_{p_2}^2} \right)^{1/2} \frac{c_{s_2}^4}{v^4} \left[-4 \left(1 - \frac{v^2}{c_{p_2}^2} \right)^{1/2} \left(1 - \frac{v^2}{c_{s_2}^2} \right)^{1/2} \right. \right.$$
$$\left. \left. + \left(2 - \frac{v^2}{c_{s_2}^2} \right)^2 \right] \right\} \tag{4.85}$$

and thus,

$$\kappa h = \left(\frac{v^2}{c_1^2} - 1 \right)^{-1/2} (m\pi - \chi_{12}) \tag{4.86}$$

The term in brackets in (4.85) is the left-hand side of the Rayleigh wave-velocity equation (2.100); it vanishes for $v = v_R$ and is negative for $v < v_R$. Therefore, there exists a dispersive mode for $m = 0$, since, for $v < v_R$, $\chi_{12} < 0$ in (4.86). It has no low-frequency cutoff. At $v = v_R$, $\kappa h = 0$. Furthermore, this branch may have roots $v < c_1$. Thus, if $c_1 < v_R$, one has, for $v < c_1$,

$$\chi_{12} = i\eta_{12} = i \arg \tanh \left\{ \frac{\rho_2}{\rho_1} \left(\frac{1 - v^2/c_1^2}{1 - v^2/c_{p_2}^2} \right)^{1/2} \frac{c_{s_2}^4}{v^4} \right.$$
$$\left. \left[\left(2 - \frac{v^2}{c_{s_2}^2} \right)^2 - 4 \left(1 - \frac{v^2}{c_{p_2}^2} \right)^{1/2} \left(1 - \frac{c_{s_2}^2}{v^2} \right)^{1/2} \right] \right\} \tag{4.87}$$

and, for $m = 0$, (4.86) becomes

$$\kappa h = - \left(1 - \frac{v^2}{c_1^2} \right)^{-1/2} \eta_{12} \tag{4.88}$$

where, for $v < v_R$, η_{12} is negative.

By (2.98) we see also that as

$$v \rightarrow v_s$$
$$-\eta_{12} \rightarrow \infty \tag{4.89}$$

and, therefore, $\kappa h \rightarrow \infty$

Thus, at high frequencies, the phase velocity of the $m = 0$ mode tends to the speed of Stoneley waves at a liquid-solid interface.

It is now clear that by assuming the medium underlying the water layer to be an elastic solid rather than a liquid, one introduces an additional, entirely new, type of waveguide mode. It has no low-frequency cutoff.

For very long wavelengths its velocity of propagation approaches the speed of Rayleigh waves, i.e., of surface waves on the free boundary of an elastic half-space; at these wavelengths, the water layer becomes a negligible surface film. For very short wavelengths, the water layer is effectively of infinite thickness and the phase velocity approaches that of Stoneley waves at a liquid-solid surface. As in Sec. 2.4, the motion is concentrated at the interface, and dies off exponentially in both directions away from it.

The higher modes $m > 0$ have a low-frequency cutoff at $v = c_{S_2}$, corresponding to the fact that total reflection of sound in the liquid is no longer possible. We have seen, however, that for small c_{S_2} the loss of energy upon reflection is small; the bottom is then treated as a liquid, and the almost totally reflected sound waves are slightly attenuated in the horizontal direction (Sec. 4.5.)† Here we are assuming c_{S_2} large enough for this approach to fail. For $c_1 < c_{S_2}$ and $m \neq 0$; $v \to c_1$ as $\kappa h \to \infty$. For

† These belong, strictly speaking, to the continuous-spectrum modes. But a complete study of this spectrum would show that the major contribution to the field at long ranges comes from modes with complex wave numbers of minimal imaginary part. The latter are essentially those calculated by Eby et al.[19] and Williams and Eby,[20] whereas the real parts are, for all practical purposes, equal to the discrete eigenvalues of the liquid-bottom waveguide. Indeed, the whole analysis of the continuous spectrum may be recast as a theory of complex eigenvalue modes.[29] A real discussion of this point of view would involve us in considerable mathematical complexities and would lengthen this presentation beyond its intended bounds.

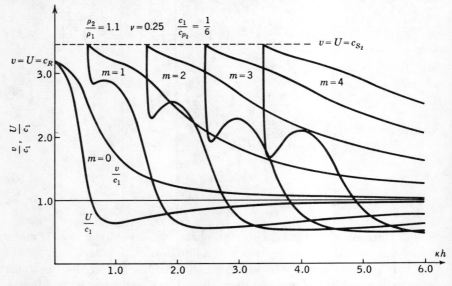

Fig. 4.33 Dispersion curves for a fluid layer overlying a semi-infinite elastic solid, for the first five modes.

$c_1 > c_{S_2}$ there are no unattenuated modes $m > 0$; only the $m = 0$ mode can propagate without attenuation.

In Figs. 4.33 and 4.34 we show some typical dispersion curves. The only reliable experimental results pertaining to this type of waveguide correspond to extremely low frequencies. Thus, seismologists have indications that the $m = 0$ Airy phase (Fig. 4.33) is observed in connection with some submarine earthquakes,[12] and is probably pertinent to the transmission of 5- to 7-sec period microseisms[8] from storms at sea. The asymptotic $v \to v_s$ and $v \to c_1$ branches are also observed (although v_s and c_1 cannot yet be distinguished from each other) on both broad-band seismographs and hydrophones[30] for submarine earthquakes,[13,30,31] nuclear underwater explosions,[13] and, perhaps, ocean bottom tremors and landslides.[32]

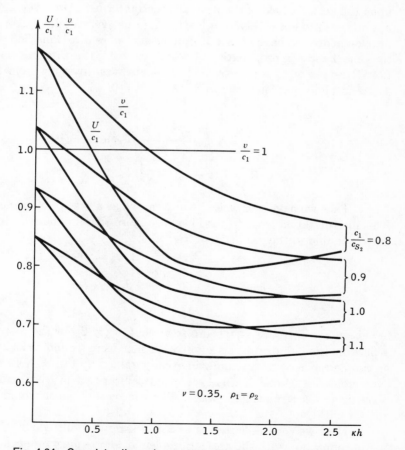

Fig. 4.34   Complete dispersion curves of fundamental mode for the cases $c_1/c_{S_2} = 0.8, 0.9, 1.0$, and 1.1.   Poisson's ratio $\nu = 0.35$ and $\rho_1 = \rho_2$.

4.8 NEAR FIELD OF POINT SOURCE IN TWO-LAYERED MEDIUM

When source and receiver are both located in a layer in which sound can be trapped by total reflection, the trapped or waveguide modes should account, at long ranges, for most of the observed acoustic field. These modes correspond to the discrete spectrum of eigenvalues, and have been examined in some detail in Secs. 4.2 to 4.7. We have shown that the theory, and thus the assumptions behind it, are largely in agreement with experiments.

Something must now be said about the contribution of partial reflections since it is clear that it can be of importance for sufficiently short source-receiver ranges. We could, for instance, attempt to evaluate the continuous-spectrum integrals, such as (3.97), and superpose the results upon the acoustic field of the discrete spectral terms. However, since it is not our wish to get involved in lengthy and not very useful mathematical developments, we have chosen a simpler and more direct method, leading to some handy approximations. We start with the integral transform (2.257) representing a system of harmonic waves diverging from a point source in a homogeneous medium at $z = z_0, r = 0$

$$\frac{e^{ikR}}{R} = i \int_0^\infty \frac{e^{\pm i\gamma(z-z_0)}}{\gamma} J_0(\kappa r) \kappa \, d\kappa \qquad (4.90)$$

$$R = [(z - z_0)^2 + r^2]^{1/2} \qquad (4.91)$$

This, we have seen, may be interpreted as a system of plane waves. This interpretation leads to the following expression for the reflected field, corresponding to the geometry of Fig. 4.35.

$$\Phi_{\text{refl}} = i \int_0^\infty \mathcal{R}_0 \frac{e^{i\gamma(z+z_0)}}{\gamma} J_0(\kappa r) \kappa \, d\kappa \qquad (4.92)$$

In Sec. 2.10, we sketched a treatment of (4.92) for the case of total reflection from a stratified section with increasing sound velocity when $\mathcal{R}_0$ can be replaced by an approximation obtained by the W.K.B. method. Numerous discussions of this type of integral appear in the literature on acoustic and electromagnetic waves,[14] an account of which would take us too far afield.

Here we confine ourselves to a very simple result which is of some use in connection with the present problem of short-range propagation in a shallow-water waveguide. Assuming still that $\kappa r \gg 1$, we use the asymp-

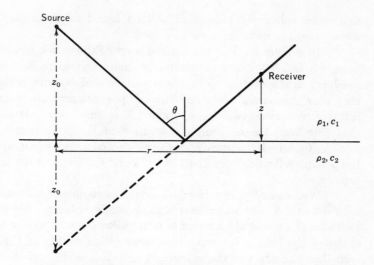

Fig. 4.35 Geometry of source and receiver near reflecting interface. The interface is at $z = 0$, and the z axis is pointing up.

totic form (2.263) so that (4.92) becomes

$$\Phi_{\text{refl}} = \frac{1}{\sqrt{2\pi r}} \text{Re} \int_0^\infty \Re_0 \frac{\sqrt{\kappa}}{\gamma} \, e^{i[\gamma(z+z_0)+\kappa r+\pi/4]} \, d\kappa \tag{4.93}$$

At this point, if one assumes that $\Re_0$ is not varying too rapidly, the principle of stationary phase (Sec. 2.8) tells us that most of the contribution to the integral comes at

$$\frac{\partial}{\partial \kappa}\left[\gamma(z + z_0) + \kappa r\right] = -\frac{\kappa}{\gamma}(z + z_0) + r = 0 \tag{4.94}$$

or

$$\frac{r}{z + z_0} = \tan \theta \tag{4.95}$$

i.e., it comes from the usual reflected-ray path.

The inclusion of higher-order terms in the stationary-phase expansion results in a correction term σ:

$$\Phi_{\text{refl}} = \frac{e^{ikR_2}}{R_2}(\Re_0 + \sigma) \qquad R_2 = [(z + z_0)^2 + r^2]^{1/2} \tag{4.96}$$

where

$$\sigma \propto \frac{c_1}{\omega R_2}\left(\frac{c_1^2}{c_2^2} - \sin^2 \theta_1\right)^{-3/2} \tag{4.97}$$

Thus, it is sufficient to multiply the spherical-image wave fronts by the plane-wave reflection coefficient as long as frequency and range are not too small and as long as θ is not close to critical. A detailed discussion of this first-order sphericity correction will be found in a number of standard works, notably in Brekhovskikh's book.[14]

In a layer such as the surface layer of the two-layered half-space of Secs. 4.3 and 4.4, there are infinitely many arrival paths from source to receiver, corresponding to multiple surface and bottom reflections. One may then reason as before and sum all possible arrivals, weighted by the suitable reflection coefficients, under the integral sign. It may be shown that this leads to the complete solution of the point-source problem.[33] In cases for which there are no totally reflected arrivals (subcritical ranges), the bottom reflection coefficient $|\mathfrak{R}| < 1$ and the terms of the series decrease rapidly.

Weinstein[15] has performed model short-range experiments in a tank with 0.3 to 0.6 m of water over a thick sandy bottom. He finds that the inclusion of a moderate number of terms allows one to predict quite well the shape of the field. We reproduce some of his results in Fig. 4.36. It is seen that the effect of the correction term σ is small and that even in the zone of critical reflections quite reasonable results may be obtained by using a plane-wave reflection coefficient. In a sense, these results were foreshadowed in some model work with elastic waves by Clay and McNeil.[36]

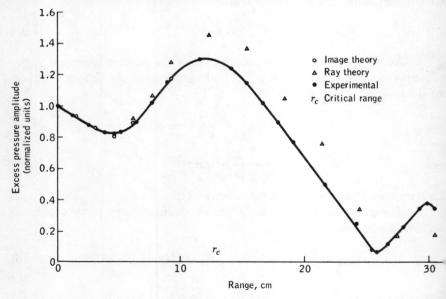

Fig. 4.36 Excess pressure amplitude on a sand bottom as a function of range for a point source of sound at a frequency of 20,000 cps located midway between the surface and bottom in water 15 cm deep. The points indicated as "Ray theory" correspond to a spherical wave diverging from an image and weighted by a plane-wave reflection coefficient. In the "Image theory" account has been taken of the correction term σ. (After Weinstein.[15])

REFERENCES

1. J. M. Ide, R. F. Post, and W. J. Fry: *U.S. Naval Res. Lab. Rept.* S-2113, 1943.
2. C. L. Pekeris: "Theory of Propagation of Explosive Sound in Shallow Water," *Geol. Soc. Am., Mem.* 27, 1948.
3. J. L. Worzel and W. M. Ewing: *Geol. Soc. Am., Mem.* 27, 1948.
4. I. Tolstoy: *J. Acoust. Soc. Am.,* **30**:348 (1958).
5. C. S. Clay, *J. Acoust. Soc. Am.,* **31**:1973 (1959).
6. F. I. Kriazhev: *Soviet Phys. Acoust.,* **6**:60 (1960); also **6**:225 (1960).
7. W. C. Knudsen: *J. Acoust. Soc. Am.,* **29**:918 (1957).
8. F. Press and W. M. Ewing: *Trans. Am. Geophys. Union,* **29**:163 (1948).
9. M. A. Biot: *Bull. Seism. Soc. Am.,* **42**:81 (1952).
10. I. Tolstoy: *Bull. Seism. Soc. Am.,* **44**:493 (1954).
11. I. Tolstoy and W. M. Ewing: *Bull. Seism. Soc. Am.,* **40**:25 (1950).
12. F. Press, W. M. Ewing, and I. Tolstoy: *Bull. Seism. Soc. Am.,* **40**:111 (1950).
13. A. R. Milne: *Bull. Seism. Soc. Am.,* **49**:838 (1959).
14. L. M. Brekhovskikh: "Waves in Layered Media," Academic Press Inc., New York, 1960.
15. M. S. Weinstein, Thesis, University of Maryland, College Park, Md., 1956.
16. A. O. Williams: *J. Acoust. Soc. Am.,* **32**:363 (1960).
17. I. Tolstoy: in "Non-homogeneity in Elasticity and Plasticity," p. 373 (IUTAM Warsaw Symposium), Pergamon Press, New York, 1960.
18. W. M. Ewing, S. Mueller, M. Landisman, and Y. Sato: *Geofis. Pura Appl.,* **44**:83 (1959).
19. R. K. Eby, A. O. Williams, R. P. Ryan, and P. Tamarkin: *J. Acoust. Soc. Am.,* **32**:88 (1960).
20. A. O. Williams and R. K. Eby: *J. Acoust. Soc. Am.,* **34**:836 (1962).
21. E. T. Kornhauser and W. P. Raney: *J. Acoust. Soc. Am.,* **27**:689 (1955).
22. A. B. Wood: in V. M. Albers (ed.), "Underwater Acoustics," p. 159, Plenum Press, New York, 1963.
23. I. Tolstoy: *Polytech. Inst. Brooklyn, Microwave Res. Inst. Symp. Ser.,* p. 43, 1964.
24. K. V. McKenzie: *J. Acoust. Soc. Am.,* **32**:221 (1960).
25. D. E. Weston, *J. Acoust. Soc. Am.,* **32**:647 (1960).
26. J. B. Hersey: Continuous Reflection Profiling, in M. N. Hill (ed.), "The Sea," vol. 3, pp. 47–71, Interscience Publishers (Division of John Wiley & Sons, Inc.), New York, 1963.
27. I. Tolstoy: *J. Acoust. Soc. Am.,* **28**:1182 (1956).
28. I. Tolstoy: *J. Geophys. Res.,* **66**:2485 (1961).

29. J. H. Rosenbaum, *J. Geophys. Res.*, **64**:95 (1959).
30. W. M. Ewing, F. Press, and J. L. Worzel: *Bull. Seism. Soc. Am.*, **42**:37 (1952).
31. J. Northrop, M. Blaik, and I. Tolstoy: *J. Geophys. Res.*, **65**:4223 (1960).
32. J. Northrop and A. Berman: *J. Acoust. Soc. Am.*, **31**: 838 (1959).
33. C. L. Pekeris and I. M. Longman: *J. Acoust. Soc. Am.*, **30**:323 (1958).
34. P. A. Barakos: *J. Acoust. Soc. Am.*, **34**:1919 (1962).
35. H. P. Bucker and H. E. Morris: *J. Acoust. Soc. Am.*, **38**:1010 (1965).
36. C. S. Clay and H. McNeil: *Geophysics*, **20**:766 (1955).

CHAPTER FIVE

PROPAGATION OF SOUND IN DEEP WATER

5.1 INTRODUCTION

As already pointed out in Chap. 4, the distinction between deep- and shallow-water propagation is primarily a matter of scale, defined by the dimensionless parameter κh, κ being the horizontal component of the wave number and h the ocean depth. In practice, deep-water acoustics concerns itself with the range $\kappa h \gg 10$ and, usually, $\kappa h > 10^2$. As a result of the great thickness of water (in terms of wavelengths), it is no longer possible to neglect the variations of c within the water layer. In the shallow case, the water layer was of the order of a wavelength thick, and a constant average value for c was taken. In deep water this is no longer permissible. This feature, perhaps more than any other, is characteristic of deep-water propagation; a continuous $c(z)$ variation in a thick layer has pronounced effects on long-range sound transmission.

Speaking very broadly, there are three main types of ocean stratification displayed by $c(z)$ (Fig. 5.1).

The sound velocity often displays a marked sound-velocity minimum, known as the SOFAR sound channel. One may neglect or average out the near-surface variations of $c(z)$. This case, labeled a in Fig. 5.1, is quite useful in predicting the major features of long-range waveguide effects, such as SOFAR propagation or the periodic focusing of energy in the "convergence zones" (Fig. 5.2). This behavior of $c(z)$ below the surface layer is typical of moderate and equatorial latitudes (see Chap. 1).

In Arctic or Antarctic regions the minimum of sound velocity becomes shallower and eventually reaches the surface, resulting in a stratification of $c(z)$ similar to that of case b in Fig. 5.1. Case c, showing a surface sound channel, is useful for visualizing the behavior of sound at shallow depths and short ranges (a few kilometers) whenever there is a pronounced trapping of sound near the surface.

The ocean bottom is often treated as a homogeneous liquid, of density $1.5 < \rho < 2.5$, of somewhat higher sound velocity than that of the ocean water at the interface (which is a maximum at that point for deep water—Fig. 5.1). It is possible that in many deep-water sediments, $c(z)$ decreases to a minimum in the first few meters and then increases rapidly with depth.[1,2] The increase of $c(z)$ has not been included adequately in the theory so far. In fact, the actual sediment structure will have an effect only on the propagation of low frequencies out to relatively short ranges ($r < 100$ km). For frequencies exceeding a few cycles per second and ranges of more than 100 km, the exact character of the bottom sediments is probably of little or no importance. The attenuation of sound within the sediment is so large that arrivals which have appreciably and repeatedly penetrated into the mud layer will be negligible. Bottom roughness likewise produces attenuation (Chap. 6).

In this chapter we display both theoretical and experimental results.

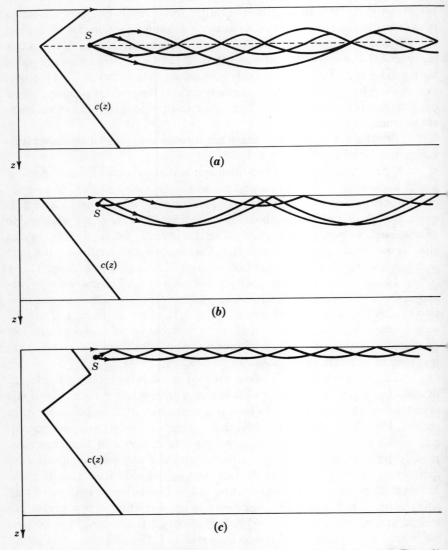

Fig. 5.1 Main types of ocean stratifications displayed by $c(z)$ (compare with Fig. 1.2). Also shown are schematic ray diagrams illustrating the waveguide effect for a source S in the deep (a) and in the surface (c) channels. Case (b) corresponds to the Arctic type of sound-velocity stratification.

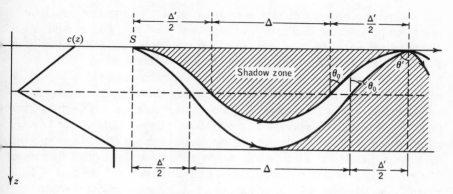

Fig. 5.2 The case in which bottom sound speeds of water and sediment are matched. If one makes the additional assumption $\rho_2 = \rho_1$, there are no reflections from the bottom. Also shown are the principal elements of the convergence-zone and shadow-zone geometry. The Δ and Δ' for the surface and bottom grazing rays are indicated above and below, respectively.

The body of available data is quite large but, as was pointed out in the foreword to this book, much of it is not suitable for comparison with theory and is therefore unusable here. On the whole, our qualitative understanding of sound transmission in the deep ocean is good, in the sense that most of the relevant physical phenomena are understood, but only a very small number of *quantitative* comparisons of theory and experiment have been published, e.g., Pedersen[3] and Barkhatov[4] (with scale models).

Since the absorption coefficient for sound in seawater is quite small for frequencies of the order of a few hundred cycles per second, extremely long ranges for propagation are possible provided the acoustic energy is totally reflected before reaching the boundaries. (Transoceanic transmission paths through the SOFAR channel are easily achieved.) This raises the question of the cumulative effect upon propagation of intrinsic uncertainties, fluctuations, and perturbations of the ocean structure. As we shall see, it appears extremely likely that these effects preclude any comparisons between theory and experiment as detailed as those that can occasionally be obtained in shallow water.

5.2 RAY OPTICS OF THE DEEP OCEAN

The oceans of the world have, on the whole, two rather frequently encountered properties, both of which have already been mentioned in Chap. 1. First is the existence, for latitudes below 50° or so, of the deep sound duct known as the SOFAR channel. In this section we shall discuss the major implications of this waveguide effect from a ray standpoint, using simplified and idealized mathematical models. The second often recurring property, the surface sound channel (appearing schematically in Fig. 5.1c), will be discussed briefly at the end of this section.

Approximations to the ocean, of the type shown in Fig. 5.1a, can be obtained in a number of ways. For ray tracing, one of the most convenient ones has $c(z)$ varying linearly, or in linear segments, on both sides of the SOFAR channel axis; whereas for mode theory, linear segments for $1/c^2$ are more convenient. The principal effects, such as the existence and spacing of convergence and shadow zones, can be adequately illustrated by means of approximations with a discontinuous derivative dc/dz at the axis. Thus we shall use the following cases, having $z = 0$ for sound channel axis:

$$c = \begin{cases} c_0 + pz & z > 0 \\ c_0 - p'z & z < 0 \end{cases} \tag{5.1}$$

and also

$$c = \begin{cases} \left(\dfrac{1}{c_0{}^2} - qz\right)^{-1/2} & z > 0 \\ \left(\dfrac{1}{c_0{}^2} + q'z\right)^{-1/2} & z < 0 \end{cases} \tag{5.2}$$

This notation has been chosen to keep p, p', q, and q' positive for $z \gtrless 0$. Let h be the distance from channel axis to the bottom, h' the distance to the surface, and $c_1 = c_0 + \Delta c$ and $c_1' = c_0 + \Delta c'$ the sound speeds in the water at the bottom and surface, respectively. Then (5.1) and (5.2) yield

$$p = \frac{\Delta c}{h} \qquad p' = \frac{\Delta c'}{h'} \tag{5.3}$$

and

$$q = \frac{1}{h}\left(\frac{1}{c_0{}^2} - \frac{1}{c_1{}^2}\right) \simeq \frac{2}{h}\frac{\Delta c}{c_0}\frac{1}{c_0{}^2}$$

$$q' = \frac{1}{h'}\left(\frac{1}{c_0{}^2} - \frac{1}{c_1'{}^2}\right) \simeq \frac{2}{h'}\frac{\Delta c'}{c_0}\frac{1}{c_0{}^2} \tag{5.4}$$

The following values were picked as giving a reasonable average picture for the western Atlantic. The reason for the oddly particularized values in the metric system is that the original calculations were carried out in British units.

$$
\begin{aligned}
h &= 3{,}597 \text{ m } (11{,}800 \text{ ft}) & c_1 &= 1{,}539.2 \text{ m/sec } (5{,}050 \text{ ft/sec}) \\
h' &= 1{,}281 \text{ m } (4{,}200 \text{ ft}) & c_1' &= 1{,}524.0 \text{ m/sec } (5{,}000 \text{ ft/sec}) \\
& & c_0 &= 1{,}487.4 \text{ m/sec } (4{,}880 \text{ ft/sec})
\end{aligned}
\tag{5.5}
$$

that is,

$$\Delta c = 51.8 \text{ m/sec}$$
$$p = 1.44 \times 10^{-2} \sec^{-1}$$
$$q = 0.876 \times 10^{-11} \text{ m}^{-1} \sec^{-2}$$
$$\Delta c' = 36.6 \text{ m/sec}$$
$$p' = 2.86 \times 10^{-2} \sec^{-1}$$
$$q' = 1.738 \times 10^{-11} \text{ m}^{-1} \sec^{-2}$$

(5.6)

This depth of the SOFAR channel, 1,281 m (4,200 ft), is fairly representative of most of the Atlantic Ocean. For the sake of clarity in discussing long-range propagation, it is convenient to eliminate reflections from the bottom. This is achieved simply by assuming the water to lie over a half-space of constant sound velocity c_2 such that $c_2 = c_1$, and that the densities are also matched, that is, $\rho_2 = \rho_1$. We thus have the example of Fig. 5.2, which will illustrate the essentials of long-range propagation in the simplest form.

Consider a source very close to the free surface (Fig. 5.2), so close that, in so far as the ray geometry goes, a negligible error is committed by making it lie at the surface. The rays leaving the source are then entirely contained between one leaving the source horizontally (the surface-grazing ray) and one leaving it at an angle θ' (with respect to the vertical)

$$\theta' = \text{Arcsin} \frac{c_1'}{c_1}$$

(5.7)

The latter ray is determined by the fact that ultimately it just grazes the bottom; i.e., it has a turning point at $z = h_1$ and $c = c_1$. Under these conditions it is clear, from the drawing in Fig. 5.2, that there exist large areas of the medium that are not irradiated at all; these are the *shadow zones*. Separating the shadow zones are regions of partial focusing, or *convergence zones*. Furthermore, by analogy with the case of Fig. 2.17, we may expect a caustic delineating the left side of the convergence region (drawn schematically in Fig. 5.3). The chief difference from the case of Fig. 2.17 lies in the fact that here the rays returning from the lower half-space are curved (convex upward). Indeed, even in a simple oceanic model such as this, a number of caustics occur in practice, depending upon the position of the source and the assumed dependence of c on z. Many of these caustics are quite weak and undetectable both in an exact mode solution and in practice. They do, however, correspond to a narrow region of divergence in the amplitudes calculated from ray tracing [Eq. (2.256)] and are a nuisance in this sort of calculation. A more detailed discussion will be found in Brekhovskikh.[5]

Thus, if in this simple picture of an ocean one considers a harmonic

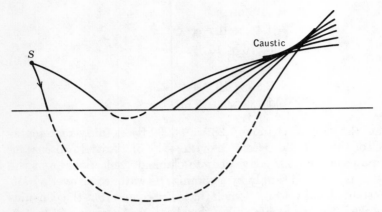

Fig. 5.3 Schematic caustic in the ocean above the SOFAR channel axis.

point source near the surface, the sound field measured by a hydrophone moving away from the source will show zones of very low intensity (shadow) separated by convergence zones of high intensity (see Sec. 5.3 and Figs. 5.23 and 5.26 for what are essentially exact calculations of the sound field). The sound-field amplitudes calculated by ray theory are shown schematically in Fig. 5.4. From the ray standpoint, the intensity in the shadow zone is zero, whereas, in fact, a measurable amount of energy diffracts into the nonilluminated region.

The separation between convergence zones is easily calculated from ray theory.

Suppose first that we approximate the stratified ocean of Fig. 5.1a by Eq. (5.1), i.e., by two linear sections of $c(z)$. Both limiting rays (Fig. 5.2) return into the convergence zone, so that examination of either one should give us the distance D between such zones.

We begin with the surface-grazing ray and note that in this case $D = 2L$, where L is given by (2.238) and (2.237). However, it is informative to obtain this result from geometrical considerations. We know from Sec. 2.10 that the rays are circles centered on the line of zero sound velocity. That is, if we make a change of vertical coordinate using the line $c = 0$ as the new origin,

$$c = pz \tag{5.8}$$

Fig. 5.4 Schematic pressure intensity vs. range in the ocean for source and receiver near the surface.

and the turning-point coordinate z_T is the radius of the circle

$$R = z_T = \frac{c_T}{p} \tag{5.9}$$

Above and below the channel axis, we have, respectively,

$$R' = \frac{c_1'}{p'} \tag{5.10a}$$

$$R = \frac{c_1'}{p} \tag{5.10b}$$

The corresponding horizontal distances covered by a complete half-cycle above or below the axis are, respectively,

$$\Delta' = 2R' \cos \theta_0 \tag{5.11a}$$

$$\Delta = 2R \cos \theta_0 \tag{5.11b}$$

$$\theta_0 = \text{Arcsin} \frac{c_0}{c_1'} \tag{5.12}$$

A complete cycle corresponds to a horizontal distance

$$D = \Delta + \Delta' = 2c_1' \cos \theta_0 \left(\frac{1}{p} + \frac{1}{p'}\right) \tag{5.13}$$

which, by virtue of (5.3) and (5.12), can also be written as

$$D \simeq 2 \sqrt{2}\, c_1' \left(\frac{\Delta c'}{c_0}\right)^{1/2} \left(\frac{h}{\Delta c} + \frac{h'}{\Delta c'}\right) \tag{5.14}$$

Substituting the constants (5.5) and (5.6) we obtain

$$D \simeq 0.698 \times 10^5 \, \text{m} \tag{5.15}$$

The other ray, grazing the bottom, gives almost the same results.   Here the horizontal distances covered above and below the sound-channel axis are, respectively,

$$\Delta' = 2R' (\cos \theta_0 - \cos \theta') \tag{5.16a}$$

$$\Delta = 2R \cos \theta_0 \tag{5.16b}$$

where θ' is the angle of incidence of the bottom-grazing ray at the free surface (Fig. 5.2).

$$\theta' = \text{Arcsin} \frac{c_1'}{c_1} \tag{5.17a}$$

$$\theta_0 = \text{Arcsin} \frac{c_0}{c_1} \tag{5.17b}$$

and how
$$R' = \frac{c_1}{p'} \tag{5.18a}$$

$$R = \frac{c_1}{p} \tag{5.18b}$$

It follows that
$$D = \Delta + \Delta' = 2c_1 \left(\frac{1}{p} + \frac{1}{p'} \right) \cos\theta_0 - 2c_1 \frac{1}{p'} \cos\theta' \tag{5.19}$$

This gives a numerical answer of
$$D \simeq 0.704 \times 10^5 \, \text{m} \tag{5.20}$$

i.e., essentially the same as that given by the surface-grazing ray.

We could also have used Eqs. (2.238) and (2.237) to obtain these results. This we shall do to estimate D for the slightly different case (5.2) [with the same numerical constants (5.5) and (5.6)]. Thus

$$D = 2L \tag{5.21}$$

where L is given by (2.238) and (2.237), that is, using the surface-grazing ray

$$L = 2a \left[\int_0^h \frac{dz}{(1/c_0{}^2 - a^2 - qz)^{1/2}} + \int_0^{h'} \frac{dz}{(1/c_0{}^2 - a^2 - q'z)^{1/2}} \right] \tag{5.22}$$

or
$$D = 4a \left(\frac{1}{c_0{}^2} - a^2 \right)^{1/2} \left(\frac{1}{q} + \frac{1}{q'} \right) \tag{5.23}$$

Since, by (2.236), we have
$$a = \frac{\sin\theta_0}{c_0} \tag{5.24}$$

we get by using (5.4)
$$D = 2 \frac{c_0{}^2}{c_1'} \cos\theta_0 \left(\frac{h}{\Delta c} + \frac{h'}{\Delta c'} \right) \tag{5.25}$$

This is the result (5.13), multiplied by

$$\frac{c_0{}^2}{c_1'^2} \simeq 1 - 2 \frac{\Delta c'}{c_0} \tag{5.26}$$

i.e., a difference of approximately 5 percent, or 3 km. This is of the same order as commonly occurring navigation errors. Thus, from a geometrical standpoint, the difference in assumed dependence of c on z does not lead to large differences in D providing the same extrema for the velocities are used at $z = 0$, h, and h'. But from another point of view, these differences are actually intolerable; uncertainties of this order preclude any possibility of correctly predicting the relative phases of two or more rays.

The fluctuations in relative phase of two rays due to small perturbations of the measured sound velocity can be estimated as follows: It is convenient to suppose that source and receiver are located at the same depth z, for example, on the SOFAR sound-channel axis. Consider two rays arriving at the receiver—one from above and the other from below (Fig. 5.5). Let us compare two slightly different cases, one in which the velocity gradient above is p and another in which it is $p + \delta p$. In both cases the velocity profile below remains unperturbed. What is the difference in phases of the ray arriving from above for the two cases?

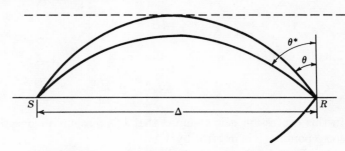

Fig. 5.5   Difference in ray paths from source S to receiver R, corresponding to small difference in velocity c_1' near the sea surface, assuming the same smooth $c(z)$ law between S–R level surface in both cases.

In the perturbed case, the angle of incidence is θ^*, and in the unperturbed it is θ:

$$\theta^* = \theta + \delta\theta \tag{5.27}$$

Since source and receiver stay fixed, Δ is an invariant:

$$\Delta = 2\frac{c_0}{p}\cot\theta = 2\frac{c_0}{p + \delta p}\cot(\theta + \delta\theta) \tag{5.28}$$

which gives, to first order,

$$\delta\theta = \frac{1}{2}\frac{\delta p}{p}\sin 2\theta \tag{5.29}$$

The phase of the ray (for one turning point only) is, in the unperturbed case,

$$S = 2s + \frac{\pi}{2} + \kappa x = 2\left(s + \frac{1}{2}\Delta\frac{\omega}{c_0}\sin\theta\right) + \frac{\pi}{2} \tag{5.30}$$

where

$$s = \int_{z_0}^{z_T}\left(\frac{\omega^2}{p^2 z^2} - \kappa^2\right)^{1/2} dz \tag{5.31}$$

z_T being the turning point. This integral gives

$$s = \frac{\omega}{p}\left(-\cos\theta + \log\frac{1 + \cos\theta}{\sin\theta}\right) \tag{5.32}$$

The perturbation of S corresponding to $\delta\theta$ and δp is, by (5.30),

$$\delta S = 2\delta s + \Delta\frac{\omega}{c_0}\cos\theta\,\delta\theta \tag{5.33}$$

where now it is easily verified that the total contribution of $\delta\theta$ vanishes and

$$\delta S = -2\frac{\delta p}{p}s \tag{5.34}$$

Finally, using (5.3), we obtain the result

$$\delta S \simeq -2\frac{\delta\,\Delta c}{\Delta c}s \tag{5.35}$$

In this expression it is assumed that h is measured correctly and that the corresponding c is in error by $\delta\,\Delta c$.

Exactly the same result can be proved for the case (5.2) with q instead of p, for the surface-grazing ray

$$\delta S = -2\frac{\delta q'}{q'}s \tag{5.36}$$

$$\frac{\delta q'}{q} \simeq \frac{\delta\,\Delta c'}{\Delta c'} \tag{5.37}$$

(5.2) is particularly convenient here, since s has the simple form

$$s = \int_{z_0}^{z_T}\left[\omega^2\left(\frac{1}{c_0^2} - q'z\right) - \kappa^2\right]^{1/2}dz = \frac{2\omega}{3c_0^3q'}\cos^3\theta \tag{5.38}$$

These results imply a high sensitivity of phase to small errors in c. Thus, suppose we are dealing with a surface-grazing ray and remember that we have assumed source and receiver to be on the SOFAR channel axis. For the orders of magnitude occurring in practice [Eq. (5.5)],

$$\cos\theta = (1 - \sin^2\theta)^{1/2} = \left(1 - \frac{c_0^2}{c_1'^2}\right)^{1/2} \simeq \left(2\frac{\Delta c'}{c_0}\right)^{1/2} \tag{5.39}$$

and it is easily seen from (5.38) that

$$s \simeq \frac{2^{3/2}}{3}\frac{\omega h'}{c_0}\left(\frac{\Delta c'}{c_0}\right)^{1/2} \tag{5.40}$$

For (5.5) therefore, by (5.37) and (5.36) we find

$$\delta S \simeq - 2f \frac{\delta \, \Delta c'}{\Delta c'} \frac{h'}{c_0} \tag{5.41}$$

as the error in estimating the phase of a ray path leaving the channel axis and recrossing it after grazing the surface (Fig. 5.5). Thus, for an error of 1 percent in $\Delta c'$ ($\simeq 0.3$ m/sec error $= 2 \times 10^{-4}$ relative error in c_1') and a frequency of 30 cps, $\delta S \simeq 0.5$. For a bottom-grazing ray, the above approximation for the error should be increased by a factor of two ($\delta \, \Delta c$ and Δc then refer to the water sound velocity at the bottom). Thus, at 30 cps the total uncertainty in phase for a ray arriving in the convergence zone may well be as high as $\pi/2$ for errors of the order of 0.3 m/sec in estimated surface and bottom sound velocities.

It appears improbable that one can estimate the proper phasing of rays arriving at a receiver a few tens of kilometers away. This is an important point; although the deep ocean can be treated as a waveguide for long-range sound transmission, one cannot expect detailed comparisons between theory and experiment to be successful. General calculations concerning average sound levels, existence of convergence zones and shadow regions, etc., are meaningful, but it is unlikely that the fine structure of an acoustic field at frequencies higher than 10 cps and at long ranges can be successfully predicted.

This point can be further emphasized by examining waveguides qualitatively similar to the SOFAR channel. We shall discuss such examples further in Sec. 5.3, but meanwhile the following ray considerations are suggestive.

Consider first the symmetric waveguide defined by

$$\frac{1}{c^2} = \begin{cases} \dfrac{1}{c_0{}^2} - qz & z > 0 \\[3mm] \dfrac{1}{c_0{}^2} + qz & z < 0 \end{cases} \tag{5.42}$$

where q is determined as in (5.4) by assuming a value of c for some selected value $z = h$.

In a sense this model is unphysical; the sound velocity is infinite at $z = \pm 1/qc_0{}^2$. But for the orders of magnitude involved here, this is a very great distance indeed from the channel axis (for example, for $\Delta c/c \simeq 10^{-2}$ it is of the order of $50h$). Since we are interested in energy that is traveling within a band of z's not exceeding $3h$ to $4h$, this feature is of no practical consequence.

The equation of the rays is here, for a source at $z = 0$,

$$x = \pm a \int_0^z \frac{dz}{(1/c_0{}^2 - a^2 \pm qz)^{1/2}} \qquad (5.43)$$

which gives, for $z > 0$,

$$x = \mp \frac{2a}{q}\left[\left(\frac{1}{c_0{}^2} - a^2 - qz\right)^{1/2} - \left(\frac{1}{c_0{}^2} - a^2\right)^{1/2}\right] \qquad (5.44)$$

That is, the rays are parabolas with vertical axes. There are no really remarkable properties apparent in this equation (Fig. 5.6).

If, on the other hand, we take a waveguide for which c has continuous derivatives dc/dz, d^2c/dz^2, . . . on the axis, such as

$$c = c_0 \cosh bz \qquad (5.45)$$

a quite different situation prevails. The rays are now given by

$$x = \pm a \int_0^z \frac{dz}{[(1/c_0{}^2)\,\mathrm{sech}^2\,bz - a^2]^{1/2}}$$

$$= \pm \frac{1}{b}\,\mathrm{Arcsin}\left[\frac{a}{\sqrt{1/c_0{}^2 - a^2}}\,\sinh bz\right] \qquad (5.46)$$

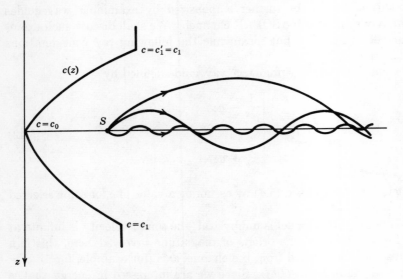

Fig. 5.6 Typical ray paths issuing from source S on the sound-channel axis, for a sound channel of the type shown on the left and corresponding to Eq. (5.42).

or
$$z = \pm \frac{1}{b} \arg \sinh \left[\frac{1}{a} \sqrt{1/c_0^2 - a^2} \sin bx \right] \tag{5.47}$$

and it is clear that all rays go through the points $z = 0$, $x = n\pi/b$ regardless of the value of a; that is, for all values of ϑ_0 at the source $x = 0$, $z = 0$, we have a periodic recurrence of *perfect* foci (Fig. 5.7).

Thus, although we may attempt to approximate the behavior of small-angle rays in the SOFAR channel by fitting curves such as (5.42) or (5.45) through the same pairs of points, the predicted results are totally different; the sound field is extremely sensitive to the type of model assumed. Note that (5.45) actually represents a broad class of approximations exhibiting periodic focusing of energy (for source and receiver on axis) corresponding to "weak cases" of (5.45). Indeed, it is only these "weak cases" that can be discussed in the present context since if bz in (5.45) becomes appreciable, the conditions of validity of the ray theory are violated.

For example, a parabolic channel

$$c = c_0 + \beta z^2 \tag{5.48}$$

will exhibit approximate periodic focusing if

$$c_0 \cosh bz \simeq c_0 + \beta z^2 \tag{5.49}$$

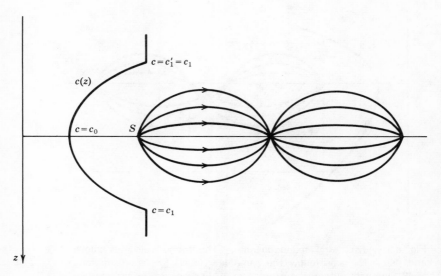

Fig. 5.7 Same general situation as in Fig. 5.6, but $c(z)$ now varies according to Eq. (5.45), or, approximately, to Eq. (5.48). Here the rays are brought into focus at an infinity of evenly spaced points.

i.e., as long as

$$\frac{\beta z^2}{c_0} \ll 1 \tag{5.50}$$

we shall have foci at points

$$z = 0 \qquad x = n\pi \left(\frac{c_0}{2\beta}\right)^{1/2} \tag{5.51}$$

Condition (5.50) implies simply that the sound-velocity gradients are not too strong, so that within the region under consideration there is no appreciable difference between cosh bz and its expansion up to second order. All functions which can be approximated by parabolas for small z will give various degrees of focusing, depending upon how well conditions such as (5.50) are met.

Finally, in an asymmetric waveguide,

$$c = \begin{cases} c_0 \cosh b_1 z & z > 0 \\ c_0 \cosh b_2 z & z < 0 \end{cases} \tag{5.52}$$

One has two series of partial foci, spaced $n\pi/b_1$ and $n\pi/b_2$ apart, with complete focusing at points $n\pi(1/b_1 + 1/b_2)$ (Fig. 5.8). The same holds true,

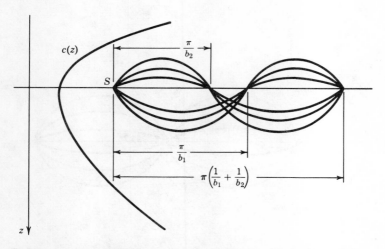

Fig. 5.8 Asymmetric sound channel. The sound velocities above and below the axis follow the same law (5.45) [or, approximately, (5.48)] but with different constants b or β. For a source on the channel axis, the rays are focused at a succession of partial and complete foci. When the situation becomes symmetrical this system of foci degenerates into the single family of Fig. 5.7.

approximately, for

$$c = \begin{cases} c_0 + \beta_1 z^2 & z > 0 \\ c_0 + \beta_2 z^2 & z < 0 \end{cases} \tag{5.53}$$

Subject to two conditions of the type (5.50) we have partial foci and complete foci spaced $n\pi(c_0/2\beta_1)^{1/2}$, $n\pi(c_0/2\beta_2)^{1/2}$, and $n\pi \sqrt{c_0/2}(1/\sqrt{\beta_1} + 1/\sqrt{\beta_2})$. Laws such as (5.52) may provide, in average terms, a fairly realistic description of sound propagation in the vicinity of the SOFAR channel axis. But in fact, $c(z)$ does not really vary this smoothly, even at these depths. Jumps of the order of 0.3 m/sec may occur giving a step-wise and often time-dependent variation of $c(z)$ both above and below the sound-channel axis[6] (Fig. 5.9).

Very little has actually been published on comparisons between experiment and ray calculations. Concerning long-range–deep-ocean propagation, we mention a review paper by Hale,[7] who quotes Pedersen as author of some ray computations giving the envelope of the convergence zones. Not much information concerning model, method of computing, or source is given. We reproduce here Hale's figure as Fig. 5.10. In Fig. 5.11 we show an experimental investigation of the convergence-zone effect performed by M. C. Rinehart of Hudson Laboratories, Columbia University (unpublished). The experiment consisted in exploding 1-kg

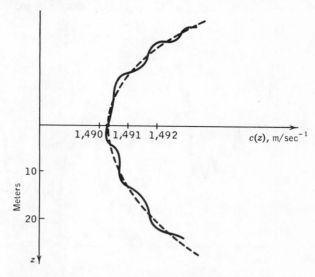

Fig. 5.9   Schematic showing the type of behavior $c(z)$ which actually occurs near the SOFAR channel.

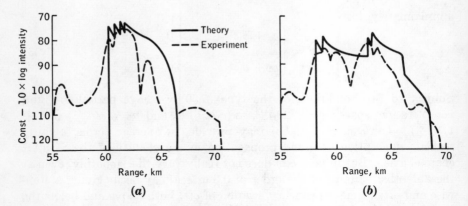

Fig. 5.10 Comparison of sound intensities observed in the first convergence zone (dashed line) with those calculated by ray theory (solid line). (After Hale.[7])

charges of TNT at 12-m depth, recording the pressure signal on a hydrophone 100 m deep, and plotting the time integral of the square of the pressure. The water depth was 8.4 km (Puerto Rico Trench). The expected convergence-zone peaks appear at 70-km intervals.

Interesting results have been published by Pedersen,[3] for the case of a surface channel. The model is shown in Fig. 5.12. A truncated sine wave was used as a pulse, being of sufficient duration to ensure interference between the various possible paths at these ranges. Several combinations

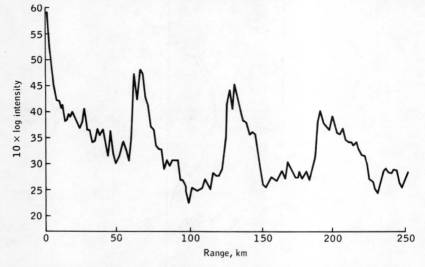

Fig. 5.11 Actually observed succession of convergence zones in a typical North Atlantic experiment. [After Rinehart (unpublished).]

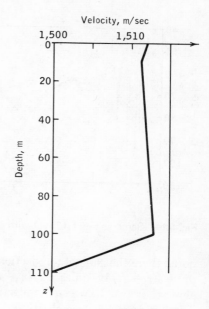

Fig. 5.12 Sound-velocity profile for surface channel used by Pedersen[3] in his calculations of the field shown in Figs. 5.13 and 5.14.

of source and receiver depths were used. The amplitudes calculated by ray theory compared quite well with observation (Figs. 5.13 and 5.14).

Some recent measurements by Parkes[8] in the Mediterranean, characterized by unusually large dc/dz values above the shallow SOFAR channel ($\simeq 150$ m), appear to offer an interesting confirmation of the effects of total reflection upon pulse shape predicted in Sec. 2.10. We

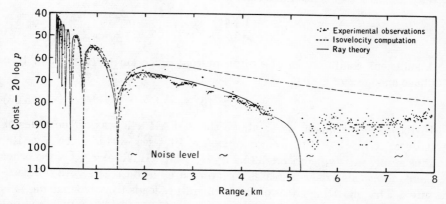

Fig. 5.13 Comparison of surface-channel experimental observations (logarithmic amplitude scale) with ray-theory calculations for a sound-velocity profile with surface channel (Fig. 5.12) (solid line) and without a channel (dashed line). The frequency is 530 cps, the receiver is at 120-m depth, and the source is at 16 m (Pedersen[3]). Amplitudes are plotted on a logarithmic scale.

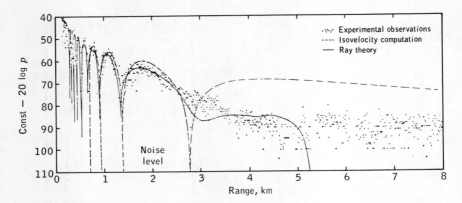

Fig. 5.14 Same as Fig. 5.13, but with frequency of 1,030 cps.

noted there that for total reflection with change in phase of $\pi/2$, an incident pulse $\delta(r - ct)$ becomes $p[1/(r - ct)]$, that is, acquires a tail (r is measured along the ray). Two such reflections produce a phase change of π and the delta function is reconstituted, but with change in sign. Elsewhere (Sec. 2.5) we indicated that total internal reflection in a continuously stratified medium, i.e., at a ray turning point, may under certain conditions be equivalent to a change in phase of $\pi/2$. Conditions under which this effect should appear are investigated in Appendix 3. It is shown there that if the horizontal distance between source and receiver is D, the pulse width is Δt, and the velocity gradient near the turning point is dc/dz, one may define the dimensionless constant

$$\Gamma = \frac{1}{c^3}\left(\frac{dc}{dz}\right)^2 D^3(\Delta t)^{-1} \tag{5.54}$$

A sufficient condition for the total internal reflection to correspond to a phase change $\pi/2$ is that

$$\Gamma > 10^3 \tag{5.55}$$

In Parkes' experiment, dc/dz above the SOFAR axis was of the order of 0.5 sec^{-1}, $D \simeq 3 \times 10^4$ m, and $\Delta t \simeq 5 \times 10^{-4}$ sec. This gives $\Gamma \simeq 10^6$, thus amply satisfying criterion (5.55) *above* the SOFAR axis. On the other hand, *below* this axis, c increases with pressure but decreases with temperature. This offsetting effect of the temperature leads to very small dc/dz— indeed this may be as much as two orders of magnitude smaller, so that (5.55) is no longer satisfied.

Figure 5.15 shows the sequence of pulses 1, 2, 3, and 4 corresponding to ray arrivals along the paths 1, 2, 3, and 4 of Fig. 5.16. We see that, as

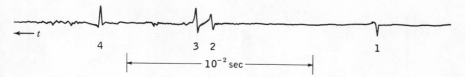

Fig. 5.15   Delta-function-type pulse 1 becomes a broader arrival with a tail and opposite sign of peak amplitude after one turning point (arrivals 2 and 3) and becomes simply a pulse of opposite polarity after 2 turning points (arrival 4).   Corresponding ray paths are indicated schematically in Fig. 5.16.

expected, pulses 2 and 3 are close to being 1 with a change in sign and a tail, whereas 4 is simply 1 with a change in sign (two turning points, both above the SOFAR axis).   Thus, our somewhat oversimplified arguments appear to be experimentally confirmed.   A fact not yet mentioned is that pulse 1, which has suffered a total internal reflection below the SOFAR channel, appears to reproduce rather faithfully the form of the original pulse near the source.   At present, one cannot go beyond the rather vague statement that since (5.55) is not satisfied, we expect the change in shape of the pulse to be much smaller than that exhibited by 2, 3, and 4.   Since criterion (5.55) is, in effect, an alternative way of expressing the fact that ray theory is valid (Appendix 3), it appears that we have here a test of the criterion for validity.

A successful model experiment was performed by Barkhatov et al.[4] Here, a $c(z)$ gradient leading to a caustic similar to that of Fig. 2.17 was produced by heat diffusion in a saltwater bath.   The measured $c(z)$ is shown in Fig. 5.17.   This corresponds to the conditions of formation of a caustic in the homogeneous section.   Thus Eq. (2.275) can be applied. Figure 5.18 shows a comparison between the amplitudes calculated by this equation and the experimental results; the agreement is seen to be good.

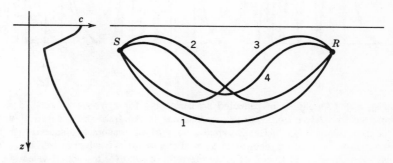

Fig. 5.16   Ray paths for arrivals of Fig. 5.15.

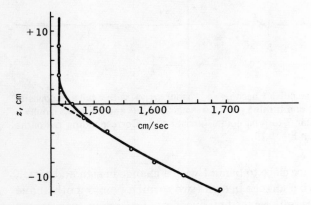

Fig. 5.17 Actually measured sound velocity $c(z)$ in Barkhatov's[4] model (points and solid curve), together with $c(z)$ approximation used for calculations [Eq. (5.2) or (2.267) for $z = 0$, dashed line].

In this section we have, among other things, emphasized the uncertainties besetting predictions of phase corresponding to travel paths of more than a few kilometers in a real ocean. This is a fundamental point, which we shall reexamine from a normal mode point of view in the following section. Nevertheless, exact and detailed calculations applied to

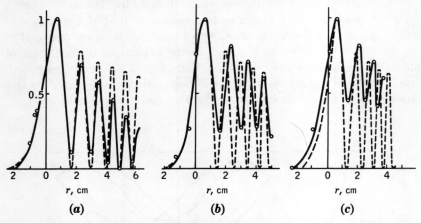

Fig. 5.18 Amplitude of reflected pressure field for a frequency of 2.75 megacycles, plotted in relative units p/p_{max} vs. distance in cm from the theoretical edge of the caustic (Fig. 2.17). (After Barkhatov.[4]) (a) Corresponds to source 4 cm above the boundary $z = 0$ and a receiver 11.5 cm above it. (b) Receiver at 14.5 cm. (c) Source at 2 cm; receiver at 10 cm. Furthermore, in (a) and (b) the sound-velocity gradient is about 20 sec^{-1}, whereas it is 30 sec^{-1} in (c). Points and solid lines are experimental. Dashed line corresponds to Eq. (2.275).

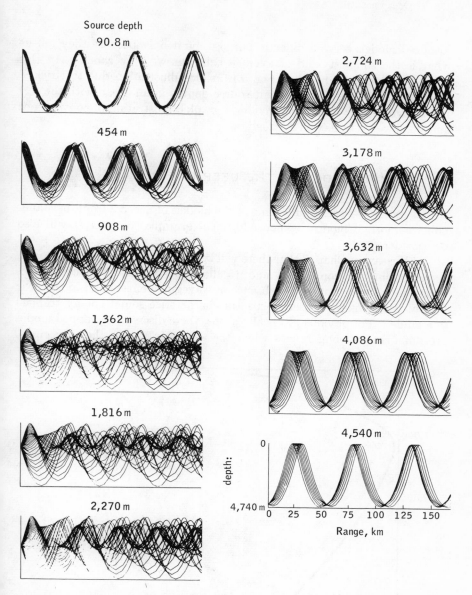

Source depth
90.8 m
454 m
908 m
1,362 m
1,816 m
2,270 m
2,724 m
3,178 m
3,632 m
4,086 m
4,540 m

depth:
0
4,740 m

Range, km
0 25 50 75 100 125 150

Fig. 5.19 Ray diagrams for source at different depths in an ocean with the sound-velocity stratification shown in Fig. 5.20. (After R. J. Urick.[23]) These diagrams illustrate the following features for a fairly typical ocean: (a) The variations of relative insonification at different depths and ranges for selected source positions.   (b) The strong convergence and shadow zones for a source near the surface or near the bottom.   (c) The importance of caustics in all cases.   This figure can be profitably compared with the results of our mode calculations shown in Figs. 5.23–5.25 for rather similar geometries. Also apparent are partial foci of the type described in the text in connection with Eq. (5.53) and corresponding to the schematic drawing of Fig. (5.8).

idealized models serve a didactic purpose, be it only because they tell us what is the simplest kind of average behavior we may expect. In this spirit we have reproduced in Fig. 5.19 a nice illustration due to Urick[23] showing ray tracings for different source depths in an ocean with the $c(z)$ law shown in Fig. 5.20. It provides a graphic illustration of convergence and shadow effects, as well as caustics.

5.3 NORMAL MODES OF THE DEEP OCEAN

In this section we reexamine some of the models of Sec. 5.2 from the standpoint of normal modes. Some additional examples of interest will also be considered.

We saw in Chap. 3 that there will be, in general, two types of modes, corresponding to continuous and to discrete spectra. The continuous spectrum is important in the absence of waveguide effects and in the near field of waveguides. Discrete spectra characterize sound energy trapped in a guide. For obvious physical reasons, these discrete or trapped modes are dominant at long ranges when the source is within the waveguide.

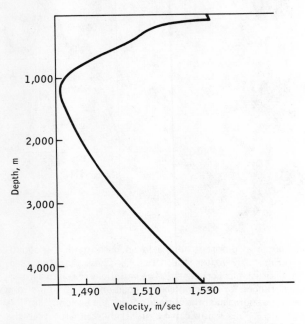

Fig. 5.20   Sound velocity vs. depth assumed by Urick in calculations shown in Fig. 5.19.

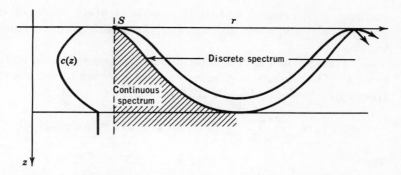

Fig. 5.21   In the case of no bottom reflection from an idealized mathematical model of deep ocean, the regions corresponding to modes with continuous and discrete spectra are fairly sharply separated by the bottom-grazing ray.

The question frequently arises in practice, as to the range r at which one may begin to neglect the contributions of the continuous spectrum. In each situation one must, of course, use judgment and physical intuition, but recollection of the correspondence between modes and rays and the sketching of pertinent rays will usually provide an answer. For example, consider Fig. 5.21 in which we assume that the sound velocity and the density at the bottom of the water column match that in the liquid sediment. Rays that do not correspond to total reflection are describable mostly in terms of the continuous spectrum. Here the distinction between regions dominated by continuous and discrete spectra, respectively, is relatively sharp and unambiguous. In other cases, e.g., Fig. 5.22, in which a bottom of relatively high sound velocity is assumed, the two regions will

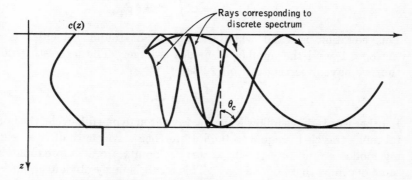

Fig. 5.22   In the case of bottom reflections, there is overlap between the regions in which the partial reflections (continuous spectrum modes) and total reflections (discrete spectrum) contribute significantly to the field.

overlap. In the case of a perfectly reflecting bottom, on the other hand, there are only totally reflected, i.e., guided modes, and no continuous spectrum at all.

This section is limited to the discussion of guided waves and discrete spectra. The pressure amplitude of the fields we shall discuss is therefore given by expressions such as (3.123)

$$p_a = \frac{\rho}{\sqrt{r}} \sum_{n \neq m} \sum_{m=1}^{M} (P_m{}^2 + P_n{}^2 + 2P_m P_n \cos \Delta\kappa_{mn}\, r)^{1/2} \qquad (5.55)$$

where

$$\Delta\kappa_{mn} = \kappa_m - \kappa_n \qquad (5.56)$$

and the eigenvalues κ_m are roots of the characteristic equation (2.142). Much useful information concerning the behavior of the κ_m's and some resulting properties of the sound field can easily be extracted from the W.K.B. approximations to the characteristic equation, i.e., the Bohr-Sommerfeld equation. For example, in the simple case of two turning points (no surface or bottom reflections) this equation has the form (2.217):

$$\int_{z'_T}^{z_T} \gamma_m\, dz = \left(m - \frac{1}{2}\right)\pi \qquad (5.57)$$

The interference wavelengths defined as in Eq. (4.21),

$$\Lambda_{mn} = \frac{2\pi}{\Delta\kappa_{mn}} \qquad (5.58)$$

between various modes are informative quantities in these problems, since they describe the space rates of oscillation of the sound field. The interference wavelengths of neighboring modes are, by Eq. (2.220),

$$\Lambda_{m-1,m} = 2 \int_{z'_T}^{z_T} \tan\theta\, dz \qquad (5.59)$$

This equation is valid when the spread of sound velocities is small ($\Delta c/c_0 \ll 1$) and the number of modes is large. The interesting point is that we have, referring to Eq. (2.238),

$$\Lambda_{m-1,m} = 2L \qquad (5.60)$$

In other words, if we follow a cycling ray through one full cycle, the horizontal range traveled is equal to the interference wavelength of two neighboring modes m and $m - 1$ whose turning points are at approximately the same depth as those of the ray. This result is fairly obvious if one recalls the discussions of Sec. 2.9 and Sec. 4.2, in which the relationship between modes and rays was considered. Selecting a given ray is nearly equivalent to selecting a set of neighboring modes, and vice versa. At the source these modes, and in particular, the two neighboring modes, $m - 1$ and m, must be in phase. As we move away from the source in a horizontal direction, these modes go out of phase and the signal level drops (the ray leaving the source no longer affects a receiver at the source depth—it has curved away). The next point at which the two modes are in phase again, giving a large signal, is, by definition, one interference wavelength $\Lambda_{m-1,m}$ away; this is in the region where the same ray, after completing a full cycle, returns to the same level and illuminates the receiver once again.

This result may, in particular, be put to use estimating the spacing of convergence zones from the eigenvalues κ_m. For this purpose, we may use the approximate Bohr-Sommerfeld equation (5.57). As an example, we consider the case (5.2), the characteristic equation of which is, for $\frac{\omega}{\kappa} = v \leq c_1'$,

$$\frac{2}{3\omega^2} \gamma_0{}^3 \left(\frac{1}{q} + \frac{1}{q'}\right) = \left(m - \frac{1}{2}\right)\pi \tag{5.61}$$

giving

$$\kappa_m{}^2 = k_0{}^2 - \omega^{4/3}\left(m - \frac{1}{2}\right)^{2/3}\frac{2}{c_0}\mu \tag{5.62}$$

$$\mu = \frac{c_0}{2}\left(\frac{3}{2}\frac{\pi}{1/q + 1/q'}\right)^{2/3} \tag{5.63}$$

$k_1 \leq \kappa_m \leq k_0$, where k_0 and k_1 differ by only a few percent, and it follows that the second term in (5.62) is small. If also $m \gg \frac{1}{2}$, use of the binomial expansion yields

$$\kappa_m \simeq k_0 - \omega^{1/3}m^{2/3}\mu \tag{5.64}$$

Thus, differentiating with respect to m, we have

$$\Delta\kappa_{m-1,m} \simeq -d\kappa_m = +\tfrac{2}{3}\mu\omega^{1/3}m^{-1/3} \tag{5.65}$$

Near $v = \omega/\kappa = c_1'$, $\kappa_m \simeq k_1'$ and (5.64) then gives

$$m^{2/3} \simeq \frac{k_0 - k_1'}{\omega^{1/3}\mu} \simeq \omega^{3/2}\frac{\Delta c'}{\mu c_0{}^2} \tag{5.66}$$

This permits us to eliminate m in (5.65):

$$\Delta\kappa_{m-1,m} \simeq \tfrac{2}{3}\mu^{3/2}c_0(\Delta c')^{-1/2} \tag{5.67}$$

Using (5.4) , (5.64), and the result (5.39) we have

$$\Lambda_{m-1,m} \simeq 2c_0 \cos\theta_0 \left(\frac{h}{\Delta c} + \frac{h'}{\Delta c'}\right) \tag{5.68}$$

which is for all practical purposes the same as (5.14) and (5.25).

Likewise $\Lambda_{M-1,M}$, that is, the interference wavelength of the cutoff mode with its neighbor, for the same model would yield (5.19).

Also of interest are the shortest rates of oscillation of the signal in the horizontal direction, i.e., the largest $\Delta\kappa_{mn}$, which obviously correspond to

$$\Delta\kappa_{1M} \simeq k_0 - k_{min} \tag{5.69}$$

where k_0 is taken on the sound-channel axis and k_{min} corresponds to the highest velocity c_{max}. In (5.1) and (5.2), k_{min} is simply k_1, and

$$\Delta\kappa_{1M} \simeq k_0 \frac{\Delta c}{c_0} = \omega \frac{\Delta c}{c_0{}^2} \tag{5.70}$$

and

$$\Lambda_{1M} \simeq \frac{c_0{}^2}{f \, \Delta c} \tag{5.71}$$

These limiting wavelengths can be observed when the lowest and highest modes interfere, i.e., when in a ray tracing the shallowest and steepest rays meet. Such a situation arises for sound propagation along the axis of a sound channel, since the horizontal or almost horizontal rays can then interfere with the critical or limiting rays at their axis crossings.

Similarly, at any other depth z, the shortest interference wavelengths observed will correspond to the locally turning mode or ray $k(z) = \omega/c(z)$ interfering with the steepest possible ray $k = k_1$, that is,

$$\Lambda(z)_{min} = \frac{2\pi}{k(z) - k_1}$$

Another interesting consequence of simple equations such as (5.61) is the possibility of estimating the total number of modes characteristic of a given problem. The maximum mode number M being $\gg 1$, corresponding to $\kappa_M \simeq k_{min}$, it follows from (5.63) and (5.61) that

$$M = \text{integral part of} \left[\frac{1}{2} + \left(\frac{k_0 - k_{min}}{\mu\omega^{1/3}}\right)^{3/2}\right]$$

or

$$M = \text{integral part of} \left(\frac{1}{2} + \omega\mu^{-3/2}\frac{\Delta c^{3/2}}{c_0{}^3}\right) \tag{5.72}$$

This is for the case when (5.61) is valid (two turning points). Suitable modifications of (5.72) are easily found to fit other circumstances.

Figures (5.23) to (5.34) exhibit the results of exact mode calculations for the case of Fig. (5.2) with the constants of Eqs. (5.2) and (5.4) to (5.6) [using Eqs. (3.129) to (3.136), and (3.123)]. The specific gravity of the bottom sediment was taken equal to 2. As long as $c_1 = c_2$, that is, when the speed of sound in the water at the ocean bottom matches that of the sediment, the assumptions $\rho_2 = \rho_1$ or $\rho_2 = 2\rho_1$ are practically equivalent. This is so because the rays or modes all have turning points above the bottom and the effect of the bottom sediment is a perturbation of the phase which vanishes exponentially [like $e^{-\zeta}$ in the case (5.2), Eq. (3.127)] with the distance of the turning point from the bottom. But if $c_2 > c_1$, some waveguide modes correspond to waves that are totally reflected from the sediment surface; these will show a visible, albeit minor, effect of the bottom density upon the results of acoustic-field calculations which are displayed below. A source frequency of 30 cps and power output of 1 watt are assumed.

We begin with cases for which $c_1 = c_2$. In Fig. 5.23, sources and receivers are at 24.4 m and 91.4 m. The great difference in sound levels is due to the rapid falloff of the field near the free surface. Both curves illustrate the smooth falloff of the theoretical field away from the convergence peaks, into the shadow zones. The shadow zone, in which the field is small (but measurable for sources of power exceeding, say, 100 watts), is

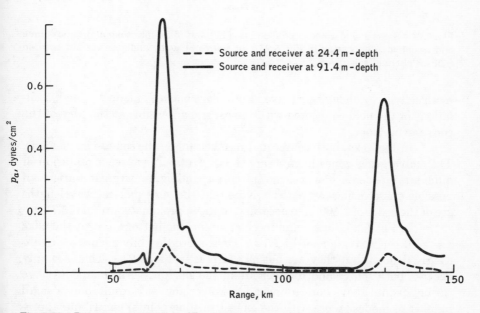

Fig. 5.23 Pressure amplitude p_a [Eq. (5.55)] vs. range for a simple harmonic source of power output 1 watt at 30 cps. The velocity profile $c(z)$ is that of Eqs. (5.2) and (5.5), with matched velocities on bottom. The solid curve corresponds to source and receiver at 91.4 m, whereas the dashed curve corresponds to depths of 24.4 m for both. Note that in the shadow zone the pressure amplitude for the first case drops to about 0.01 dyne. It would take a 100-watt source to raise the level to 0.1 dyne. This should be visible above background noise level.

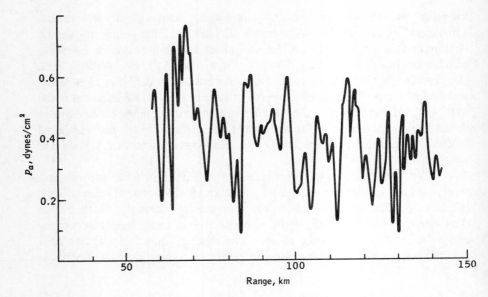

Axis label (vertical): p_a, dynes/cm^2
Axis label (horizontal): Range, km

Fig. 5.24 Same sound-velocity profile [Eqs. (5.2) and (5.5)] for ocean and same source and frequency (30 cps) as in Fig. 5.23, but source (1 watt) and receiver are both on SOFAR channel axis $z = 0$.

essentially a region of destructive interference between modes. Small oscillations of the field connected with the caustic are visible at the edge of the convergence zone.

In Fig. 5.24, both source and receiver are on the sound-channel axis. The convergence zones have disappeared. Instead, we see a profusion of different interference wavelengths, corresponding to a great variety of possible crisscrossing ray paths. Note that the very shortest wavelengths are of the order of 1,500 m in accord with the approximate formula (5.71).

In Fig. 5.25, source and receiver are on the bottom, i.e., at the edge $z = z_1$ of the waveguide of Fig. 5.2. Once more the convergence zones are clearly defined, but they are not as sharp as in Fig. 5.23. This is simply because both source and receiver are in the shadow. All the modes have turning points above both source and receiver and, as a result, only a small number of modes (those with the closest turning points) contribute appreciably to the field. For the same reason, the average sound levels are appreciably less than in Figs. 5.23 and 5.24.

In the following samples of acoustic-field calculations, we have assumed $c_2 > c_1$. In this manner, we include a number of bottom reflections in the waveguide spectrum, corresponding to total reflection of sound from the sediment surface.

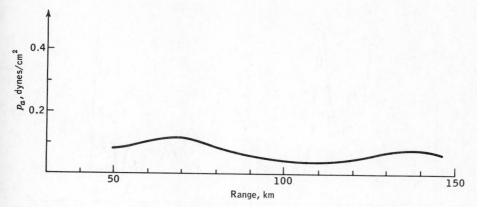

Fig. 5.25   Same as Fig. 5.24 but with source and receiver on bottom interface.

Thus in Fig. 5.26 we have the same source and receiver geometry as in Fig. 5.23, but we have chosen a bottom velocity of $c_2 = 1,546.1$ m/sec. In Fig. 5.27, $c_2 = 1,556.0$ m/sec. We see clearly how, as the bottom velocity is increased, the number of reflections and modes increases, and the field becomes more and more complicated.

Figure 5.28 shows comparisons of the same sort, for source and receiver on the bottom. The cases $c_2 = 1,542.7$ m/sec and $c_2 = 1,546.1$

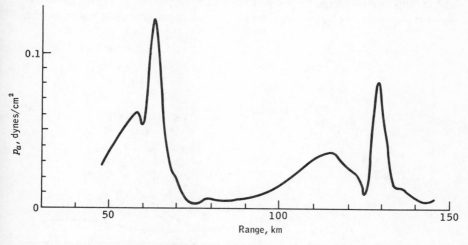

Fig. 5.26   Similar model but with unmatched bottom sound velocity (sediment sound velocity $c_2 = 1,546.10$ msec^{-1}). Same source ($\Pi = 1$ watt, $f = 30$ cps) and source and receiver depth of 24.4 m. Compare with dashed curve of Fig. 5.23, for which $c_2 = c_1 = 1,539.2$ msec^{-1}. Increasing the sediment sound velocity by only 6.9 msec^{-1} has produced an appreciable change of shape for the $p_a(r)$ curve, because of the introduction of bottom reflections.

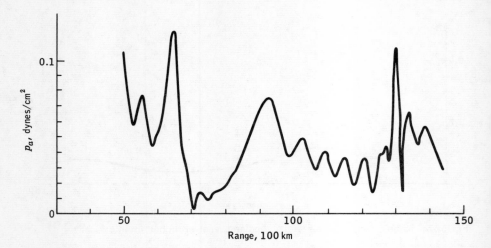

Fig. 5.27 Same as Fig. 5.26, but with $c_2 = 1,556.0$ msec^{-1}. The $p_a(r)$ curve is now appreciably more complex, owing to many additional totally reflected arrivals bouncing off the bottom.

m/sec are shown together with that of Fig. 5.25 ($c_2 = 1,539.2$ m/sec) to illustrate the greater complexity of the sound field as c_2 is increased. If $c_2 = 1,572.8$ m/sec, Fig. 5.29, the field has become very complex indeed; all trace of the convergence zone effect has disappeared. In this case, the shortest interference wavelengths correspond to interference between the

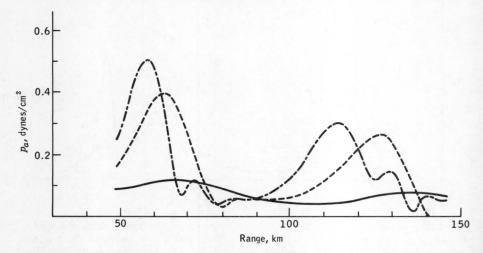

Fig. 5.28 Source and receiver on the bottom. Comparison of different bottom velocities. Solid line: matched $c_2 = c_1 = 1,539.2$ msec^{-1}; dashed line: $c_2 = 1,542.67$ msec^{-1}; dotted and dashed line: $c_2 = 1,546.10$ msec^{-1}. Illustrates the effect of small velocity increments in the sediment.

grazing mode $(\kappa_m \approx k_1 = \omega/c_1)$ and the steepest totally reflected mode (cutoff mode $\kappa_M \approx k_2 = \omega/c_2$), giving approximately

$$\Lambda_{mM} \simeq \frac{c_1{}^2}{f(c_2 - c_1)} \tag{5.73}$$

i.e., about 2,400 m, which is what we measure around $r = 61$ km on Fig. 5.29.

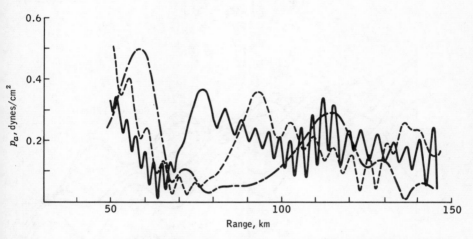

Fig. 5.29   Same as Fig. 5.26, but dotted and dashed line: $c_2 = 1{,}546.10$ msec^{-1} (as in Fig. 5.28); dashed line: $c_2 = 1{,}556.0$ msec^{-1}; solid line: $c_2 = 1{,}572.8$ msec^{-1}. The pressure field rapidly becomes more complicated as the number of bottom reflections is increased.

The vertical fluctuation rates of the sound field are also of great practical interest.   The most rapid rates, in particular, are of concern for feasibility studies and the design of systems.   It is clear from (5.55) that these correspond to the oscillations of the P_m and P_n functions.   Since γ varies slowly enough for the W.K.B. and ray theories to be usable everywhere except near turning points, it follows that a good estimate for the maximum local rate of amplitude oscillation gives

$$\Lambda_{zM} \simeq \frac{2\pi}{\gamma_M} \tag{5.74}$$

where γ_M is the local maximum value of γ.

Thus, on the SOFAR channel axis, we find

$$\gamma_M \simeq (k_0{}^2 - k_2{}^2)^{1/2} \simeq k_2 \left(2\,\frac{c_2 - c_0}{c_0}\right)^{1/2} \tag{5.75}$$

or
$$\Lambda_{zM} \simeq \frac{c_0}{f}\left[\frac{c_0}{2(c_2 - c_0)}\right]^{1/2} \tag{5.76}$$

but on the bottom of our model ocean

$$\gamma_M \simeq (k_1^2 - k_2^2)^{1/2} \simeq k_1\left(2\frac{c_2 - c_1}{c_1}\right)^{1/2} \tag{5.77}$$

or
$$\Lambda_{-M} \simeq \frac{c_1}{f}\left[\frac{c_1}{2(c_2 - c_1)}\right]^{1/2} \tag{5.78}$$

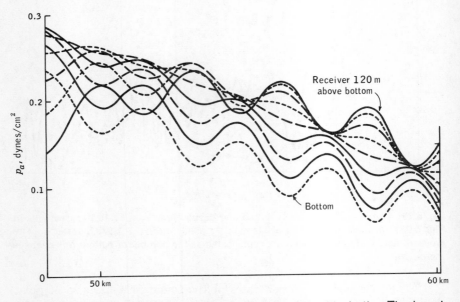

Fig. 5.30 Variation of acoustical pressure amplitude $p_a(r)$ with depth. The lowest curve corresponds to the left-hand-side extremity of the solid curve in Fig. 5.27. Everything remains the same except that each curve corresponds to receiver levels about 15 m apart.

Figure 5.30 provides an illustration of the variation of the acoustic-field amplitudes with depth. It shows a series of $p_a(r)$ curves computed from Eq. (5.55) at depths 15.2 m apart, starting with the case where both source and receiver are at the bottom. The latter case simply corresponds to the $p_a(r)$ shown at the left-hand side of Fig. 5.29 ($r \leq 6.10^4$ m). Examining these curves, we see that in spanning 120 m we have covered approximately $\frac{1}{2}\Lambda_z$. This is in good agreement with Eq. (5.78), which gives

$$\Lambda_{zM} \simeq 240 \text{ m}$$

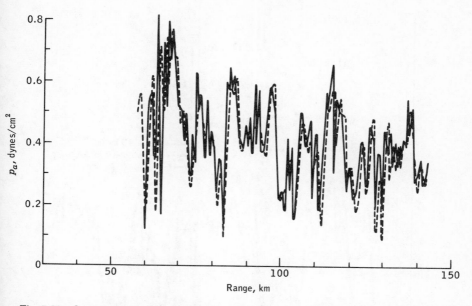

Fig. 5.31   Same source with source and receiver on SOFAR channel axis.   Comparison of $p_a(r)$ curve of Fig. 5.24 (matched bottom velocities $c_2 = c_1 = 1{,}539.2$ msec^{-1}, dashed line) with case $c_2 = 1{,}572.77$ msec^{-1} (solid line).   The increased space rate of oscillation in the latter case, because of arrivals totally reflected from bottom, matches the approximate estimate provided by Eq. (5.71).

In Fig. 5.31, the source and receiver are on the sound-channel axis.   The case of Fig. 5.24 (with $c_2 = c_1$) is also shown for comparison; the average features of the sound field, i.e., the long wavelength oscillations (due primarily to interferences between the lower modes), are very much the same, but we now have fluctuations of very short wavelength superimposed upon them.   Equations (5.69) to (5.71), with $\Delta c = c_2 - c_0$, give here, for the shortest horizontal-fluctuation wavelength,

$$\Lambda_{1M} \simeq 900 \text{ m}$$

which is what we see in Fig. 5.31 near $r = 9 \times 10^4$ m.

We conclude this series of numerical samples with a few more cases of source and receiver on the axis of model sound channels, where, for simplicity, we assume the channels to be symmetric above and below the axis.

Figure 5.32 shows the on-axis field of a 400-cps 1-watt point source in the sound channel of Fig. 3.7.   By (5.72), the total number of modes is $M = 90$.   However, for source and receiver on axis and for a symmetric channel, only the symmetric pressure modes are excited, thus reducing the

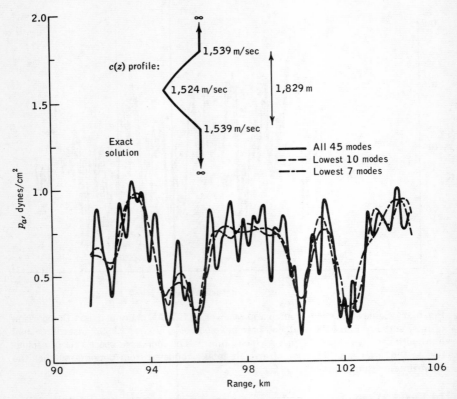

Fig. 5.32   The case of source $\Pi = 1$ watt and $f = 400$ cps in symmetrical sound channel is shown in inset.   Source and receiver are both on axis.   Illustrates the type of approximation one obtains by neglecting some of the modes.

pertinent number to 45.   Furthermore, it is seen from Fig. 5.32 that a partial sum, up to $M = 7$ or 10, provides an adequate picture of an average, smoothed-out sound field from which the more rapid oscillations, of wavelength $\Lambda_{1M} \simeq 400$ m, have been removed entirely.

Figure 5.33 shows the on-axis sound field for a similar sound channel, but with the velocity law

$$\frac{1}{c^2} = \frac{1}{c_0{}^2} - a^2z^2 \tag{5.79}$$

The calculation of the pressure amplitude involved, in this case, the use of Eqs. (3.157), (3.165), and (5.55).   We chose $c_1 = 1,539.2$ m/sec at $|z| \geq h = 914.4$ m, $c_0 = 1,524$ m/sec (Fig. 3.8), $f = 400$ cps, and $\Pi = 1$ watt.   In other words, we are using the same numerical constants as in the example of Fig. 5.32.   In particular, the extrema of sound velocity c_0

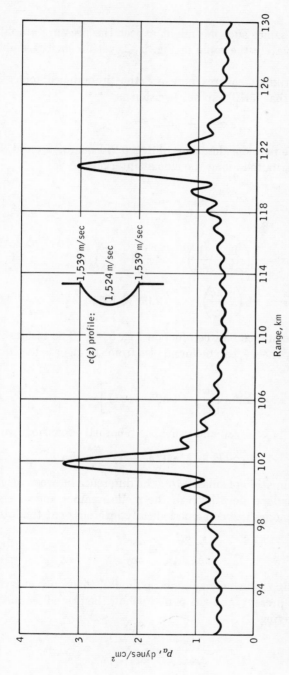

Fig. 5.33 Same source and receiver, but with "parabolic" sound channel [Eq. (5.79)] shown in inset. Although the two channels shown in the insets of this figure and Fig. 5.32 are, in some sense, approximate versions of one another, there is little, if any, resemblance between the predicted sound fields. Note here the strong focusing effects, as predicted by approximate ray and mode theories.

and $c_1 = c_1'$ are the same, and one might expect the pressure amplitudes $p_a(r)$ to be approximately the same in Fig. 5.32, yet no such resemblance is visible.

The most striking features here are the pronounced foci. Since $az \ll 1/c_0$, it follows that (5.79) can be rewritten as

$$c \simeq c_0 + \tfrac{1}{2}a^2 c_0{}^3 z^2 \tag{5.80}$$

and therefore, by the ray considerations of Sec. 5.2, Eqs. (5.49), and (5.51), one expects foci distributed along the axis at intervals

$$x = \frac{\pi}{ac_0} \tag{5.81}$$

In the present case,

$$a = \frac{1}{h}\left(\frac{1}{c_0{}^2} - \frac{1}{c_1{}^2}\right)^{1/2} \simeq \frac{1}{hc_0}\left(2\frac{\Delta c}{c_0}\right)^{1/2}$$

$$x \simeq \pi h\left(2\frac{\Delta c}{c_0}\right)^{-1/2} \simeq 2.03 \times 10^4 \text{ m} \tag{5.82}$$

which is about the distance between foci on Fig. 5.33. The results (5.81), which are due to ray theory, can be found also from the eigenvalue equation (3.157):

$$\kappa_m = \alpha_m = \left[\frac{\omega^2}{c_0{}^2} - \omega a(2m + 1)\right]^{1/2} \tag{5.83}$$

Assuming $\omega a(2m + 1) \ll \omega^2/c_0{}^2$ and using the binomial expansion, we have

$$\kappa_m \simeq k_0 - \tfrac{1}{2}ac_0(2m + 1) \tag{5.84}$$

Thus, in the approximation of small $\Delta c/c_0$, the difference between neighboring eigenvalues is independent both of the mode number and of the frequency. Thus *all* modes will come periodically into phase at the intervals

$$\Delta r = \frac{2\pi}{\Delta\kappa_{m-1,m}} = \frac{2\pi}{ac_0} \tag{5.85}$$

But if one is exciting exclusively symmetric modes, then only every other mode (5.84) will be present, and the period is half the preceding one. We must use $\Delta\kappa_{m-2,m}$, giving

$$x = \frac{2\pi}{\Delta\kappa_{m-2,m}} = \frac{\pi}{ac_0} \tag{5.86}$$

This is the result (5.81) previously established by ray theory.

At this point the following question might well be asked: Since all approximate estimates based upon W.K.B. and ray approximations, such as numerical values for κ_m, vertical or horizontal rates of fluctuations of the sound field, and distribution of convergence, shadow, and focal zones, turn out to be quite satisfactory in practice, why bother with exact solutions in these problems? This is a legitimate question, one which becomes even more so when one examines, as we shall do shortly, the experimental limitations on measurements. So far, we have used exact solutions for the sound field for eclectic reasons; at the ranges involved, the errors incurred by using, for example, the Bohr-Sommerfeld equation for computing κ_m are too large, and we needed reliable illustrations of what the sound field can be expected to look like under ideal conditions. Although the Bohr-Sommerfeld equation is surprisingly accurate and quite sufficient for describing qualitative features of the field such as Λ_{mn}, Λ_z, D, etc., it may often be inadequate for calculating the precise phasing of the modes when adding them to obtain the detailed shape of the sound field. Thus we saw in Sec. 3.8 that in using the Bohr-Sommerfeld equation for the case of Fig. 3.7, errors in κ_m are of the order of 5×10^{-5} for κ_1, 10^{-5} for κ_2, etc. For the first two modes $\Delta\kappa_{mn} = \Delta\kappa_{12}$ is in error by the order of several units in 10^{-5} m^{-1}, and in computing $\cos(\Delta\kappa_{12}r)$ to better than 10 percent, r cannot be allowed to exceed 1.5×10^4 m or so! This is brought home by the calculations exhibited in Fig. 5.34 showing the same case as Fig. 5.32 but calculated by the W.K.B. method. We see that although the sound field exhibits the same typical rates of oscillation (as one would expect from the discussion above), the field is incorrectly predicted at these great ranges. The discrepancies shown in Figs. 5.34 and 5.32 are for $f \simeq 400$ cps and for the constants shown in the insert. A slight improvement should occur if f is increased and dc/dz is decreased. But for frequencies $f \leq 1$ kcps and for values of dc/dz likely to be actually encountered in the ocean, these results should be fairly typical. Therefore, if one wishes to calculate the sound field at long ranges for models approximating a typical ocean, one must use the exact wave functions and eigenvalues; the W.K.B. and ray methods are not sufficiently accurate. In the light of our discussion of Sec. 2.9 this means that for ranges exceeding 10 km or so, the neglected effects of continuous reflection of energy along a ray are making themselves felt.

Surface-channel computations can also be performed by the normal mode methods we have used so far. Thus, consider Fig. 5.35, which falls into the class of cases labeled c in Fig. 5.1. It is obvious that for a source in the surface layer, rays can be trapped by total reflection. From the mode standpoint, these trapped rays correspond simply to a subfamily of modes of the complete spectrum, in particular to modes such that $c_2' < v = \omega/\kappa < c_1'$. If we limit ourselves to ranges outside the shaded region of

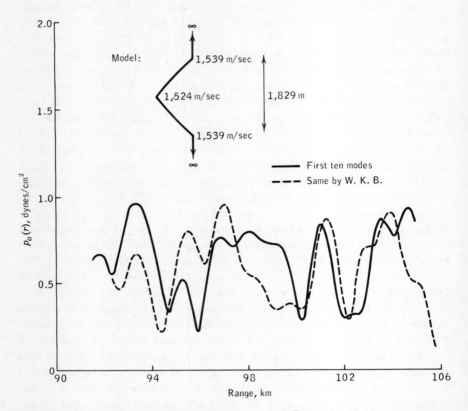

Fig. 5.34 Comparison of the 10-mode $p_a(r)$ curve of Fig. 5.32 with the same curve calculated by the W.K.B. method.

Fig. 5.35, that is, to the discrete spectrum, an accurate description of the sound field will result by the use of Eqs. (5.55), (3.123), and (3.129) to (3.136). Also, in view of our previous discussions, it is clear that a complete sum of all the modes is not necessary; it would be quite sufficient merely to add a small number of modes corresponding to the appropriate range of phase velocities $c_2' < v < c_1'$. An alternative method would be to consider a waveguide such as that in Fig. 5.35, but with a perfectly reflecting bottom. If this waveguide is sufficiently thick, the contribution from the bottom reflections will be negligible in comparison with the surface-trapped arrivals (for source and receiver in surface channel), out to ranges of the order of a few kilometers.

A third method consists of treating the surface channel as an imperfect or "leaky" waveguide in which small but measurable losses occur upon

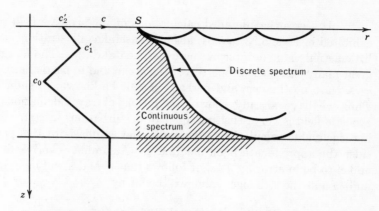

Fig. 5.35   For the velocity profile shown at left, the modes trapped in the surface channel are those with phase velocities $v: c_2' \leq v \leq c_1'$ corresponding to the cycling rays shown here.   For the case of matched bottom-sediment velocities and densities, the surface-channel field would be represented by a small number of modes, i.e., a subspectrum, to a high degree of accuracy.

each internal reflection by "tunneling" through an intervening high-velocity section, into the lower-velocity region below.   This effect can be calculated in a number of fairly straightforward ways, which we shall not go into here.   A recent paper by Pedersen and Gordon[9] displays some interesting comparisons of mode theory with experiment in this type of waveguide. We have reproduced one of their results in Fig. 5.36; the agreement between theory and experiment is quite good, and there is considerable improvement in using the mode theory as against the ray results.

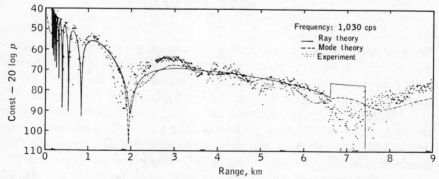

Fig. 5.36   The comparison, for a model of the type shown in Fig. 5.12, of mode calculations, ray calculations, and experiment.   The source is at 15-m depth; the receiver is at 70 m.   The amplitude scale is logarithmic.   (From Pedersen and Gordon[9]).

It seems that detailed calculations of the acoustic field such as are exhibited in Figs. 5.23 to 5.34, although useful as illustrations, are often of little actual value in interpreting experimental data.   The fact is that in a great many cases, the properties of the ocean and in particular the curve of c vs. z are not known, and perhaps cannot be known, in sufficient detail. Thus we have already shown, by means of ray calculations, that the acoustic field is very sensitive to small perturbations in $c(z)$.   The following eigenvalue calculations give additional emphasis to this point.   Consider the approximate equation (5.62).   Assuming c_0 and c_1 to be correct and c_1' to be in error by $\delta \Delta c_1'$, it follows that q' and μ will be in error by $\delta q'$ and $\delta \mu$ and the mth eigenvalue will be off by

$$|\delta \kappa_m| \simeq \omega^{1/3}(m - \tfrac{1}{2})^{2/3}|\delta \mu| \simeq (k_0 - \kappa_m)\frac{|\delta \mu|}{\mu} \tag{5.87}$$

Thus the effect on low modes ($\kappa_m \simeq k_0$) is negligible, as one would expect, since they correspond to rays traveling close to the minimum velocity axis with only small excursions to the side.   The largest errors are for $\kappa_m \simeq k_1'$ for which the rays spend a good part of their path in regions where the errors on c' are large, i.e.,

$$\frac{\delta \kappa_m}{\kappa_m} \simeq \frac{\Delta c'}{c_1'}\frac{|\delta \mu|}{\mu} \tag{5.88}$$

But, by (5.64),

$$\frac{|\delta \mu|}{\mu} \simeq \frac{2}{3}\frac{q'}{q + q'}\frac{|\delta q'|}{q'} \simeq \frac{2}{3}\frac{q'}{q + q'}\frac{\delta \Delta c'}{\Delta c'} \tag{5.89}$$

And (5.4) gives, approximately, using (5.5) and (5.6)

$$\frac{\delta \kappa_m}{\kappa_m} \simeq \frac{\Delta c'}{c_1'}\frac{1}{2}\frac{\delta \Delta c'}{\Delta c'} \simeq \frac{1}{2}\frac{\delta \Delta c'}{c_1'}$$

An error of 0.3 m/sec in estimating c' (assuming everything else to be correct) implies an error of the order of 1×10^{-4}, that is, in the fourth significant figure, of κ_m.   Thus, at ranges exceeding 10^4 m, the computed phases of individual mode terms in (5.55) are going to be quite random.

Naturally occurring fluctuations of 0.3 m/sec in the sound velocity are not uncommon;[6,10] inhomogeneities along a ray path (particularly near the surface), internal waves, and large-scale turbulence all conspire to give a distribution of sound velocities c which is both unpredictable and variable.

It appears, therefore, that in the light of our present knowledge of the oceans, detailed calculations of the sound field at long ranges ($r > 20$ km or so) in typical deep ocean models have only a theoretical, illustrative interest.   One must not expect to perform comparisons between theory and experiment of the type possible in shallow water (Chap. 4). Less ambitious goals have to be set; these will be described in Chaps. 6 and 7.

An effort to compare experiment with mode theory at the very low frequency of 10 cps, for long ranges, was made by Guthrie, Tolstoy, and Shaffer[11] in the northwestern Atlantic, using instrumentation essentially similar to that used in the shallow-water experiments described in Chap. 4. In Fig. 5.37, we show the calculated and observed curves of $p(r)$. There is agreement for the oscillation rates, but the details of the observed field bear little resemblance to those calculated. Even though some sections, in particular toward the end of the run, do show fair agreement, this is not too convincing; subsequent efforts to repeat such results have not been uniformly successful.

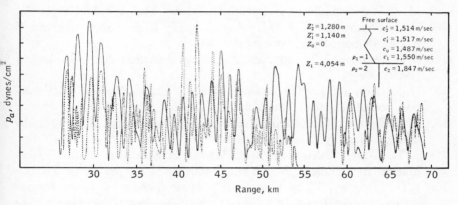

Fig. 5.37   An effort to compare theory (solid line) and experiment (dotted line) by use of theoretical sound-velocity profile shown in insert, for a source of 10 cps, source depth of 24.4 m, and receiver depth of 41.6 m.   The amplitude scale is linear in arbitrary units. The high space rate of oscillation, that is, the shortness of mode-interference wavelengths, is due to either total reflection from high-velocity bottom or to the fact that partial reflections have not yet been damped out.   (Guthrie et al.[11])

The theoretical treatment of deep-water problems is, on the whole, very similar to that of electromagnetic waves in the atmosphere, and for further developments of general interest, we may refer the reader to general texts[12-14] and, in particular, to Budden's book[15] in which the mode approach is emphasized throughout. Papers by Tolstoy[16,17] and Pekeris[18] refer more specifically to ocean acoustics. Further material relevant to the relationships between mode and ray theories has been discussed by Carter and Williams,[19] Williams and Horne,[20] and Hirsch and Carter.[21]   A fine review of the field has been published recently by Frosch.[22]

REFERENCES

1. J. E. Nafe and C. L. Drake: Physical Properties of Marine Sediments, in M. N. Hill (ed.), "The Sea," Vol. 3, pp. 794–815, Interscience Publishers (Division of John Wiley & Sons, Inc.), New York, 1963.
2. J. C. Fry and R. W. Raitt: *J. Geophys. Res.*, **66**:589 (1961).
3. M. A. Pedersen: *J. Acoust. Soc. Am.*, **34**:1197 (1962).
4. A. N. Barkhatov and I. I. Shmelev: *Soviet Phys. Acoust.*, **4**:101 (1958).
5. L. M. Brekhovskikh: "Waves in Layered Media," Academic Press Inc., New York, 1960.
6. A. T. Piip: *J. Acoust. Soc. Am.*, **36**:1948 (1964).
7. F. E. Hale: *J. Acoust. Soc. Am.*, **33**:456 (1961).
8. I. Tolstoy: *J. Acoust. Soc. Am.*, **37**:1153 (1965).
9. M. A. Pedersen and D. F. Gordon: *J. Acoust. Soc. Am.*, **37**:105 (1965).
10. E. J. Skudrzyk: in V. M. Albers (ed.), "Underwater Acoustics," p. 199, Plenum Press, New York, 1963.
11. A. N. Guthrie, I. Tolstoy, and J. Shaffer: *J. Acoust. Soc. Am.*, **32**:645 (1960).
12. D. E. Kerr (ed.): "Propagation of Short Radio Waves," McGraw-Hill Book Company, New York, 1951.
13. H. Bremmer: "Terrestrial Radio Waves," American Elsevier Publishing Company, New York, 1949.
14. J. R. Wait: "Electromagnetic Waves in Stratified Media," The Macmillan Company, New York, 1962.
15. K. G. Budden: "The Wave-Guide Mode Theory of Wave Propagation," Logos Press Ltd., London, and Academic Press Inc., New York, (1961).
16. I. Tolstoy and J. May: *J. Acoust. Soc. Am.*, **32**:655 (1960).
17. I. Tolstoy: *Polytech. Inst. Brooklyn, Microwave Res. Inst. Symp. Ser.*, **14**:43 (1964).
18. C. L. Pekeris: *J. Acoust. Soc. Am.*, **18**:295 (1946).
19. A. H. Carter and A. O. Williams: *J. Acoust. Soc. Am.*, **34**:1985 (1962).
20. A. O. Williams and W. Horne: *J. Acoust. Soc. Am.*, **36**:1997 A (1964).
21. P. Hirsch and A. H. Carter: *J. Acoust. Soc. Am.*, **37**:90 (1965).
22. R. A. Frosch: *Science*, **146**:889 (1964).
23. R. J. Urick: *J. Acoust. Soc. Am.*, **38**:348 (1965).

CHAPTER SIX

THE EFFECT OF IRREGULARITIES OF THE MEDIUM

6.1 INTRODUCTION

In this chapter we discuss some of the complications that arise in dealing with more realistic models of the ocean. Our efforts in previous chapters to compare experimental data with theoretically calculated pressure fields have been limited by the fact that the ocean is not an ideal stratified waveguide. Both the surface and internal movements perturb this picture.[1-3]

In transmission experiments, the inhomogeneities in the ocean increase the attenuation and cause the radiation propagating in different modes to become incoherent. The signal reflected by irregular boundaries loses its similarity to the incident signal and part of the radiation is scattered into other directions. Inhomogeneities within the ocean have a similar effect. The problem is extremely complicated, and it is necessary to use approximate solutions.

The effect that a particular inhomogeneity has on acoustical transmission depends strongly upon the frequency of the signal. Basically, if an inhomogeneity is small compared with the acoustic wavelength, the radiation scattered by this inhomogeneity is also small. In ocean acoustics we encompass a range of wavelengths from a fraction of a meter to a few kilometers and inhomogeneities that vary from a few centimeters to tens of kilometers.

As a practical matter, it is convenient to consider separately the various types of inhomogeneity. First we shall briefly discuss the propagation of signals in a random inhomogeneous medium with isotropic statistical properties. Since this model is too simple to describe long-range sound propagation in a stratified medium, we will develop an approximate theory for sound propagation in an irregular waveguide. The reflection at irregular boundaries and a statistical description of the reflected signals constitute the middle sections. The derivation of the coherent reflection coefficient from an irregularly stratified layer leads to the discussion of propagation in an irregular stratified waveguide.

6.2 SCATTERING OF RADIATION BY RANDOM INHOMOGENEITIES

In transmission experiments at sea it is generally found that signal levels fluctuate under what appear to be constant transmission conditions. The fluctuations are sometimes attributed to the scattering of radiation by random inhomogeneities in the water. Experiments made in the mixed layer at very high frequencies, i.e., greater than 10,000 cps, have shown that the signal level changes in a random manner. The corresponding optical phenomenon of twinkling stars has been observed for thousands of years. However we have been aware of these acoustical fluctuations only since the 1940s.[4]

The mixed layer near the surface of the ocean can be assumed to have an isotropic statistical description. The mean acoustic velocity and mean density together with their mean-square fluctuations are assumed constant throughout the region. The mean dimensions of the irregularities, i.e., correlation function, are constant in the region. In the mixed layer, the mean-square fluctuations of acoustic velocity and density are assumed to be very small.[5]

Geometrical optical approximations were used by Krasilnikov[6] and Bergmann[7] in their studies of the problem. They applied perturbation techniques to the eikonal equation (Sec. 2.10) and obtained formulas for the mean-square fluctuations of phase and amplitude as functions of range. The intensity of radiation scattered by random inhomogeneities was also studied with wave theory, about the same time, by Pekeris.[8] He derived a general formula for scattered radiation with the assumption of small random fluctuations of the index of refraction. Mintzer[9-11] applied wave theory to the transmission experiments of Sheehy.[12] Although the scatter of the data is large, the theory describes the dependence of the fluctuations of the signal amplitude upon range. More recently, Stone and Mintzer have demonstrated excellent agreement between theory and small-scale model experiments.[13] The effects that would be expected for the focusing and defocusing of acoustic waves by spherical inhomogeneities in water have been discussed by Skudrzyk.[14] Experiments to study thermal microstructure and forward scattering of sound were made in the water off Key West, Florida. The small thermal inhomogeneities were found to affect the fluctuation of sound transmission approximately as predicted by theory.[15]

The scattering of radiation in an isotropic inhomogeneous medium has been extensively treated using both wave and ray theoretical methods in a book by L. A. Chernov;[16] thus there is no need for a detailed development of the subject here. We shall, however, discuss some of the results and the application of the theory to acoustic signal transmissions in an inhomogeneous ocean.

The inhomogeneities in the ocean usually change slowly compared with acoustical frequencies, and for high-frequency experiments in the mixed layer, the medium can be assumed to be essentially fixed during a measurement. Since the inhomogeneities can change between measurements, the received signals also change for repeated source transmissions. Although we discuss the statistical properties of signals subject to random fluctuations in more detail in Sec. 6.5, it is sufficient for now to state that the mean amplitude, mean phase, and mean-square fluctuations of the amplitudes and phases can be determined for the set of signals.

For an approximately plane-wave signal propagating in an inhomogeneous medium, we let the signal $p(t)$ have the amplitude A relative to A_0 and the phase fluctuation ΔS as follows:

$$\frac{p(t)}{A_0} = \frac{A}{A_0} e^{i\Delta S + i(kx - \omega t)}$$

$$= e^{B + i\Delta S} e^{i(kx - \omega t)} \tag{6.1}$$

The fluctuation of the absolute amplitude ΔA as given in terms of B is

$$B = \ln \frac{A}{A_0} = \ln \frac{A_0 + \Delta A}{A_0} \simeq \frac{\Delta A}{A_0} \qquad \text{for } \Delta A \ll A_0 \tag{6.2}$$

Chernov used the method of Rytov (which permits large total phase fluctuation) to calculate a theoretical value of $\overline{B^2}$ (ref. 16, p. 75).

$$\overline{B^2} = \alpha L \tag{6.3}$$

$$\alpha \simeq \frac{\sqrt{\pi}}{2} \overline{\mu^2}\, ak^2 \qquad \text{for } ka \gg 1,\, \overline{\mu^2} \ll 1 \tag{6.4}$$

where a is the correlation parameter of the inhomogeneity as defined by the correlation function $\psi(r)$:†

$$\psi(r) = e^{-r^2/a^2} \tag{6.5}$$

where $\overline{\mu^2}$ is the mean-square fluctuation of the index of refraction, and L is the transmission distance.

He also calculated the mean-square phase fluctuations $\overline{\Delta S^2}$ to be

$$\overline{\Delta S^2} = \alpha L = \frac{\sqrt{\pi}}{2} \overline{\mu^2}\, ak^2\, L \tag{6.6}$$

The mean-square phase fluctuations are proportional to range. (In Sec. 6.9, the same range dependence of phase fluctuations is obtained for a stratified medium with random irregularities.) Measurements of $\overline{B^2}$ and $\overline{\Delta S^2}$ are used to determine the fluctuation parameter α. Estimates of $\overline{\mu^2}a$ can be made with (6.4) for the high-frequency case. The correlation of phase fluctuations with absolute amplitude fluctuations for a single receiver, and two-receiver correlation functions, are also discussed in the

† The correlation function for isotropic inhomogeneities is defined as the following:

Let $\Delta c(r) = $ fluctuation of velocity

$$\psi(r) = \frac{1}{\overline{\mu^2} V} \int_V \frac{\Delta c(r')\, \Delta c(r' + r)\, dv'}{c^2} \qquad dv' \text{ element of volume}$$

$$\overline{\mu^2} = \frac{\overline{\Delta c^2}}{c^2}$$

book. The parameters $\overline{\mu^2}$ and a are a property of the microstructure of the water.

The theory of scattering by inhomogeneities usually assumes that the statistical properties of the inhomogeneities are isotropic in the scattering region. This assumption requires a body of water that has the same constant mean sound velocity throughout the region of the experiments. The implications of this assumption will be seen shortly.

The acoustical transmission between a source and receiver depends upon the position of the source and receiver relative to the nonuniform medium, and a change of source position, receiver position, or translation of the source and receiver also causes a change in the signal transmission. At sea it is extremely difficult to fix instruments at constant positions in the medium, and even if the source and receiver are attached to the bottom, internal waves and tides cause the medium to change relative to the source and receiver. Without belaboring the point, it should be clear that it is extremely difficult to study transmission fluctuations due to random inhomogeneities in a stratified ocean.

Sagar made an extensive series of experiments to study intensity fluctuations due to temperature microstructure in the sea.[17-19] Extraneous effects such as motions of the transducers and changes of the mean acoustic velocity were minimized by the selection of good trials, data analysis, and care during the experiments. For a frequency of 14.5 kcps, a 2,000-m maximum range, and a maximum depth of 48 m, Sagar[19] reports the following range of values of $\overline{\mu^2}a$

$$\overline{\mu^2}a \simeq 5 \times 10^{-7} \text{ to } 11 \times 10^{-7} \text{ cgs units} \tag{6.7}$$

The linear dependence of amplitude and phase fluctuations upon range predicted by Eq. (6.3) has been verified with high-frequency experiments. We can then consider the possibility of measuring transmission fluctuations with low-frequency sound. To do this, we use Sagar's larger value of $\overline{\mu^2}a$ and calculate α with (6.4) for a 100-cps signal.

$$\alpha \simeq 16 \times 10^{-12} \text{ cm}^{-1} \tag{6.8}$$

The amplitude variation $\Delta A/A_0$ at 10 km is 0.4 percent, and a tenfold increase of range increases the amplitude variation to only about 1.2 percent. It is evident that fluctuation experiments conducted at the lower frequencies require source-receiver separations that are many times the thickness of the ocean. If we recall the discussion of the propagation of signals in a stratified ocean, it is obvious that the ocean cannot be regarded as being statistically homogeneous even if the bottom and top are ignored. Because of the importance of stratification in the propagation of low-frequency sound over large distances, we conclude that the theory of scattering in a statistically homogeneous medium is not directly applicable to this problem.

Let us reconsider the nature of a dynamically stable ocean, to better specify the acoustic problem. The ocean is approximately horizontally stratified and its density increases with depth even though currents and internal waves can perturb the stratification. The ocean surface is horizontal with time-dependent waves superimposed upon it. The bottom of the ocean varies from areas having steep slopes to areas having smooth, horizontal bottoms. It is apparent that reflections at the irregular surface and the irregularly stratified bottom are required to describe acoustical propagation in the ocean. Even if one uses modes that do not interact with the surface or bottom, the transmission is perturbed as the stratification within the ocean varies.

6.3 REFLECTION OF ACOUSTIC SIGNALS AT A ROUGH BOUNDARY

We commence our study of propagation in an irregular oceanic waveguide by first examining the reflection at an irregular boundary. All real interfaces and boundaries are rough for radiation with short enough wavelength, and the apparent roughness at surfaces also depends upon the viewing conditions. For example, at grazing incidence light reflected in the specular direction by an unpolished surface has about the same characteristics as the reflection from a mirror. The same surface viewed from directions near vertical incidence would scatter light and appear rough. Many qualitative aspects of the scattering of light can be demonstrated in a darkened room with a flashlight and surfaces of different roughness such as a blotter, newsprint, glossy paper, and a mirror.

In more sophisticated experiments we might observe regularities in the scattered radiation from a corrugated surface. Further investigation might show that when this surface is illuminated, the light is scattered into other particular directions. In one direction, the specular direction, incident white light is reflected as white light. In the other directions, incident white light is separated into its spectrum ranging from violet to red. It is obvious that the surface has the properties of an optical grating. We shall now examine the scattering of radiation by three types of surfaces.

The light reflected by a *plane-mirror surface* has the same properties as the incident light. No light is scattered in any direction except the specular direction. The plane mirror scatters radiation coherently since there are definite phase relations between the incoming and scattered waves.[20] Translation of the mirror in its plane does not alter reflected radiation.

An *optical grating* scatters light into particular directions. The phases of the scattered waves are related to the phases of the incident waves by the familiar grating equation. Translation of the grating in its plane by 1, 2, . . . , n grating spaces does not alter the scattered radiation. A periodic surface such as an optical grating scatters radiation coherently.

A *randomly rough surface* such as a blotter scatters light in all directions; i.e., an illuminated spot is visible in any direction. Translation of the surface in its plane may change the intensity in a particular direction. If we translated the surface and measured the phases of the scattered waves, we would observe that these phases are random and unrelated to the incident radiation; the radiation is incoherently scattered.

The preceding qualitative descriptions are adequate for many purposes because if the boundaries are reasonably smooth, little radiation is lost by reflections and the radiation is trapped in the waveguide. If the boundaries are rough, most of the radiation is lost and one has little transmission. Thus, as we shall show, the attenuation caused by irregularities can be included in the transmission equations rather simply, and the modes that interact with very rough boundaries can be ignored at large range. Unfortunately, quantitative statements about what is rough or what is reasonably smooth require a good deal of mathematical analysis and a number of approximations.

A first formulation of the scattering of acoustic waves by a periodic surface was made by Rayleigh.[21] He postulated that the reflection consists of an infinite set of outgoing waves and the incident and reflected waves are fitted to the boundary conditions on the sinusoidal boundary. Brekhovskikh[22] and Eckart[23] used the Helmholtz integral[24] to formulate the scattering problem. The former examined the periodically rough surface and the latter studied reflections from a statistically rough surface. The Helmholtz integral requires the values of the normal derivatives of the incident and reflected waves on the boundary. These were estimated with the Kirchhoff approximation, which assumes that the wave is locally reflected by a plane surface, an approximation useful for surfaces that are not too rough and are not shadowed. An iterative solution of the Helmholtz equation gives the Kirchhoff approximation as the first term,[25] and the other terms can be neglected if the minimum radius of curvature of the surface is much greater than the acoustic wavelength.[26] Beckmann and Spizzichino discuss this matter in detail in the context of the scattering of electromagnetic waves.[27] Our development is similar to Eckart's and Beckmann and Spizzichino's in that we use the Helmholtz integral, a directional source, and the Kirchoff approximation.

Many acoustic experiments are made with transient signals, directional sources, and directional receivers. Source and receiver directivity can be used to limit the area of surface that is illuminated. Effectively, a limitation of the area can be had by transmitting short transient signals and then permitting the receiver to pass the signals during a suitable time. Reflected radiation can be separated from incident radiation by both source directivity and travel-time differences.

Gated sine-wave trains or "pings" are frequently used in experiments. The longer the ping, the more the spectrum of this type of signal is peaked at the angular frequency of the wave train. For theoretical calculations, the actual spectrum can be approximated by a single frequency. Thus, for this development the simple harmonic source is adequate. The far-field acoustical pressure at R due to a simple harmonic source with power output Π and source directivity D_0 is

$$p\ (x,y,z,t)\ =\ \frac{BD_0}{R}\ e^{i(kR-\omega t)} \qquad \text{for } kR \gg 1 \tag{6.9}$$

where by Eq. (2.49)

$$B^2\ =\ \frac{\Pi\rho c}{2\pi}$$

The scattered acoustical pressure is by the Helmholtz theorem[24]

$$p(R')\ =\ -\ \frac{1}{4\pi} \int \left(p|_s\, \frac{\partial\psi}{\partial n}\ -\ \psi\, \frac{\partial p}{\partial n}\bigg|_s \right) dS \tag{6.10}$$

where

$$\psi\ =\ \frac{e^{i(kR'-\omega t)}}{R'} \tag{6.11}$$

n is the normal drawn toward the source, S is the irregular surface, and $p|_s$ and $\partial p/\partial n|_s$ are the values of p and its normal derivatives on the surface. The origin of the coordinate system is in the center of the illuminated area (Fig. 6.1). The xy plane coincides with the mean of the rough surface as averaged over the illuminated area. The source and receiver are at distances R_1 and R_2, respectively, from the origin. R_1 is in the xz plane and makes an angle of θ_1 with the z axis. R_2 makes the angle θ_2 with the z axis, and the projection of R_2 on the xy plane has the angle θ_3 relative to the x axis.

Development of the theory is simpler if R_1 and R_2 are much larger than the acoustic wavelength and the dimensions of the illuminated area. Then both the incident wave on the area and the scattered waves are nearly

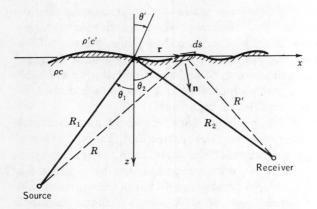

Fig. 6.1 Geometry for reflection at a rough surface. The dependence upon y is not shown.

plane waves. The time dependence can be ignored and the incident pressure wave p_1 and the corresponding scattered field ψ are

$$p_1 = \frac{BD_0}{R_1} \exp\left[i\mathbf{k}_1 \cdot (\mathbf{R}_1 + \mathbf{r})\right] \tag{6.12}$$

$$\psi = \frac{\exp\left[i\mathbf{k}_2 \cdot (\mathbf{R}_2 - \mathbf{r})\right]}{R_2} \tag{6.13}$$

where $\mathbf{r}$ gives the location of the scattering area dS relative to the origin. The differences in *direction* between R and R_1, and R' and R_2, are neglected in the plane-wave approximation.

The Kirchhoff approximation is used to evaluate p and $\partial p/\partial n$ in terms of p_1 on the boundary. The usual plane boundary conditions described in Sec. 2.4 are applied at the local area dS. The values of p and $\partial p/\partial n$ are

$$p|_s = \Re p_1 \tag{6.14}$$

$$\left.\frac{\partial p}{\partial n}\right|_s = -\Re \left.\frac{\partial p_1}{\partial n}\right|_s \tag{6.15}$$

where

$$\Re = \frac{\rho' c' \cos\theta - \rho c \cos\theta'}{\rho' c' \cos\theta + \rho c \cos\theta'}$$

θ is the angle of incidence at dS and θ' is given by Snell's law. Substitution of (6.12), (6.13), and (6.14) into (6.10) gives

$$p = -\frac{1}{4\pi} \int \Re \frac{\partial}{\partial n} (p_1 \psi)\, dS$$

$$p \simeq \frac{-iBe^{ik(R_1+R_2)}}{4\pi R_1 R_2} \int D_0 \Re (\mathbf{k_1} - \mathbf{k_2}) \cdot \mathbf{n} \exp [i(\mathbf{k_1} - \mathbf{k_2}) \cdot \mathbf{r}] \, dS$$

$$\text{for } \begin{array}{l} R_1 k_1 \gg 1 \\ R_2 k_2 \gg 1 \end{array} \quad (6.16)$$

The reduction and evaluation of (6.16) requires that the products of the vectors be expanded in terms of θ_1, θ_2, θ_3, and $\mathbf{n}$, the normal to dS. The elevation of the surface ζ is relative to the mean level $z = 0$. The components of $\mathbf{n}$ are

$$n_x = -\zeta_x n_z \qquad n_y = -\zeta_y n_z \qquad n_z = (1 + \zeta_x^2 + \zeta_y^2)^{-1/2} \quad (6.17)$$

where

$$\zeta_x = \frac{\partial \zeta}{\partial x}$$

$$\zeta_y = \frac{\partial \zeta}{\partial y}$$

$$dS = \frac{dx \, dy}{n_z}$$

The differences of the horizontal and vertical components of the incident and reflected wave numbers are †

$$\begin{aligned} 2\alpha &= (k_1 - k_2)_x = k (\sin \theta_1 - \sin \theta_2 \cos \theta_3) \\ 2\beta &= (k_1 - k_2)_y = -k (\sin \theta_2 \sin \theta_3) \\ 2\gamma &= (k_1 - k_2)_z = -k (\cos \theta_1 + \cos \theta_2) \end{aligned} \quad (6.18)$$

In the specular direction α and β are zero and γ is $-k \cos \theta$.

Substitution of (6.17) and (6.18) into (6.16) yields

$$p = \frac{iBe^{ik(R_1+R_2)}}{2\pi R_1 R_2} \int \int \Re D_0 (\alpha \zeta_x + \beta \zeta_y - \gamma) e^{2i(\alpha x + \beta y + \gamma \zeta)} \, dy \, dx \quad (6.19)$$

Evaluation of (6.19) requires specification of the illumination function, D_0. A desirable function should be unity over the area and decrease to zero outside the area. The slit or aperture function, that is, $D_0 = 1$ for $|x| \leq X$ and $D_0 = 0$ otherwise, is frequently used. However, it gives a scattered acoustic field of the form $\sin kX/kX$. The gaussian illumination function is more convenient for calculations because it does not have side lobes. Throughout the discussion, we use gaussian illumination functions to minimize the confusion between side lobes due to the irregular surface and the side lobes due to the surface illumination function.

† α, β, γ are now defined as differences between incident and reflected wavenumber components, and are not to be confused with our previous use of these symbols. We shall adhere to this convention throughout Secs. 6.3 to 6.7.

In polar coordinates, D_0 is

$$D_0 = e^{-r^2/R^2} \tag{6.20}$$

and in rectangular coordinates

$$D_0 = \exp\left(-\frac{x^2}{2X^2} - \frac{y^2}{2Y^2}\right) \tag{6.21}$$

X, Y, and R define the effective dimensions of the illuminated area. Subject to the condition of large kX and kY or R, (6.19) can be simplified by an integration by parts of the terms involving ζ_x and ζ_y.[27] For integration of the term ζ_x, we form the product of a function of x and a function of ζ as follows:

$$\int_{-\infty}^{\infty} \alpha D_0 e^{2i\alpha x} \left(e^{2i\gamma\zeta} \frac{\partial\zeta}{\partial x} dx\right) = \frac{\alpha}{2i\gamma} D_0 e^{2i(\alpha x + \gamma\zeta)} \Big|_{-\infty}^{\infty}$$

$$- \int_{-\infty}^{\infty} D_0 \frac{\alpha^2}{\gamma} e^{2i(\alpha x + \gamma\zeta)} dx - \int_{-\infty}^{\infty} \frac{\alpha}{2i\gamma} e^{2i(\alpha x + \gamma\zeta)} \frac{\partial D_0}{\partial x} dx$$

Substitution of (6.21) for D_0 gives the following form for the result of integration:

$$\int_{-\infty}^{\infty} \alpha D_0 e^{2i(\alpha x + \gamma\zeta)} \frac{\partial\zeta}{\partial x} dx = 0 - \int_{-\infty}^{\infty} D_0 \frac{\alpha^2}{\gamma} e^{2i(\alpha x + \gamma\zeta)} dx$$

$$+ \int_{-\infty}^{\infty} D_0 \frac{\alpha x}{2i\gamma X^2} e^{2i(\alpha x + \gamma\zeta)} dx \tag{6.22}$$

$$= F(X) + G(X)$$

Inspection shows that $G(X)$ will, for large kX, fall off faster than $F(X)$. This may be checked by the use of Schwarz's inequality, which shows that

$$\frac{|G(X)|}{|F(X)|} \propto (kX)^{-1}$$

We see that the third term on the right side of (6.22) is negligible when the dimensions of the illuminated area are much larger than the acoustic wavelength. A similar analysis can be made for the term in the integrand involving ζ_y. The result of the integration by parts is

$$p \simeq \frac{-iBe^{ik(R_1+R_2)}}{2\pi R_1 R_2} \int\!\!\int_{-\infty}^{\infty} \Re D_0 \frac{(\alpha^2 + \beta^2 + \gamma^2)}{\gamma} e^{2i(\alpha x + \beta y + \gamma\zeta)} \, dy \, dx \tag{6.23}$$

The reflection coefficient $\Re$ depends upon the incident angle. $\Re$ can be removed from the integral for a free surface or an infinitely rigid surface.

It is also independent of the angle at the interface of two media having the same velocity and different densities. In many practical situations one can use average values for $\mathcal{R}$, α, β, and γ, since the incident radiation can be restricted to a small range of angles by a directional source. We use the average values in the integral, and the scattered and reflected acoustical pressure on substitution of (6.18) is

$$p \simeq \frac{ikBf(\theta)\mathcal{R}e^{ik(R_1+R_2)}}{2\pi R_1 R_2} \int\!\!\int_{-\infty}^{\infty} D_0 e^{2i(\alpha x + \beta y + \gamma \zeta)}\, dy\, dx \qquad (6.24)$$

where

$$f(\theta) \equiv \frac{1 + \cos\theta_1 \cos\theta_2 - \sin\theta_1 \sin\theta_2 \cos\theta_3}{\cos\theta_1 + \cos\theta_2} \qquad (6.25)$$

$f(\theta)$ is $\cos\theta$ in the specular direction; $\theta_1 = \theta_2$ and $\theta_3 = 0$. The function $f(\theta)/\cos\theta$ has been tabulated (ref. 27, p. 25). The scattered and reflected radiation is given by (6.24), and this expression is used to calculate the radiation scattered by both corrugated and random surfaces in subsequent sections.

It is convenient to measure the scattered signal relative to the signal reflected by a mirror-like surface when the illumination factor, source position, receiver position, etc., are the same. The signal reflected by a mirror surface $\zeta = 0$ is

$$p_0 = \frac{ikBf(\theta)\mathcal{R}e^{ik(R_1+R_2)}}{2\pi R_1 R_2} \int\!\!\int_{-\infty}^{\infty} D_0 e^{2i(\alpha x + \beta y)}\, dy\, dx \qquad (6.26)$$

This represents the reflection by a mirror surface of the illumination function *with its side lobes*. It is important to distinguish these side lobes from the diffraction effects of a rough surface.

6.4 PERIODIC SURFACE

The ocean surface frequently has the appearance of a corrugated surface although it is in fact a random surface with a highly peaked frequency spectrum. In Sec. 6.6, we show that such a randomly corrugated surface has scattering characteristics similar to the periodic corrugated surface. It is desirable to examine the radiation scattered by a periodic corrugated surface because the scattering integral (6.24) can be evaluated and directly compared with experiments. The comparison is particularly important because a number of approximations were made in the derivation of (6.24), the validity of which should be tested.

Let us assume the surface has corrugations parallel to the y axis according to the following equation:

$$\zeta = \sigma \cos Kx \qquad (6.27)$$

The substitution of (6.27) for ζ in the scattering integral yields an exponential function that can be expressed as the following series of Bessel functions:[28]

$$e^{2i\gamma\sigma \cos Kx} = J_0 (2\gamma\sigma) + 2 \sum_1^\infty (i)^n J_n (2\gamma\sigma) \cos n Kx \qquad (6.28)$$

The substitution of (6.28) and the source directivity (6.21) into (6.24) yields an integral that can be evaluated. The result is

$$p = \frac{ik\, BXY \, \Re e^{-2\beta^2 Y^2}}{R_1 R_2} \, [\cos \theta_1 J_0 (2\gamma\sigma) \, e^{-2\alpha^2 X^2}$$

$$+ \sum_1^\infty (i)^n f(\theta_1, \theta_n) \, J_n (2\gamma_n\sigma) \, e^{-(2\alpha_n - nK)^2 X^2/2}$$

$$+ \sum_1^\infty (i)^n f(\theta_1, \theta_n) \, J_n (2\gamma_n\sigma) \, e^{-(2\alpha_n + nK)^2 X^2/2}] \qquad (6.29)$$

$f(\theta_1, \theta_n)$ is given by (6.25), and θ_n refers to the direction of the nth scattering order, i.e., $\theta_2 = \theta_n$ in (6.25).

The corrugated surface diffracts the radiation into many different directions or orders. At large distance, the angular width of a particular order depends upon the width of the illuminated area. For very large X and Y, the pressure is zero in all directions other than

$$\beta = 0$$
$$\alpha = 0$$

or

$$2\alpha_n = \pm nK \qquad (6.30)$$

$\beta = 0$ and $\alpha = 0$ correspond to the direction for specular reflection. The condition $2\alpha_n = \pm nK$ specifies the directions of the scattered radiation in directions other than specular.†

Extensive experimental studies of the acoustic waves scattered by corrugated surfaces have been made in the acoustics laboratory at

---

† Our development gives the far-field scattered radiation. Radiation scattered along the plane of the rough surface and surface waves are not determined in the approximation. Surface waves have been observed in the studies of light scattered from gratings.[29-30] Theoretical studies of surface waves, the effect of shadowing, and the fields near the irregularities require different developments from the Kirchhoff approximation.[31-36] The radiation scattered by special surfaces such as small bosses on a rigid plane can be calculated without the Kirchhoff approximation.[37,38] Biot studied this type of surface and was able to replace the rough surface by a boundary condition.[39]

Brown University.[40] The experiments were done in a water tank having pressure-release surfaces that consisted of thin sheets of cork cemented to the corrugated surfaces. The pressure-release surfaces were irradiated with nearly plane waves from a directional transducer, and the scattered radiation was observed with a probe hydrophone. The frequency range covered 80 to 300 kcps, corresponding to a range of $k\sigma$ from 0.34 to 4.0. Unwanted reflections from the tank walls were eliminated by transmitting pings from the source and observing the signal at the proper time.

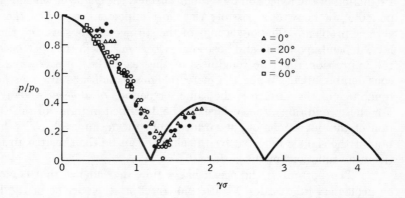

Fig. 6.2 Reflection from a sinusoidal corrugated surface in the specular direction. (From La Casce and Tamarkin.[40]) $\sigma = 0.15$ cm, $K = 3.12$ cm^{-1}, and the k range is 3.4 to 6.3 cm^{-1}. The original notation has been altered.

Some of the experimental results are compared with theoretical calculations and shown in Fig. 6.2. The amplitudes p/p_0 are normalized relative to a plane pressure-release surface. The incident and reflected angles range from 0 to 60°. The results of similar experiments are given by Leporskii.[41] His comparisons of experimental p/p_0 and theory as a function of θ_n are shown in Fig. 6.3. Leporskii also shows excellent com-

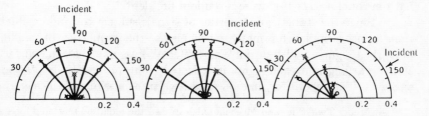

Fig. 6.3 Polar-coordinate plot of the reflection from a sinusoidal corrugated surface. (From Leporskii.[41]) $\sigma = 0.108$ cm, $K = 4.14$ cm^{-1}, and $k = 13.3$ cm^{-1} (×—theory, o—experiment).

parisons between theory and experiment for a sawtooth surface. The latter result is surprising since sharp edges of the sawtooth corrugations obviously violate the conditions for use of the Kirchhoff approximation.†

6.5 FIRST AND SECOND MOMENTS OF SIGNALS SCATTERED BY RANDOMLY IRREGULAR INTERFACES

Prediction of the reflection by a rough surface, the shape of which is neither periodic nor known, is possibly the most important aspect of the rough-surface problem. The deviations of the surface of the sea from the mean level depend upon time and position. Observations in the open ocean give the impression that the roughness of the sea surface is the same over a considerable area. When the meteorological conditions are constant, the roughness of the surface is the same for periods of at least several hours. For these conditions, the surface can be described in terms of the distribution of the deviations of the surface from the mean level. The distribution of the signals reflected by the surface can be then related to the distribution functions of the surface.[43,44]

The bottom of the ocean has a time dependence that is measured on geological time scales. With enough effort the surface of the bottom can be measured and the problem can be treated as a deterministic one. This would require numerical integration of the scattering integral for the source and receiver positions. It is obvious that the scattered field changes with translation of the source and receiver relative to the bottom. Each pair of source and receiver positions requires a calculation. Assembling such a set of calculations would be a formidable task for even a very small experiment. Assuming that the source and receiver are translated as a pair between each transmission, the set of signals at the receiver could be described by a mean signal and distribution of the individual signals about the mean. Although the ocean bottom is not random and time dependent like the surface, it is convenient, and practically necessary, to consider bottom roughness as if it were a random problem.

Since the statistical properties of signals subject to random fluctuations appear similar for many mechanisms, the properties of randomly perturbed signals will be examined first. We assume that the surface is slowly varying and each signal is reflected from an essentially stationary surface. The repetition time of successive transmissions of the signal can

---

† Proud, Tamarkin, and Meecham also studied the radiation scattered by a sawtooth surface.[42] They used calculations based upon Meecham's variational treatment[31] in which the square of the error in the boundary condition is minimized. The experimental results were in agreement with this theory.

be so chosen that each transmission observes a statistically independent, new surface. Let the source transmit the same signal at the times $T_1, T_2, \ldots, T_N$ and, correspondingly, the signals at the receiver are $p_1(T_1 + t), p_2(T_2 + t), \ldots, p_N(T_N + t)$. The signals are recorded and aligned by inserting the time delays $(T_N - T_1)$ into p_1, $(T_N - T_2)$ into p_2, etc. Dropping T_i for convenience, we can write the signals as $p_1(t)$, $p_2(t), \ldots, p_N(t)$. The mean or first moment of the sequence is†

$$\langle p(t) \rangle_N = \frac{1}{N} \sum_1^N p_n(t) \qquad (6.31)$$

Suppose the signal is dependent upon a fluctuation parameter τ and the probabilities $\mathcal{P}(\tau_n)$ of the fluctuations (τ_n) are known [$\mathcal{P}(\tau_n)$ is the probability that τ has the value τ_n]. Then, the expected average signal is the following:[45]

$$\langle p(t) \rangle_\tau = \sum_1^N p(t|\tau_n) \mathcal{P}(\tau_n)$$

The acoustical pressure for a particular travel-time fluctuation τ is $p(t|\tau)$. For a very large sample, the summation can be replaced by an integral. We let $W(\tau) \, d\tau$ be the probability that the variable τ has the particular value τ in the infinitesimal interval between τ and $\tau + d\tau$.[46 p.124] The average pressure is the sum of the products of all pressures times the probability of occurrence of that pressure. Integration over all values of τ yields the average pressure as follows:

$$\langle p(t) \rangle_\tau = \int_{-\infty}^{\infty} p(t|\tau) \, W(\tau) \, d\tau \qquad (6.32)$$

The determination of $\langle p(t) \rangle_\tau$ requires measurement of the phases of the signals. $\langle p(t) \rangle_\tau$ tends to zero when there are large fluctuations between transmissions. Many experimenters have measured $\langle pp^* \rangle$ or $\langle |p| \rangle$ for instrumental reasons. Neither of these should be confused with $\langle p \rangle$. The distribution of pp^* can be described in terms of the first, second, and higher moments of p. Even though the fluctuations may be gaussian, the distribution of pp^* is not gaussian.[46]

The second moment of the set of signals about the mean is

$$s^2(t) = \frac{1}{N} \sum_1^N [p_n(t) - \langle p(t) \rangle_N]^2$$

or
$$s^2(t) = \frac{1}{N} \left[\sum_1^N p_n{}^2(t) - N \langle p(t) \rangle_N{}^2 \right] \qquad (6.33)$$

---

† The mean value or average of a quantity f is denoted as $\langle f \rangle_\tau$. The subscript τ in $\langle \ \rangle_\tau$ refers to average on τ. Occasionally, when a more compact notation is desirable, we use $\bar{f}$ to denote the average of f.

The average of the second moment over the duration of the arrival T is a measure of the mean-square deviations over the whole signal. [All squares in (6.33) are absolute squares.] The average of the second moment is defined as follows:

$$\langle s^2 \rangle_T \equiv \frac{1}{T} \int_0^T s^2(t) \, dt \qquad (6.34)$$

where $\qquad\qquad s^2(t) \simeq 0 \qquad \text{for } t > T$

Before we can make an estimate of the expected value of $(1/N) \sum p_n{}^2$, we must consider the operation of squaring the signals. The set of signals is unlabeled and each signal is subject to random fluctuations. Thus in forming the square of the signal there is some probability that we have chosen the pair $p(t|\tau_m) \, p(t|\tau_n)$. With $W_{mn}(\tau_m,\tau_n)$ defined as the bivariate distribution function of the fluctuations τ_m and τ_n, the expected average value of p^2 is[45]

$$\langle pp^* \rangle_{\tau_1,\tau_2} = \int\!\!\!\int_{-\infty}^{\infty} p(t|\tau_1) \, p^*(t|\tau_2) \, W_{12}(\tau_1, \tau_2) \, d\tau_1 \, d\tau_2 \qquad (6.35)$$

With (6.32) to (6.35) the expected value of the mean-square second moment is

$$\langle s^2 \rangle_T = \langle \overline{pp}^* \rangle_T - \langle \bar{p}\bar{p}^* \rangle_T$$

or

$$\langle s^2 \rangle_T = \frac{1}{T} \int_0^T \langle pp^* \rangle_{\tau_1,\tau_2} \, dt - \frac{1}{T} \int_0^T \langle p(t) \rangle \, \langle p^*(t) \rangle \, dt \qquad (6.36)$$

As the fluctuations tend to zero, the first term on the right side of (6.36) becomes equal to the second term, and the mean-square second moment tends to zero. For very large fluctuations, the second term on the right tends to zero and the mean-square second moment is the average absolute square of the signal.

The distribution functions for a randomly rough surface are obtained by replacing τ by ζ/c since the travel-time fluctuation is the distance fluctuation associated with the irregular boundary. If the fluctuations are gaussian, the distribution function is

$$W(\zeta) = \frac{1}{\sigma\sqrt{2\pi}} \, e^{-\zeta^2/2\sigma^2} \qquad (6.37)$$

The bivariate distribution function $W_{12}(\zeta_1,\zeta_2)$ assumes that one path involves the surface at (x,y,z) with displacement ζ_1. The second path involves the surface at (x',y',z') with the displacement ζ_2. Again we assume a gaussian distribution function and $W_{12}(\zeta_1,\zeta_2)$ is [45]

$$W_{12}(\zeta_1,\zeta_2) = \frac{1}{2\pi\sigma^2(1-\psi^2)^{1/2}} \exp\left[-\frac{1}{2(1-\psi^2)\sigma^2} (\zeta_1{}^2 + \zeta_2{}^2 - 2\zeta_1\zeta_2\psi) \right] \tag{6.38}$$

with

$$\psi(\xi,\eta) \equiv \frac{1}{\sigma^2} \langle \zeta_1\,(x,y,z,t)\, \zeta_2(x',y',z',t)\rangle \tag{6.39}$$

$$\xi \equiv x - x' \qquad \eta \equiv y - y' \qquad \langle \zeta \rangle = 0 \tag{6.40}$$

Expressions (6.38), (6.39), and (6.40) are a description of a randomly rough surface with a gaussian distribution. The shape of the surface enters as the surface correlation function ψ.

The mean signal and the mean second moment of the signals have been expressed for the repeated transmission of transient signals in a fluctuating medium. The scattering calculation given in Secs. 6.3 and 6.4 are for a continuous-wave signal. The problem we would like to consider is the reflection of wave trains of simple harmonic signals or pings. Pings of sufficient length have a narrow spectrum centered at the frequency of the wave train and we use this fact to simplify the expressions.

On recalling that the time dependence of p has been suppressed, we note that the phase $\gamma\zeta$ in (6.24) represents the time fluctuation. On inversion of the order of integration, the mean of the signals reflected at a sequence of randomly rough surfaces is obtained by the substitution of (6.24) into (6.32) as follows:

$$\langle p \rangle_\zeta \simeq \frac{ikBf(\theta)\Re e^{ik(R_1+R_2)}}{2\pi R_1 R_2} \int \int D_0 e^{2i(\alpha x + \beta y)} \langle W(\zeta)e^{2i\gamma\zeta}\rangle_\zeta \, dx \, dy \tag{6.41}$$

The average within the integrand is the characteristic function. For a surface with a gaussian distribution function (6.37) it is

$$\langle W(\zeta)\, e^{2i\gamma\zeta}\rangle_\zeta = e^{-2\gamma^2\sigma^2} \tag{6.42}$$

The result of the integration of (6.41) with (6.42) and (6.21) is

$$\langle p \rangle_\zeta \simeq \frac{ikBf(\theta)\Re XY}{R_1 R_2} e^{ik(R_1+R_2)-2(\gamma^2\sigma^2+\alpha^2 X^2+\beta^2 Y^2)} \tag{6.43}$$

$\langle p \rangle$ tends to zero for large X and Y in all directions except the specular direction, $\alpha = \beta = 0$. Much of the complication in (6.43) is due to the combination of the Helmholtz formulation of the problem and the directional illumination function.

The effect due to the rough surface is more apparent if the factors common to the reflection from a rough surface and a smooth surface are eliminated. Thus, the mean reflected signal can be expressed with p_0, (6.26), and (6.43), as follows:

$$\langle p \rangle_{\zeta} \simeq p_0 e^{-2\gamma^2\sigma^2} \tag{6.44a}$$

The mean signal differs from the mirror-reflected signal by the factor $e^{-2\gamma^2\sigma^2}$.

The mean signal $\langle p \rangle_{\zeta}$ tends to zero with large fluctuations and large $\gamma^2\sigma^2$ because the phase of each reflected signal is random relative to the incident signal. The whole set of signals have random phases so that the sum tends to zero. Under such conditions, the scattered radiation is incoherent.

The mean signal tends to p_0 as $\gamma^2\sigma^2$ tends to zero. The set of signals reflected by a smooth interface are all identical. The reflected signals have definite phases relative to the incident radiation and the reflected radiation is coherent.

The exponential factor in (6.44a) is unity for coherent reflection and zero for incoherent reflection. If we follow the suggestion of Eckart,[23] $e^{-2\gamma^2\sigma^2}$ is identified as being a measure of the coherence of scattered radiation. The reflection coefficient $\mathfrak{R}$ in (6.43) and the coherence factor can be combined to form a *coherent reflection coefficient* as follows:

$$\text{Coherent reflection coefficient} \equiv \langle \mathfrak{R} \rangle \equiv \mathfrak{R} e^{-2\gamma^2\sigma^2} \tag{6.44b}$$

In the Kirchhoff approximation, the coherent reflection coefficient is *dependent upon the distribution* of the surface roughness and *independent* of the *shape* of the surface.

The mean second moment $\langle s^2 \rangle$ follows from the substitution of (6.24), (6.41), and (6.42) into (6.36). $\langle s^2 \rangle$ is

$$\langle s^2 \rangle \simeq \frac{k^2 B^2 f^2(\theta) \mathfrak{R}^2}{4\pi^2 R_1^2 R_2^2} \int\int\int\int D_0 D_0' e^{2i[\alpha(x-x')+\beta(y-y')]}$$

$$[\langle W_{12}(\zeta_1,\zeta_2) e^{2i\gamma(\zeta_1-\zeta_2)} \rangle_{\zeta_1,\zeta_2} - e^{-4\gamma^2\sigma^2}] \, dy \, dy' \, dx \, dx' \tag{6.45}$$

The first term in the bracket is the characteristic function of the bivariate distribution. For a gaussian distribution (6.38) the characteristic function is

$$\langle W_{12}(\zeta_1,\zeta_2) e^{2i\gamma(\zeta_1-\zeta_2)} \rangle_{\zeta_1,\zeta_2} = e^{-4\gamma^2\sigma^2(1-\psi)} \tag{6.46}$$

The mean second moment is

$$\langle s^2 \rangle \simeq \frac{k^2 B^2 f^2(\theta) \Re^2}{4\pi^2 R_1{}^2 R_2{}^2} \int\int\int\int D_0 D_0' \, e^{2i(\alpha\xi+\beta\eta)} \left[e^{-4\gamma^2\sigma^2(1-\psi)} - e^{-4\gamma^2\sigma^2} \right] dy \, dy' \, dx \, dx'$$

$$x - x' = \xi \text{ and } y - y' = \eta \quad (6.47)$$

We recall that the ocean surface is random and that ψ tends to zero for large ξ and η. We may define ξ_0, η_0 as values of ξ, η such that ψ becomes essentially negligible for $\xi > \xi_0, \eta > \eta_0$. For many acoustic experiments, the dimensions of the illuminated area are much greater than ξ_0 and η_0. These considerations permit the following approximate integration of (6.47) over x and y:

$$\langle s^2 \rangle \simeq \frac{k^2 B^2 f^2(\theta) \Re^2 XY}{2\pi R_1{}^2 R_2{}^2} \int\int_{-\infty}^{\infty} D_0' e^{2i(\alpha\xi+\beta\eta)} \left[e^{-4\gamma^2\sigma^2(1-\psi)} - e^{-4\gamma^2\sigma^2} \right] d\xi \, d\eta \quad (6.48)$$

where

$$D_0' = e^{-\xi^2/2X^2 - \eta^2/2Y^2}$$

and

$$|X| \gg |\xi_0| \qquad |Y| \gg |\eta_0|$$

The expression for $\langle s^2 \rangle$ in rectangular coordinates is useful for surfaces that are rough along one direction and nearly uniform in the other.

ψ is independent of direction when the surface is isotropically rough. Transformation of (6.47) to polar coordinates and integration give

$$\langle s^2 \rangle \simeq \frac{k^2 B^2 f^2(\theta) \Re^2 R^2}{4\pi R_1{}^2 R_2{}^2} \int_0^\infty \int_0^{2\pi} D_0 e^{2ir(\alpha \cos \varphi + \beta \sin \varphi)}$$

$$\left[e^{-4\gamma^2\sigma^2[1-\psi(r)]} - e^{-4\gamma^2\sigma^2} \right] d\varphi \, r \, dr \quad (6.49)$$

where

$$\xi = r \cos \varphi \qquad \eta = r \sin \varphi$$

The integral over φ can be transformed by the use of $(2.258)^{(47)}$ with the aid of the change of variable

$$\alpha = \kappa \cos \theta \qquad \beta = \kappa \sin \theta \qquad (6.50)$$

The result of the transformation is

$$\langle s^2 \rangle \simeq \frac{k^2 B^2 f^2(\theta) \Re^2 R^2}{2R_1{}^2 R_2{}^2} \int_0^\infty D_0 \, J_0 \, (2\kappa r) \left[e^{-4\gamma^2\sigma^2(1-\psi)} - e^{-4\gamma^2\sigma^2} \right] r \, dr \quad (6.51)$$

Both expressions (6.48) and (6.51) have the same dependence on $\gamma^2\sigma^2$. For a rough surface, $\gamma^2\sigma^2$ is very large and the second term in the bracket is negligible. For a smooth surface, $\gamma^2\sigma^2$ is zero and the whole bracket is zero. Neither (6.48) nor (6.51) can be integrated directly for the usual forms of ψ. It is customary to consider small $\gamma\sigma$ and large $\gamma\sigma$ separately.

6.6 RANDOM SURFACE AND LOW ACOUSTICAL FREQUENCIES — SMALL $\gamma\sigma$

The scattered radiation for small $\gamma\sigma$ can be obtained by expansion of the exponentials in (6.48) and (6.51):

$$\langle s^2 \rangle \simeq \frac{k^2 B^2 f^2(\theta) \mathcal{R}^2 XY \, e^{-4\gamma^2\sigma^2}}{2\pi R_1^2 R_2^2} \int\!\!\int_{-\infty}^{\infty} D_0 e^{2i(\alpha\xi + \beta\eta)}$$

$$\left[4\gamma^2\sigma^2\psi + \frac{(4\gamma^2\sigma^2\psi)^2}{2!} + \cdots \right] d\xi \, d\eta \quad (6.52)$$

and for the isotropic expression

$$\langle s^2 \rangle \simeq \frac{k^2 B^2 f^2(\theta) \mathcal{R}^2 R^2}{2R_1^2 R_2^2} e^{-4\gamma^2\sigma^2} \int_0^{\infty} D_0 J_0 (2\kappa r)[4\gamma^2\sigma^2\psi + \cdots] r \, dr$$

$$(6.53)$$

Although (6.52) and (6.53) converge for all values of $\gamma\sigma$, many terms are required, and the expansion is useful only for $(2\gamma\sigma)^2$ less than unity. Equation (6.53) can be evaluated for the isotropic gaussian correlation function

$$\psi = e^{-r^2/2r_0^2} \quad (6.54)$$

by use of the following integral[48],[28]

$$\int_0^{\infty} J_0 (br) \, e^{-r^2/2a^2} \, r \, dr = a^2 e^{-a^2 b^2/2} \quad (6.55)$$

The incoherent scattered radiation is

$$\langle s^2 \rangle \simeq \frac{2k^2 B^2 f^2(\theta) \mathcal{R}^2 R^2 (r_0')^2 \gamma^2\sigma^2}{R_1^2 R_2^2} e^{-4\gamma^2\sigma^2 - 2(\kappa r_0')^2} \quad (6.56)$$

where

$$\frac{1}{(r_0')^2} = \frac{1}{r_0^2} + \frac{2}{R^2}$$

Often the scattered radiation is referred to the incident pressure p_1 at the scattering area, and (6.56) may be written in the following form. Let

$$p_1 = \frac{B_1}{R_1} \exp [i\mathbf{k}_1 \cdot \mathbf{R}]$$

$$\langle s^2 \rangle = \langle p_1 p_1^* \rangle \frac{A}{R_2^2} S_{if} \quad (6.57)$$

where S_{lf} is the low-frequency scattering function

$$S_{lf} \equiv \frac{2}{\pi} \, \mathcal{R}^2 \gamma^2 \sigma^2 f^2(\theta) k^2 (r_0')^2 e^{-4\gamma^2 \sigma^2 - 2(\kappa r_0')^2} \tag{6.58}$$

and

$$A \equiv \pi R^2 \tag{6.59}$$

The square of the coherent signal scattered by an irregular surface also can be expressed in a form similar to (6.57). Transformation of (6.41) to polar coordinates with (6.20) and integration with (6.55) yields

$$\langle \bar{p}\bar{p}^* \rangle = \langle p_1 p_1^* \rangle \frac{A}{R_2{}^2} S_{coh} \tag{6.60}$$

where

$$S_{coh} \equiv \frac{\mathcal{R}^2 k^2 A f^2(\theta)}{4\pi^2} \, e^{-4\gamma^2 \sigma^2 - 2\kappa^2 R^2} \tag{6.61}$$

The form of the coherent scattering function S_{coh} is different from the form S_{lf}. S_{coh} *depends upon the illuminated area*, whereas S_{lf} does not. It is evident that the experimental determination of S_{lf} requires the measurement of $\langle s^2 \rangle$. If $\langle pp^* \rangle$ is measured, $\langle p \rangle$ must also be determined.

Experimental studies of the radiation scattered by randomly rough surfaces were made in the acoustics laboratory of Brown University.[49] The equipment and procedure were the same as described in Sec. 6.4. The surfaces consisted of irregular corrugations that were a function of x and independent of y. Surface I was made with 1-cm-wide cork strips. The surface had a gaussian amplitude distribution and small correlation for ξ greater than 1 cm. For our purpose, a suitable approximate ψ is (6.39)

$$\psi \simeq e^{-\xi^2/2\xi_0^2} \tag{6.62}$$

with $\xi_0 = 0.6$ cm, $\sigma = 0.082$ cm.

Their measurements of $\langle pp^* \rangle$ were the sum of the coherent (6.44) and the incoherent scattered radiation (6.52). The substitution of (6.62) into these expressions and evaluation of the integral for specular direction yield

$$\langle pp^* \rangle \simeq p_0 p_0^* e^{-4\gamma^2 \sigma^2} \left[1 + \frac{4 \, \xi_0 \gamma^2 \sigma^2}{X} \right] \tag{6.63}$$

for $\xi_0 \ll X$, $4\gamma^2 \sigma^2 < 1$, $\theta_1 = \theta_2$.

The first term in the bracket is the coherent $\langle p \rangle^2$ and the second term the incoherent $\langle s^2 \rangle$. Theoretical curves of $\langle p \rangle^2$ and $\langle pp^* \rangle$ are shown on Fig. 6.4. The average reflected signals in the specular direction for several incident angles are also shown on Fig. 6.4.[49] For measurement of the average scattered radiation, the transducers were fixed and the rough surface was displaced along the x direction between each ping. Proud, Beyer, and Tamarkin report that ten readings were usually sufficient to determine $\langle p\, p^* \rangle$. The comparison of experimental data with theory shows excellent agreement over a range of incident angles from 0 to 60°. For $2\gamma\sigma$ less than 1, most of the scattered radiation is coherent, $\langle p \rangle^2$. At large values of $2\gamma\sigma$, the scattered radiation is largely incoherent.

The second surface studied by Proud, Beyer, and Tamarkin was a corrugated pressure-release surface, and its profile is shown on Fig. 6.5.

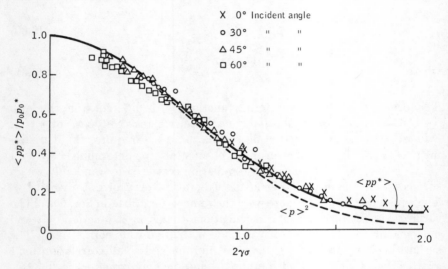

Fig. 6.4 Mean radiation scattered by a rough surface. The radiation scattered in the specular direction for 0°, 30°, 45°, and 60° was measured by Proud, Beyer, and Tamarkin.[49] Their data for the different directions have been combined in one figure, and the original notation is changed.

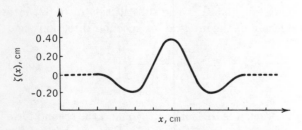

Fig. 6.5 Profile of Surface II. The profile of Surface II is shown as a function of x.[49] The correlation function has the form of (6.64) with $a = 2.6$ cm and $K = 1.30$ cm^{-1}.

The surface is approximately a damped cosine wave and its approximate correlation function, $\psi(\xi)$, is

$$\psi(\xi) = e^{-\xi^2/2a^2} \cos K\xi \tag{6.64}$$

A surface having this type of correlation function is in a sense related to the periodic corrugated surface we discussed in Sec. 6.4; i.e., as a tends to infinity, ψ tends to $\cos K\xi$ and $\psi = \cos K\xi$ is the correlation function of a sinusoidal corrugated surface. Thus for aK very large, one would expect the scattered radiation to be very similar to that scattered by a periodic corrugated surface. Substitution of (6.64) in (6.52) gives

$$\langle s^2 \rangle \simeq \frac{2k^2 B^2 f^2(\theta) \Re^2 X Y^2 \ell \gamma^2 \sigma^2}{R_1^2 R_2^2} e^{-4\gamma^2\sigma^2 - 2\beta^2 Y^2}$$

$$\{\exp[-(2\alpha - K)^2 \ell^2/2] + \exp[-(2\alpha + K)^2 \ell^2/2]\} \tag{6.65}$$

where

$$\frac{1}{\ell^2} = \frac{1}{X^2} + \frac{1}{a^2}$$

The two terms with $(2\alpha \pm K)$ correspond to the first scattering orders in (6.29). The term corresponding to the zeroth order is $\langle p \rangle^2$, and it is the absolute square of (6.43). Inclusion of higher-order terms such as ψ^2, ψ^3, $\ldots$, ψ^n in evaluation of (6.52) leads to terms involving $(2\alpha \pm nK)$.

The total scattered and reflected radiation $\langle pp^* \rangle$ was measured in the experiment. Constant terms such as source amplitude, etc., were eliminated by measuring $\langle pp^* \rangle$ relative to the plane-surface reflection $\langle p_0 p_0^* \rangle$. The relative scattered radiation is obtained by combining (6.26), (6.43), and (6.65) for $\beta = 0$. Taking p_0 for the specular case $\alpha = 0$:

$$\frac{\langle pp^* \rangle}{\langle p_0 p_0^* \rangle} = \frac{1}{\langle p_0 p_0^* \rangle} (\langle p \rangle \langle p^* \rangle + \langle s^2 \rangle)$$

$$\frac{\langle pp^* \rangle}{\langle p_0 p_0^* \rangle} \propto \frac{f^2(\theta)}{\cos^2 \theta_1} e^{-4\gamma^2\sigma^2} (e^{-4\alpha^2 X^2}$$

$$+ \frac{2\ell}{X} \gamma^2 \sigma^2 \{\exp[-(2\alpha - K)^2 \ell^2/2] + \exp[-(2\alpha + K)^2 \ell^2/2]\}) \tag{6.66}$$

Their experimental results for surface II are shown in Fig. 6.6, together with the theoretical curve given by (6.66).† The small humps on both sides of the peak ($\alpha = 0$) are the forward- and backscattered orders.

† Proud, Beyer, and Tamarkin used the Eckart theory without slope correction and found the first factor to be $[(\cos \theta_1 + \cos \theta_2)/2 \cos \theta_1]^2$ instead of $(f(\theta)/\cos \theta_1)^2$. The effect of the slope correction is small and can be neglected near specular reflection. For these calculations it is less than 20 percent over the range of 2α shown on Fig. 6.6.

These comparisons of theory and experiment were made for small $\gamma\sigma$ and the coherent components were large in the specular direction for surfaces. Since the coherent reflection coefficient and $\langle s^2 \rangle$ depend upon ψ and σ^2, it is evident that measurements of the scattered radiation can be used to measure σ^2 and to estimate ψ.[49-51]

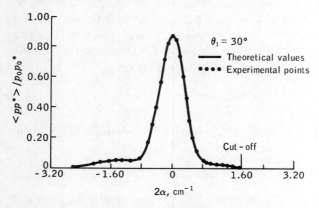

Fig. 6.6 Radiation scattered by Surface II. The data points were observed by Proud, Beyer, and Tamarkin.[49] The experimental parameters are the following: $\theta_1 = 30°$, $k = 3.40$ cm^{-1}, $\gamma^2 h^2 = 0.17$, and $X = 1.6$ cm. The theoretical curve was calculated for the surface with a correlation function (6.64). The notation has been changed.

6.7 RANDOM SURFACE AND THE HIGH-FREQUENCY LIMIT

The reflection of very high-frequency signals by the sea surface yields scattered radiation that is incoherent. Although the radiation is primarily scattered in the specular direction, part is scattered in all directions. As we shall show, the scattered radiation is primarily dependent upon the distribution of the slopes of the sea surface and independent of frequency for $2\gamma\sigma$ large enough. At intermediate frequencies, that is, $2\gamma\sigma \sim 1$, one would expect the scattered radiation to depend upon frequency. The intermediate values of $2\gamma\sigma$ are difficult to treat; however, upper limits of $\langle s^2 \rangle$ or $\langle pp^* \rangle$ can be estimated by comparison of the expansion with summable series.[27]

To estimate $\langle s^2 \rangle$ for very high frequencies, we return to the expression for the scattered radiation (6.51). The coherent component is negligible and can be dropped. On ignoring D_0, the constants, and dropping the second term, we note that $\langle s^2 \rangle$ is

$$\langle s^2 \rangle \simeq \langle pp^* \rangle \propto \int_0^\infty J_0(2\kappa r)e^{-4\gamma^2\sigma^2[1-\psi(r)]} r\,dr \qquad \text{for } \gamma^2\sigma^2 \gg 1$$

The integrand consists of the product of an oscillatory function and an exponential function. At very high frequencies, the main contribution to the integral is near $r = 0$ because of the rapid oscillations of $J_0(2\kappa r)$ for large argument. Near $r = 0$, the phase changes slowly and the expression can be evaluated by the method of stationary phase.[23,27] The expansion of ψ about $r = 0$ is

$$\psi \simeq 1 + \psi''(0) \frac{r^2}{2} + \cdots \tag{6.67}$$

$\psi''(0)$ may be related to the characteristics of the surface as follows:[23]

$$\frac{\partial \psi}{\partial r'} = \frac{1}{\sigma^2} \left\langle \zeta(r) \frac{\partial \xi(r + r')}{\partial r'} \right\rangle \tag{6.68}$$

r is replaced by $(r - r')$, and the operation is repeated to give

$$\frac{\partial^2 \psi}{\partial r'^2} = -\frac{1}{\sigma^2} \left\langle \frac{\partial \xi(r - r')}{\partial r'} \frac{\partial \xi(r)}{\partial r} \right\rangle \tag{6.69}$$

thus

$$\psi''(0) = -\frac{1}{\sigma^2} \langle \zeta'^2 \rangle \tag{6.70}$$

Substitution of (6.70) and (6.67) and inclusion of the constants in (6.51) give

$$\langle s^2 \rangle \simeq \frac{k^2 B^2 f^2(\theta) \Re^2 R^2}{2 R_1^2 R_2^2} \int_0^\infty D_0 J_0(2\kappa r) e^{-2\gamma^2 \langle \zeta'^2 \rangle r^2} r \, dr \tag{6.71}$$

The evaluation of (6.71), with the aid of (6.55), is

$$\langle s^2 \rangle \simeq \frac{k^2 B^2 f^2(\theta) \Re^2 R^2}{8 R_1^2 R_2^2 \gamma^2 \langle \zeta'^2 \rangle} e^{-\kappa^2/(2\gamma^2 \langle \zeta'^2 \rangle)} \tag{6.72}$$

for $2\gamma^2 \langle \zeta'^2 \rangle \gg R^{-2}$, $4\gamma^2 \sigma^2 \gg 1$.

Expressed with a scattering function S_{hf} and the incident radiation p_1, $\langle s^2 \rangle$ is

$$\langle s^2 \rangle \simeq \langle p_1 p_1^* \rangle \frac{A}{R_2^2} S_{\mathrm{hf}} \tag{6.73}$$

where

$$S_{\mathrm{hf}} \equiv \frac{f^2(\theta) \Re^2}{2\pi \, (\cos \theta_1 + \cos \theta_2)^2 \langle \zeta'^2 \rangle} e^{-\kappa^2/(2\gamma^2 \langle \zeta'^2 \rangle)} \tag{6.74}$$

The scattering function S_{hf} is independent of frequency in the high-frequency limit. S_{hf} depends upon the mean-square slope of the surface, but neither the mean-square wave height nor the correlation distance affect it. This expression is similar to one obtained by Eckart although he made an additional approximation by dropping ζ_x and ζ_y in (6.19). In the specular direction, (6.74) reduces to the expression given by Eckart.[23]

Experimental studies of the scattering function are frequently made with a "reverberation" experiment, illustrated in Fig. 6.7. The source and receiver are usually at the same position and $\theta_2 = -\theta_1$. Measurements of radiation backscattered from the sea surface are made as follows: The surface is illuminated with a transient signal, and the reflected signals are displayed on an oscillograph. The reflected signal has a "tail" that is presumably due to radiation scattered by inhomogeneities; sometimes it has arrivals that can be attributed to scattering from the medium beneath the surface. With omnidirectional sources and receivers, it is difficult to separate the surface scattering from the volume scattering of radiation.

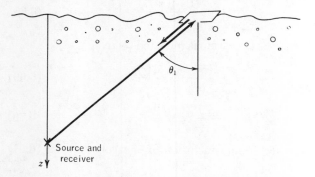

Fig. 6.7 Source and receiver position for the backscattering or reverberation experiment. The scatterers (bubbles) near the surface also contribute to the backscattering of radiation.

Experiments of this kind were made by Urick and Hoover using a technique that permitted separation of the surface- and volume-scattered radiation near normal incidence.[52] The carrier frequency of the pings was sufficiently high for the high-frequency scattering theory to be used. They illuminated the surface with a directional source and observed the backscattered radiation from the illuminated area with a receiver next to the source.

The backscattering function is obtained by letting $\theta_2 = -\theta_1$ in (6.74). S_{hf} is

$$\text{backscatter } S_{hf} = \frac{\mathcal{R}^2}{8\pi \cos^4 \theta \langle \zeta'^2 \rangle} e^{-\kappa^2/(2\gamma^2 \langle \zeta'^2 \rangle)} \tag{6.75}$$

Theoretical curves for several values of wind speed are shown in Fig. 6.8. $\langle \zeta'^2 \rangle$ was calculated from the following relation due to Cox and Munk:[53]

$$\langle \zeta'^2 \rangle \simeq (3 + 5.12w) \times 10^{-3} \tag{6.76}$$

where w is wind speed in m/sec. The experimental data have the same shape as the theoretical curves for incident angles out to about 45°. The amplitude of the theoretical curve could have been adjusted to better fit the data; however, this was not done. The scattered radiation at greater angles can be attributed to bubbles near the surface.[54,55]

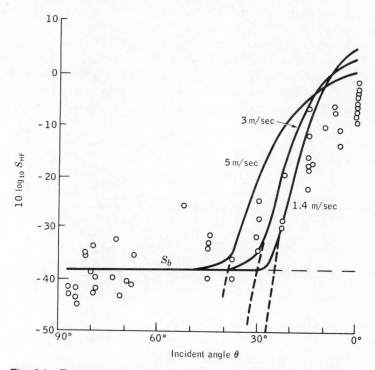

Fig. 6.8 Experimental and theoretical surface-scattering function for very large $\gamma^2 h^2$. The scattering functions are shown for the surface. Bubbles near the surface can scatter radiation. The radiation scattered by 10^{-2} bubbles/cm^{-2} has been estimated by Clay and Medwin[55] and is labeled S_b. The experimental data are from Urick and Hoover, for a 4 to 5 m/sec wind speed.[52] The source and receiver were 43 m beneath the surface.

6.8 REFLECTION FROM A SLIGHTLY IRREGULAR STRATIFIED MEDIUM

The reflection of radiation by a slightly irregular stratified section over a uniform half-space can be obtained in a manner that is similar to the problem of a single interface. We use a concept developed in Chap. 2, that is, that the reflection from a stratified half-space can be expressed with a single complex coefficient. The latter has the form of the reflection coefficient for the two interface problems. The reflection at the second interface depends upon the ρ_i, c_i, and h_i of all succeeding layers.

The source and receiver are assumed to be at a very large distance from the illuminated area. The Kirchhoff approximation is adapted to the assumption of a thin stratified section as follows: First, the incident, reflected, and transmitted waves are assumed to satisfy locally plane-wave boundary conditions at the element of area dS. Second, the interfaces cut by the projection dS can be considered parallel over the local area. Third, the thickness of the stratified section is small compared with the source and receiver distances. The model is illustrated in Fig. 6.9. About

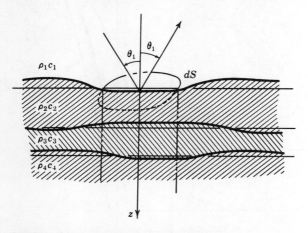

Fig. 6.9 Slightly irregular stratified medium.

15 km of a geophysical profile that was taken in the Hatteras Abyssal Plain is shown on Fig. 6.10. It is evident that the signals reflected by the ocean bottom indicate the presence of many shallow interfaces over thick sections and that the subbottom interfaces are the same for distances of at least a kilometer. Thus our assumptions appear to be compatible with the geophysical properties of sediments in deep ocean basins.

We consider the reflection from a layer with a homogeneous half-space above and beneath it. If we restrict the discussion to the specular direction, the notation can be the same as used with the stratified medium. The model is illustrated in Fig. 6.11. Snell's law gives the relation between γ_1 and γ_2. From (2.86), the plane-wave reflection and transmission coefficients at each interface are R_{12}, R_{21}, R_{23}, T_{12}, and T_{21}. The reflection coeffi-

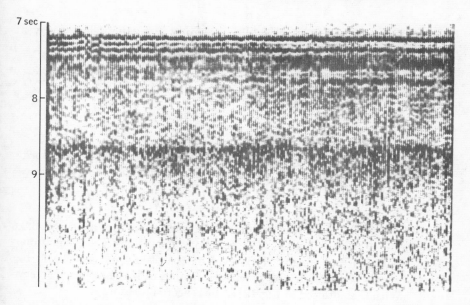

Fig. 6.10 Geophysical profile. Continuous geophysical profile taken in the Hatteras Abyssal Plain near 31°N, 72°W. About 15 km of profile are shown. The times are two-way travel times. The source frequency was centered about 130 cps. The display is in sequence of intensity-modulated signals and each vertical trace is a single transmission. The transmissions are about 75 m apart. The data were furnished by Rona, Liang, and Clay.

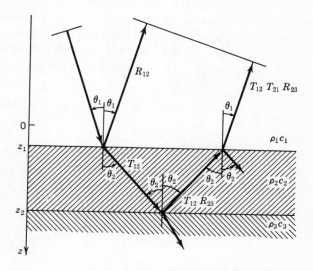

Fig. 6.11 Reflection at a layer.

cient of the layer $\mathcal{R}_{12}$ obtained by adding and multiplying the reflected waves with their proper phases is, relative to the plane $z = 0$,

$$\mathcal{R}_{12} = R_{12}e^{2i\gamma_1 z_1} + (1 - R_{12}{}^2)R_{23}e^{2i\gamma_1 z_1} \sum_0^\infty (-R_{12}R_{23})^n e^{2i(n+1)\gamma_2(z_2 - z_1)} \quad (6.77)$$

where
$$1 - R_{12}{}^2 = T_{12}T_{21}$$
$$R_{12} = -R_{21}$$

The second term on the right is a geometric progression. The usual form of the reflection coefficient (2.114) can be obtained by summing the series with

$$z_1 = 0 \quad \text{and} \quad z_2 - z_1 = h_2$$

For the irregular layer, we follow the same procedure as in Sec. 6.3. The Kirchhoff approximation and boundary conditions yield equations similar to (6.16) and (6.19). It is evident that the slope terms can be dropped if p is observed in the specular direction or if the slopes are very small. With the notation of Fig. 6.11, the reflected pressure is

$$p \simeq \frac{iBe^{ik(R_1 + R_2)}}{2\pi R_1 R_2} \int\int \gamma_1 D_0 \mathcal{R}_{12} \, dy \, dx \quad (6.78)$$

Note: $\gamma_1 = k \cos \theta_1$.

The average of a sequence of signals can be developed in the same manner as discussed in Sec. 6.5. Since the bottom is not time dependent, we assume that the source and receiver are translated between each two signal transmissions. As shown in Fig. 6.10, each transmission is made at a different location, and a slightly different layer thickness might be observed with each transmission. The interfaces are assumed to have random fluctuations of depth ζ_1 as follows:

$$\langle \zeta_n \rangle = 0 \quad \text{where } z_n - \sum_1^n h_i = \zeta_n \quad (6.79)$$
$$\langle \zeta_n{}^2 \rangle = \sigma_n{}^2$$

We assume, for simplicity, that the correlation of the fluctuations ζ_i and ζ_{i+1} should be considered and that the correlations of ζ_i and ζ_{i+2} are negligible. For a gaussian distribution of ζ_i, the bivariate distribution is[45]

$$W_{12}(\zeta_1, \zeta_2) = \frac{1}{2\sigma_1\sigma_2\pi\sqrt{1-\psi^2}} \exp\left[-\frac{1}{2(1-\psi^2)} \left(\frac{\zeta_1^2}{\sigma_1^2} + \frac{\zeta_2^2}{\sigma_2^2} - 2\psi\frac{\zeta_1\zeta_2}{\sigma_1\sigma_2} \right) \right]$$
$$(6.80)$$

$$\psi \equiv \frac{1}{\sigma_1\sigma_2} \langle \zeta_1\zeta_2 \rangle \quad (6.81)$$

The characteristic function is

$$\langle W_{12}e^{i(a\zeta_1+b\zeta_2)}\rangle = \int\int e^{i(a\zeta_1+b\zeta_2)}\, W_{12}(\zeta_1,\zeta_2)\, d\zeta_1\, d\zeta_2 \tag{6.82}$$

Substitution of (6.80) in (6.82) and integration yield

$$\langle W_{12}e^{i(a\zeta_1+b\zeta_2)}\rangle = e^{-\frac{1}{2}[\sigma_1{}^2 a^2 + \sigma_2{}^2 b^2 + 2ab\sigma_1\sigma_2\psi]} \tag{6.83}$$

The average of p, (6.78), over the distribution function (6.80) is

$$\langle p\rangle \simeq \frac{iBe^{ik(R_1+R_2)}}{2\pi R_1 R_2}\int\int \gamma_1 D_0\langle\mathcal{R}_{12}\rangle\, dy\, dx \tag{6.84}$$

The average $\langle\mathcal{R}_{12}\rangle$,

$$\langle\mathcal{R}_{12}\rangle = \int\int \mathcal{R}_{12}W_{12}\, d\zeta_1\, d\zeta_2$$

is evaluated with the help of (6.77) and (6.82), and is represented by a series of functions of the type (6.83).   We let D_0 be the gaussian illumination function (6.21), and then the average signal can be written in the following form

$$\langle p\rangle \simeq \frac{iB\gamma_1 e^{ik(R_1+R_2)}}{R_1 R_2}\langle\mathcal{R}_{12}\rangle A \tag{6.85}$$

where $A = XY$ and, for $z_1 = 0$,

$$\langle\mathcal{R}_{12}\rangle = R_{12}e^{-2\gamma_1{}^2\sigma_1{}^2} + (1 - R_{12}{}^2)R_{23}e^{2i\gamma_2 h_2}e^{-2[\gamma_2{}^2\sigma_2{}^2 + (\gamma_2-\gamma_1)^2\sigma_1{}^2]}$$

$$\frac{1}{2\pi A}\int\int D_0 e^{-4\gamma_2(\gamma_2-\gamma_1)\sigma_1\sigma_2\psi}\, dy\, dx + \cdots \tag{6.86}$$

The integral in (6.86) can be approximated for a particular ψ with the techniques used in Secs. 6.6 and 6.7.

If the fluctuations of the depths of the interfaces are uncorrelated, $\psi = 0$ and $\langle\mathcal{R}_{12}\rangle$ is

$$\langle\mathcal{R}_{12}\rangle_{\psi=0} = R_{12}e^{-2\gamma_1{}^2\sigma_1{}^2} + (1 - R_{12}{}^2)R_{23}e^{2i\gamma_2 h_2}e^{-2[\gamma_2{}^2\sigma_2{}^2 + (\gamma_2-\gamma_1)^2\sigma_1{}^2]} + \cdots \tag{6.87}$$

Often the thin layers appear to conform to the irregularities of a deeper layer.   We approximate this case as $\psi = 1$; then $\langle\mathcal{R}_{12}\rangle$ is

$$\langle\mathcal{R}_{12}\rangle_{\psi=1} = R_{12}e^{-2\gamma_1{}^2\sigma_1{}^2} + (1 - R_{12}{}^2)R_{23}e^{2i\gamma_2 h_2}e^{-2[\gamma_2\sigma_2 + (\gamma_2-\gamma_1)\sigma_1]^2} + \cdots \tag{6.88}$$

The effect of irregularities in the depths of the interfaces will now be demonstrated with an example resembling the first layer in deep ocean sediments.   Precision echo-sounder studies indicate the presence of several reflection interfaces at subbottom depths of the order of 5 to 20 m.[56]

Geophysical data indicate that the sediments near the water interface frequently have nearly the same speed of sound as the water and that the density and velocity increase as a function of depth.[57] For our example we assume that in the first layer $\rho_2 > \rho_1$, $c_1 = c_2$, and that the medium beneath the second interface is uniform. The reflection coefficient of the uniform layer is the solid curve on Fig. 6.12. To examine the effect of

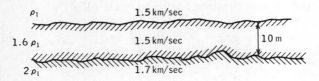

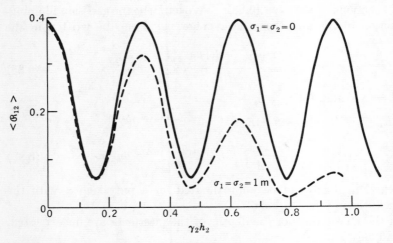

Fig. 6.12 Reflection from a layer. The solid curve is the reflection from a uniform layer $\sigma_1 = \sigma_2 = 0$. The dashed curve is the reflection from a slightly irregular layer $\sigma_1 = \sigma_2 = 1$ m.

irregularities, let us assume that both interfaces have the fluctuations $\sigma_1 = \sigma_2 = 1$ m. The result of the calculation for $\psi = 0$ is the dashed line in Fig. 6.12.

The reflection coefficient from Fig. 6.12 demonstrates the dependence of the reflected signal upon stratification and roughness. Obviously, without change of other properties, roughness of the bottom decreases the coherent reflection coefficient. Geophysical studies indicate that the roughness depends upon the physiographic province. In the Hatteras Abyssal Plain, σ_1 is less than 0.5 m.[73]

Intrinsic absorption also alters the reflection coefficient.[76] We regard the dependence of absorption upon frequency as being known (from experiments) for the particular material, and confine our analysis to a single frequency.[59] The absorption of plane waves can be treated by letting the propagation constant become complex as follows. With

$$k = k' + ik'' \tag{6.89}$$

$$p \backsim e^{i(k'R - \omega t) - k''R} \tag{6.90}$$

In a purely formal way, the reflection coefficients can be calculated with complex wave numbers.[76] Snell's law takes the form

$$\alpha_1 = \alpha_2 = \cdots = \alpha_n$$

$$\alpha_1 = k \sin \theta_1 = k' \sin \theta_1 + ik'' \sin \theta_1 \tag{6.91}$$

Although θ_1 may be real, $\theta_2, \theta_3, \ldots, \theta_n$ are complex angles. The complex reflection coefficient R_{12} is given by

$$R_{12} = \frac{\rho_2 \gamma_1 - \rho_1 \gamma_2}{\rho_2 \gamma_1 + \rho_1 \gamma_2} \tag{6.92}$$

$$\gamma_n = \gamma_n' + i\gamma_n''$$

Formal substitution of (6.91) and (6.92) in (6.77) yields

$$\mathcal{R}_{12} = R_{12} e^{2i\gamma' z_1 - 2\gamma'' z_1} + (1 - R_{12}^2) R_{23} e^{2i\gamma' z_1 - 2\gamma'' z_1}$$

$$\sum (-R_{12}R_{23})^n e^{2i(n+1)\gamma_2'(z_2 - z_1) - 2(n+1)\gamma_2''(z_2 - z_1)} \tag{6.93}$$

or with $z_1 = 0$ and $z_2 - z_1 = h_2$

$$\mathcal{R}_{12} = \frac{R_{12} + R_{23} e^{-2(\gamma_2'' h_2 + i\gamma_2' h_2)}}{1 + R_{12}R_{23} e^{-2(\gamma_2'' h_2 + i\gamma_2' h_2)}} \tag{6.94}$$

As the absorption $\gamma_2'' h_2$ increases, the effect of the second interface decreases. In the limit of very large $\gamma_2'' h_2$, $\mathcal{R}_{12}$ tends to R_{12}. Figure 6.13 illustrates the dependence of R_{12} upon $\gamma_2 h_2$. Comparison of Figs. 6.13 and 6.12 shows considerable difference in the behavior of $\langle \mathcal{R}_{12} \rangle$ and $\mathcal{R}_{12}$ with absorption. The coherent reflection tends to zero with increasing roughness, whereas the reflection coefficient with absorption tends to become independent of the properties of succeeding layers.

The reflection of sound from multiple absorbing layers has been studied in the laboratory[74] and in the deep ocean.[58,75] Both experiments demonstrated agreement between theory and experiment.

The coherent reflection coefficient for n layers with irregular interfaces is obtained upon substitution of $\mathcal{R}_{23}$ for R_{23}. $\mathcal{R}_{23}$, $\mathcal{R}_{34}$, etc., are continued through the sequence of layers by the recursion formula given in Chap. 2. It may be convenient to write $\mathcal{R}_{23}$ in the expanded form (6.77) for evaluation of the integral because subbottom sediments usually have rather low contrasts of ρc and the resulting series should converge rapidly when the incident waves are near vertical incidence.

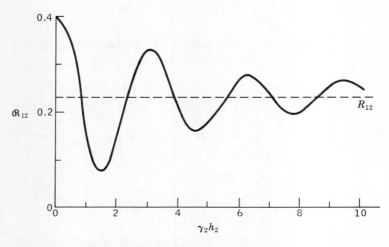

Fig. 6.13 Reflection from a layer with absorption. The layer is the same as that shown in Fig. 6.12. $\sigma_1 = \sigma_2 = 0$ and $\gamma_2''h = 0.2\gamma_2'h$.

6.9 WAVEGUIDE WITH SLIGHTLY IRREGULAR INTERFACES

The ocean is horizontally stratified, but the stratifications are irregular and the surface and bottom are rough. A sound-velocity profile along 24°N was calculated from oceanographic data.[60,61] As shown in Fig. 6.14, the depths of the isovelocity lines *vary slowly as a function of distance* along the profile. In addition to these variations there are time-dependent perturbations such as internal waves, deep currents, etc. Thus a more accurate model of the ocean should include the slowly varying space- and time-dependent properties together with a rough surface and bottom.

To proceed, we assume that the radiation within any particular mode remains in that mode. This assumption is commonly used in microwave literature[62,63] and may be expressed as the following:

1. The eigenvalues of the characteristic equation correspond to the local stratification.
2. The stratification varies slowly from one local region to another.

3. There are no reflections or appreciable scattering of energy from one mode to another in transition regions.

These assumptions can be applied to waveguides in which the stratification is a function of position.[64-67]

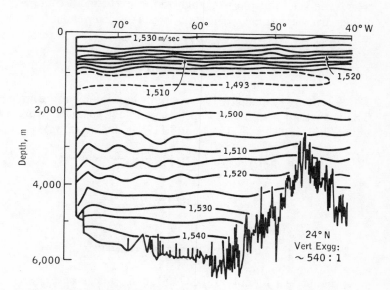

Fig. 6.14 Sound-velocity and bottom profile along 24°N.[60,61] The bottom profile is used with the permission of F. C. Fuglister.

From Sec. 2.2, we recall that the solution of the wave equation Φ can be written as the product of a radial function and a z-dependent function as follows:

$$\nabla^2\Phi + \frac{\omega^2}{c^2}\Phi = 0$$

$$\Phi = R(r)\,\varphi(z)$$

$R(r)$ and $\varphi(z)$ satisfy the following wave equations:

$$\nabla_r^2 R(r) + \kappa^2 R(r) = 0$$

$$\frac{\partial^2}{\partial z^2}\varphi(z) + \gamma^2\varphi(z) = 0 \tag{6.95}$$

where

$$\kappa^2 + \gamma^2 = \frac{\omega^2}{c^2}$$

The solution $\varphi(z)$ was expanded in normal modes $\varphi(\gamma_m,z)$ (or φ_m), and these functions are discrete for trapped modes. The characteristic equation for trapped modes is (Sec. 2.6)

$$\theta = m\pi \tag{6.96}$$

where θ is the total phase change and m is the mode number. The eigenvalues are the vertical, γ_m, and horizontal, κ_m, components of wave number, and these are related as follows:

$$\gamma_m{}^2 + \kappa_m{}^2 = \frac{\omega^2}{c^2}$$

The solution was evaluated for a simple harmonic point source at depth z_0. The acoustical pressure at depth z and range r can be expressed with the aid of (2.5), (3.115), (3.118), and (3.119) as the following:

$$p(t) = \frac{-i\rho}{\sqrt{r}} \sum_{m=1}^{M} P_m e^{-i(\kappa_m r - \omega t - \pi/4) - \delta_m r} \tag{6.97}$$

where
$$P_m \equiv \frac{p_m \varphi_m(z_0) \varphi_m(z)}{\rho_0}$$

$$\frac{p_m}{\rho_0} = \frac{2\pi}{\nu_m \sqrt{\kappa_m}} (\rho_0 c_0 \Pi)^{1/2} \tag{6.98}$$

δ_m is the mode attenuation (Sec. 4.5), and ν_m is given by (3.115). Expression (6.97) can be used as the basis for our estimation of the effect of irregularities on the transmission of signals.

Assumption 1 means that $\varphi_m(z)$ satisfies the z-separated wave equation everywhere and thus γ_m is a function of position. For a single mode, the power radiated by the source into that mode is dependent upon the stratification at the source. Similarly, the acoustical level at the receiver depends upon the stratification at the receiver. In view of assumption 3, i.e., no scattering, it seems reasonable to use the suggestion of Williams and Lewis and approximate $\bar{P}_m$ for the irregular waveguide as follows:[64]

$$\bar{p}_m = [p_m \text{ (source) } p_m \text{ (rcv.)}]^{1/2} \tag{6.99}$$

$$\rho \bar{P}_m = \bar{p}_m \varphi_m[z_0, \gamma_m \text{ (source)}] \, \varphi_m[z, \gamma_m \text{ (rcv.)}]$$

Source and rcv. refer to the local stratifications at the source and receiver.

The phase of the signal (6.97) for the mth mode is dependent upon $\kappa_m r$ where κ_m is a function of r (or x and y). Variations of the stratification cause κ_m to vary, and one would observe phase fluctuations ΔS_m in the transmitted signal. To estimate ΔS_m and relate it to the variations of the stratification, we can use a perturbation solution of the plane-wave equation.

Let κ_m be expressed as follows:

$$\kappa_m(r) = \bar{\kappa}_m + \epsilon_m(r) \tag{6.100}$$

and

$$\bar{\kappa}_m = \langle \kappa_m(r) \rangle_r$$

The substitution of (6.100) in (6.95) yields, in the plane-wave approximation (large κr)

$$\frac{\partial^2 R_m}{\partial r^2} + \bar{\kappa}_m{}^2 R_m + 2 \bar{\kappa}_m \epsilon_m R_m + \epsilon_m{}^2 R_m = 0 \tag{6.101}$$

The approximate solution of (6.101) can be written as

$$R_m = e^{-i(\bar{\kappa}_m r + \Delta S_m)} \tag{6.102}$$

Substitution of (6.102) into (6.101) yields, after dropping the higher-order terms, the following:

$$\frac{d(\Delta S_m)}{dr} = \epsilon_m \tag{6.103}$$

or

$$\Delta S_m = \int_0^r \epsilon_m \, dr$$

The approximate phase fluctuation is the integral of the phase fluctuation along the path. The substitution of $(\bar{\kappa}_m r + \Delta S_m)$ in (6.97) gives the acoustical pressure

$$p(t) \simeq \frac{-i\rho}{\sqrt{r}} \sum_{m=1}^{M} \bar{P}_m e^{-i(\bar{\kappa}_m r - \omega t - \pi/4 + \Delta S_m) - \delta_m r} \tag{6.104}$$

Expression (6.104) can be used to calculate the acoustical pressure in a nonuniform or irregular waveguide as long as the assumptions 1, 2, and 3 hold. A typical example is the transmission of sound in shallow water over a sloping bottom.† The amplitude of the signal in each mode depends upon $\bar{P}_m$. From (3.115), (4.17), (4.61), or (4.81), it is evident that $\bar{P}_m \propto (h_{\text{source}} h_{\text{rev.}})^{-1/2}$, and thus the signal level at the receiver depends upon the reciprocal square root of the water depth at the receiver. Caution in the application of (6.104) to sound propagation up or down slopes in the ocean is necessary. First, one should remember that hydrographic charts are prepared for the navigation of ships and not for acoustic experiments. If possible the experimenter should study the original echo-sounding data to estimate the slope and roughness of the bottom. Continuous seismic pro-

† The source and receiver in a wedge was discussed by Biot and Tolstoy, ref. 4, chap. 3. Much of the difficulty in this problem is due to the diffraction at the apex of the wedge. As a matter of practice in ocean acoustics, the diffraction can be ignored and image techniques or Eq. (6.104) can be used to estimate the sound field.

files should be made along the transmission path because sedimentation and erosional processes can bury many important features such as stream beds, different rock strata, and faults. A major change of the subsurface structure in a waveguide can be regarded as the junction of two different waveguides, and one would expect part of the radiation to be scattered at the junction. Fortunately in areas like the shallow water south of Fire Island, New York, the bottom and subbottom layers are slowly varying over several kilometers of range and these locations can be used as field laboratories to compare theory and experiment.

Let us return to the transmission of signals in a slowly varying ocean and consider repeated transmissions of signals as discussed in Sec. 6.5. At the time of each signal transmission, one has a particular set of isovelocity surfaces, ϵ_m's, and integrated phase ΔS_m. Each repeated transmission can encounter a different set of isovelocity surfaces. From many signal transmissions, we can obtain the distribution of ΔS_m, i.e., $W(\Delta S_m)$. Given sufficient oceanographic data, ϵ_m, ΔS_m, and $W(\Delta S_m)$ can be calculated numerically and then (6.32) can be used to estimate the average (coherent) signal. *Given insufficient* data, we can only *guess* the statistical properties and proceed.

We now wish to determine an approximate relation between $\overline{\epsilon_m{}^2}$ and $\overline{\Delta S_m{}^2}$. We assume that all unknown statistical functions are gaussian, and

$$\overline{\Delta S_m{}^2} = \left\langle \int_0^r \epsilon_m(x)\, dx \int_0^r \epsilon_m(x')\, dx' \right\rangle_r \qquad (6.105a)$$

where

$$\langle \Delta S_m \rangle = 0$$

$$W(\Delta S_m) = (2\pi\, \overline{\Delta S_m{}^2})^{-1/2}\, e^{-\Delta S_m{}^2/2\, \overline{\Delta S_m{}^2}} \qquad (6.105b)$$

The product of integrals can be expressed as a double integral, and the average can be moved inside the integral signs to form $\langle \epsilon_m(x)\, \epsilon_m(x') \rangle_r$. On making the assumption that $\langle \epsilon_m(x)\, \epsilon_m(x') \rangle_r$ depends upon $(x - x') = \xi$, we note that $\overline{\Delta S_m{}^2}$ can be expressed as the following integral of a correlation function:[16]

$$\overline{\Delta S_m{}^2} = \overline{\epsilon_m{}^2} \int_0^r \int_{-x'}^{r-x'} \psi_{\epsilon m}(\xi)\, dx'\, d\xi \qquad (6.106)$$

where

$$\overline{\epsilon_m{}^2}\, \psi_{\epsilon m}(\xi) \equiv \langle \epsilon_m(x + \xi)\, \epsilon_m(x) \rangle_x$$

If $\psi_{\epsilon m}(\xi)$ tends to zero for $\xi \ll r$, $\overline{\Delta S_m{}^2}$ is approximately the following:

$$\overline{\Delta S_m{}^2} \simeq r\, \overline{\epsilon_m{}^2} \int_{-\infty}^{\infty} \psi_{\epsilon m}(\xi)\, d\xi \qquad (6.107)$$

The correlation coefficient $\psi_{\epsilon m}(\xi)$ is determined from oceanographic data and the corresponding set of eigenvalues κ_m. It is apparent that the calculation of $\psi_{\epsilon m}(\xi)$ requires knowledge of the correlation function of the isovelocity surfaces in the ocean. Without such knowledge, we assume $\psi_{\epsilon m}(\xi)$ is gaussian and has a correlation distance a_m as follows:

$$\psi_{\epsilon m}(\xi) = e^{-\xi^2/a_m^2} \tag{6.108}$$

The evaluation of $\overline{\Delta S_m^2}$ for the gaussian function (6.108) gives

$$\overline{\Delta S_m^2} \simeq \sqrt{\pi} r \, a_m \, \overline{\epsilon_m^2} \tag{6.109}$$

At large range, the mean-square phase fluctuation is proportional to the range and to $a_m\overline{\epsilon_m^2}$.†

The mean acoustic signal is the average of $p(t)$ over all phase fluctuations. The average of (6.104) with the aid of the distribution function is

$$\overline{p(t)} \simeq \frac{-i\rho}{\sqrt{r}} \sum_{m=1}^{M} \int_{-\infty}^{\infty} \bar{P}_m e^{-i(\bar{\kappa}_m r - \omega t - \pi/4 + \Delta S_m) - \delta_m r} \, W(\Delta S_m) \, d(\Delta S_m) \tag{6.110}$$

Let us ignore the fluctuations of $\bar{P}_m$ and use a gaussian distribution for $W(\Delta S_m)$. With the aid of (6.105), $p(t)$ is

$$\overline{p(t)} \simeq \frac{-i\rho}{\sqrt{r}} \sum_{m=1}^{M} \bar{P}_m e^{-i(\bar{\kappa}_m r - \omega t - \pi/4) - \delta_m r - \overline{\Delta S_m^2}/2} \tag{6.111}$$

The phase fluctuations decrease the coherence of the signal and for $\psi_{\epsilon m}$ given by (6.108), $\overline{p(t)}$ is

$$\overline{p(t)} \simeq \frac{-i\rho}{\sqrt{r}} \sum_{m=1}^{M} \bar{P}_m e^{-i(\bar{\kappa}_m r - \omega t - \pi/4) - \delta_m r - (\sqrt{\pi}/2) r a_m \overline{\epsilon_m^2}} \tag{6.112}$$

Expression (6.112) shows that the fluctuations cause the coherent signal to tend to zero as $\exp -[(\sqrt{\pi}/2) r a_m \overline{\epsilon_m^2}]$ at large range. As an example, we let $\epsilon_m = 0.001 \, \bar{\kappa}_m$ and $a_m = 10 \, \lambda$. Since $\bar{\kappa}_m$ is roughly $2\pi/\lambda$, we find that the coherent signal is attentuated by e^{-1} at a distance of 2,500 acoustic wavelengths.

The mean-square pressure is the absolute square of (6.104). pp^* consists of two types of terms, the mean-square pressure for each mode and the cross-product or mode-interference terms. The latter terms are of considerable interest for they give the detailed dependence of the sound field upon range. Since these terms depend upon $[(\bar{\kappa}_m - \bar{\kappa}_n)r + \Delta S_m - \Delta S_n]$, one would expect the mode-interference terms to be very strongly dependent

---

† This result has about the same range and frequency dependence as that obtained by Chernov [Sec. 6.2, Eq. (6.6)] since $\epsilon_m^2 \propto \omega^2$. In our development, amplitude fluctuations were ignored and the absolute square of ΔS_m was calculated. Bourret also ignored the amplitude fluctuations and obtained a similar result.[72]

upon the correlation of ΔS_m and ΔS_n. The average of the absolute square of
(6.105) with the aid of the bivariate distribution function, $W_{12}(\Delta S_m, \Delta S_n)$, is

$$\langle pp^* \rangle \simeq \frac{\rho^2}{r} \sum_{m=1}^{M} \bar{P}_m{}^2 e^{-2\delta_m r} + \frac{\rho^2}{r} \sum_{m \neq n} \int\int_{-\infty}^{\infty} P_m P_n$$

$$e^{-i(\bar{\kappa}_m - \bar{\kappa}_n)r - (\delta_m + \delta_n)r - i(\Delta S_m - \Delta S_n)} W_{12}(\Delta S_m, \Delta S_n)\, d(\Delta S_m)\, d(\Delta S_n) \quad (6.113)$$

For any particular waveguide, $W_{12}(\Delta S_m, \Delta S_n)$ can be determined numerically. The fluctuations ΔS_m and ΔS_n might be correlated because the
deviations from the mean stratification that cause an increase in ΔS_m could
also cause a corresponding change in ΔS_n.

The mean-square signal can be evaluated for the bivariate gaussian
distribution function (6.80) in which $\sigma_1{}^2 = \overline{\Delta S_m{}^2}$, $\sigma_2{}^2 = \overline{\Delta S_n{}^2}$, and $\psi = \psi_{Smn}$.
The integration of (6.113) with the help of (6.82) and (6.83) is

$$\langle pp^* \rangle \simeq \frac{\rho^2}{r} \sum_{m=1}^{M} \bar{P}_m{}^2 e^{-2\delta_m r} + \frac{\rho^2}{r} \sum_{m \neq n} \bar{P}_m \bar{P}_n$$

$$\exp\left[-i(\bar{\kappa}_m - \bar{\kappa}_n)r - (\delta_m + \delta_n)r - \tfrac{1}{2}\left(\overline{\Delta S_m{}^2} + \overline{\Delta S_n{}^2} - 2|\Delta S_m| \cdot |\Delta S_n|\psi_{Smn}\right)\right]$$

where
$$|\Delta S_m| \cdot |\Delta S_n|\psi_{Smn} = \langle \Delta S_m \Delta S_n \rangle$$
$$|\Delta S_m| = +\, (\overline{\Delta S_m{}^2})^{1/2} \quad (6.114)$$

From the expression involving $\overline{\Delta S_m{}^2}$, $\overline{\Delta S_n{}^2}$, and $2|\Delta S_m| \cdot |\Delta S_n|\psi_{Smn}$ it is
evident the amplitudes of the mode-interference terms are largest when
$\psi_{Smn} \simeq 1$ and they decrease as ψ_{Smn} tends to zero. We can express ψ_{Smn}
as a function of ϵ_m and ϵ_n by following a procedure similar to that used to
estimate $\overline{\Delta S_m{}^2}$. Thus $\langle \Delta S_m \cdot \Delta S_n \rangle$ is

$$\langle \Delta S_m \cdot \Delta S_n \rangle = \left\langle \int_0^r \epsilon_m(x)\, dx \int_0^r \epsilon_n(x')\, dx' \right\rangle$$

$$= \int_0^r \int_0^r \langle \epsilon_m(x)\, \epsilon_n(x') \rangle\, dx\, dx' \quad (6.115)$$

On making the assumption that $\langle \epsilon_m(x)\, \epsilon_n(x') \rangle$ is a function of $\xi = x - x'$,
we note that the average can be expressed as the following cross-correlation
function:

$$\langle \epsilon_m(x)\, \epsilon_n(x + \xi) \rangle = |\epsilon_m| \cdot |\epsilon_n|\, \psi_{\epsilon mn}(\xi) \quad (6.116)$$

where
$$|\epsilon_m| = +\, (\overline{\epsilon_m{}^2})^{1/2}$$

Again we assume that ψ tends to zero for $\xi \ll r$ and then (6.115) is

$$\langle \Delta S_m \cdot \Delta S_n \rangle = |\Delta S_m| \cdot |\Delta S_n|\psi_{Smn} \simeq |\epsilon_m| \cdot |\epsilon_n|r \int_{-\infty}^{\infty} \psi_{\epsilon mn}(\xi)\, d\xi \quad (6.117)$$

The substitution of (6.117) into (6.114) shows that fluctuations of the stratification cause the amplitude of the mode-interference terms to decrease as range increases. $\psi_{\epsilon mn}$ would probably have about the same correlation distance, a_m or a_n, as $\psi_{\epsilon m}$. For a large number of modes such as in the deep ocean, the difference between the effect of the fluctuations on the mth and $(m-1)$th modes would probably be very small. The differences would increase as $|m-n|$; thus, $\psi_{\epsilon mn}$ would tend to zero as $|m-n|$ increases.

In principle, the ocean waves on the surface and irregularities of the ocean bottom have been included in the development. But there may be several orders of magnitude of difference between the wavelengths of internal waves and waves on the surface of the ocean; i.e., internal wavelengths are of the order of kilometers whereas surface waves are measured in meters. If we were to include the surface in the calculation of $\overline{\Delta S_m{}^2}$, oceanographic data would be required every few meters along the transmission path because the surface wavelengths are so short. It is obvious that the numerical effort can be reduced tremendously by handling the effect of the irregular surface separately.

The reflection at an irregular surface can be regarded as an *incomplete reflection* in that the modulus of the coherently reflected signal is less than the modulus of the incident signal. In the sense of the discussion of the reflection of signals by a dissipative bottom (Sec. 4.5), the loss caused by reflection from an irregular surface can be treated as a mode attenuation. The procedure is identical to that given in Sec. 4.5. The reflection loss b_m for incident angles corresponding to the mth mode is given by

$$|\langle \mathfrak{R} \rangle| = 1 - b_m$$

where $\langle \mathfrak{R} \rangle$ is given by (6.44b) or (6.86) and $\mathfrak{R}$ is the reflection coefficient for smooth interfaces, (2.114), (6.15), or (6.77). The attenuation of signal transmission due to these boundary losses can be calculated with the aid of Eqs. (4.69) to (4.72) (let $\epsilon = b_m$). The signal amplitude $A_m(r)$ in a waveguide of thickness h is, for an initial amplitude A,

$$A_m = A e^{-\delta_m' r} \tag{6.118}$$

where
$$\delta_m' \equiv \frac{b_m \gamma_m}{2h \kappa_m} \tag{6.119}$$

and
$$\frac{\kappa_m}{\gamma_m} = \tan \theta_m$$

The attenuation δ_m' is proportional to the number of reflections per unit length of waveguide and the loss per reflection.

The coherent reflection coefficient (6.44b) can be used to give δ'_m for the ocean surface as follows:

$$|\langle\Re\rangle| = 1 - b_m = \Re e^{-2\gamma_m^2\sigma^2}$$

$$b_m \simeq 2\gamma_m^2\sigma^2 \quad \text{for} \quad 2\gamma_m^2\sigma^2 \ll 1$$

and
$$\delta'_m \simeq \frac{\gamma_m^3\sigma^2}{h\,\kappa_m} \tag{6.120}$$

For a given roughness σ, the attenuation increases with increasing mode number since γ_m increases with the mode number. The lowest modes would have the least attenuation, and therefore at very large range most of the radiation would be in these modes. The total attenuation δ_m is the sum of the individual attenuations due to surface roughness, bottom roughness, and transmission into the bottom.

The theoretical results of our consideration of acoustical propagation in an irregularly stratified ocean are given by expressions for $\overline{p(t)}$, (6.112), and $\langle pp^*\rangle$, (6.114). In the following, we apply the theory to deep- and shallow-water experiments.

For an example of sound transmission in deep water, we estimate the phase fluctuations that would be expected for experiments in the Hatteras Abyssal Plain (30°N, 71°W). Let us assume the simplified velocity profile shown in Fig. 6.15 and let the depth of the mixed layer fluctuate

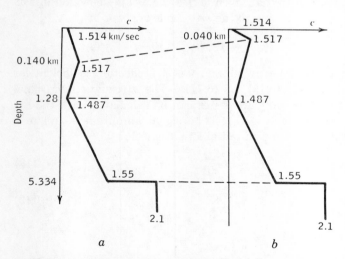

Fig. 6.15 Velocity profiles. The mixed layer is assumed to fluctuate at a depth between 0.14 and 0.04 km.

from 40 to 140 m. The profile is composed of segments having the form of (5.2), i.e.,

$$c(z) = \left(\frac{1}{c_0^2} - qz\right)^{-1/2} \tag{6.121}$$

We use the W.K.B. approximation (Sec. 2.9) to calculate eigenvalues for the two velocity profiles and obtain an estimate of the perturbation ϵ_m. From (2.209) and (2.142), the phase integral can be written as

$$\theta_m = \int_{z_t}^{z_b} \gamma_m \, dz + \chi_m = m\pi \tag{6.122}$$

where χ_m is the total phase change caused by reflections at the top z_t, bottom z_b, or turning points. By Snell's law, κ is constant for all z and thus $\gamma(z)$ can be obtained as follows:

$$\gamma^2 = k^2 - \kappa^2 = \frac{\omega^2}{c^2(z)} - \frac{\omega^2}{c_0^2} \sin^2 \vartheta_0 \tag{6.123}$$

Substitution of the velocity function (6.121) for $c(z)$ gives

$$\gamma^2 = \gamma^2(0) - q\omega^2 z \tag{6.124}$$

where

$$\gamma(0) = \frac{\omega}{c_0} \cos \vartheta_0$$

The total phase change from the top to the bottom of the ocean is the sum of all segments and χ_m. The evaluation of (6.122) is straightforward when $\gamma \, dz$ is integrable, and numerical values of γ_m can be obtained with the aid of a desk calculator.

Approximate values of $\bar{\kappa}_m$ and $|\epsilon_m|$ were calculated for the velocity profiles shown on Fig. 6.15. The sums and differences of the eigenvalues were used to estimate $\bar{\kappa}_m$ and $|\epsilon_m|$. Numerical values of the fluctuation

Table 6.1 Fluctuations caused by change of surface-channel depth, velocity profiles of Fig. 6.15. $a_m = 1\,\text{km}$, $r = 100$ km.

Freq.	Mode	κ_m	$|\epsilon_m|$	$\dfrac{\sqrt{\pi}}{2} a_m \overline{\epsilon_m^2}$	$\dfrac{\overline{\Delta S_m^2}}{2}$
10	20	$40.5\ \text{km}^{-1}$	$8 \times 10^{-3}\ \text{km}^{-1}$	$5.7 \times 10^{-5}\ \text{km}^{-1}$	5.7×10^{-3}
10	21	$40.4\ \text{km}^{-1}$	$11 \times 10^{-3}\ \text{km}^{-1}$	$10.7 \times 10^{-5}\ \text{km}^{-1}$	10.7×10^{-3}
100	200	$405\ \ \text{km}^{-1}$	$8 \times 10^{-2}\ \text{km}^{-1}$	$5.7 \times 10^{-3}\ \text{km}^{-1}$	0.57
100	210	$404\ \ \text{km}^{-1}$	$11 \times 10^{-2}\ \text{km}^{-1}$	$10.7 \times 10^{-3}\ \text{km}^{-1}$	1.07

parameters for 10- and 100-cps signals are given in Table 6.1. The phase fluctuation at the receiver ΔS_m depends upon the correlation distance a_m of the irregularity and the range r (6.109). The mean or coherent signal is proportional to $\exp -(\overline{\Delta S_m{}^2}/2)$, and for a 10-cps signal, the twentieth mode is about 99.4 percent coherent at 100 km. Similarly the 200th mode of a 100-cps signal would be 57 percent coherent.

If the fluctuations of the mixed layer were the only perturbation, one would expect repeated transmissions to be nearly alike. Three repeated segments of the 10.04-cps transmission experiment made by Guthrie and Shaffer are shown in Fig. 6.16.[68] (A longer but unrepeated set of data from the same experiment is shown in Fig. 5.37.) The average of the

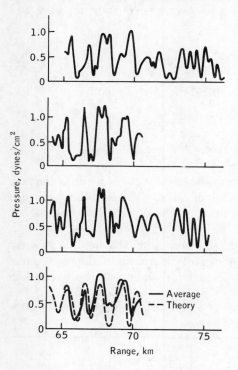

Fig. 6.16 Average signal level as a function of range for repeated trials. The data were taken at a water depth of 5.38 km. The source frequency was 10.04 cps. A. N. Guthrie and J. Shaffer furnished the illustration.[68] Theoretical calculation of Tolstoy and May is the dashed curve.[77]

three segments is the solid line at the bottom of the figure. The dashed line is a theoretical calculation of Tolstoy and May[77] for the (a) velocity profile shown in Fig. 6.15. The high bottom velocity used in these calculations does not mean that the bottom velocity is 2.1 km/sec, but it is a simple way to include partial reflections in the computation, at least to a first approximation.

In shallow-water experiments, the main perturbations are most likely to be changes of water depth.† Often the fluctuations are ocean waves and these occur so rapidly that the average signal level versus range is obtained during one experiment.[(70,71)] As an example we shall apply Eqs. (6.114) and (6.120) to experiments made in the shallow water south of Fire Island, New York. The experiments were part of the series described in Chap. 4 and the waveguide parameters are shown in Fig. 4.32. Signal levels versus range data were taken under very calm conditions with wave heights nearly zero, that is, $\sigma \simeq 0$. As is evident in Fig. 6.17, the receiver, source depth, and frequency were such that only the first and second modes were observed. (The experimental data are the solid curves.) The acoustic signal in mode 1 was obviously very nearly equal to the signal in mode 2 because the mode interference minima are nearly zero. The experiment was repeated several days later when the root-mean-square height of the surface waves was about 0.5 m. As shown in Fig. 6.17, the interference minima are very pronounced when the surface was nearly flat. The mode interference effect is much smaller when the root-mean-square wave height is about 0.5 m. It is evident from Eqs. (6.114) and (6.115) that a decrease of mode-interference effects could be expected.

Theoretical pressure levels for the experimental conditions can be calculated with the aid of (6.114) and (6.115). We know the fluctuation of the sea surface from which we must first calculate the fluctuations of κ_m. An estimation of the distribution of κ_1 and κ_2 can be made with the characteristic equation for a shallow-water waveguide in the following form:

$$\gamma_m \left(h_1 + \zeta \right) + \chi_m = m\pi \tag{6.125}$$

where χ_m is the reflection phase angle at the interface, h_1 is the mean water depth, and ζ is the fluctuation of the water depth. Equation (6.125) can be solved for γ_m and expressed in terms of ζ as follows:

$$\gamma_m = \frac{m\pi - \chi_m}{h_1 + \zeta} \simeq \frac{m\pi - \chi_m}{h_1} \left(1 - \frac{\zeta}{h_0} \right) = \bar{\gamma}_m \left(1 - \frac{\zeta}{h_1} \right) \tag{6.126}$$

where

$$\bar{\gamma}_m = \frac{m\pi - \chi_m}{h_1}$$

and

$$|\zeta| \ll h_1 \tag{6.127}$$

† The sensitivity of signal transmission to the position of an isolated surface irregularity was nicely demonstrated by Scrimger.[(69)] He observed the transmission between a fixed source and receiver in shallow water and then caused the bow wave from a small boat to pass over the receiver, the transmission path, and the source. Simultaneous recordings were made of the signal transmission and surface wave heights at both source and receiver. The fluctuations of the signal level occurred when the surface water wave was above the source or receiver. The fluctuation was small when the surface water wave was entirely between the source and receiver.

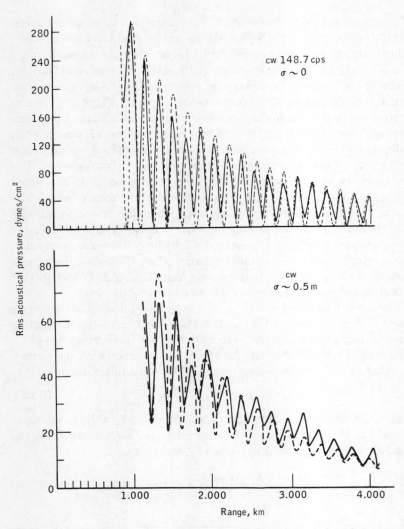

Fig. 6.17 Comparison of theoretical and experimental data as a function of range and mean wave heights. The dashed curves are theoretical data and the solid curves are experimental data. The nearly flat, calm data ($\sigma \sim 0$) are shown on the upper part of the figure. A repeat of the same experiment was made with about sea state 2 and root-mean-square wave height about 0.5 m ($\sigma \sim 0.5$ m). The data and theory for this case are on the lower part of the figure.[71]

The horizontal component of the acoustic wave number and its fluctuation ϵ_m can be obtained as follows:

$$\kappa_m{}^2 = k^2 - \gamma_m{}^2$$

$$\simeq k^2 - \bar{\gamma}_m{}^2 \left(1 - \frac{\zeta}{h_1}\right)^2$$

$$\simeq \bar{\kappa}_m{}^2 + \frac{2\bar{\gamma}_m{}^2 \zeta}{h_1} \tag{6.128}$$

where

$$\bar{\kappa}_m{}^2 = k^2 - \bar{\gamma}_m{}^2$$

With the aid of the binomial theorem and (6.100) ϵ_m is

$$\epsilon_m \simeq \frac{\bar{\gamma}_m{}^2 \zeta}{\bar{\kappa}_m h_1} \tag{6.129}$$

If the probability density of ζ is known, the probability density of ϵ_m can be obtained by transformation of probability densities. As given by Lee,[46] the transformation from $W(x)$ to $W(y)$ with $y = f(x)$ is

$$W(y) = \frac{1}{a} W \left(\frac{y}{a}\right) \qquad y = ax$$

Thus the assumption of a gaussian sea-surface distribution with a root-mean-square wave height σ gives a gaussian distribution for the fluctuation of the horizontal component of wave number. The root-mean-square of ϵ_m is

$$(\bar{\epsilon}_m{}^2)^{1/2} \simeq \frac{\overline{\gamma_m{}^2}\sigma}{\bar{\kappa}_m h_1} \tag{6.130}$$

The calculation of the mean-square phase fluctuations $\overline{\Delta S_m{}^2}$ requires knowledge of the correlation function $\langle \epsilon_m(x)\, \epsilon_m(x + \zeta)\rangle$ *along the transmission path*. The signals were transmitted along a path of constant water depth and roughly parallel to the crests or trough of the sea surface waves. The length of a wave crest was of the same order of magnitude as the length of the transmission path. We assert that $\langle \epsilon_m(x)\, \epsilon_m(x + \zeta)\rangle$ is approximately constant and ϵ_m is independent of x. From (6.105a), $\overline{\Delta S_m{}^2}$ is

$$\overline{\Delta S_m{}^2} \simeq r^2\, \overline{\epsilon_m{}^2} \tag{6.131}$$

The bivariate distribution of ΔS_m and ΔS_n is obtained by the substitution of (6.131) into (6.113). The attenuation δ'_m can be calculated by means of (6.120).

Numerical values of $|\epsilon_m|$ and δ'_m were calculated for the Fire Island shallow-water waveguide. Values of κ_1 and κ_2 are given at the end of

Sec. 4.6. For root-mean-square wave height of 0.5 m, $(\overline{\epsilon_m^2})^{1/2}$ and δ_m' are the following:

$$\bar{\kappa}_1 \simeq 0.57 \text{ m}^{-1} \qquad (\overline{\epsilon_1^2})^{1/2} \simeq 0.4 \times 10^{-3} \text{ m}^{-1} \qquad \delta_1' \simeq 0.2 \times 10^{-4} \text{ m}^{-1}$$

$$\bar{\kappa}_2 \simeq 0.54 \text{ m}^{-1} \qquad (\overline{\epsilon_2^2})^{1/2} \simeq \ 2 \times 10^{-3} \text{ m}^{-1} \qquad \delta_2' \simeq \ 2 \times 10^{-4} \text{ m}^{-1}$$

The attenuation δ_m' caused by the irregular surface is added to the attenuation given in Sec. 4.6.

The acoustical pressure as given by (6.114) also depends upon the correlation of ΔS_m and ΔS_n. We assume the fluctuation in depth affects γ_1 at the same time as it affects γ_2, or correspondingly κ_1 and κ_2. From (6.128) an increase of ζ increases κ_1 and κ_2. We assume ψ_{Smn} is one. However, the contribution of $2|\Delta S_1| \cdot |\Delta S_2| \, \psi_{S12}$ is small compared with $\overline{\Delta S_2^2}$. The theoretical dashed curves shown in Fig. 6.17 were calculated with (6.114). The source was not calibrated for these experiments, and so the theoretical curves were multiplied by constants to match the experimental data at 1 km for $\sigma \simeq 0$ and at 1.5 km for $\sigma \simeq 0.5$ m. The main effects of the sea surface were to decrease the mode interference and to cause a small increase of the attenuation.

In summary, ocean surface waves and time-dependent irregularities of the stratification produce two effects on the transmission of signals. First, the attenuation is increased. Second, signals in different modes become incoherent relative to time and position. These effects are mode dependent and they can preclude a detailed theoretical duplication of experimental acoustical pressure level versus range data in the deep ocean.

REFERENCES

1. J. C. Swallow: *Deep-Sea Res.*, **3**:74–81 (1955).
2. T. E. Pochapsky: *Tellus*, **15**:352–362 (1963).
3. E. C. LaFond: *J. Geophys. Res.*, **67**:3573 (1962).
4. "Physics of Sound in the Sea," pt. I, Transmission, National Research Council, Research Analysis Group (1946).
5. L. N. Liebermann: *J. Acoust. Soc. Am.*, **23**:563–570 (1951).
6. V. A. Krasilnikov: *Doklady Akad. Nauk. SSSR*, **58**:1353 (1947).
7. P. G. Bergmann: *Phys. Rev.*, **70**:486 (1946).
8. C. L. Pekeris: *Phys. Rev.*, **71**:268 (1947).
9. D. Mintzer: *J. Acoust. Soc. Am.*, **25**:922 (1953).
10. D. Mintzer: *J. Acoust. Soc. Am.*, **25**:1107 (1953).
11. D. Mintzer: *J. Acoust. Soc. Am.*, **26**:186 (1954).

12. M. J. Sheehy: *J. Acoust. Soc. Am.*, **22**:24 (1950).
13. R. G. Stone and D. Mintzer: *J. Acoust. Soc. Am.*, **34**:647–653 (1962).
14. E. Skudrzyk: *J. Acoust. Soc. Am.*, **29**:50–60 (1957).
15. D. C. Whitmarsh, E. Skudrzyk, and R. J. Urick: *J. Acoust. Soc. Am.*, **29**:1124–1143 (1957).
16. L. A. Chernov: "Wave Propagation in a Random Medium" (Translated by R. A. Silverman), McGraw-Hill Book Company, New York, 1960.
17. F. H. Sagar: *J. Acoust. Soc. Am.*, **27**:1092 (1955).
18. F. H. Sagar: *J. Acoust. Soc. Am.*, **29**:948 (1957).
19. F. H. Sagar: *J. Acoust. Soc. Am.*, **32**:112-120 (1960).
20. "International Dictionary of Physics and Electronics," D. Van Nostrand Company, Inc., Princeton, N.J., 1956.
21. Lord Rayleigh: "The Theory of Sound," vol. II, 2d ed., 1896. Reprinted by Dover Publications, Inc., New York, 1945, p. 89.
22. L. M. Brekhovskikh; *J. Exptl. Theor. Phys. USSR*, **23**: 275, 289 (1952).
23. C. Eckart: *J. Acoust. Soc. Am.*, **25**:566–570 (1953).
24. B. B. Baker and E. T. Copson: "The Mathematical Theory of Huygens' Principle," pp. 23–28, Oxford University Press, London, (1939).
25. A. W. Maue: *Z. Physik*, **126**:601–618 (1949).
26. W. C. Meecham: *J. Rational Mech. Anal.*, **5**:323–333 (1956).
27. P. Beckmann and A. Spizzichino: "The Scattering of Electromagnetic Waves from Rough Surfaces," The Macmillan Company, New York, 1963.
28. M. Abramowitz and I. Stegun: Handbook of Mathematical Functions, *Nat. Bur. Std., Appl. Math. Ser.* 55 (1965).
29. R. W. Wood: *Phil. Mag.*, **4**:396 (1902).
30. C. H. Palmer, Jr.: *J. Opt. Soc. Am.*, **42**:269 (1952).
31. W. C. Meecham: *J. Appl. Phys.*, **27**:361–367 (1956).
32. H. W. Marsh: *J. Acoust. Soc. Am.*, **33**:330–333 (1961).
33. C. E. Jordon (ed.): "Symposium on Electromagnetic Theory and Antennas, Copenhagen, 1962" Pergamon Press, New York, 1963.
34. J. L. Uretsky: *J. Acoust. Soc. Am.*, **35**:1293–1294 (1963).
35. S. R. Murphy and G. E. Lord: *J. Acoust. Soc. Am.*, **36**:1598 (1964).
36. J. G. Parker: *J. Acoust. Soc. Am.*, **28**:672–680 (1956).
37. V. Twersky: *J. Appl. Phys.*, **22**:852 (1951).
38. V. Twersky: *J. Acoust. Soc. Am.*, **29**:209 (1957).
39. M. A. Biot: *J. Acoust. Soc. Am.*, **29**:1193–1200 (1957).
40. E. O. La Casce and P. Tamarkin: *J. Appl. Phys.*, **27**:138–148 (1956).
41. A. N. Leporskii: *Soviet Phys. Acoust.*, **2**:185–189 (1956).
42. J. M. Proud, Jr., P. Tamarkin, and W. C. Meecham: *J. Appl. Phys.*, **28**:1298–1301 (1957).

43. G. Neumann: *Tech. Mem.* 43, Beach Erosion Board, Dept. of the Army, (1953).
44. H. W. Marsh, M. Schulkin, and S. G. Kneale: *J. Acoust. Soc. Am.*, **33**:334–340 (1961).
45. J. V. Uspensky: "Introduction to Mathematical Probability," Chaps. 9 and 15, McGraw-Hill Book Company, New York, 1937.
46. Y. W. Lee: "Statistical Theory of Communication," p. 190, John Wiley & Sons, Inc., New York, 1960.
47. A. Sommerfeld: "Partial Differential Equations in Physics," p. 86, Academic Press Inc., New York, 1949.
48. G. N. Watson: "A Treatise on the Theory of Bessel Functions," 2d ed., p. 393, Cambridge University Press, London, 1952.
49. J. M Proud, Jr., R. T. Beyer, and P. Tamarkin: *J. Appl. Phys.*, **31**:543 (1960).
50. M. V. Brown and J. Riccard: *J. Acoust. Soc. Am.*, **32**:1551 (1960).
51. C. S. Clay: *J. Acoust. Soc. Am.*, **32**:1547–1551 (1960).
52. R. J. Urick and R. M. Hoover: *J. Acoust. Soc. Am.*, **28**:1038 (1956).
53. C. Cox and W. Munk: *J. Opt. Soc. Am.*, **44**:838–850 (1954).
54. R. J. Urick: *J. Marine Res.*, **15**:134–148 (1956).
55. C. S. Clay and H. Medwin: *J. Acoust. Soc. Am.*, **36**:2131–2134 (1964).
56. B. C. Heezen, M. Tharp, and W. M. Ewing: *Geol. Soc. Am. Spec. Papers*, No. 65, p. 53, 1959.
57. C. S. Clay and P. A. Rona: *J. Geophys. Res.*, **70**:855–870 (1965).
58. T. G. Bell: *J. Acoust. Soc. Am.*, **36**:2003 (1964).
59. A. B. Wood and D. E. Weston: *Acustica*, **14**:156–162 (1964).
60. F. C. Fuglister: Atlantic Ocean Atlas, Woods Hole Oceanographic Institution, Woods Hole, Mass. (1960).
61. W. D. Wilson: *J. Acoust. Soc. Am.*, **32**:641 (1960).
62. J. C. Slater: "Microwave Transmission," McGraw-Hill Book Company, New York, 1942.
63. C. G. Montgomery, R. H. Dicke, and E. M. Purcell (eds.): "Principles of Microwave Circuits," p. 191, McGraw-Hill Book Company, New York, 1948.
64. A. O. Williams and M. N. Lewis: "Approximate Normal Mode Methods of Calculation for Sound Propagation in Shallow Water," *Tech. Rept.* 56–1, Brown University, Providence, R.I., 1956.
65. D. E. Weston: *Proc. Phys. Soc. (London)*, **73**:365–384 (1959).
66. R. K. Eby, A. O. Williams, R. P. Ryan, and P. Tamarkin: *J. Acoust. Soc. Am.*, **32**:88–99 (1960).
67. A. D. Pierce: *J. Acoust. Soc. Am.*, **37**:19–27 (1965).
68. A. N. Guthrie and J. Shaffer: *J. Acoust. Soc. Am.*, **38**:1060 (1965).
69. J. A. Scrimger: *J. Acoust. Soc. Am.*, **33**:239–247 (1961).

70. L. N. Zakharov, V. S. Nesterov, and E. G. Fedoseeva: *Soviet Phys. Acoust.*, **9**:188–190 (1963).
71. C. S. Clay: *J. Acoust. Soc. Am.*, **36**:833–837 (1964).
72. R. C. Bourret: *J. Acoust. Soc. Am.*, **33**:1793–1797 (1961).
73. C. S. Clay: *J. Geophys. Res.*, **71**:2037–2046 (1966).
74. G. R. Barnard, J. L. Bardin, and W. B. Hempkins: *J. Acoust. Soc. Am.*, **36**:2119–2123 (1964).
75. F. R. Menotti, S. R. Santaniello, and W. R. Schumacher: *J. Acoust. Soc. Am.*, **38**:707–714 (1965).
76. L. M. Brekhovskikh, "Waves in Layered Media," Academic Press Inc., New York and London, 1960.
77. I. Tolstoy and J. May: *J. Acoust. Soc. Am.*, **32**:655 (1960).

CHAPTER SEVEN

MEASUREMENTS IN THE OCEAN AS A PROBLEM IN FILTER THEORY

7.1 INTRODUCTION

The acoustic field due to a source in the ocean has been discussed in previous chapters. Theory and experiment were compared, and the results support the theoretical development reasonably well. However, such comparisons are often difficult to make because both theory and experiment are extremely sensitive to minor variations in the stratification of the waveguide. In this chapter we shall examine another approach that is suggested by the form of the expressions for the acoustic field, which are *linear*. Since they relate the received signal at one position to the input or source, we can regard them as filter functions. It is convenient to consider the propagation problem as a linear filter because we can use many of the techniques developed in statistical communication theory.

The techniques of linear filter theory are useful for making input-output calculations with the impulse response or the phase and frequency response of the system. The response of a filter can be determined either experimentally or theoretically. In the "black box" approach to the study of passive filters, one measures the frequency response or impulse response between the input terminals and the output terminals and does not ask what is inside the box. The ocean can be regarded as a filter inside a black box, and we have only to measure the input-output functions between points of interest. However, the immensity of the ocean and the almost infinite number of input-output positions necessitate another approach, namely, that we make a limited number of measurements and determine a theoretical model. Calculations based upon the model may be used (in principle) to interpolate the response between observation points.

7.2 TRANSFER FUNCTIONS IN A LINEAR SYSTEM

Acoustic experiments consist of measuring at a receiver the signal due to a source, and thus may be considered as a filter problem in which we measure the transfer function. The mathematical tools of filter theory are the Fourier integral transformations, convolution integrals, and correlation integrals.[1,2] We shall illustrate the application of these techniques to acoustic problems. Since measurements are always made in the presence of noise, some discussion of filters, signals, and noise is also given.

For an arbitrary acoustical environment, assumed to be linear, the acoustical pressure observed at a receiver due to an *impulse* of pressure radiated by a source is $p_I(t)$. The notation of a lower-case letter for the time function and an upper-case letter for the frequency function is used in this chapter. $p_I(t)$ and $P_I(\omega)$ have the following Fourier transformations:

$$p_I(t) = \frac{1}{2\pi} \int_{-\infty}^{\infty} P_I(\omega) e^{i\omega t} \, d\omega \tag{7.1}$$

$$P_I(\omega) = \int_{-\infty}^{\infty} p_I(t)e^{-i\omega t}\, dt \tag{7.2}$$

subject to the condition

$$\int_{-\infty}^{\infty} |p(t)|\, dt \text{ is finite}$$

The acoustical pressure $p_0(t)$ at the receiver for an arbitrary source drive $f_s(t)$ is given by the convolution of $f_s(t)$ with the impulse response $p_I(t)$.[1]

$$p_0(t) = \int_{-\infty}^{\infty} p_I(\tau)f_s(t-\tau)\, d\tau$$

or

$$p_0(t) = \int_{-\infty}^{\infty} f_s(\tau)p_I(t-\tau)\, d\tau \tag{7.3}$$

Substitution of the Fourier transformations of f_s and p_I, $F_s(\omega)$ and $P_I(\omega)$, and use of the Dirac delta function

$$\delta(\alpha) = \frac{1}{2\pi}\int_{-\infty}^{\infty} e^{ix\alpha}\, dx \tag{7.4}$$

yield p_0 as a function of $F_s(\omega)$ and $P_I(\omega)$,

$$p_0(t) = \frac{1}{2\pi}\int_{-\infty}^{\infty} P_0(\omega)e^{i\omega t}\, d\omega$$

with

$$P_0(\omega) = P_I(\omega)F_s(\omega) \tag{7.5}$$

(7.5) states the useful result that $P_0(\omega)$ of the output signal is the product of the spectrum function of the source and $P_I(\omega)$.

The correlation function is used in Chap. 6 for the description of randomly irregular surfaces. It is also extremely useful in the analysis of linear systems, signals in noise problems, and array computations. The correlation integral for two functions $p_1(t)$ and $p_2(t)$ is†

$$\psi_{12}(\tau) = \int_{-\infty}^{\infty} p_1^*(t)p_2(t+\tau)\, dt \tag{7.6}$$

and with the aid of (7.2) and (7.4), $\psi_{12}(\tau)$ can be expressed in terms of the spectrum functions of $p_1(t)$ and $p_2(t)$ as follows:

$$\psi_{12}(\tau) = \frac{1}{2\pi}\int_{-\infty}^{\infty} \Psi_{12}(\omega)e^{i\omega\tau}\, d\omega \tag{7.7}$$

with

$$\Psi_{12}(\omega) \equiv P_1^*(\omega)P_2(\omega) \tag{7.8}$$

Here asterisks denote complex conjugates.

† The correlation is referred to as the autocorrelation if the two functions are the same and as the cross correlation if the two functions are different. Although we do not make this distinction, some authors define the correlation as a normalized quantity and use the term covariance for unnormalized operations. We use the subscript notation ψ_{ab} to mean the correlation of the functions f_a and f_b. The corresponding spectrum function is Ψ_{ab}.

If p_1 equals p_2, Ψ_{11} is termed the energy density spectrum. For p_1 not equal to p_2, $\Psi_{12}(\omega)$ is sometimes called the cross-energy density spectrum or the cross spectrum.

For the results stated up to this point it is assumed that the Fourier integral transforms (7.1) and (7.2) exist. The techniques of correlation can be applied to nonperiodic functions that do not have the usual Fourier transformations.[(2)] The random function for which the integral

$$\lim_{T \to \infty} \frac{1}{2T} \int_{-\infty}^{\infty} |f(t)|^2 \, dt \tag{7.9}$$

exists and is finite (not zero) can be used to determine the correlation functions. The correlation function is defined as the following integral:

$$\psi_{ff}(\tau) = \lim_{T \to \infty} \frac{1}{2T} \int_{-T}^{T} f^*(t) f(t + \tau) \, dt \tag{7.10}$$

$\psi_{ff}(\tau)$ tends to zero as τ tends to infinity if the random function contains no constant or periodic components.

The correlation function can be expressed as the following Fourier transformations: [(2) or (1), p. 96]

$$\psi_{ff}(\tau) = \frac{1}{2\pi} \int_{-\infty}^{\infty} \Psi_{ff}(\omega) e^{i\omega\tau} \, d\omega \tag{7.11}$$

$$\Psi_{ff}(\omega) = \int_{-\infty}^{\infty} \psi_{ff}(\tau) e^{-i\omega\tau} \, d\tau \tag{7.12}$$

ψ_{ff} is analogous to a power and Ψ_{ff} as given by (7.11) and (7.12) is referred to as the power-spectrum density.

The cross-correlation function of two different functions, f_1 and f_2, is the following integral:

$$\psi_{12}(\tau) = \lim_{T \to \infty} \frac{1}{2T} \int_{-T}^{T} f_1^*(t) f_2(t + \tau) \, dt \tag{7.13}$$

The cross-correlation function expressed as a Fourier integral is [(1) p. 78]

$$\psi_{12}(\tau) = \frac{1}{2\pi} \int_{-\infty}^{\infty} \Psi_{12}(\omega) e^{i\omega\tau} \, d\omega \tag{7.14}$$

$$\Psi_{12}(\omega) = \int_{-\infty}^{\infty} \psi_{12}(\tau) e^{-i\omega\tau} \, d\tau \tag{7.15}$$

Equations (7.12) and (7.15) give the power-spectrum density Ψ_{ff} and cross-spectrum density as the Fourier transform of the correlation function. Thus, the power spectrum $\Psi_{ff}(\omega)$ of a random function $f(t)$ can be specified even though the Fourier transformation of $f(t)$, that is, $F(\omega)$, does not exist.

The input-output relations of linear systems driven by random functions can be expressed with correlation functions.[(1) p. 348] The responses at two detectors due to an impulse source are $p_{Ia}(t)$ and $p_{Ib}(t)$. Ordinarily, the source function is assumed to be the same for both detectors a and b. However, the source may be directional, so we assume that detector a observes the signal $p_a(t)$ due to $f_1(t)$ at the source and detector b observes the signal $p_b(t)$ due to $f_2(t)$ at the source. The acoustical pressures p_a and p_b at detectors a and b due to source functions $f_1(t)$ and $f_2(t)$ with the aid of (7.3) are

$$p_a(t) = \int_{-\infty}^{\infty} p_{Ia}(\nu)f_1(t - \nu)\, d\nu$$
$$p_b(t) = \int_{-\infty}^{\infty} p_{Ib}(\sigma)f_2(t - \sigma)\, d\sigma \tag{7.16}$$

On inversion of the order of integration, the cross-correlation function of p_a with p_b is

$$\psi_{ab}(\tau) = \int_{-\infty}^{\infty} p_{Ia}(\nu)\, d\nu \int_{-\infty}^{\infty} p_{Ib}(\sigma)\psi_{12}(\tau + \nu - \sigma)\, d\sigma \tag{7.17}$$

where $\quad \psi_{12}(\tau) = \lim_{T \to \infty} \frac{1}{2T} \int_{-T}^{T} f_1^*(t)f_2(t + \tau)\, dt$

p_{Ia}, p_{Ib}, and ψ_{12} can be replaced by their Fourier transformations where the spectrum functions are the following:

$$P_{Ia}(\omega) = \int_{-\infty}^{\infty} p_{Ia}(\nu)e^{-i\omega\nu}\, d\nu \tag{7.18}$$

$$P_{Ib}(\omega') = \int_{-\infty}^{\infty} p_{Ib}(\sigma)e^{-i\omega'\sigma}\, d\sigma \tag{7.19}$$

$$\Psi_{12}(\omega'') = \int_{-\infty}^{\infty} \psi_{12}(\mu)e^{-i\omega''\mu}\, d\mu \tag{7.20}$$

With the aid of (7.4), the transformation of (7.17) follows directly and is

$$\psi_{ab}(\tau) = \frac{1}{2\pi} \int_{-\infty}^{\infty} \Psi_{ab}(\omega)e^{i\omega\tau}\, d\omega$$
$$\Psi_{ab}(\omega) = P_{Ia}^*(\omega)P_{Ib}(\omega)\Psi_{12}(\omega) \tag{7.21}$$

The transformation pair ψ_{ab} and Ψ_{ab} expresses the correlation properties of signals observed at different receivers, a and b. The spectrum density of the signal is in $\Psi_{12}(\omega)$ and the acoustical propagation is in the function $P_a^*(\omega)P_b(\omega)$.

The correlation of p_a and p_b [Eq. (7.17)] can also be expressed in terms of the time functions. With a change of variable $t = \sigma - \nu$, and with inversion of the order of integration, ψ_{ab} becomes

$$\psi_{ab}(\tau) = \int_{-\infty}^{\infty} \psi_{Ia,Ib}(t)\psi_{12}(\tau - t)\, dt \qquad (7.22)$$

where
$$\psi_{Ia,Ib}(t) = \int_{-\infty}^{\infty} p_{Ia}^*(\tau)p_{Ib}(\tau + t)\, d\tau \qquad (7.23)$$

$\psi_{Ia,Ib}$ has Fourier transformation relations like (7.14) and (7.15). Equations (7.21) and (7.22) express the correlation function of the signals at a and b.

The purpose of developing the transformation relationships above has been twofold. First, they are extremely useful in discussion of the detection and measurement of signals in the presence of noise. Second, they are convenient for the study of propagation in waveguides with general-type source and receiver functions. We proceed with a brief treatment of the detection of signals in noise.

7.3 MATCHED FILTERS AND MATCHED SIGNALS

Acoustic experiments are done in a noisy environment using somewhat noisy equipment. Frequently the signal bandwidth is much less than the noise band, and it is customary to pass the signals through filters in order to reduce the interference of noise with the measurements. One may then ask, for a given signal what is the "best" filter to use? There are many answers, and they depend upon what is meant by the term "best." Wiener has given a technique for the design of optimum filters[2] in which the function of the filter is to minimize the mean-square difference between the filtered signal plus noise and the desired output. The theory is frequently used to design a filter that yields an output signal that is as similar to the input signal as possible. The Wiener theory is very general and has become an important part of modern filter theory.

In many acoustic experiments *the signal is known* and we want the filter output to be as large as possible relative to the noise. This criterion is particularly useful if one is using an oscilloscope to determine the presence or absence of a particular transient signal in the presence of noise.[3] The problem is to find a filter having a frequency response $F(\omega)$ that produces at the output a signal with a maximum value relative to the average noise level. We use the method given by Van Vleck and Middleton[4] in our analysis and assume that the signal $s(t)$ and its transform $S(\omega)$ are known and given by (7.1) and (7.2).   The output signal is

$$s_0(t) = \frac{1}{2\pi} \int_{-\infty}^{\infty} S(\omega)F(\omega)e^{i\omega t}\, d\omega \tag{7.24}$$

The input-noise time function $n_i(t)$ is assumed to be stationary and uncorrelated with the signal.   Since the usual Fourier transform of $n_i(t)$ does not exist, the power-spectrum $\Psi_{nn}(\omega)$ is given by the Fourier transformation of the autocorrelation function of $n_i(t)$ as follows:

$$\psi_{nn}(\tau) = \lim_{T\to\infty} \frac{1}{2T} \int_{-T}^{T} n_i^*(t)n_i(t+\tau)\, dt \tag{7.25}$$

$$\Psi_{nn}(\omega) = \int_{-\infty}^{\infty} \psi_{nn}(\tau)e^{-i\omega\tau}\, d\tau \tag{7.26}$$

The mean-square noise output of the filter can be obtained with $F(\omega)$, $\Psi_{nn}(\omega)$, and an expression similar to (7.21). Equation (7.21) expresses the output of a system in terms of the input-signal (power) spectrum $\Psi_{12}(\omega)$ and the cross spectrum of the system response $P_{Ia}^*(\omega)P_{Ib}(\omega)$.   If we let the noise be the input with $\Psi_{nn}(\omega) = \Psi_{12}(\omega)$ and let $F(\omega) = P_{Ia}(\omega) = P_{Ib}(\omega)$, the mean-square noise out of the filter is

$$\langle n_0{}^2 \rangle = \psi_{fn,fn}(\tau)|_{\tau=0} \tag{7.27}$$

with
$$\psi_{fn,fn}(\tau) = \frac{1}{2\pi} \int_{-\infty}^{\infty} F^*(\omega)F(\omega)\Psi_{nn}(\omega)e^{i\omega\tau}\, d\omega \tag{7.28}$$

The ratio of the square of peak output signal $|s_0(t)|^2$ to the mean-square noise output $\langle n_0{}^2 \rangle$ is

$$\frac{|s_0(t_0)|^2}{\langle n_0{}^2 \rangle} = \frac{1}{2\pi} \frac{\left| \int_{-\infty}^{\infty} S(\omega)F(\omega)e^{i\omega t_0}\, d\omega \right|^2}{\int_{-\infty}^{\infty} F^*(\omega)F(\omega)\Psi_{nn}(\omega)\, d\omega} \tag{7.29}$$

At a time t_0, the output signal is a maximum.   If $\Psi_{nn}(\omega)$ is not zero in the region of integration, so that multiplication and division by $\sqrt{\Psi_{nn}(\omega)}$ is permitted, a best filter can be specified.[5]   Let us rewrite (7.29) as follows:

$$\frac{|s_0(t)|^2}{\langle n_0{}^2 \rangle} = \frac{1}{2\pi} \frac{\left| \int_{-\infty}^{\infty} [S(\omega)/\sqrt{\Psi_{nn}(\omega)}]\, F(\omega)\, \sqrt{\Psi_{nn}(\omega)}e^{i\omega t_0}\, d\omega \right|^2}{\int_{-\infty}^{\infty} |F(\omega)|^2\Psi_{nn}(\omega)\, d\omega} \tag{7.30}$$

We use Schwarz's inequality in the following form:[6]

$$\left| \int f(x)g(x)\, dx \right|^2 \leq \int |f(x)|^2\, dx \int |g(x)|^2\, dx \tag{7.31}$$

in which the equality holds for $f^*(x) \propto g(x)$. The application of (7.31) to (7.30) yields

$$\frac{|s_0(t_0)|^2}{\langle n_0^2 \rangle} \leq \frac{1}{2\pi} \int_{-\infty}^{\infty} \frac{|S(\omega)|^2}{\Psi_{nn}(\omega)} \, d\omega \tag{7.32}$$

Omitting the constant of proportionality, the maximum value of the left-hand side of (7.32) occurs for the equality and for

$$\frac{S(\omega)}{\sqrt{\Psi_{nn}(\omega)}} = [F(\omega) \sqrt{\Psi_{nn}(\omega)} \, e^{i\omega t_0}]^* \tag{7.33}$$

or

$$F(\omega) = \frac{S^*(\omega)}{\Psi_{nn}(\omega)} e^{-i\omega t_0} \tag{7.34}$$

$F(\omega)$ is the response of the matched or conjugate filter.

The substitution of (7.34) in (7.24) gives the output signal

$$s_0(t) = \frac{1}{2\pi} \int_{-\infty}^{\infty} \frac{S^*(\omega)S(\omega)}{\Psi_{nn}(\omega)} e^{i\omega(t-t_0)} \, d\omega \tag{7.35}$$

If $\Psi_{nn}(\omega)$ is constant, (7.35) is

$$s_0(t) = \frac{1}{2\pi\Psi_{nn}} \int_{-\infty}^{\infty} S^*(\omega)S(\omega) \, e^{i\omega(t-t_0)} \, d\omega \tag{7.36}$$

or

$$s_0(t) = \frac{1}{\Psi_{nn}} \int_{-\infty}^{\infty} s^*(\tau)s(\tau + t - t_0) \, d\tau \tag{7.37}$$

With the aid of (7.6), $\psi_{ss}(\tau) = \int_{-\infty}^{\infty} s^*(t)s(t + \tau) \, dt$ and the output signal is the autocorrelation of the input signal with an added time delay t_0. The output of the filter is a maximum at the time t_0. The comparison of (7.36) with (7.32) shows that for the matched filter,

$$\frac{|s_0(t_0)|^2}{\langle n_0^2 \rangle} = \frac{\psi_{ss}}{\Psi_{nn}} \tag{7.38}$$

The peak signal-to-noise ratio depends upon ψ_{ss} as a measure of the total energy in the signal received by the detector. Since the magnitude of ψ_{ss} depends upon the duration of the signal, the peak signal-to-noise ratio is improved with an increase of the duration time of the signal. A filter and signal are matched to each other, and the matched filter response is the conjugate of the signal spectrum. We consider the interrelationship of matched signals and matched filters by first examining the impulse response of the matched filter.

For constant noise-spectrum density, the matched filter is $S^*(\omega)e^{-i\omega t_0}$. With the signal $s(t)$ and the Fourier transform (7.2), we can write the conjugate of $S(\omega)$ as follows:

$$S^*(\omega) = \int_{-\infty}^{\infty} s(t)\, e^{i\omega t}\, dt \tag{7.39}$$

and for Ψ_{nn} a constant, we have

$$\frac{S^*(\omega)}{\Psi_{nn}}\, e^{-i\omega t_0} = \frac{1}{\Psi_{nn}} \int_{-\infty}^{\infty} s(t) e^{i\omega(t-t_0)}\, dt \tag{7.40}$$

The change of variable $(t_0 - t) = t'$ yields

$$\frac{S^*(\omega)e^{-i\omega t_0}}{\Psi_{nn}} = \frac{1}{\Psi_{nn}} \int_{-\infty}^{\infty} s(t_0 - t')\, e^{-i\omega t'}\, dt' \tag{7.41}$$

The comparison of (7.41) with (7.2) shows that the impulse response of the matched filter is $s(t_0 - t)$. *The response is delayed by t_0 and is the time reverse of the signal.*

The matched signal can be obtained by making a tape recording of the impulse response of the filter and then replaying the signal backward.[7-9] Except for an arbitrary time delay, this is $s(-t)$ and the signal is matched to that particular filter. Whether one uses a matched signal or a matched filter is largely a matter of experimental convenience.

7.4 CORRELATION AND FILTERING OF AN IMPULSE SOURCE IN A PERFECT WAVEGUIDE

The correlation of the signal in a perfect waveguide due to an impulsive source is given in this section. In connection with the study of signal correlations, we discuss in a somewhat more general context the use of filters and matched signals to reduce the phase distortion caused by propagation in the waveguide.

The impulse response of source and receiver in the perfect waveguide can be expressed by means of images or as a sum of modes. For the first example, we choose the case of a waveguide with perfectly reflecting rigid walls. The waveguide thickness is h, and the source and receiver are placed at $h/2$. Retaining the notation of the previous section, $p(t)$ is the acoustical pressure due to a $\delta(t)$ pressure source with strength A_0 at unit distance. The delta function can be considered as a very narrow impulsive signal with a very large bandwidth.

In the image formulation, the acoustical pressure and spectra at radial distance r from the source are

$$p(t) = A_0 \sum_{m=-\infty}^{\infty} \frac{\delta(t - R_m/c)}{R_m} \qquad (7.42)$$

where $R_m{}^2 = m^2 h^2 + r^2$, and

$$P(\omega) = A_0 \sum_{m=-\infty}^{\infty} \frac{e^{-i\omega R_m/c}}{R_m} \qquad (7.43)$$

The autocorrelation $\psi_{11}(\tau)$ is

$$\psi_{11}(\tau) = A_0{}^2 \sum_{m=-\infty}^{\infty} \frac{\delta(0)}{R_m{}^2} + A_0{}^2 \sum_{\substack{-\infty \\ m \neq n}}^{\infty} \frac{\delta[(R_m - R_n)/c + \tau]}{R_m R_n} \qquad (7.44)$$

The correlation function is written as two summations; the first one is the peak at $\tau = 0$ and the second represents the side lobes. For the impulse pressure source and infinite bandwidth, the peaks in the side lobes are distinct. The following summation[(10)no.858] can be used to evaluate the first term on the right side of (7.44):

$$\sum_{-\infty}^{\infty} \frac{1}{(n + x)^2 + y^2} = \frac{\pi}{y} \frac{\sinh 2\pi y}{\cosh 2\pi y - \cos 2\pi x}$$

The peak of the correlation function occurs at $\tau = 0$, and the cross terms, that is, $m \neq n$, are zero. Thus, $\psi_{11}(0)$ is the first term on the right-hand side of (7.44) and with the aid of the summation it can be expressed as follows:

$$\psi_{11}(0) = \frac{\pi A_0{}^2}{rh} \coth \frac{\pi r}{h} \qquad (7.45)$$

As discussed in Sec. 7.3, the autocorrelation function can also be obtained by passing the signal through a matched filter with an impulse response $p(t_0 - t)$. The convolution (7.3) of $p(t)$ and $p(t_0 - t)$ is

$$\psi_{11}(t_0 - t) = \int_{-\infty}^{\infty} p(t_0 - \tau) p(t - \tau)\, d\tau \qquad (7.46)$$

and since ψ_{11} is symmetric,

$$\psi_{11}(t - t_0) = \psi_{11}(t_0 - t)$$

The correlation operation or matched filter yields the same output signal.[(3)] In Sec. 7.3, the signal was assumed to be $s_i(t)$ at the receiver and the filter was chosen to match it. Here, the signal has been shaped by propagation in the waveguide.[(11)] The filter that matches this signal is matched to the impulse response of the waveguide.

Applications of matched filter or correlation technique to the propagation of an impulse in a waveguide are shown in Fig. 7.1. Figure 7.1a illustrates the acoustic waveguide as a linear filter. The correlation operation $p(t)$ gives the correlation function $\psi_{11}(\tau)$ shown in Fig. 7.1b. Figure 7.1c shows the result of passing the signal through its matched filter. The output $\psi_{11}(t - t_0)$ has the same form as the correlation function except that it is a function of t and has an additional time delay. Figure 7.1d demonstrates the use of matched signals in a waveguide.[12]

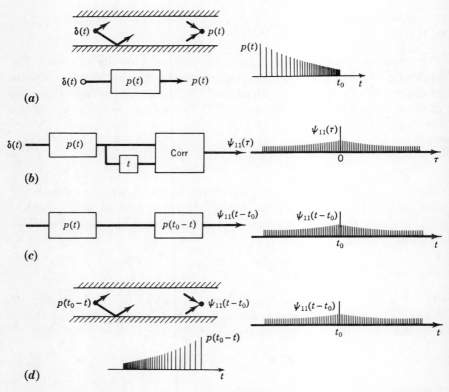

Fig. 7.1 Application of linear filter theory to propagation in a waveguide. (a) Impulse source $\delta(t)$ with waveguide as a filter; (b) correlation of $p_I(t)$; (c) matched filter with impulse response $p_I(t_0 - t)$; (d) matched signal $p_I(t_0 - t)$.

We conclude this section with a few general comments about the properties of $\psi_{11}(\tau)$ as a function of position. As the distance r between the source and receiver is increased, $\psi_{11}(0)$ decreases and the amplitude of $\psi_{11}(0)$ is asymptotic to r^{-1}. The correlation of the signals observed at two different positions, that is, r_1, z_1 and r_2, z_2, does not show the correlation maximum that corresponds to the first term in (7.44). The correlation function consists entirely of terms similar to the second term of (7.44). If we regard the correlation as a matched-filter operation, the matched filter is matched for particular source and receiver positions (r_1,z_1) in the waveguide. Displacement of the receiver to (r_2,z_2) yields a signal that is not matched to the filter and the output of the filter has the same form as the correlation of the signals $p(r_1,z_1)$ and $p(r_2,z_2)$.

7.5 AUTOCORRELATION OF SIGNALS IN SHALLOW WATER

The previous section examined the correlation of the signal in a perfect waveguide due to an impulse. This section presents the autocorrelation for a transient in a multilayered waveguide. The fields in the multilayered waveguide due to a simple harmonic source are given as a function of ω, (3.118), and (3.119).† The acoustical pressure $p(t)$ is $-\rho\ddot{\varphi}$ in terms of the displacement potential φ. For a source at $(0,z_0)$, receiver at (r,z), and for long ranges r, we have

$$p(r,z,t) = \frac{\rho}{2\pi} \int_{-\infty}^{\infty} \omega^2 G(\omega)\Phi(r,z,\omega)e^{i\omega t}\, d\omega \tag{7.47}$$

$$\Phi(r,z,\omega) = \frac{-i}{\rho\omega^2\sqrt{r}} \sum_{1}^{M} p_m\phi_m(z_0)\phi_m(z)e^{-i(\kappa_m r - \pi/4)-\delta_m r} \tag{7.48}$$

where $\qquad G(\omega) = S(\omega)F(\omega)$

$\qquad\qquad \delta_m = $ mode attenuation

$\qquad\qquad F(\omega) = $ receiver filter frequency response

$\qquad\qquad S(\omega) = $ source spectrum function

$\qquad\qquad p_m = $ excitation function (4.81)

The autocorrelation of the acoustical pressure, with the aid of (7.21), is found to be

$$\psi(r,z,\tau) = \frac{\rho^2}{2\pi} \int_{-\infty}^{\infty} \omega^4 GG^*\Phi\Phi^* e^{i\omega\tau}\, d\omega \tag{7.49}$$

† Following the notation of Sec. 7.2, we let the displacement potential be $\varphi(t)$ and then $\varphi(t) = \Phi(\omega)e^{i\omega t}$.

Insertion of (7.48) into the last expression and expansion of the product give

$$\psi(r,z,\tau) = \sum_1^M \psi_{m,m} + \sum_{\substack{1 \\ m \neq n}}^M \psi_{m,n} \tag{7.50}$$

where
$$\psi_{m,m}(r,z,\tau) = \frac{e^{-2\delta_m r}}{2\pi r} \int_{-\infty}^{\infty} p_m{}^2 GG^* \phi_m{}^2(z_0) \phi_m{}^2(z) e^{i\omega\tau} \, d\omega \tag{7.51}$$

$$\psi_{m,n}(r,z,\tau) = \frac{e^{-(\delta_m+\delta_n)r}}{2\pi r} \int_{-\infty}^{\infty} p_m GG^* \phi_m(z_0) \phi_m(z) p_n \phi_n(z_0) \phi_n(z) e^{-i[(\kappa_m - \kappa_n)r - \omega\tau]} \, d\omega \tag{7.52}$$

Equation (7.49) gives the autocorrelation of the acoustic signal as a function of the source-receiver positions and the spectrum density of the source and receiver filters. We recall from Sec. 7.2 that the correlation function and its spectrum have the same transformation relationship for both transients (7.7) and random functions (7.14). Thus, the correlation function of the signal in the waveguide (7.50) has the same form for both transient and noise excitation. $\psi(r,z,0)$ or $\int pp^* \, dt$ is measured in many signal-transmission experiments in both deep and shallow water.

Experiment and theory for the propagation of band-limited noise† have been compared for shallow water.[13] The experiments were done south of Fire Island in 22.6 m of water over about 600 m of sediments (Fig. 4.32 shows the waveguide parameters used for calculations). The source had a 10-cps bandwidth at about 150 cps (942 ± 31.5 rad/sec). In this frequency range, calculations of $p_m(\omega)$, $\gamma_m(\omega)$, and $\kappa_m(\omega)$, as shown in Fig. 7.2, indicate that linear approximations are adequate for these functions over the limited bandwidth. Four discrete modes could propagate, and of these, the third mode has small excitation in the frequency band at 942 rad/sec as shown in Fig. 7.2. The fourth mode was eliminated because the source was towed at depth 10.7 m, a node for the fourth mode. The approximate calculation of $\psi(r)$ is simple because in the frequency band the first and second modes have nearly equal and constant excitation, γ_1 and γ_2 are nearly constant, and κ_1 and κ_2 are nearly linear in ω. Thus κ_m, γ_m, and p_m are approximately the following:

$$\kappa_m \simeq \left. \frac{(\omega - a_m)}{U_m} \right|_{\omega = \omega_0}$$

$$\gamma_m \simeq f_m(\omega - g_m)|_{\omega = \omega_0} \tag{7.53}$$

$$p_m \simeq \bar{p}_m|_{\omega = \omega_0}$$

† Random noise signals that have been passed through bandpass filters are referred to as band-limited noise.

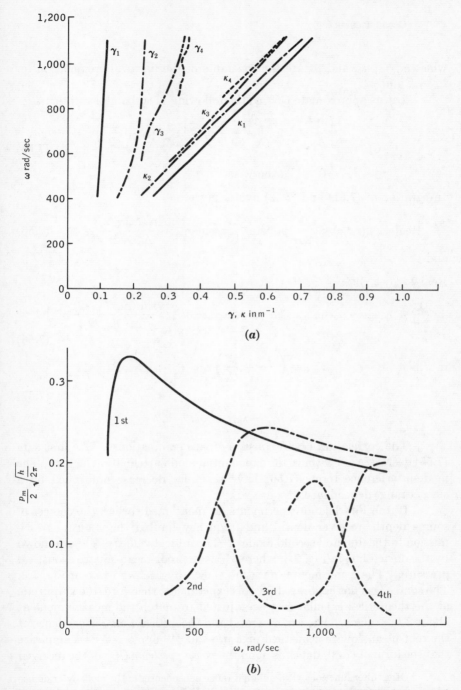

(a)

(b)

Fig. 7.2 (a) Curves of the angular frequency ω vs. the horizontal component κ_m and the vertical component γ_m of the wave number. (b) Mode excitation p_m vs. angular frequency. The waveguide parameters are given in Fig. 4.32, p. 133.

where a_m, f_m, g_m, and $\bar{p}_m$ are the constants of the linear approximation for k_m, γ_m, and p_m.

Let us approximate GG^* as the following ideal bandpass filter:

$$GG^* = \begin{cases} \dfrac{1}{\Delta\omega} & \text{for } \left(\omega - \dfrac{\Delta\omega}{2}\right) \leq \omega \leq \left(\omega + \dfrac{\Delta\omega}{2}\right) \\[2mm] 0 & \text{otherwise} \end{cases} \tag{7.54}$$

Integration of (7.51) and (7.52) over ω gives

$$\text{Real } \psi_{m,m}(r,z,\tau) \simeq \frac{1}{2\pi r}\, \bar{p}_m{}^2 \sin^2 \gamma_m z_0 \sin^2 \gamma_m z \frac{\sin (\Delta\omega\, \tau/2)}{\Delta\omega\, \tau/2} e^{-2\delta_m r} \tag{7.55}$$

and

$$\text{Real } \psi_{m,n}(r,z,\tau) \simeq$$

$$\frac{1}{2\pi r}\, \bar{p}_m \bar{p}_n \sin \gamma_m z_0 \sin \gamma_m z \sin \gamma_n z_0 \sin \gamma_n z \cos \xi_{mn} \frac{\sin (\Delta\omega\, T_{mn}/2)}{(\Delta\omega\, T_{mn}/2)} e^{-(\delta_m + \delta_n)r} \tag{7.56}$$

in which

$$T_{mn} \equiv \left(\frac{1}{U_m} - \frac{1}{U_n}\right) r - \tau \Bigg|_{\omega=\omega_0} \tag{7.57}$$

$$\xi_{mn} \equiv (\kappa_m - \kappa_n)r - \omega_0 \tau \Big|_{\omega=\omega_0}$$

The correlation (7.50) consists of two summations. The first sum (7.55) decreases as r^{-1} times the exponential mode-attenuation factor. The mode-interference terms (7.56) have a similar decrease multiplied by a $\sin x/x$ range dependence.†

In the Fire Island experiments, as mentioned earlier, the choices of source depth, receiver depth, and frequency limited the acoustic transmission to the first and second modes. Theoretical values of $\psi^{1/2}$ are shown by the dotted line in Fig. 7.3, where $\psi^{1/2}$ is the root-mean-square acoustical pressure. The experimental data are shown by the solid line in Fig. 7.3. The source was not calibrated for this experiment; therefore, the amplitude of the theoretical calculation was adjusted to match the measurement at about 2-km range. The experimental and theoretical range dependence of the root-mean-square acoustical pressure and $\psi^{1/2}$ agree. We reemphasize that the form of (7.50) depends upon the *power spectrum GG^** of the received

---

† Other filter functions yield different range dependences of the mode-interference terms. For example, the narrow gaussian filter, $GG^* \propto e^{-(\omega-\omega_0)^2/2(\Delta\omega)^2}$ and $\Delta\omega \ll \omega_0$, yields the following range dependence for real ψ_{mn}: Real $\psi_{m,n} \propto \dfrac{1}{r} \cos \xi_{mn} e^{-(\Delta\omega)^2 T_{mn}{}^2/2}$.

signal.   If the signals from impulsive sources, i.e., explosions, are filtered to have the *same spectrum* as the signals from a band-limited noise source, ψ would have the *same range dependence* for both sources.   The impulsive source would be operated at the same depth as the band-limited source. It is not difficult to fire explosive charges at fixed depth.   The gas bubble, however, acts as a secondary source at shallower depths ("bubble pulse").

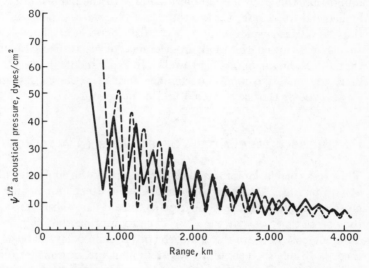

Fig. 7.3   The acoustical pressure vs. range for band-limited noise, 12.2-m hydrophone depth.   The solid lines are experimental data for a hydrophone at 12.2 m and a source at 10.7 m.   The bandwidth of the source was 10 cps at 147.8-cps center frequency.   The amplitude of the theoretical curve is the dashed line.   The water depth was 22.6 m.   The amplitude of the theoretical curve was multiplied by a constant (i.e., source strength) to correspond to the experimental data.   The simple harmonic-source data for calm sea ($\sigma \sim 0$) shown on Fig. 6.17 were taken on the same day as the data shown above.

The use of a noise source in the measurement of the propagation between the source position and receiver position yields a result that is averaged over the frequency band, and the effects of the mode-interference terms are reduced.   The mode interferences between high and low modes become negligible at large range.   The principal contributions would be the $\psi_{m,m}$ terms and the mode-interference terms $\psi_{m,m-1}$.   We have already seen that there are many factors which, in practice, severely limit the precision to which it is meaningful to calculate the acoustic field.   For example, in Sec. 6.9 we discussed the effect of irregularities within the waveguide. These caused the signals in different modes to lose their phase relationships. In an irregular waveguide the average of mode-interference terms decreased with range. This, we have just seen, is also the effect of using band-limited noise sources in a uniform waveguide. A comparison of Figs. 6.17 and 7.3 shows that for the two cases, the acoustical fields as a function of range are similar. Both continuous-wave and band-limited noise-transmission studies were made under different sea conditions. We found that the transmission data made with the band-limited noise source looked like that from the continuous-wave source when the roughness of the sea surface was about 0.5 m. The increase of signal bandwidth to 10 percent caused the mode-interference terms to decrease more rapidly than r^{-1} as the range was increased. In experiments it appears that we can limit the effective mode-interference terms to the $\psi_{m,m-1}$ and, perhaps, $\psi_{m,m-2}$ type by the use of a band-limited noise source.

7.6 CROSS CORRELATION OF SIGNALS IN A WAVEGUIDE

The cross correlation of signals is a measure of the similarity of the signals at two points. If the signals are the same except for a time delay τ, the cross correlation has the same form as the autocorrelation of the signal with the correlation peak at time τ. The assumption that signals observed at different positions are the same except for time delays is basic to all array theory. Since the uses of arrays are important in propagation studies, the cross-correlation properties of signals in a waveguide are particularly relevant to the use of arrays in a waveguide.[14]

The cross correlation $\psi(1,2,\tau)$ of the acoustical pressures $p_1(r_1,z_1,t)$ and $p_2(r_2,z_2,t+\tau)$ is, with the aid of (7.7), (7.8), and (7.21),†

$$\psi(1,2,\tau) = \text{Real}\left\{\sum_{m=1}^{M}\psi_{m,m}(1,2) + \sum_{m\neq n}\psi_{m,n}(1,2)\right\} \tag{7.58}$$

$\psi_{m,n}(1,2,\tau)$

$$= \frac{e^{-(\delta_m r_1 + \delta_n r_2)}}{2\pi\sqrt{r_1 r_2}}\int_{-\infty}^{\infty} G_1^* G_2 p_m p_n \phi_m^*(z_0)\phi_n(z_0)\phi_m^*(z_1)\phi_n(z_1)\, e^{-i[(\kappa_m r_1 - \kappa_n r_2)-\omega\tau]}\, d\omega \tag{7.59}$$

G_1 and G_2 include the filters for receivers 1 and 2.

Except for a small change in the form of the integrand, (7.59) is the same as (7.51), so that numerical approximation in the preceding section also applies here.

† $\psi(1,2,\tau)$ means the cross correlation of acoustic signal at position 1, (r_1,z_1), and position 2, (r_2,z_2,τ).

The integration of (7.59) over the narrow band $\Delta\omega$ with the linear approximations (7.53) yields

$$\text{Real } \psi_{m,n}(1,2,\tau) \simeq \frac{e^{-(\delta_m r_1 + \delta_n r_2)}}{2\pi\sqrt{r_1 r_2}}\; \bar{p}_m \bar{p}_n \sin \gamma_m z_0 \sin \gamma_n z_0 \sin \gamma_m z_1 \sin \gamma_n z_2$$

$$\times \cos \xi_{m,n}(1,2) \frac{\sin (T_{m,n}(1,2)\Delta\omega/2)}{(T_{m,n}(1,2)\Delta\omega/2)} \quad (7.60)$$

with

$$T_{m,n}(1,2) \equiv \left(\frac{r_1}{U_m} - \frac{r_2}{U_n} - \tau\right)\bigg|_{\omega=\omega_0}$$

$$\xi_{m,n}(1,2) \equiv (\kappa_m r_1 - \kappa_n r_2 - \omega_0\tau)\big|_{\omega=\omega_0} \quad (7.61)$$

$$G_1^* G_2 = \begin{cases} \dfrac{1}{\Delta\omega} & \text{for } (\omega - \Delta\omega/2) \le \omega L(\omega + \Delta\omega/2) \\ 0 & \text{otherwise} \end{cases}$$

The layered waveguide corresponding to the Fire Island area is also used for the numerical examples that illustrate the cross correlation of signals in a waveguide. For purposes of calculation, we assume that the source of Sec. 7.5 is at 7-m depth and the receivers are at 19-m depth. The receivers are assumed to be far enough from the source that the cross-mode terms can be neglected. With these simplifying assumptions, the first, second, and third modes have nearly equal excitation and the normalized cross correlation is

$$\frac{\psi(\Delta r,\tau)}{\psi(0)} \simeq \frac{1}{3}\sum_{m=1,2,4} \cos (\omega_0\tau - \kappa_m \Delta r) \frac{\sin [\Delta\omega/2(\tau - \Delta r/U_m)]}{\Delta\omega/2(\tau - \Delta r/U_m)} \quad (7.62)$$

$$r_1 - r_2 \equiv \Delta r$$

The results of the calculation are shown in Fig. 7.4. Figure 7.4a shows the cross correlation of a single mode. $\psi_{mm}(\tau)$ for $\Delta r = 0$ is essentially the same as $\psi_{mm}(\Delta r)$ for $\tau = 0$. Figure 7.4b shows the total cross correlation $\psi(\Delta r)$ of the three modes for $\tau = 0$. The sharp maximum at $\Delta r = 0$ and the lack of the $\sin x/x$ form of the envelope of the total cross-correlation function are due to the difference between the κ_m's of the different modes. The total cross correlation $\psi(\Delta r,0.3)$ for the case $\tau = 0.3$ sec is shown in Fig. 7.4c. The cross-correlation function for each of the modes is similar in appearance to that in Fig. 7.4a. The reason for the irregular form of Fig. 7.4c is that the correlation functions for the modes constructively and destructively interfere with each other. The phase and group velocities are not equal and the phase of the cosine wave is not zero at a time such that the term $\sin x/x$ is a maximum. Since the group and phase velocities are different, the envelopes of the cross-correlation functions

$\sin x/x$ are maximum at different values of time delay. The positions of the maxima of the envelopes for the three modes are indicated.

The cross correlation of an acoustical pressure as a function of the vertical separation of receivers in shallow water was also measured during the Fire Island studies of the propagation of band-limited noise.[13] The source was 5.5 km from the vertical string of receivers, and this is far enough to ignore the cross-mode terms in (7.58) and (7.59). The cross correlation was calculated by letting $r_1 = r_2$ and using the linear approximations for

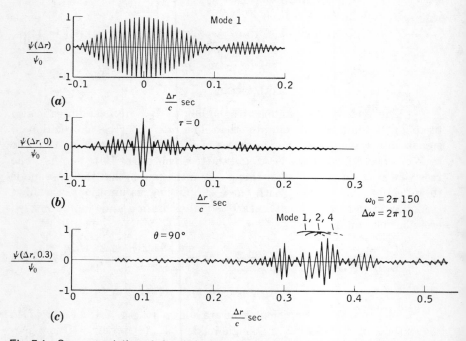

Fig. 7.4 Cross correlation of signals in a waveguide. (*a*) A single mode as a function of Δr, or τ; (*b*) three modes as a function of Δr, $\tau = 0$; (*c*) three modes as a function of Δr, $\tau = 0.3$ sec. The waveguide parameters are given in Fig. 4.32, p. 133.

p_m, γ_m, and κ_m in the frequency range 942 ± 31.5 rad/sec. Actually, the polarity coincidence, which is the cross correlation of infinitely clipped signals, was measured. The transformation of the cross correlation to the polarity coincidence $R(\tau)$ is[15]

$$R(\tau) = \frac{2}{\pi} \arcsin[\psi(\tau)] \tag{7.63}$$

The experimental data and the theoretical curve are shown in Fig. 7.5. Discrepancies are believed to be mainly due to incoherent noise in the amplifiers and hydrophones. The signal-to-instrument noise ratio was about 3:1 at this source range, and the corresponding polarity coincidence was about 0.9.[16]

7.7 REPRODUCIBILITY AND CROSS CORRELATION OF SIGNAL TRANSMISSIONS IN DEEP WATER

In filter theory, it is sometimes convenient to use the frequency or wavenumber response and at other times impulse-response measurements are better. In the preceding section, normal mode theory was used to calculate the correlation properties of signal transmissions in shallow water.

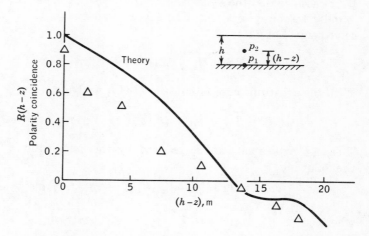

Fig. 7.5 Polarity coincidence for a distant noise source. The experimental polarity coincidence as a function of detector separation is shown for the source at a distance of 5.5 km. The bandwidth of the source was 10 cps and the center frequency was 147.8 cps. The source depth was 10.7 m and the water depth was 22.6 m. The theoretical curve is that for the first and second modes.

These methods can be used in deep water and are especially useful for transmissions from simple harmonic or band-limited sources. Here we illustrate an application of the impulse-response technique (Sec. 7.4) to a transmission experiment in the ocean. Let us assume that between the source and receiver a the impulse response of the ocean is $p_{Ia}(t)$. The signal is stored and then reproduced reversed in time [i.e., the signal is recorded on magnetic tape and replayed backward[9,17]]. As a practical matter, it may be necessary to use an initial source transmission $f(t)$ instead of an impulse function. (Electromechanical sources are convenient to use and reproducible but they have limited signal bandwidth.) In the following we extend (7.46) to two receiver positions and an input function $f(t)$.

A source function $f(t)$ is transmitted by the source and received at the receiver. The signal $s_{af}(t)$ at the receiver is with the aid of (7.3)

$$s_{af}(t) = \int_{-\infty}^{\infty} f(t - \tau) p_{Ia}(\tau) \, d\tau \tag{7.64}$$

The signal $s_{af}(t)$ is stored on magnetic tape and replayed in reversed time with the time delay t_0 to give

$$s_{af}(t_0 - t) = \int_{-\infty}^{\infty} f(t_0 - t - \tau) p_{Ia}(\tau) \, d\tau \tag{7.65}$$

Let us assume that the signal is received at position b, for which the source-b impulse response is $p_{Ib}(t)$. The source transmits $s_{af}(t_0 - t)$, and the received signal at b is

$$s_{abf}(t) = \int_{-\infty}^{\infty} s_{af}(t_0 - t + \tau') p_{Ib}(\tau') \, d\tau' \tag{7.66}$$

With the substitution of (7.65) into (7.66), we have

$$s_{abf}(t) = \int\int_{-\infty}^{\infty} p_{Ib}(\tau') p_{Ia}(\tau) f(t_0 - t + \tau' - \tau) \, d\tau \, d\tau' \tag{7.67}$$

This last expression can be reduced by the substitution $\tau'' = \tau' - \tau$ to the following:

$$s_{abf}(t) = \int_{-\infty}^{\infty} \psi_{ab}(\tau'') f[t_0 - (t - \tau'')] \, d\tau'' \tag{7.68}$$

where

$$\psi_{ab}(\tau'') \equiv \int_{-\infty}^{\infty} p_{Ia}(\tau + \tau'') p_{Ib}(\tau) \, d\tau \tag{7.69}$$

If one transmits a function $f(t)$ and obtains $s_{af}(t)$, the time-reversed transmission $s_{af}(t_0 - t)$ yields a signal that is the convolution of $f(-t)$ and the cross correlation of the impulse responses of the waveguide to positions a and b. The autocorrelation of the signal s_{aaf} follows directly by letting $b = a$.

Parvulescu and Clay used the matched-signal technique to study the reproducibility of signal transmissions across the Tongue of the Ocean, 24°30′N, 77°30′W.[18] The source ship was anchored on the west side, and the receiving ship was anchored 36 km away on the east side. A simplified diagram of equipment and the experimental procedure is shown in Fig. 7.6. Figure 7.7 is a set of photographs that were made of signal transmissions during the experiments. The received signal from a shot consists of about 10 predominant arrivals and the overall time duration of the received signal was about 2 sec.   With a 400-cps source and 1.5-kw power amplifier, the signal-to-noise ratio at the receiver was about 2:1 for a single-ping transmission.   The recording of the matched signal was noisy. The transmission of the matched signal included this noise which was not matched to the travel path and did not correlate at the receiver.   The peak signal output for matched transmission was 10 times the peak level for a single ping.   Most of the increase of the side-lobe level is due to the transmission of the recorded noise along with the matched signal.

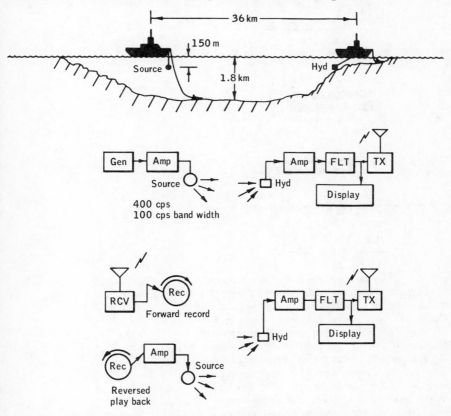

Fig. 7.6   Matched-signal experiment in the Tongue of the Ocean.   A placement of the source and receiver and a simplified diagram of the equipment are shown.   The source had approximately a 100-cps bandwidth at 400 cps and was driven by a 1.5-kw power amplifier.   The source transmitted a 15-msec ping.   The signal was received at the listening ship.   The received signals were transmitted by radio back to the source where the signals were recorded.   The recorded signal was replayed reversed in time into the source to produce the matched signal.   The correlation of the travel path was received at the receiving hydrophone.[18]

The source ship was anchored in water 1.8-km deep with about 2 or 3 km of scope. The ship moved slowly in a generally north-south direction (roughly perpendicular to the acoustical travel path). Matched-signal transmissions or the cross correlations of various source positions were observed as functions of time and source position. Initial matched-signal transmissions were made about one minute after the short pings were transmitted. The peak amplitude of the single-ping transmitted

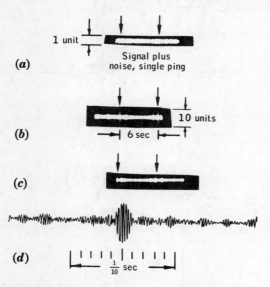

Fig. 7.7 Data taken to show the reproducibility of signals. The data were taken during the matched-signal experiment in the Tongue of the Ocean.[18] The original ping was a 15-msec 400-cps ping. (*a*) Transmitted signals from two single 15-msec 400-cps pings, transmitted 6 sec apart. (*b*) Hydrophone signal for matched-signal transmission from the source. This transmission was made about 2 min after the first. The amplitudes of the peaks are 10 times the signal shown in Fig. 7.7*a*. (*c*) Hydrophone signal for an unmatched signal, that is, the ship had drifted to a new position about 450 m from matched position. This transmission was made after 40 min elapsed time. (*d*) Expanded time-scale trace of the hydrophone signal for a matched signal. The peak amplitude is 10 units. These data were taken after 10 min and an estimated source displacement of 150 m.

signal is unity. The peak of the correlation signal decreased from 10 to 6 units after 10 minutes and a source displacement of about 150 m. The peak was not observable when the source was displaced about 450 m after 40 minutes elapsed time. The matched-signal transmissions were extremely sensitive to changes of the source depth. The amplitude of the peak remained the same when the source depth was changed from 40 to 41.5 m for a signal matched at 40-m depth, but a change of 3 m in the source depth caused the peak to be lost in the noise.

If we examine the cross-correlation function [(7.58) and (7.59)], it is evident that the correlation function is less sensitive to radial displacements than to the vertical displacements of a receiver. The radial part of the mode-interference term (7.59) depends upon $(\kappa_m - \kappa_n)r$ and $(\kappa_m - \kappa_n)$ is usually small compared to k. γ_m is also a fraction of k; however, γ_m and γ_n are in (7.59) and (7.60) as $\sin \gamma_m z \sin \gamma_n z$. A change of the source or receiver depths that is sufficient to increase $\gamma_m z$ by $\pi/2$, or greater, causes large changes in the amplitudes and phases of the mode-interference terms. In the Tongue of the Ocean at 400 cps, we estimate the number of modes to be about 250 and γ_{max} to be about 0.5 m^{-1}. The change of source depth of 1.5 m increased $\gamma_{max} z$ by about $\pi/4$, and the peak of the correlation function remained about the same. The 3-m change of depth changed $\gamma_{max} z$ by about $\pi/2$, and the correlation peak disappeared. The correlation function was an order of magnitude less sensitive to horizontal displacements than to vertical displacements.

In summary, the cross-correlation properties of signals in a waveguide have demonstrated several important differences between transmission in an infinite homogeneous medium and in a stratified medium. In a stratified medium, the use of time delays in a signal-processing system is limited because the information in different modes propagates with different group velocities. In a deep-water waveguide, that is, with many modes, small differences in the vertical positions of two receivers can cause the signals to become uncorrelated. Filters and signals that are matched to the propagation between two points in a waveguide can be used to improve the peak signal to noise of the transmission.

We have shown that the average of the mode-interference terms tends to zero for band-limited noise and large range. This applies to a particular type of measurement and does not mean that the signals are generally incoherent. Low-frequency signal transmissions appear to be coherent and reproducible over ranges of several hundred kilometers. It would appear from the sensitivity of transmission to source depth (in the Tongue of the Ocean) that lack of reproducibility in data is often the result of our inability to repeat the same experiment.

REFERENCES

1. Y. W. Lee: "Statistical Theory of Communication," John Wiley & Sons, Inc., New York, 1960.
2. Norbert Wiener: "Extrapolation, Interpolation, and Smoothing of Stationary Time Series," The Technology Press of the Massachusetts Institute of Technology, Cambridge, Mass., and John Wiley & Sons, Inc., New York, 1950.
3. G. L. Turin: An Introduction to Matched Filters, *IRE Trans. Inform. Theory*, IT-6, 311–329 (1960). (This issue is devoted to matched filters, and the complete issue is of interest.)
4. J. H. Van Vleck and D. Middleton: *J. Appl. Phys.*, **17**:940–971 (1946).
5. B. M. Dwork: *Proc. IRE*, **38**:771–774 (1950).
6. R. Courant and D. Hilbert: "Methoden der Mathematischen Physik," vol. I, p. 40, Interscience Publishers (Division of John Wiley & Sons, Inc.), New York, 1937.
7. Carl Eckart: The Theory of Noise Suppression by Linear Filters, *Scripps Inst. Oceanog.*, 51–44 (1951).
8. M. K. Smith: *Geophysics*, **23**:44–57 (1958).
9. A. Parvulescu: *J. Acoust. Soc. Am.*, **33**:1674 (1961).
10. L. B. W. Jolley: "Summation of Series," Dover Publications, Inc., New York, 1961.
11. M. M. Backus: *Geophysics*, **24**:233–261 (1959).
12. K. Walther: *J. Acoust. Soc. Am.*, **33**:681 (1961).
13. C. S. Clay: *J. Acoust. Soc. Am.*, **31**:1473–1479 (1959).
14. C. S. Clay: *J. Acoust. Soc. Am.*, **33**:865–870 (1961).
15. J. L. Lawson and G. E. Uhlenbeck (eds.): "Threshold Signals," p. 58, McGraw-Hill Book Company, New York, 1950.
16. B. S. Melton and P. R. Karr: *Geophysics*, **22**:553–564 (1957).
17. H. Kuttruff: *Acustica*, **13**:120 (1963).
18. A. Parvulescu and C. S. Clay: *Radio Elec. Eng.*, **29**:223–228 (1965).

CHAPTER EIGHT

SOME CONCLUSIONS

8.1 OCEAN ACOUSTICS AND GEOPHYSICS

Ocean acoustics is, in the final analysis, a branch of geophysics. The oceans are a major surface feature of the earth, and the study of sound propagation in the sea is intimately related to many allied fields such as oceanography, seismology, and geology. Ocean acoustics supplies and extracts information to and from these fields. It may be used as a tool for investigating the ocean's stratification and structure, the nature of bottom sediments and rocks, and so forth; at the same time, this sort of knowledge is needed for the analysis of sound propagation in the ocean.

Knowledge of the environment is essential, and considerable strides have been made in this direction during the last two decades. The development of continuously recording velocimeters (Greenspan and Tschiegg[1]) for investigating ocean structure and continuous "seismic profilers" for bottom studies (Hersey[2] and Clay et al.[3]), as well as the accumulation of data on sediment velocity and structure (Nafe and Drake[4] and Ewing et al.[5]), are among the more noteworthy accomplishments. This type of information makes it possible at times to describe the environment in terms of stratified media with plane parallel boundaries. It has shown us that on the average, the ocean is simple enough to allow significant comparisons between theory and experiment to be made on this basis.

Thus the experimental and theoretical work of Pekeris,[6] Ewing and Worzel,[7] Tolstoy,[8] Clay,[9] Kriazhev,[10] Kriazhev and Petrov,[11] and Brekhovskikh[12] shows that the mode theory is a useful, valid tool for the interpretation of shallow-water propagation experiments at low frequencies (i.e., small κh, κ being horizontal wave number and h the water depth); this is further emphasized by model studies (Knudsen[13]). Of particular interest in this connection is the Brown University work (Eby et al.[14] and Williams and Eby[15]) wherein the mode theory is used as a framework to show that an important mechanism of attenuation under typical shallow-water conditions is due to bottom reflection losses brought about both by the sound-absorbent properties of the bottom and by partial transformation of the incident sound energy into shear waves. Boundary roughness is another cause of attenuation since it reduces the coherent signal. In connection with the general problem of reflection from rough surfaces, the work of Proud et al.[16] and Leporskii[17] seems to have settled the question of the usefulness of the Kirchhoff approximation, since their comparisons of theory and experiment show that this method can be applied even beyond its nominal limits of validity. The theory has also been developed in the case of shallow-water waveguide propagation by Williams and Eby[15] and Clay.[18] The latter has shown the similarity of transmission patterns for band-limited noise in a calm sea and simple harmonic sound in a rough sea.

In all of this, both experiment and theory emphasize the great importance of bottom parameters and, in particular, of the layering and sound velocity. Relatively small perturbations of these quantities may completely change the behavior of the sound field. Thus one of the simplest and most basic features of a low-frequency, harmonic sound field in shallow water, namely, the interference wavelengths of the lowest modes, is strongly influenced by the nature of the bottom (Fig. 8.1). In a typical deep-water

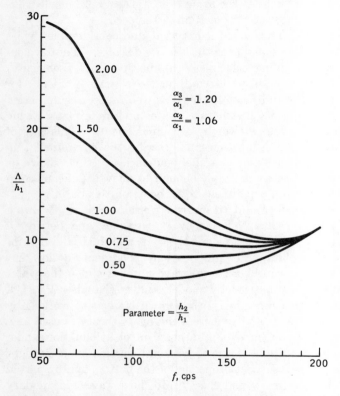

Fig. 8.1 Interference wavelength (ratio to water-layer thickness h_1) for the first two modes vs. frequency f for a three-layer waveguide consisting of a layer of water of $h_1 = 19.8$ m thick and of sound velocity $\alpha_1 = 1,508$ m sec; over a layer of sediment of sound velocity $\alpha_2 = 1.06 \, \alpha_1$, of varying thickness h_2 (h_2/h_1 has the constant values indicated for each curve), and of density $\rho_2 = 2$; over a half-space of sound velocity $\alpha_3 = 1.20\alpha_1$ and of density $\rho_3 = \rho_2$. This demonstrates the sensitivity of Λ/h_1 to h_2/h_1.

case, the sound field is very sensitive to the stratification. From a ray standpoint, this briefly says that for long paths, small differences in the sound-velocity profile $c(z)$ may produce large cumulative phase changes.

As an example, consider the behavior of low modes in a sound channel. Figure 8.2 shows a comparison, for two different cases, of the calculated behavior of the acoustical pressure amplitudes p vs. horizontal range r, for a frequency of 400 cps, source and receiver on the channel axis $z = 0$, and a source power of 1 watt. In case (a) the assumed $c(z)$ law is

$$c = \left(\frac{1}{c_0^2} - a^2|z| \right)^{-\frac{1}{2}} \tag{8.1}$$

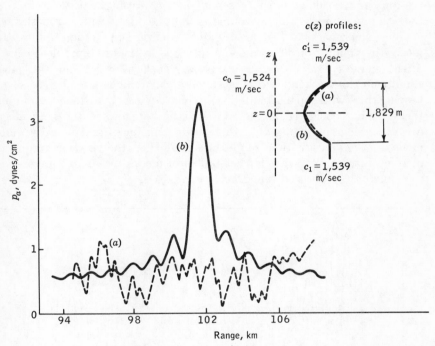

Fig. 8.2 Difference in long-range fields (calculated from exact solutions of the wave equation) for the two slightly different waveguides shown in insert and corresponding to Eqs. (8.1) and (8.2) in text. The case (b), with continuous derivatives of the sound velocity $c(z)$ on the waveguide axis, shows strong focusing, whereas (a) shows none. This demonstrates the sensitivity of the sound field to small errors in the assumed $c(z)$ law.

whereas in case (b) we assume that

$$c = \left(\frac{1}{c_0^2} - b^2z^2 \right)^{-\frac{1}{2}} \tag{8.2}$$

The values c_0 and $c(z)$ at $z = \pm h = \pm 914.5$ m are identical in both cases. In other words, the end and middle points of the $c(z)$ profile are the same.

Yet in case (*b*) we have strong periodic focusing, whereas in case (*a*) there is no trace of it. The analysis of sound propagation in the oceans is thus, at best, a touchy business; *if* we happen to have obtained a suitable approximation for the stratification, we *may* be able to calculate an acoustic field similar to that which is in fact observed. In such calculations, two complementary points of view are possible. The ocean may be analyzed in terms of modes or in terms of rays. On the whole the former is perhaps more rigorous and easier to use in cases involving focusing, caustics, etc., but both points of view are, of course, valid. In deep water, the surface-channel experiments of Pedersen[19] and Pedersen and Gordon[20] illustrate nicely the validity of mode and ray methods in the same problem; this is often characteristic of ocean acoustics (Tolstoy[21]). From the mode standpoint this work involved a relatively small number of modes ($M < 40$) propagating (with some attenuation) to relatively short distances and must therefore be considered as an intermediate step toward the truly deep-ocean problem involving the whole water thickness and a great many modes. The investigations of Guthrie et al.[22] at the very low frequency of 10 cps used a somewhat larger number of modes ($M \simeq 10^2$) in an effort to explain a complicated sound field (Fig. 8.3).

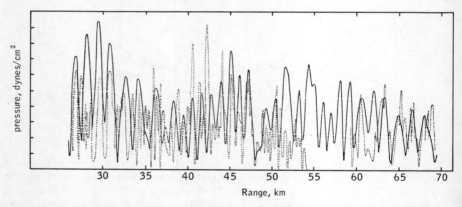

Fig. 8.3 Experimental (dotted line) and calculated (solid line) pressure amplitude vs. range for a simple harmonic source at 10.04 cps at a depth of 24 m in a deep section of the ocean. This shows the complicated nature of the field variations that are found even at such low frequencies; at 10 cps we already have almost 100 guided modes in the model assumed for the calculations (see Guthrie et al.[22]).

All the work we have just mentioned illustrates the fully deterministic point of view in which certain assumptions are made about the medium; the sound field due to a source is calculated in detail and the resulting curves are compared with experiments with at least a modicum of success. But it would seem that this approach has been carried about as far as it will go. The oceans, and the deep ocean in particular, are subject to unpredictable fluctuations in space and time. As a result the reproducibility of deep-ocean acoustic data is often poor; that is, it is very difficult to repeat an experiment and obtain the same results when the acoustic field varies rapidly with range r.

For example, consider Fig. 8.3 showing a typical plot of the acoustical pressure amplitude vs. r for a frequency of 10 cps. An idea of the complication involved at higher frequencies f is obtained by multiplying the rates of oscillation shown by $f/10$; thus, at 300 cps, the acoustic field varies 30 times as fast. Many modes are involved — of the order of 10^2 at 10 cps, 10^3 at 100 cps, etc. These modes are sensitive to small variations of c in time and space, e.g., to departures of actual conditions in an ocean from our idealized assumption of constant horizontal stratification. Orders of magnitude of these effects are such (Tolstoy[21]) that one can hardly expect a high order of reproducibility for long-range data at frequencies $f > 10$ cps for a deep ocean ($\kappa h \gg 10^2$). The reproducibility is certainly not sufficient to allow comparisons between theory and experiment of the quality obtained by Pedersen[19] and Pedersen and Gordon[20] in surface channels or by Clay[9] and Tolstoy[8] in shallow-water waveguides. In these experiments, the wavelengths were within an order of magnitude of the vertical dimensions of the waveguide, the total number of excited modes M was not inordinately large ($M < 40$ for Pedersen and Gordon's[20] highest frequency and $M \leq 4$ in the Clay[9] and Tolstoy[8] work), and the data could be reproduced, within acceptable limits of error, from one experiment to the next. In the work reported by Guthrie et al.,[22] $M \simeq 10^2$ and reproducibility was localized and marginal, suggesting that some sort of limit for this kind of work was being reached. Further improvements in our understanding of deep-water propagation along the lines of Pedersen's,[19] Pedersen and Gordon's,[20] or Guthrie's[22] work are possible; but these improvements will probably be limited to short ranges or to small numbers of modes M and, effectively, to narrow waveguides ($\kappa h \leq 10^2$) with steady, easily measured properties.

We are approaching definite limits imposed not so much by what is analytically or numerically possible as by the intrinsic uncertainties imposed by the medium itself. We do not know and may never know the properties of the medium accurately enough because they are not fixed in time and space. Currents, tides, turbulence, and internal waves (Skudrzyk,[23] Crease,[24] and Pochapsky[25]) are forever disturbing whatever idealized, average picture one assumes for the medium. This state of affairs is, to some extent, typical of geophysical research; we cannot control all the pertinent factors in an experiment. As a result, we may start out to test a theory and we end up by using the theory to determine the environment or, at least, to refine our knowledge thereof. But essentially the problem remains incompletely determined.

In the ocean, in addition, one cannot fully control either instrument position or its motion in time and space. For a more or less constant source-receiver distance, the properties of the actual paths followed by the sound may vary; however, the experiments of Parvulescu and Clay[26] indicate that over short time periods of the order of minutes, oceanic fluctuations are not sufficient to destroy phase coherence and reproducibility. Extreme care must be used in the design of acoustic experiments at sea; the design should be dictated by the nature of the problem rather than by preconceived notions of what the experimenter intends to discover. Mastering the fundamentals of propagation theory and instrumentation is not enough; an understanding of the importance of fluctuations, the meaning of statistical methods, and sampling theory is essential. Excellent accounts of these and allied fields will be found in books by Lumley and Panofsky,[27] Brillouin,[28] and Blackman and Tukey.[29]

Of particular importance to the sampling of fluctuating radiation fields in the ocean is the Nyquist criterion which says, in effect, that one must sample at a rate at least double that of the highest-frequency component in the spectrum to avoid aliasing the data and introducing fictitious frequency terms. Consider, for instance, the experimental results at $f = 10.04$ cps of Guthrie et al.[22] shown in Fig. 8.3. The sampling occurs in space, and the fluctuation rate is a space rate. The shortest fluctuation distance Λ_{min} is of the order of 0.5 km. Note that the smallest Λ's probably correspond to partial reflections and thus to damped modes, which are not included in the discrete spectrum of the ocean waveguide, and that these must eventually disappear because of their higher rate of attenuation. $\Lambda_{min} \simeq 0.5$ km means spacing the points closer than 0.25 km apart. Likewise the sample must be several times longer than the longest expected interference wavelength, e.g., five times Λ_{max}. In a typical Atlantic Ocean experiment Λ_{max} is essentially the convergence zone spacing, of the order of 70 km. We are thus led to the conclusion that at 10 cps one requires 1.4×10^3 points spaced 0.25 km apart over 350 km. At 300 cps, no less than 4.2×10^4 points are needed. Problems of this scope are within the capabilities of modern computers and data-processing procedures. One may envision an experiment similar to that of Guthrie et al.[22] in which a recorded field of the kind shown in Fig. 8.3 is subjected to a spectrum analysis in wave-number space, and the extracted mode-interference wave-number spectrum may be compared with theory. This would be somewhat analogous to the spectroscopic problem of determining energy levels from the emission spectrum of an atom. It represents a fundamental change in emphasis in analyzing acoustic fields in the ocean. This procedure would considerably diminish the amount of computing to be done by the experimenter and would not require, in these calculations, so high a degree of accuracy — in consonance with the intrinsic limitations of the experiments. In experiments such as these one could also extract directly the κ_m spectrum out of the acoustic field.

Fluctuations in the structure of the medium will affect neither the number nor the wavelengths of the spectral lines. The matched-signal technique applied to ocean acoustics by Parvulescu and Clay[26] enables one to determine quantitatively some of the effects of such fluctuations, essentially by measuring the coherence and "repeatability" of signal transmissions.

Certainly future progress in ocean acoustics will rely heavily on both the acquisition of better data and the improvement of our knowledge of the oceans. But it appears equally certain that, in the interpretation of experiments, progress in ocean acoustics will also lean heavily on modern statistical and data-processing methods. An entirely deterministic description of events is not possible. Determinism in the traditional sense of the word was, it seems, an illusion. Indeed, information theory tells us that even under laboratory conditions a certain margin of uncertainty is intrinsic to all knowledge (Brillouin[30]). This should be especially clear to workers in geophysics, where, by the standards of a laboratory physicist, agreement between theory and experiment is often marginal and where uncontrollable and unpredictable effects are a familiar feature of our environment (Tukey[31]).

REFERENCES

1. M. Greenspan and C. E. Tschiegg: in V. M. Albers (ed.), "Underwater Acoustics," Plenum Press, New York, 1963.
2. J. B. Hersey: Continuous Reflection Profiling, in M. N. Hill (ed.), "The Sea," Vol. 3, pp. 47–71, Interscience Publishers (Division of John Wiley & Sons, Inc.), New York, 1963.
3. C. S. Clay, W. L. Liang, and S. Wisotsky: *J. Geophys. Res.*, **69**:3419–3428 (1964).
4. J. E. Nafe and C. L. Drake: Physical Properties of Marine Sediments, in "The Sea," Vol. 3, pp. 794–815, Interscience Publishers (Division of John Wiley & Sons, Inc.), New York, 1963.
5. W. M. Ewing, J. L. Ewing, and M. Talwani: *Geol. Soc. Am. Bull.*, **75**:17–36 (1964).
6. C. L. Pekeris: in "Propagation of Sound in the Ocean," *Geol. Soc. Am. Mem.* 27, 1948.

7. W. M. Ewing and J. L. Worzel: in "Propagation of Sound in the Ocean," *Geol. Soc. Am. Mem.* 27, 1948.
8. I. Tolstoy: *J. Acoust. Soc. Am.*, **30**:348–361 (1958).
9. C. S. Clay: *J. Acoust. Soc. Am.*, **31**:1473–1479 (1959).
10. F. I. Kriazhev: *Soviet Phys. Acoust.*, **6**:60–70 (1960).
11. F. I. Kriazhev and N. A. Petrov: *Soviet Phys. Acoust.*, **6**:225–232 (1960).
12. L. M. Brekhovskikh: "Waves in Layered Media," Academic Press Inc., New York, 1960.
13. W. C. Knudsen: *J. Acoust. Soc. Am.*, **29**:918–924 (1957).
14. R. K. Eby, A. O. Williams, R. P. Ryan, and P. Tamarkin: *J. Acoust. Soc. Am.*, **32**:88–99 (1960).
15. A. O. Williams, Jr., and R. K. Eby: *J. Acoust. Soc. Am.*, **34**:836–843 (1962).
16. J. M. Proud, Jr., R. T. Beyer, and P. Tamarkin: *J. Appl. Phys.*, **31**:543–552 (1960).
17. A. N. Leporskii: *Soviet Phys. Acoust.*, **2**:185–189 (1956).
18. C. S. Clay: *J. Acoust. Soc. Am.*, **36**:833–837 (1964).
19. M. A. Pedersen: *J. Acoust. Soc. Am.*, **34**:1197–1203 (1962).
20. M. A. Pedersen and D. F. Gordon: *J. Acoust. Soc. Am.*, **37**:105–118 (1965).
21. I. Tolstoy: *Quasi-Optics*, 43–56, *Polytech. Inst. Brooklyn*, New York, 1964.
22. A. N. Guthrie, I. Tolstoy, and J. Shaffer: *J. Acoust. Soc. Am.*, **32**:645–647 (1960).
23. E. J. Skudrzyk: in V. M. Albers (ed.), "Underwater Acoustics," p. 199, Plenum Press, New York, 1963.
24. J. Crease: in V. M. Albers (ed.), "Underwater Acoustics," pp. 129–139, Plenum Press, New York, 1963.
25. T. E. Pochapsky: *Tellus*, **15**(4):352–362 (1963).
26. A. Parvulescu and C. S. Clay: *Radio Elec. Engr.*, **29**(4):223–228 (1965).
27. J. L. Lumley and H. A. Panofsky: "The Structure of Atmospheric Turbulence," Interscience Publishers (Division of John Wiley & Sons, Inc.), New York, 1964.
28. L. Brillouin: "Science and Information Theory," Academic Press Inc., New York, 1956.
29. R. B. Blackman and J. W. Tukey: "The Measurement of Power Spectra," Dover Publications, Inc., New York, 1958.
30. L. Brillouin: "Scientific Uncertainty and Information," Academic Press Inc., New York, 1965.
31. J. W. Tukey: *Science*, **148**(3675):1283–1289 (1965).

APPENDIX 1

Consider the case of a homogeneous half-space of sound velocity c_0, density ρ_0 ($z \geq 0$), in contact with a half-space ($z \leq 0$) of the same desnity but with the variable sound velocity

$$c(z) = \left(pz + \frac{1}{c_0{}^2} \right)^{-1/2} \qquad p > 0 \qquad\qquad (A1.1)$$

We note that at $z = -1/pc_0{}^2$, c becomes infinite! One might conclude from this that we have chosen an unsuitable model. However, for the problems occurring in practice (see Chap. 5), the values of the constants p and c_0 are such that in the range of possible z values, c varies only within quite moderate bounds. A physical boundary usually interrupts the medium at values of $z \gg -1/pc_0{}^2$, that is, long before this effect becomes obnoxious [see remark following Eq. (5.42)].

Thus, we may safely assume a medium $z < 0$ stratified according to the law (A1.1), providing we limit ourselves to angles of incidence i such that the rays turn long before reaching the singular plane $z = -1/pc_0{}^2$. From remarks made at the end of Sec. 2.10 this implies $i > 45°$.

The wave functions corresponding to a medium of indefinite extent can then be used (see Sec. 3.8):

$$\phi = A\gamma[J_{1/3}(\zeta) + J_{-1/3}(\zeta)] \qquad\qquad (A1.2)$$

$$\frac{d\phi}{dz} = A\gamma^2[-J_{2/3}(\zeta) + J_{-2/3}(\zeta)] \qquad\qquad (A1.3)$$

where
$$\zeta = \int_{z_T}^{z} \gamma \, dz = \frac{2}{3\omega^2 p} \, \gamma^3(z) \, \Big|_{z_T}^{z} \qquad\qquad (A1.4)$$

z_T is the value of z for which $\gamma = 0$ (that is, the turning point)

To obtain the value of θ at $z = z_0$, we evaluate (A1.4), (A1.3), and (A1.2) at $z = z_0$ and apply (2.117):

$$\theta = \arctan \left(\frac{J_{1/3} + J_{-1/3}}{J_{2/3} - J_{-2/3}} \right)_{\zeta=\zeta_0} \qquad\qquad (A1.5)$$

If we now assume vanishingly short wavelengths and large wave numbers so that $\zeta_0 \to \infty$, we may apply to (A1.5) the asymptotic formula

$$J_\nu(x) \to \left(\frac{2}{\pi x} \right)^{1/2} \cos\left[x - \left(\nu + \frac{1}{2} \right) \frac{\pi}{2} \right] \qquad \text{as } x \to \infty \qquad (A1.6)$$

Applying this result to (A1.5) gives

$$\theta = \arctan \left[\frac{\cos (\zeta - 5/12 \, \pi) + \cos (\zeta - 1/12 \, \pi)}{\cos (\zeta - 7/12 \, \pi) - \cos (\zeta + 1/12 \, \pi)} \right] \tag{A1.7}$$

and thus

$$\theta = - \left(\zeta + \frac{\pi}{4} \right) \tag{A1.8}$$

If now ζ is redefined as in Eq. (2.119), its sign in (A1.8) is changed. Similarly, $-\pi/4$ becomes $+\pi/4$ for consistency with coordinates and direction of travel. This proves the result (2.123) and (2.119) in the asymptotic limit of high frequencies for a stratification of the type (A1.1). This result is then usually accepted for other $c(z)$ laws (see ref. 1, Chap. 2). In order for (A1.8) to be a good approximation, (A1.6) must be valid, i.e., ζ must be large. As is well known, (A1.6) neglects terms of the order of ζ^{-1} and smaller. To be sure that the relative error in (A1.8) is less than 1 percent we take

$$\zeta > 40\pi \tag{A1.9}$$

that is,

$$\frac{2}{3\omega^2 p} \gamma_0^3 > 40\pi \tag{A1.10}$$

But the distance D between source and receiver, when these are at the same depth and connected by a ray of incident angle θ_0 having one turning point, as in Fig. 2.18, is

$$D = \frac{2}{pc_0^2} \sin 2\theta_0 \tag{A1.11}$$

For rays that are not too steep,

$$\theta_0 \simeq \frac{\pi}{2} - \epsilon$$

$$D \simeq \frac{4}{pc_0^2} \cos \theta_0 \tag{A1.12}$$

This gives at least the correct order of magnitude for D in most situations occurring in practice. Since now

$$\gamma_0 = \frac{\omega}{c_0} \cos \theta_0 \tag{A1.13}$$

and, since, by (A1.1),

$$p = \frac{2}{c^3} \left| \frac{dc}{dz} \right| \tag{A1.14}$$

it follows that (A1.10) may be rewritten as

$$\frac{1}{24} \omega D^3 \frac{1}{c_0^3} \left(\frac{dc}{dz} \right)^2 > 40\pi \tag{A1.15}$$

If now we wish to apply this to essentially all the spectral components of a pulse of duration Δt, we assume that the lowest frequency of practical interest in the spectrum is of the order of $f = 1/2\Delta t$. If (A1.15) is satisfied for this frequency, it will be satisfied *a fortiori* for all other components. Thus, writing

$$\Gamma = (\Delta t)^{-1} D^3 \frac{1}{c^3} \left(\frac{dc}{dz}\right)^2 \tag{A1.16}$$

it follows that, if

$$\Gamma > 10^3 \tag{A1.17}$$

then (A1.8) applies to all spectral components of the pulse.

APPENDIX 2

To obtain the result (3.83) from Eq. (3.82), we utilize the following properties of the delta function (see ref. 3, Chap. 3),

$$\delta\left[(x - x_1)\,(x - x_2)\right] = \frac{\delta\,(x - x_1) + \delta(x - x_2)}{|x_1 - x_2|} \tag{A2.1}$$

$$\delta\,(cx) = \frac{1}{c}\,\delta\,(x) \tag{A2.2}$$

and the definition by the periodic (period $2h$) series:

$$\sum_{n=0}^{\infty} \delta\,(x + 2nh) = \frac{1}{h} \sum_{m=0}^{\infty} \cos\frac{m\pi}{h}\,x \tag{A2.3}$$

To make the notation more concise, we define ρ as

$$(c^2 t^2 - r^2)^{1/2} = \rho \tag{A2.4}$$

and we write (3.82) in the form

$$\frac{\partial \Phi}{\partial t} = -\frac{c}{4\pi h\rho} \sum_{m=0}^{\infty} [\cos \gamma_m(z - z_0 + \rho) + \cos \gamma_m(z - z_0 - \rho) - \cos \gamma_m(z + z_0 + \rho)$$
$$- \cos \gamma_m(z + z_0 - \rho)] \tag{A2.5}$$

where, by (3.76),

$$\gamma_m = \frac{m\pi}{h}$$

We have, therefore, by (A2.3), omitting for simplicity the $2nh$ in the arguments of the δ functions,

$$\frac{\partial \Phi}{\partial t} = -\frac{c}{4\pi\rho} \sum_{n=0}^{\infty} [\delta(z - z_0 + \rho) + \delta(z - z_0 - \rho) - \delta(z + z_0 + \rho) - \delta(z + z_0 - \rho)] \tag{A2.6}$$

Using (A2.1) this gives

$$\frac{\partial \Phi}{\partial t} = -\frac{c}{2\pi} \sum_{n=0}^{\infty} \{\delta[(z - z_0 + 2nh)^2 - \rho^2] - \delta[(z + z_0 + 2nh)^2 - \rho^2]\} \tag{A2.7}$$

Or, by (A2.4),

$$\frac{\partial \Phi}{\partial t} = -\frac{c}{2\pi} \sum_{n=0}^{\infty} [\delta\,(R_n{}^2 - c^2 t^2) - \delta\,(R_n'{}^2 - c^2 t^2)] \tag{A2.8}$$

Where
$$R_n{}^2 = (z - z_0 + 2nh)^2 + r^2 \tag{A2.9}$$
$$R_n'{}^2 = (z + z_0 + 2nh)^2 + r^2$$

Since
$$R_n{}^2 - c^2t^2 = (R_n - ct)(R_n + ct)$$

we use (A2.1) again:

$$\frac{\partial \Phi}{\partial t} = -\frac{1}{4\pi t} \sum_{n=0}^{\infty} [\delta(R_n - ct) + \delta(R_n + ct) - \delta(R_n' - ct) - \delta(R_n' + ct)] \tag{A2.10}$$

But since $t > 0$ and $R_n > 0$ and $\delta(R_n - ct)$ and $\delta(R_n' - ct)$ are zero everywhere except at $t = R_n/c$ and $t = R_n'/c$,

$$\frac{\partial \Phi}{\partial t} = -\frac{c}{4\pi} \sum_{n=0}^{\infty} \left[\frac{1}{R_n} \delta(R_n - ct) - \frac{1}{R_n'} \delta(R_n' - ct) \right] \tag{A2.11}$$

and finally, using (A2.2),

$$\frac{\partial \Phi}{\partial t} = -\frac{1}{4\pi} \sum_{n=0}^{\infty} \left[\frac{1}{R_n} \delta\left(\frac{R_n}{c} - t\right) - \frac{1}{R_n'} \delta\left(\frac{R_n'}{c} - t\right) \right] \tag{A2.12}$$

Since $\delta(x)$ is an even function of x, Eq. (3.83) follows.

APPENDIX 3

We will show that our Eqs. (4.59), (4.58), and (4.60) are consistent, respectively, with Pekeris' Eqs. (A.104), (A.105), and (A.118) in his classic treatment of the problem in *Geol. Soc. Am. Mem. 27*.

Note first of all that Pekeris uses a *velocity potential* source having the time dependence

$$f(t) = \begin{cases} e^{-\lambda t} & t > 0 \\ 0 & t < 0 \end{cases} \tag{A3.1}$$

whereas (Sec. 3.5) we *essentially* use a time dependence $-1(t)$ for the displacement potential,

$$f(t) = \begin{cases} -1 & t > 0 \\ 0 & t < 0 \end{cases} \tag{A3.2}$$

If one makes $\lambda \to 0$ in Pekeris' source function and if one applies it to the homogeneous medium, he would obtain a velocity potential $(1/R)\ 1\ (t - R/c)$, $R = (x^2 + y^2 + z^2)^{1/2}$, whereas our source function would give us the result (3.55), that is, a displacement potential $-(1/4\pi)\ (1/R)\ 1\ (t - R/c)$. In other words, in order to make our results directly comparable to Pekeris', we take his results and

1. we make $\lambda \to 0$

2. we multiply by $-\dfrac{1}{4\pi}$

Pekeris' velocity potential then becomes identical to our displacement potential.

Applying 1 and 2 to Pekeris' Eq. (A.104) and using our notation gives

$$\Phi_m = \frac{1}{\pi h r} \cdot \frac{1}{[\kappa_m |\partial^2 \kappa / \partial \omega^2|_m]^{1/2} \omega_m} \, T_m \sin\left(\kappa_m r - \omega_m t\right) \tag{A3.3}$$

where

$$T_m = \frac{\gamma_{1m} h \sin \gamma_{1m} z \sin \gamma_{1m} z_0}{\gamma_{1m} h - \sin \gamma_{1m} h \cos \gamma_{1m} h - a^2 \sin^2 \gamma_{1m} h \tan \gamma_{1m} h} \tag{A3.4}$$

and (A3.3) is valid for

$$\frac{\partial^2 \kappa_m}{\partial \omega^2} < 0 \tag{A3.5}$$

but since

$$\frac{\partial^2 \kappa}{\partial \omega^2} = -\frac{1}{U^3} \frac{\partial U}{\partial \kappa} \tag{A3.6}$$

282

the condition (A3.5) is equivalent to

$$\frac{\partial U_m}{\partial \kappa} > 0 \tag{A3.7}$$

and we must compare (A3.3) with (4.59).

Using (A3.6) transforms (A3.3) into

$$\Phi_m = \frac{1}{\pi h r \left| U_m^{-1} \, \partial U_m / \partial \kappa \right|^{1/2}} \frac{U_m}{\omega_m \kappa_m^{1/2}} T_m \sin\left(\kappa_m r - \omega t\right) \tag{A3.8}$$

In order for this to be identical with (4.59), it is necessary that

$$\frac{1}{\omega_m \kappa_m^{1/2}} U_m T_m = c_1^2 \frac{\kappa_m^{1/2}}{\omega_m^2} S_m \tag{A3.9}$$

i.e., writing

$$\frac{\omega_m}{\kappa_m} = v_m \tag{A3.10}$$

we must have

$$\frac{U_m v_m}{c_1^2} = \frac{S_m}{T_m} \tag{A3.11}$$

But by virtue of (4.41) and (4.42) this is our group-velocity identity:

$$U_m v_m = \frac{\nu_m}{\sigma_m} \tag{A3.12}$$

We have thus demonstrated that Pekeris' result (A.104) yields our Eq. (4.59), providing the proper allowances are made for the difference in source functions. A similar proof can be made in the case of the Airy phase solutions, i.e., our Eq. (4.60) and Pekeris' Eq. (A.118).

We take his (A.118), make $\lambda \to 0$, and multiply by $-1/4\pi$, obtaining

$$\Phi_m = -\frac{1}{\pi h 3^{2/3}} \frac{E(v)}{\left[(\kappa_{0m}/2\pi)\omega_{0m}^2\right]^{1/2}} \frac{1}{r^{5/6}\left[-\partial^3\kappa_{0m}/\partial\omega^3\right]^{1/3}} T_{0m} \sin\left(\omega_{0m} t - \kappa_{0m} r - \frac{\pi}{4}\right) \tag{A3.13}$$

but

$$\frac{\partial^3 \kappa}{\partial \omega^3} = \frac{1}{U} \cdot \frac{\partial}{\partial \kappa}\left(\frac{\partial^2 \kappa}{\partial \omega^2}\right) \tag{A3.14}$$

and since $\partial U/\partial \kappa = 0$, we may use (A3.6) to obtain

$$\frac{\partial^3 \kappa}{\partial \omega^3} = -\frac{1}{U^4} \cdot \frac{\partial^2 U}{\partial \kappa^2} \tag{A3.15}$$

Using the formula

$$\sin\left(x - \frac{\pi}{4}\right) = -\cos\left(-x - \frac{\pi}{4}\right)$$

Eq. (A3.13) becomes

$$\Phi_m = \frac{2}{(2\pi)^{1/2}} \frac{1}{h3^{2/3}} \frac{1}{r^{5/6}} \frac{U_{0m}{}^{4/3}}{\kappa_{0m}{}^{1/2}\omega_{0m}} \frac{E(v)}{|\partial^2 U_{0m}/\partial\kappa^2|^{1/3}} T_{0m} \cos\left(\kappa_{0m}r - \omega_{0m}t - \frac{\pi}{4}\right) \quad (A3.16)$$

For this to be identical with Eq. (4.60) requires that we have

$$\frac{U_{0m}{}^{4/3}}{\kappa_{0m}{}^{1/2}\omega_{0m}} T_{0m} = c_1{}^2 U_{0m}{}^{1/3} \frac{\kappa_{0m}{}^{1/2}}{\omega_{0m}{}^2} S_{0m} \quad (A3.17)$$

or

$$\frac{U_{0m}v_{0m}}{c_1{}^2} = \frac{S_{0m}}{T_{0m}} \quad (A3.18)$$

which we have just seen to be true.

NAME INDEX

SUBJECT INDEX